INSURRECTION, CORRUPTION &
MURDER
IN
EARLY
VERMONT

INSURRECTION, CORRUPTION & MURDER IN EARLY VERMONT

LIFE ON THE WILD NORTHERN FRONTIER

GARY G. SHATTUCK

Foreword by H. Nicholas Muller III

Charleston · London

THE History PRESS

Published by The History Press
Charleston, SC 29403
www.historypress.net

Front cover: Lake Champlain. *Library of Congress Prints and Photographs Division, LC-DIG-pga-05472.*

Back cover, bottom: From Burlington Bay on Lake Champlain. In this circa 1811 view, six lake sloops make their way to and from the harbor between (left to right) Shelburne Point, Rock Dunder and Juniper Island. *Private collection.*

First published 2014

Manufactured in the United States

ISBN 978.1.62619.656.8

Library of Congress CIP data applied for.

To Kate, my wife and companion

CONTENTS

FOREWORD

Gary Shattuck's prodigious research that underlies *Insurrection, Corruption and Murder in Early Vermont: Life on the Wild Northern Frontier* has brought to the surface interesting and detailed information about the early years of Vermont in the second and third decades after statehood in 1791. He demonstrates how leading residents wrestled for fortune within the new trade rules created by the sudden imposition of Jefferson's Embargo of 1807 in December of that year and during the War of 1812. He demonstrates how those who occupied the highest social and economic strata in northwestern Vermont hid behind those less well connected and fortunate who did the "dirty" work. He lays bare the dysfunctions of institutions, particularly in the legal area, in the young state of Vermont and the efforts to improve them. This important book advances the understanding of Vermont in the opening years of the nineteenth century.

The standard treatments of the *Black Snake* affair, during which, in 1808, smugglers shot it out with revenue officers on the banks of the Winooski River, paint it as a colorful incident sparked by constraints and opportunities created by the embargo. Aside from the lawlessness, the accounts see the incident as symptomatic of the deep split in Vermont between the Federalists and Jefferson's Democratic Republicans. Not satisfied with the modern historical accounts of the notorious *Black Snake* incident, Gary Shattuck began his extensive research in a little-used collection in the archives of the Vermont Historical Society. Exploiting his experience in legal records honed as an assistant U.S. attorney for Vermont, Shattuck examined judicial and trial records largely ignored by historians. This productive research enabled him to reconstruct the activities of the participants in a gripping day-by-day, hour-by-hour narrative of the events leading to the deadly encounter, the details of the alcohol-fueled fight and the tangled legal aftermath. More importantly, it also led his investigation beyond the bloody fight to peel back the layers in historical research to reveal the institutional adolescence and growing pains of the young state of Vermont.

The commerce of northwestern Vermont centered on trade across the United States–Canada border on Lake Champlain and overland to reach Montreal and Quebec and often the European market beyond. When Jefferson's 1807 embargo and the land embargo that followed in early 1808 placed legal barriers on trade across the border and disrupted this commerce, merchants turned to widespread smuggling to evade them. The War of 1812, with armies and navies contesting control of the Champlain Valley, which often made the movement of material across the border treasonous activity, intensified the commercial disruption. The restrictions on commerce created opportunities for large financial returns. They also magnified efforts to enforce the laws. In teasing out the details of these activities, Shattuck has provided little-known detail about the legal system with the porous jails, the first state of Vermont prison, the militia, the revenue agents and the merchants. He has also provided detail on a fascinating cast of characters.

Not surprisingly, political leanings and affiliation played into the story. The Jefferson and Madison administrations appointed their Republican allies to the key roles of U.S. attorney, collector of customs and militia officers. Much of the population—and certainly the merchants, many part of the Burlington elite—actively opposed the federal restraints on trade that exacerbated the partisan conflict and smuggled with impunity. They shielded themselves behind men like the *Black Snake* crew with little resources or legal sophistication. Along with delineating the events, Shattuck introduces rich portraits of the *personae dramatis*. He describes the trials of Chittenden County sheriff Daniel Staniford, charged with building, maintaining and staffing a jail that could not hold any determined prisoner, including those charged in the *Black Snake* affair. The porous county jails helped induce Vermont to erect the state prison at Windsor, where Samuel Mott, one of the leaders of the smugglers, would serve time. Lieutenant Alexander Miller of Wallingford received orders to lead his company in the Vermont militia to the north to assist the revenue agents. His letters to his wife, Lucretia, provide detail of the difficulties, dangers and political intrigue in confronting the smuggling where Jeffersonian and Federalist adherents worked at cross purposes. His depiction of the upstanding, hardworking, litigious and financially meticulous William C. Harington, variously attorney, justice of the peace, state's attorney and member of the state council, who prosecuted the *Black Snake* crew, allows him to probe the rudimentary but developing Vermont legal apparatus.

Shattuck, in a chapter entitled "Vannessed," follows the evidence he uncovered to question the integrity of the well-connected Jeffersonian Republican Cornelius P. Van Ness, who came to Vermont in 1806 with high expectations. He practiced law in Franklin County until his appointment as U.S. attorney in 1810 and as collector of customs in 1813. He eventually served in the Vermont General Assembly, as governor and as chief justice of the Vermont Supreme Court. He ended his career in a cloud as minister to Spain, where he consorted with a Spanish woman while his wife died at home. A wealthy man by the standards of the time, he apparently spent beyond his means. Driven by financial necessity and a certain veniality, Van Ness figured out how to game the system for its financial rewards. Shattuck asks why an ambitious man would leave the more prestigious position of U.S. attorney to become collector of customs. He unearths the documentary record and definitively answers the question: money. This story includes other local notables and characters, including Nathan B. Haswell, Jabez Penniman (married to Ethan Allen's widow), the hapless *Black Snake* participant Francis Ledgard, the shadowy smuggler Ramon Manzuco and the much beset Samuel Buel, who with determination and little success dogged Van Ness until his own death.

This richly researched book, densely populated with fresh information, will command a place on the shelf of the history of Vermont in the first decade and a half of the nineteenth century.

H. NICHOLAS MULLER III

Long a student of Vermont's past, Dr. Muller has published articles on Vermont and the embargo and smuggling on Lake Champlain and overland during the War of 1812 among his books and other publications on Vermont.

PREFACE

In 1997, the largest and longest criminal trial in Vermont history took place over the course of four months in Burlington at the United States District Court for the District of Vermont, with Judge William K. Sessions presiding. It concerned a huge, sophisticated international drug-smuggling operation involving tons of hashish being moved by many individuals, including members of organized crime, between Pakistan, Africa's west coast, the Netherlands, Canada and, of all places, Vermont. The organization was so far-reaching and well connected that it even used the huge oil industry barge *Giant 4*, the Dutch vessel that raised the sunken Russian submarine *Kursk* in 2001.[1]

The role played by the Vermont participants concerned, primarily, providing the strong backs needed to shepherd many dozens of large plastic barrels full of hashish, strapped together and floating in unwieldy rafts out on the St. Lawrence River, up onto Canadian shores. Those rafts had been previously assembled and then set adrift by *Giant 4* crew members as the ship made its way upriver toward Montreal. Meanwhile, the Vermonters, who had already established a base of operations on the north side of the river, waited with their Zodiac boats to go out to intercept and manhandle the rafts ashore, break them apart and then convey their contents southward to smuggle into Vermont. Their efforts went astray when frightened Asian workers panicked and set the rafts loose before it was time, at which point vigilant coast watchers reported the suspicious activities to the Canadian Coast Guard, causing everyone to abandon their efforts and flee homeward. After many months of investigation by the U.S. Attorney's Office, the Drug

Enforcement Administration and the U.S. Customs Service, the Vermonters were caught and finally brought to court.

I was privileged to serve as one of two Department of Justice assistant United States attorneys prosecuting the case, and it was certainly one of the highlights of my thirty-five years in the law enforcement arena. Since retiring from that work, I have been extraordinarily fortunate to be able to combine those prior experiences with my deep love of the past as I went off in pursuit of an advanced degree in military history. Delving deep into obscure legal documents became my focus, and it surprisingly resulted in the uncovering of some important information, allowing me to write my first book recasting a bit of important Massachusetts history that took place in the first months of the Shays' Rebellion. That effort was so successful that I turned my attention to early Vermont history to determine whether there might be some period in its past vulnerable to similar inquiry. And much to my delight, indeed there was.

As I began my initial research, reading about the times surrounding Thomas Jefferson's ill-conceived Embargo of 1807 and the significant impact it had on Vermonters living on the northern frontier, it became clear that there were several aspects of the era ripe for further examination—particularly the incredible situation existing on Lake Champlain involving various smuggling groups brazenly operating between Vermont and Quebec in defiance of the embargo and challenging the ineffective measures taken by authorities to stem their illicit trade.

When the two factions did meet, it frequently resulted in a physical confrontation of some kind. Unfortunately, one such confrontation, the so-called *Black Snake* Affair, ended in the vicious murders of three officials. Two of them were militiamen from Rutland, the first two individuals named in a heartbreakingly long list of those giving their lives in service to the U.S. Department of the Treasury over the past two hundred years.[2] Because of my experiences working with the Treasury's Customs Service on many cases, my familiarity with smuggling between Vermont and Quebec and learning from the Shays-era book that accounts of the past are not always accurate, I was curious to know if those tumultuous times in the state's history, and the deaths of these men in particular, had been fully and accurately reported. As it turned out, they had not.

John Quincy Adams's observation that "posterity delights in details" is just the kind of wise counsel that a historian relishes, and it was to the details that I then looked. Fortunately, with access to the important resources at various institutions around New England, a close examination of documents revealed substantial new facts, recasting exactly what took place before, during and after the murders and providing a vibrant contextual picture of these times awash in rich detail.

As with the Massachusetts project, legal documents—ranging from routine papers filed by a sheriff's deputy in the normal course of his duties to decisions rendered by the Vermont and United States Supreme Courts that involved some of the participants in the events of 1808 and thereafter—became my primary focus. This proved a most interesting journey, as it brought me to voluminous state and federal court files, many covered with black soot and untouched for over two centuries. It was indeed a rare privilege to examine these important documents for the many untapped treasures they revealed and to then reconstruct in these pages these tumultuous times.

I was totally unprepared for the story that was about to unfold and which involved, incredibly, not only extensive smuggling along the state's border with Quebec in locations with which I was already familiar but also early members of the agencies for and with which I worked—the Office of the United States Attorney (then called the District Attorney) for the District of Vermont and Customs Service, as well as the state and federal courts in which I practiced and the cities where I presented many cases to grand juries.

But this turned out to be a story much more interesting than just these murders, for they occurred at a critical moment in Vermont's history when numerous other challenges were also taking place. It was their senseless and vicious manner that stood out, accentuating those moments and providing the modern-day student with a very raw and stark lesson of what it meant to be a Vermonter at the time. Many opportunities presented themselves to creative individuals, both criminals and professionals alike (sometimes indistinguishable), and some rose into, while others fell out of, positions of prominence in these few years. To fully understand what took place following the end of the War of 1812 with the Treaty of Ghent in 1815, one must first pause and consider deeply these particular years because they constitute a pivotal moment connecting the state's infancy, two decades earlier, with its future.

During the course of researching and traveling, I had the pleasure of meeting many wonderful people who unfailingly provided much important assistance, allowing this project to reach fruition. Unquestionably high on my list is one of Vermont's most distinguished historians, Dr. H. Nicholas Muller III, himself a recognized scholar of these particular times. Over the course of many conversations, and too few lunches, Nick was an enthusiastic early supporter of my work, immediately recognizing the incredible value that legal documents provide. He unstintingly provided positive feedback and guidance, allowing me to confidently venture out and make the observations and conclusions that follow. It was only through his probing and questioning that I came to refine what was at first an acceptable thesis into one I hope others will find of value and interest as well.

I am also most thankful to Nick for introducing me to his longtime associate in academia, research and writing, another of Vermont's esteemed historians Dr. John J. Duffy. Even as these two busy men were in the throes of completing their most recent publication concerning Ethan Allen, they graciously took time to provide me with much support. Together with Art Cohn, historian, archaeologist, co-founder and former executive director of the important Lake Champlain Maritime Museum, each took time to read drafts of this manuscript, and it is unquestionably better than it would otherwise have been without their input. It was through Art's many contacts that we were able to locate and procure two potash barrels (modern-day re-creations of a very difficult object to find), which will be an important addition to the museum's collections, for they represent, in tangible form, why those three individuals senselessly lost their lives.

But none of this would have been possible without having access to the primary source documents that shed so much incredible light onto these times. For that, I am exceedingly thankful for the riches lying within the Vermont State Archives and Records Administration in Middlesex, particularly its many untouched legal documents. They constitute true gold to a researcher and are ably overseen by archivists Mariessa Dobrick, Scott Reilly and, in particular, Susan Swaska, the person in charge of efforts to centralize and index the state's old legal documents. I also have Sue to thank for guiding me to some unusual cases I certainly would never have found on my own. Rutland Superior Court clerk Therese Corsonnes and Franklin County Superior Court operations manager James Pelkey also provided me with much help in allowing access to their files.

One of the most interesting repositories I visited was the National Archives at Boston, located in nearby Waltham, Massachusetts, where all New England federal court files are held. For that assistance, I am indebted to archives specialist Walter Hickey for guiding me through its many, incredible resources, which allowed me to flesh out this story in ways that would not have otherwise been possible.

Librarian Paul Carnahan at the Vermont Historical Society in Barre; Prudence Doherty and her staff manning the Special Collections at the University of Vermont's Bailey/Howe Library in Burlington; Eva Garcelon-Hart of the Henry Sheldon Museum in Middlebury; the staff of the Fletcher Free Library in Burlington; James Davidson of the Rutland Historical Society in Rutland; and Palmer E. Martin, grand secretary of the Grand Lodge of Vermont, Free and Accepted Masons, all made their various collections available, affording me many opportunities to discover yet additional seldom-seen gems hiding deep within.

I was also fortunate to meet Catherine Becker Wiest Desmarias, owner of Stone House Historical Research in Essex Junction. We had several conversations regarding early warning out methods in New England, and it was through her help that I was able to more fully appreciate what this meant to the down and out living in Burlington during these times. Additionally, local historian David Blow was most helpful, and it was his map of period Burlington, hanging at the Fletcher Free Library, that made much of this story come alive, thanks to his careful reconstruction of the town's early roads and buildings.

I am also most thankful for the insights provided by Ranger Richard Colton, historian and historic weapons safety officer of the National Park Service's Springfield Armory in Springfield, Massachusetts. Through Rich's extensive knowledge of firearms and the history of their manufacture in Vermont, I came to better understand the particulars of the truly extraordinary weapon that was used in the murders.

Of course, none of this could have been so admirably and competently put into book form without the able assistance of those in the publishing industry, specifically Whitney Tarella Landis, commissioning editor, and Jaime Muehl, editorial department manager, of The History Press. I am most grateful for their wonderful insights and recommendations, as well as the work of their design team, in bringing this project to fruition.

The actual event took place on the Winooski (also called the Onion) River, within earshot of the Ethan Allen Homestead, located on the Intervale on the north side of Burlington. In attempting to re-create exactly what happened, I visited the area on a couple occasions and met with Tom McHugh, a member of the homestead's board of directors, and museum director Dan O'Neil. Tom and I walked the river when it was on the verge of flood stage, slipping and sliding across its banks, which were oozing mud and infested with so many mosquitoes that our first venture had to be curtailed to await the dropping of leaves from lush undergrowth in the coming fall. It was only then that we were able to return and, as close as I think possible, identify the stretch of river where the incident unfolded. As this book reached publication, arrangements were being completed with officials to erect appropriate signs in the area to commemorate this tragedy.

As hard as I worked to research and write the book on early Massachusetts history, this project was many times more complicated. The fact that few have delved deeply into the personal lives of prominent, and not so prominent, individuals living in Burlington at the time made the work all the more intense, as there were few secondary resources available revealing the underlying context of their personal travails. I have no doubt that much more information remains hidden in legal files never opened (after all, at some point, a researcher has to stop researching and start writing), but I hope that this story provides sufficient facts to allow the modern reader to begin to appreciate the difficulties that Jefferson's embargo and the War of 1812 posed for those living on Vermont's northern border. And on that note, of course, any and all errors that might ensue, I wholeheartedly embrace as my own.

In the end, it has been a richly rewarding experience, and I have loved every minute of it.

1
KING POTASH

The estimate from Content C. Hallock and Israel Williams for the rope, yard and frame used to support the weight of the falling prisoner's body came in at $10.00. Additional materials, such as various timbers and 304 feet of planking, held in place by necessary nails and spikes, added another $16.80 to the cost. On top of that, the manpower needed to raise the entire structure ran $6.00 more. When one includes the cost of assembling the coffin ($2.00), clothing its inhabitant ($4.25) and digging the grave and covering it all up (another $2.00), then, overall, that part of the process was actually quite reasonable. However, when taking into account the additional costs of having so many soldiers employed as guards for months on end, it really became a rather expensive undertaking. Nevertheless, when one further considers that this was the first hanging since Vermont became a state in 1791 (the first having taken place in Bennington in 1778 upon "prosecutor" Ethan Allen's dubious conviction of David Redding for "inimical conduct"), that should count for something.[3]

Chittenden County's high sheriff, Daniel Staniford (circa 1768–1847), was already familiar with Hallock at the time, having experienced the pleasure of his company in his jail on at least two prior occasions. In 1804, Hallock was arrested for debt-related reasons and then once again in January 1808 for an undisclosed matter, managing to escape only two weeks later.[4] He appears to have mended his ways in the next few months, and while the most recent suit remained pending, he was allowed to provide a much-needed service to his jailor. Staniford accepted the two men's estimate for the gallows and directed them to a spot just north of Burlington Village, a sparsely populated area little serviced by roads, and out onto a small knoll in a field of second-growth pine.[5] The work was quickly completed over the next few days, and a final bill for services was submitted on October 18, 1808, detailing their efforts, including those of their two assistants, James Tyler and William Hinkson.

While it would be some time before Staniford finally received a limited reimbursement from the state legislature for his efforts, he could no longer be distracted by the needs of the soon-to-be-dead and returned his attention to dealing with the many other prisoners recently placed under his care. Composed of the likes of the two Taylors, the three Hoxies and that vicious band headed by Truman Mudget and Samuel I. Mott, responsible for the recent savage ambush and murders of three individuals (two of them government officials), the rebellious group of smugglers was vigorously threatening to destroy his jail—to literally pull it apart—if the hanging proceeded, and a riot and escaping criminals were the last things he needed.

Before becoming sheriff in 1803 and assuming the honorific "Esquire" after his name, Staniford had operated a successful distillery and brewery, also located on the north side, immediately south of the execution site. His was just one of thirty such operations in Chittenden County at a time when, according to the Department of the Treasury, charged with collecting revenue from such ventures based on their number of gallons produced, there were an estimated twenty-two thousand, abetted by thirteen thousand retailers of their products, operating within the current sixteen states. Of the thirty-four taverns and houses of public entertainment licensed in the county in 1801, only three (those of John Doxey, Nathan Smith and Widow Comstock) operated within the town, revealing that the rural folk were never far from a drink. In fact, in the five miles separating Burlington from Shelburne to the south, there was one tavern for each mile.[6] Unfortunately, the presence of so many opportunities to indulge proved one of the most significant factors contributing to the violence that Staniford encountered in the summer of 1808.

A native of Bennington, Staniford arrived in town from North Carolina after several years of trading and took up his craft in alcohol, boasting to all in April 1803 that he had "on hand, a considerable quantity of GIN, of his own manufacturing of an excellent quality & allowed by the best Physicians to be as healthy as any imported liquors." He was similarly proud of his beer-producing prowess, "flatter[ing] himself that he shall be able to brew as good Beer, Ale or Porter, as any imported from Foreign Countries." He had every reason to be pleased, for similar operations around the state were each turning out an estimated fifty gallons of their various products every day, or some six hundred barrels a year. But he also had to apologize at the moment for his inability to produce sufficient concoctions because of a lack of barley due to the bad season, promising to expand his operations as the summer progressed. Business was, in fact, so good that he sought "a smart active Boy, of fourteen or fifteen years of age" as an apprentice, as well as "a smart and faithful man, for six or twelve months."[7]

Careful, attentive employees were always in demand to help in manufacturing the substantial amount of alcohol the community craved. It was a dangerous and difficult vocation, particularly for the "rectifier," the person responsible for applying measured amounts of heat from open fires to fermenting liquid, producing combustible alcohol and, not infrequently, resulting in the destruction of the entire operation. Captain Joseph Bowman lost six hundred bushels of rye and three hundred gallons of gin in his Montpelier business in 1803, while the "peculiarly unfortunate" Captain Jabez Rogers of Middlebury lost his in 1805, wherein "it will be recounted that it is but a few years since his distillery was twice burnt, and property to a great amount destroyed." However, none of those events compared to the bizarre circumstances that, in 1807, enveloped Colonel Joseph Jones, of St. Albans, who passed on after "slipping into a vat of hot liquor in his distillery." To avoid those problems, more recently, Lewis Wood, in Hinesburg, echoed Staniford's call for careful employees, advertising in April 1809 for a distiller to take control of the local distillery: "To such an [sic] one Generous Wages will be given."[8]

Notwithstanding any of Staniford's successes for the moment, he did experience some difficulties paying his debts, forcing two New York creditors to file suit against him in July 1805 for failure to settle a $1,500 claim for goods sold to him, resulting in their attaching two five-acre lots he owned, including a "dwelling house, barn & distillery and other buildings," to ensure payment; he subsequently defaulted on the claim and was ordered to pay $1,282.[9] With those days behind him, Staniford now found himself overseeing a recently built jail, one made necessary when it became clear that lodging the town's various miscreants more than twenty miles away in Vergennes (where Vermont's notorious congressman Matthew Lyon had served time in 1798 upon his conviction for violating the Alien and Sedition Acts) proved an unacceptable inconvenience to a growing population.

The structure might have been of recent vintage, but challenges remained. Only months earlier, on November 17, 1807, Moses Rice, recently sentenced for theft, and then again on January 22, 1808, Richard

Wheeler, just sentenced for counterfeiting money, "broke gaol," forcing Staniford to take out notices in the local newspaper requesting information leading to their arrests, with a promise to those coming forward of being "handsomely rewarded."[10] And as if those incidents were not embarrassing enough, only two weeks before Wheeler's departure, on January 5, the county grand jury determined that the facility was "~~totally~~ insufficient for the safe, or even comfortable keeping of prisoners, ~~and that the same does no honor to the County~~ [strikethroughs in original]."[11] Ironically, Staniford had himself recently experienced these conditions firsthand as a prisoner but had been allowed his freedom on October 5, 1807, after satisfying another $1,800 debt-related judgment rendered against him. The possibility that the experience might have undermined his authority within the community was of such concern to the head judge of the county court that he issued a notice to all that Staniford had fulfilled his debt obligations, and the public was "to take due notice thereof and govern themselves accordingly."[12]

Now he found himself in the center of a much larger and quickly unfolding drama, one that had been building for the past several months and had the full attention of officials in Washington, including President Thomas Jefferson.

THE SEVERAL YEARS BETWEEN 1808 and 1815, ending with the demise of the Federalist Party and the onset of the so-called Era of Good Feelings at the close of the War of 1812, provided some of the most challenging and defining moments in Vermont's history. Taking place within the larger Age of the Democratic Revolution, running from the conclusion of the Seven Years' War in 1763 to the mid-1800s as democratic governments supplanted monarchal rule, they marked the end of a twenty-five-year period of "good years" for the state. Its unique birth and ensuing peculiar growth pattern witnessed it moving from, arguably, a state of nature into self-declared independence in 1777 and on to admission to the Union in 1791. Throughout, settlers moved in from states to the immediate south and began their intensive attack on the environment, withholding all restraint in their efforts to wrest a livelihood from its abundant forests and waters. The population grew, towns were formed, rudimentary governance was instituted, opportunities and the economy expanded and many relished their special moment, "when striving was buoyant and small successes seemed to justify great visions of the future."[13] However, these more recent times brought unanticipated challenges and severely tested their positive feelings, forcing them to accommodate change from outside as they could never have imagined.

On the national level, unraveling relations between Britain and France, attended by Bonaparte's invasion of Spain, were of high concern, forcing myriad, complex decisions on Jefferson's administration. Following closely on the heels of Aaron Burr's riveting treason trial in 1807, the administration was also dealing with legislation seeking to end America's involvement in the international slave trade, as dictated by the ratification of the U.S. Constitution in 1788. Additionally, its attention was increasingly drawn to the unwieldy, expansive northern border, where, from New York's Oswego and Sackets Harbor on Lake Ontario to Maine's Passamaquoddy Bay, violence began to break out. But none came close to the ferocity about to play out in Vermont.

There, notwithstanding the perambulations of the legislature finally coming to an end and its settling into its new home in Montpelier, and attended by such advancements as the building of the *Vermont*, the world's second steamboat (launched the following year), and the erection of a state prison in Windsor (a facility Staniford unsuccessfully proposed to build in Burlington in 1805), 1808 marked the start of this unattractive, disruptive and troublesome time. It would not be until the seemingly never-ending slavery issue came to consume the country's collective attention and Vermont sent its boys southward to fight the battles of the 1860s that the nation would again be so focused on events as it was this particular year, followed closely by the next few.

All members of Vermont's frontier society suddenly and without warning became embroiled by the decisions of others located in far-off places casting them as pawns in an international game. Without a tradition of democratic governance, many of these second-generation pioneers, separated from the ideals their fathers had experienced firsthand during the Revolution and possessing new perspectives and expectations, assumed a defensive, parochial attitude toward those outside influences challenging their cherished equilibrium. In the state's early years, they had no need for an intrusive formalized government, relying on the towering reputations of individuals such as Ira and Ethan Allen and Governors Thomas Chittenden and Moses Robinson to guide their immediate futures as they witnessed the humbling of Great Britain and successfully retained possession of lands sought by intruding settlers from New York. The times now demanded that they focus their attention on unfamiliar and unsettling national events, brought on by Thomas Jefferson, and severely tested their understanding of place within the overarching federal government, a concept they had never experienced in the past, let alone understood.

Many factors contributed to the internal discord, but none was of such significance as economics, fanned by political flames of national and foreign import. In this particularly contentious election year, when one was either a Jeffersonian Democrat (alternatively called a Republican) or a Hamiltonian Federalist, virtually all communal and business relationships were filtered by how one neighbor viewed another through a political lens. This constituted a severe and radical ideological division that cut deeply through Vermont society, one in which Democrats steadfastly pursued the Revolution's promises as they understood them, seeking to reconcile classical Republican concepts of civic virtue with the dictates of Jefferson's domestic agrarian policy while also fearing the prospect that political and religious forces beyond their control would derail their success. Meanwhile, conservative Federalists, advocates of strong government, international trade and a strong military, shuddered at what those populist upheavals meant to their own ideals.[14]

No institution in Vermont, still in the process of conceptualizing and implementing its particular needs, was immune to the impact of politics, penetrating deeply into all aspects of the economy. Businessmen, merchants, farmers and consumers alike felt its force just as the state was trying to put into place a credible banking system to replace a preexisting bartering tradition. This preoccupation with financial matters was deemed so important that counterfeiters threatening the state's work toward this end received draconian sentences of many years' imprisonment, while those inflicting egregious physical harm on others were fined but a few dollars. All faculties concerned with safety and security became deeply affected, including the state's developing court system and attending enforcement mechanisms—the constables and sheriffs, aided, as needed, by the militia. County jails were unable to provide the services that these new times demanded, and authorities were forced to build their new state prison. This was the particular focus of Vermont policymakers in these years when they didn't have to deal with the discord imposed on them by outsiders.

Prior accounts have acknowledged, in passing, the difficulties Vermonters experienced in these years, but few have attempted to explore deeply the individual participants who became embroiled in them as they sought to negotiate their way, incurring the least amount of harm upon themselves. Recognizing the rare opportunities for exploitation that vulnerable Vermont represented, those with less than good intentions came north seeking personal advancement. In years prior, crime had been relatively limited, local in scope and non-threatening to society at large, and it did not require sophisticated enforcement. But now, the times had become unsettled, and the state became a haven for opportunists, allowing for the arrival of not only a more determined criminal element, such as the many counterfeiters and smugglers fueled by readily available alcohol, but also those aspiring to high social, professional and political ranks in pursuit of personal gain. This was a time when many found themselves participating in varying degrees of, if not wholly illegal, then at least marginally moral conduct that had become so much a part of everyday life. For some, it was simply a question of who had the strongest will to succeed and who could survive the rough-and-tumble challenges coming their way, and for those unable or unwilling to adjust, they were destined to suffer their failures.

The conditions deteriorated so much that concepts of tolerance, trust and respect among the inhabitants were easily cast off, and foreboding, unforeseen consequences were unleashed. As communities along Vermont's northern border revealed a distasteful tolerance for lawbreaking from within and businessmen relentlessly pursued the bottom line, those charged with enforcing unpopular, ineffectual laws increasingly found themselves outmanned, outgunned and victimized by creative and resourceful gangs and wily entrepreneurs. This was a distinctly freewheeling frontier, one fueled by the alcohol that Staniford and others produced, where personal inclinations found little reason for restraint. Unfortunately, in the ensuing mêlée, not only were violent deaths (including at least one terrible disfigurement) visited on the enforcers, but also the incipient presence of distrust arose even among themselves. There simply were no gray areas, no places to hide, and people, regardless of social, political or military rank, wore their allegiances on their sleeves as they went about, openly praising and condemning one another, frequently in a vicious manner. In its removed frontier status, Vermont represented perhaps the starkest example of this in the country, revealing the deep division existing between the political parties. Their mutual animosity was so raw and palpable that even instances of murder were not far off.

Greed and competition for place consumed many, launching the careers of some while shattering those of others. Conflicting issues of state and federal concern were exposed in unseemly ways as local judges issued orders obstructing national interests and federal customs officials were threatened by members of the state's militia, men who were themselves alleged to have engaged in criminal behavior up to and including advocating the murder of those government officials. Even those in Washington counseled violence against state officers in order to preserve the sanctity of federal interests.

To add insult to their self-inflicted travails, they found themselves having to defend against lawsuits brought by the very people they had arrested and charged with wrongdoing. Suspicion spawned egregious recriminations as enforcers found themselves pitted against one another, and allegations of favoritism and illegal acts were exchanged, requiring the intervention of two presidents, the U.S. Congress and the Supreme Court. It was a system turned in on itself, and lives were lost in the process.

And it was in the midst of this roiling caldron that Daniel Staniford, together with his overworked deputies, found himself that summer. Over in Caledonia County, Sheriff David Elkins already had an inkling of problems about to explode and, in May 1807, "absconded…& placed himself under the protection of his Britannic Majesty's government of Upper Canada," whereupon High Bailiff David Tilton, "following the tracks & example of his predecessor," did the same in October.[15] Staniford remained and could only watch as Burlington and the surrounding area erupted with gangs moving across the countryside and over the waters, bold enough to do so even while companies of militia troops passed through his town in response and took up residency in his jail to guard the most violent taken into custody.

It was a sea of unrest that the government was attempting to quell, an effort then questionably within the control—or competence—of its feeble militia. All was as Jefferson had roundly condemned months earlier when he, in truth the actual author of these trials, proclaimed to the nation that this part of Vermont was in a state of insurrection.

NONE OF VERMONT'S PROBLEMS during this time make sense unless one seriously factors in the important roles played by unique geographical features, those gifts bestowed by nature, and the presence of an international border, one created by politicians and soldiers. For, despite the state's grandiose motto of "Freedom and Unity," actually only the former was in evidence in these years when the single common—and overriding—interest all newcomers shared was "the lure of the land," the one tangible resource capable of sustaining in them "a spirit of enterprise and hope."[16]

The first state admitted into the Union following the close of the Revolutionary War, this irregular, wedge-shaped, 9,250-square-mile tract of land had constituted not much more than a dark, indistinguishable shadow on a New England map between two states—New Hampshire (founded in 1623, became a colony in 1679) and New York (1664 and 1685, respectively)—each with well over a century of history behind them.

Period maps prominently display the many landmark features of these areas, particularly major watercourses that naturally attracted the attention of explorers, settlers and traders. For those residing along the Atlantic seaboard, the place of first impression for so many English transplants, there were no more important routes than those waterways that ran down from the interior and emptied into the ocean, paths that did not require the backbreaking work of carving out roads from a wooded wilderness. Easily accessible, the course of New England's early settlement and ensuing economic success closely reflected their ready access.

Straddling this dark mass of land are two major river systems, each integral parts of their own watersheds and each in keeping with what a map-dependent person would perceive as the course a river is supposed to run; that is, from north to south. And indeed, that is exactly what the Connecticut River does, defining the state's entire eastern border, flowing from its headwaters in the upper reaches of New Hampshire, through Massachusetts and Connecticut and ending at Long Island Sound. To the west, across the border and a short distance into New York, the Hudson River follows in the same manner, ending its southerly journey in New York Bay. However, in between these two drainage systems, running through the Valley of Vermont situated between the Green and Taconic Mountains, is one of much smaller dimension and taking a counterintuitive route, one that goes entirely in the opposite direction. With headwaters in the general area of the town of Peru, at 2,600 feet, the state's longest river, the Otter Creek begins its northward flow of just over one hundred miles, dropping to an elevation of some 95 feet when it empties into Lake Champlain, that body of water the Iroquois called *Caniaderi Guarunte*, the "Lake that is the Gate of the Country."[17]

For an early, western impression of this expanse of water, let Champlain himself explain what he saw in July 1609 as he finished ascending the 106-mile-long Richelieu River, passing over those northbound waters rushing toward him and into the St. Lawrence River behind him:

> *The next day we entered the lake…where I saw four fine islands, ten, twelve, and fifteen leagues long, which were formerly inhabited by the savages…There were also many rivers falling into the lake, bordered by many fine trees of the same kinds as those we have in France, with many vines finer than any I have seen in any other place; also many chestnut trees on the border of this lake, which I have not seen before…*
>
> *Continuing our course over this lake on the western side, I noticed, while observing the country, some very high mountains on the eastern* [Vermont]

side, on the top of which there is snow [rock outcroppings]. *I made inquiry of the savages whether these localities were inhabited, when they told me that the Iroquois dwelt there, and that there were beautiful valleys in these places, with plains productive in grain, such as I had eaten in this country, together with many kinds of fruit without limit.*[18]

Looking on Vermont's mountains was a sight that never failed to impress, as attested to by a member of Burgoyne's invading army in 1777 upon his own entry onto the lake:

Here a scene of indescribable sublimity burst upon us. Before us lay the waters of Lake Champlain, a sheet of unruffled glass, stretching away some ninety miles to the south, widening and straightening as rocks and cliffs projected in the most fantastic shapes into its channel. On each side is a thick and uninhabited wilderness, now rising up into mountains, now falling into glens, while a noble background is presented towards the east by the Green Mountains, whose summits appear even to pierce the clouds. On the west mountains [the Adirondacks] *still more gigantic in loftiness, pride and dignity. I cannot by any powers of language do justice to such a scene.*[19]

A part of the massive Lake Champlain–St. Lawrence watershed tilting northward, the Otter Creek constitutes but a small contribution to this, the sixth-largest body of fresh water in the United States. The watershed occupies 435 square miles of surface area (an impressive 19:1 ratio of drainage area to surface area), is 115 miles in length, varies in width from 1 to 12 miles, reaches down to a depth of some four hundred feet and is dotted by no fewer than seventy islands. Many other rivers contribute to this basin, 56 percent of them located within Vermont, 37 percent in New York and 7 percent in Quebec.[20] Those principal rivers on the east side of the lake in Vermont include the Onion (also called the Winooski), the Missisquoi and the Lamoille. All of this water, as well as that draining south from Missisquoi Bay extending into Quebec, finds an outlet through a narrowing in the lake where it flows down the Richelieu River, finally emptying into the St. Lawrence River in Sorel, fifty miles downstream from Montreal.

There are no natural outlets from the lake to the south, which would have afforded surrounding lands the ability to become a part of important trading networks such as those communities existing along the Connecticut and Hudson Rivers experienced. That deficiency was finally remedied in 1823, when, during New York's canal-building frenzy (the Erie Canal opened two years later) and well after the events of 1808, the sixty-mile Champlain Canal opened, allowing for shipping costs to drop a dramatic 80 percent virtually overnight and affording those living in the interior ready access to markets they had only dreamed of. But until that happened, there was only one direction for settlers to look toward for survival, and that was the one in which nature sent those lake waters.[21]

AFTER CHAMPLAIN AND BURGOYNE left the Richelieu and glided out onto the lake, they soon came upon an impinging geologic feature to their immediate left. While the shores on each side, separated by less than a mile, had begun to flare outward, those to the east suddenly jutted back into the channel, creating a short peninsula that then turned abruptly to the south, much like a bent finger, and had the effect of partially enveloping the adjoining waters to its south in a shallow bay.

The earliest settlement of these particular lands occurred in approximately 1741, when, pursuant to a royal grant, or seigniory, allowed by French king Louis XV, "councilor to the Supreme Council of Quebec and principle [*sic*] scrivener to the Marine" Francois Foucault arranged for several settlers to take up residency and begin construction of a mill. The stone structure they raised within the following two years was wind-driven, thereby providing the more recent, and still in use, name of Windmill Point and Windmill Bay. The land itself was not particularly conducive to farming, making its permanent occupation difficult, as it was repeatedly taken up and abandoned with the shifting military and political fortunes dictated by alternating French and British overseers.

Upon the conclusion of the Seven Years' War in 1763 and France's removal from North America, the following year, Foucault sold all of his interests to Quebec's British governor James Murray. In 1774, Murray leased the lands to Henry Caldwell of Quebec City. With the later delineation of an international border cutting through this locale, those lands to the north became known as Caldwell's Manor, while those to the south on Windmill Point (located "upriver") were called Caldwell's Upper Manor. Caldwell refurbished the mill and other structures that had fallen into disrepair and moved settlers into the area in the 1780s. The lands subsequently passed on to his heirs, but it was not until the 1830s, after contentious proceedings that included land speculator Ira Allen (who received a grant of the same lands from Vermont governor Thomas Chittenden in 1781), that those holding disputed titles in what was now the town of Alburgh were finally able to cease worrying about their validity.

Windmill Point continued to maintain its strategic importance in the coming years, receiving the attention of various governments because of its proximity to the border, as well as being a short, watery distance from New York's shores. The forty-fifth parallel (which extends to Vermont's eastern border, ending at the Connecticut River) separating the United States from British Canada in this particular area had been proscribed in the original grant made by James I in 1606, but because of inaccurate surveys in the intervening years, it remained a point of contention between the two countries until finally resolved in 1842.[22] As the terms of the peace of 1783 at the conclusion of the Revolutionary War did not fully describe which country had control of the area, British troops continued to maintain a presence extending southward, taking in all of Caldwell Manor and Windmill Point, positioning their posts at Dutchman's Point in North Hero, Vermont, and Pointe au Fer, New York.

Not fully aware that foreign troops remained in occupation at the time, upon Vermont's resolution of competing land claims with neighboring New York and its becoming part of the Union in 1791, Congress drafted the very first legislation for its fourteenth state.[23] Three issues were addressed: the application of federal law, its enforcement through the naming of a federal court judge and U.S. marshal and the establishment of a critically important revenue-gathering location to monitor international trade between the two countries. On March 2, 1791, President Washington signed into law "An Act Giving Effect to the Laws of the United States, within the State of Vermont," providing, in part:

> *Sec. 1…That from and after the third day of March next, all the laws of the United States, which are not locally inapplicable, ought to have, and shall have, the same force and effect within the state of Vermont, as elsewhere in the United States;* [and]…
>
> *Sec. 8…that for the due collection of* [customs] *duties, there shall be in the said state of Vermont, one district; and a collector shall be appointed, to reside at Alburgh, on Lake Champlain, which shall be the only port of entry or delivery within the said district, of any goods, wares or merchandize, not the growth or manufacture of the United States.*[24]

As the federal government sought to establish a physical presence in this remote area, those living in Alburgh proceeded in their own attempts to create a town government, one that would have authority over the same lands the British claimed as their own. Significant problems began to arise between the various interests, fueled by Governor Chittenden himself. On May 16, 1792, exasperated with the inability of the town to move forward in its efforts, apparently because of the questionable loyalty of some residents toward the new Vermont government he headed, Chittenden admonished local authorities:

> *In case there are any of the inhabitants of said town that have sworn allegiance to the King and government of Great Britain, such obligations cease with the government and can be no obligation* [objection] *to a submission to the laws of this and the United States. Would those people chuse* [sic] *to be under the British government, they must move within its limits, otherwise they ought to submit to the government of the state in which they live.*[25]

Two months later, the problem remained but now threatened to adversely affect the country's relationship with Great Britain. On July 12, 1792, Secretary of State Jefferson deemed it necessary to write to Chittenden seeking his cooperation in calming down the situation:

> *Sir…I must renew my entreaties to your Excellency that no innovation in the state of things may be attempted for the present. It is but lately that an opportunity has been afforded of pressing on the court of Gt. Britain our rights on the question of posts, and it would be truly unfortunate if any premature measures on the part of your state should furnish a pretext for suspending the negotiations on this subject. I rely therefore that you will see the interest even of your own state in leaving to the federal government the measures for recovering its rights…*[26]

Tensions continued, and two years later, in 1794, Ira Allen expressed his own frustrations with those living in the town named after him, calling them "such a pack of people" that he dared not trust even the town clerk with the original copies of deeds he sought to record.[27] Fortunately, upon John Jay's treaty, concluded that same year, the posting of British troops was finally resolved, and they agreed to remove to above the parallel by June 1, 1796. Notably, only one year after achieving statehood, the people along this northern frontier had already established a reputation for pursuing their own self-interests, and it was something that Jefferson could not have forgotten.

DESPITE THE CRITICAL IMPORTANCE that Canada played in the upcoming years, those most directly involved in settling Vermont's frontier came from the south, moving their way northward from Connecticut and Massachusetts up the Connecticut River in the years immediately following the Seven Years' War (only somewhat restrained by the 1763 Proclamation line, drawn diagonally through the wilderness, that was meant to stop settlers from going any farther), accelerating their pace after 1783. Accordingly, alliances toward Hartford and Boston remained strong for these adventurers, while those settling in the southwest part of the state looked toward Albany and the Hudson River for commercial outlets. Even so, one interested Bennington observer at the time, seeking to catalogue the state's various attributes, took the trouble in 1787 to approach other towns to answer such questions as: "What trade hath your town with…Canada…?"; "What are the articles usually imported and exported and how do you judge the balance of trade?"; and "What is the quality of the timber, and do you export any, how much, and where to?"[28] These interesting questions aside, a substantial portion of the state, some three-quarters of it, lacked any real need to deal with Canadian markets, and it became an important factor contributing to the rise of domestic sectionalism taking place early in the next century.

With the southern areas becoming tamed, the next region to see settlement was the Champlain Valley. The first census taken in 1792 revealed a statewide population of 85,341, spread out over a seven-county area. This climbed to 154,465 by 1800, with residents living in eleven counties, and to 217,719, residing in thirteen counties, by 1810. This last was the year that Alburgh's county, Grand Isle, was first listed as possessing a population of 3,445, whereas Staniford's Chittenden County numbered 18,120. For the town of Burlington, that number had risen more than five-fold between 1790 and 1810, from 300 to 1,689 (it was not listed as one of the top five population centers until 1830). Notwithstanding those impressive increases, Vermont witnessed a marked outpouring of its people in the following decade, precipitated by the travails of 1808, the War of 1812 and incipient signs of forest degradation and soil depletion. Some sixty towns experienced a decrease in population, attended by a miserly growth rate of only 8 percent compared to the nation's 32 percent.[29] Compounding the problem, for those seeking to own land in the northwest part of the state, things remained terribly confusing, brought on by the unilateral actions of New Hampshire's governor Benning Wentworth years earlier when he made so many grants of his own while giving short shrift to competing New York claims to the same tracts. Together with the aggressive actions taken by members of the

Allen family and their associates, clear ownership for much of these lands remained highly uncertain for many years as continuous litigation took place to set matters right.

The attraction for these lands is certainly understandable. A 1794 account describes the staggering number of trees available for consumption before the cutting began:

> *In some parts of the country they are so thick, that it is with difficulty we can ride among them. In other places, they have resolved themselves into trees of large dimensions, which are generally at the distance of eight or ten feet from each other. On one acre, the number of the trees is commonly from one hundred and fifty to six hundred and fifty…Estimating a cord to be four feet in height, and width, and eight feet in length, the quantity of wood which is generally found on one acre, is from fifty to two hundred cords; where the large pines abound, the quantity of wood is much larger than what is here stated…*[30]

That wide variety of trees is further described as consisting of pine, maple, buttonwood, elm, hemlock, oak, basswood, ash and birch, attaining dimensions of up to 6 feet in diameter, reaching to a height of 247 feet and being upward of four hundred years old.[31]

To those living farther to the north, the potential these lands held was so attractive that covetous Canadian merchants looked on them as an integral part of what they envisioned as their own "Commercial Empire of the St. Lawrence." It was a worthy goal recognized by the Legislative Council of Quebec in 1788 when it allowed for the free importation of timber from Vermont, together with lumber, naval stores, cereals, dairy products, cattle, poultry and fish, all coming in by way of Lake Champlain. Quebec's surveyor of woods, Jonathan Coffin, actively sought out massive oaks at the time for the largest ships being built in Britain; these would play an important role when its navy faced Bonaparte's threats years later. Quebec's readiness to accept Vermont's trade with minimal governmental interference was also based on pragmatic reasoning. Recognizing the difficulty presented by the long frontier separating the two countries, it not only sought to exploit an economic benefit but also implicitly acknowledged that to have done otherwise—to have impeded or prohibited such imports—would have made it virtually powerless to prevent any ensuing smuggling operations rising in opposition.[32] It was an observation prescient in the extreme.

Quebec's desire to accommodate Vermont's trade was actively reciprocated by the Allens, similarly inclined to see that this wilderness, landlocked in much the way Switzerland was and needing accommodation from neighboring powers allowing it to conduct business, was subdued. Accordingly, even while efforts were being taken by others to incorporate Vermont into the Union, the family moved ahead with separatist overtures of their own to append it to Quebec, which would have allowed the fruits of their many holdings ready access to British markets.

In 1789, Levi Allen traveled to London to speak with authorities in hopes of advancing the proposition further. His goal was to negotiate "a Commercial and Friendly Intercourse between Vermont and His Majesty's Dominions." In opening his petition, Allen made note that during the war many people from New England, New York and New Jersey had fled to Vermont "in order to avoid being driven into arms against their Sovereign, by the Revolters," and lamented the ensuing separation from Britain. He then moved on to the reason for traveling so far and provided significant insights concerning the opportunities afforded by the proximity of Vermont to Canada:

> *The locality of Vermont, as well as the disposition of its inhabitants, renders its connections with Canada the most natural as well as the most advantageous of any, as the waters of Lake Champlain are the principal means by which they can export their produce, or receive their manufactures they stand in need of from this Country, on this account they earnestly hoped to have been incorporated as an appendage to the Province of Quebec, but those hopes were defeated by the boundary line of the United States as settled by the late Peace.*
>
> *…the Inhabitants of Vermont is* [sic] *computed to be one hundred and sixty thousand souls…; their vicinity to Canada and particularly the bordering of Lake Champlain, the principal entrance to that Province from the south, cannot fail…to render their Friendship and Commerce useful and acceptable, and as they are for the most part people who were (and continue to be) loyally disposed…* [to seek] *His Majesty's Royal Benevolence and Regards.*[33]

Allen's inflated assessments of the numbers of inhabitants and their purported degree of loyalty notwithstanding, his observations concerning the potential for commercial profit were accurate as he continued in a vein with which Quebec merchants could not have disagreed:

> *The produce of Vermont consists in lumber, naval stores, corn and grain of all sorts, pot and pearl ashes, pig and bar iron, cattle and provisions of*

*all kinds, horses and mules, hemp, flax, tallow, bees wax and honey, with
many more articles which the inhabitants early wish to be permitted to send
to or through the Canadian market, and to receive in exchange such goods
and manufactures as they have occasion for.*

Echoing those sentiments, one Canadian government official similarly
observed that "their situation makes them dependent on us for their
necessary supplies of European manufactures and West India commodities.
The whole of the surplus of their lands around Lake Champlain & Lake
George must pass down the River St. Lawrence in British ships, or remain
on hand and perish."[34]

London was clearly long aware of the value of having access to North
American forests. They had been an important part of its overall trade policy
for decades and played a role in the creation of its various navigation acts,
in which colonial raw materials were transported to England for processing
and then reshipped out into the vast Atlantic trading network. Certainly,
their value is reflected in no small part by the course of the wars between
England and France for over a century's time. An earlier treatise from 1755
urged officials at that time to exploit the natural resources of their colonies,
noting the importance of these woods to England's economic well-being:

*Lumber is another very valuable staple in North America, and begins to
show itself very interesting to Great Britain…And that such a country as
North America, covered with the best woods in the world; and extremely
wanted in Great Britain, should so long be without a proper encouragement
that would create a vast number of ships and make a vast number of sailors
is marvelous indeed…*

*Potash, another valuable commodity, and for making it, there is not on
the globe, a more suitable country than North America…*[35]

While Allen's negotiations were in the end unavailing, the continued
importance of Vermont's forests to England's economic well-being was a
factor not lost on even the simplest of the state's residents. They were resources
deserving of the most aggressive protection, and resorting to lawsuits was
not uncommon. As Ira Allen sought to assert his Alburgh ownership rights
in 1789, he sued two men for cutting down more than three thousand oak
trees of varying dimensions, one reportedly valued at £500. Farther to the
east, in St. Albans, Eldad Butler and Wanton Vorthrop stole five hundred
rods of rail fence and one hundred trees from Roswell Wickwire's land in

July 1804, resulting in Wickwire also filing suit.[36] Months later, in January 1805, landowner Francis Childs, of Colchester, instituted a suit against local businessman Moses Catlin (1770–1842) over the loss of some of his timber. The allegation concerned Catlin's removal of five hundred white pine, five hundred yellow pine and five hundred oak trees, together with two hundred cartloads of nondescript timber, two hundred cartloads of new-growth trees, two hundred cartloads of "under wood" and two hundred cartloads of brush, totaling $1,200. Only a week later, Childs filed a second suit alleging that Catlin stole an additional one hundred trees, one hundred cartloads of wood and fifty rods of rail fences and destroyed another five thousand of the same. While resorting to lawsuits for trespass is not particularly surprising in this regard, the presence of significant amounts of timber in these virgin lands is certainly of note. Indeed, as Ira's brother, Levi, wrote in 1785, all of this wood had quite an intoxicating effect, "timber & all lumber is quite a drug…," a situation he lamented at that particular moment for having overly relied on it for anticipated returns in a failing Quebec market.[37]

Their timber certainly constituted an important source of income. An 1810 estimate of the value of the area's Norway pines alone—those destined for ships' spars spanning lengths of between fifty and seventy feet—was set at between twelve and forty dollars each, and those squared off for other uses came in at fifty-five dollars per thousand board feet.[38] The peoples living on New England's seacoasts had their vaunted fisheries, and the South had its rice, indigo and tobacco, but these towering gifts of nature constituted a most important resource to the Vermont locals and deserved close protection. But before they could harvest their bounty, those first settlers took up residency on hilltops where there was less obstructing underbrush and better drainage, later moving to the valleys to take advantage of numerous mill sites along the rivers. They erected their crude wooden shelters and set out their first crops of wheat, a vital commodity required not only for subsistence but also as a medium of exchange to purchase goods in an economy lacking currency.

With the arrival of freezing temperatures allowing the ground to harden, the winter months served as the most opportune time to take on the herculean task of felling those many nearby behemoths, thereby creating the state's first major non-agricultural industry. Men vigorously attacked their forests, girdling, felling and burning their way through great swaths of wood, a task with which Horace Greeley had firsthand experience:

> *When we first attacked it, the snow was just going, and the water and slush were knee-deep. We were all indifferent choppers…Cutting trees and*

bushes; chopping up great trunks into manageable lengths, drawing them together, rolling up and burning great heaps of logs; saving out here and there a log that would do to saw; digging out rotten pines from the soil wherein they had embedded themselves, so that they might dry sufficiently to burn; piling and burning brush and rotten or worthless sticks, and carting home such wood as served for fuel, we persevered until the job was done.[39]

His experiences replicated those of Canadian settlers vigorously cutting through their own woods. One period visitor wrote of seeing "a profusion of decayed and half-burnt timber [lying] around, and the serpentine roots of trees, blown down by tempests, stretch[ing] into the air, in the most fantastic forms." Then, "piles of blazing timber sent forth columns of smoke, which enveloped the forests far and wide. Axes rung in every thicket, and the ear was occasionally startled by the crashing trees falling to the ground." When newly appointed governor John Graves Simcoe and his wife, Elizabeth, passed through Upper Canada in 1792, they witnessed the massive clearing efforts taking place, prompting her to write excitedly, "Perhaps you have no idea of the pleasure of walking in a burning wood, but I found it so great that I think I shall have some woods set on fire for my Evening walks."[40]

In one of the earliest descriptions of what it was these men did with their trees, in 1789, the Reverend Nathan Perkins noted, while traveling along the shores of Lake Champlain, that "a raft of lumber went off for Canada, which covered an acre of water & had two little huts on it." As impressive as that sight may have been, he concluded "the rafting business unprofitable for the state and for individuals that undertake it." Nonetheless, with the continuing arrival of settlers and the development of lands, a robust wood-related trade did indeed develop between Quebec and Vermont. In 1794, Stephen Mallett, of Colchester, sent north the first raft of oak timber destined for shipbuilding, and in 1796, John Thorp, of Charlotte, provided the first shipment of Norway pine. By 1806, one observer noted that "the commerce of Burlington is greater, I suspect than any other town in this state. It is carried on with Boston, New York, Troy, Montreal, and Quebec. Lumber, floated principally to Quebec, is one of the most considerable articles." Steady progress ensued, and in 1810 alone, some $600,000 in timber was transported in this fashion, a volume so large that Burlington was then the third-largest lumber port in America.[41] This was an activity that attracted not just those lumbermen able to realize the most direct profit but also numerous others who provided the necessary manpower in this difficult, backbreaking trade.

Transporting logs over the water was not for the faint of heart, and between cutting, assembling and floating a raft downriver to Quebec City, it was a task that could take up to a year to complete. During the winter months, those marketable logs not destined for processing at local mills were rolled out onto the ice and gathered up along the lake's edge—or, when there was no ice, floated downriver until they reached the lake and could be gathered together. In the immediate Burlington area, that particular location happened to be a few miles up the Onion River, where traffic was halted by the presence of waterfalls.

In pulling a raft together, men first assembled more manageable, individual units called "cribs," each some twenty-five feet square, which were formed by topping an initial course of logs with perpendicular bracing bound with treenails. Once the cribs were pulled and tied together, they formed a vast expanse of wood, which was then equipped with up to four masts, each bearing square sails, a capstan, an anchor, a warping cable, oars to steer, a cabin and, sometimes, a fireplace while trailing a small boat or canoe. Because of the unwieldy nature of such an assembly, large numbers of men were required to man the oars on each of the four sides, and small huts were constructed around the perimeter to protect them from the elements. It is no wonder that land-bound spectators found it difficult to express in words the phenomena they were witnessing as those vast structures were pulled together and floated out.

Once a raft traveled northward down the lake—some coming from as far away as Whitehall at the southern end and taking weeks to do so, passing Windmill Point on the right—it halted at St. John, Lower Canada, where customs officials inspected it for smuggled goods. These inspections hardly deterred woodsmen otherwise inclined to illegal activity, as they had already removed any contraband onto shore and taken it inland and around the customhouse, where it would be re-boarded farther downstream after the raft had passed through inspection. Once a raft reached the rapids, its cribs were separated and floated over individually, reassembled at Sorel and then sent on the rest of the way out into the St. Lawrence River and down to Quebec City.[42]

The number of rafts making the trip will never be known, but it is clear that the northern market's appetite for timber was voracious. In the seven-month period that the St. Lawrence was open in 1807, a staggering 340 rafts of timber and 701 cribs of firewood (estimated at 6,300 cords) made the passage between Chateauguay and Montreal.[43] Making the most of these trips, rafts also transported other commodities such as livestock, wool, fish, cheese, grain, flour, distilled spirits and tobacco. One 1810 trip from Vermont reveals further that for the personal consumption of the men riding aboard, they took with them twenty barrels of pork, thirteen bushels of peas, eight bushels of potatoes and, predictably, 115 gallons of rum.[44] For these rough-and-tumble men, including those who came from Alburgh, it was certainly not uncommon for strong, or ardent, distilled spirits to be a part of any of their endeavors, including such noteworthy events as violent fisticuffs, called "knockdowns"; horse races (one resulted in the death of two of the steeds when they collided and their necks broke); and the death, in December 1804, of one local, who "being intoxicated and missing his way home, perished with the cold."[45] As one commentator noted, "Rum was at the bottom" of such incidents, and it remained so in the approaching years.[46]

One rafting expedition of the time is noteworthy both for its sheer size and the fact that it involved an important individual who would appear again on several occasions in the near future. Samuel Mix (?–1828), later a colonel of the local militia, arrived in South Hero sometime around 1792 from an unknown location. Two years later, he had a home and a successful potash operation utilizing two iron kettles and four coolers, making the area so well known that it was called "Pot Ash Point." In the spring of 1805, Mix put together a raft destined for the Quebec market; he headed northward past Windmill Point and across the border, where he began the seventy-mile, ninety-five-foot drop in elevation down the Richelieu toward the St. Lawrence, coming to a halt at the rapids twenty miles in. There, he encountered Stirling Adams, of Addison, together with his own men floating a larger raft arriving just ahead of Mix's after their own sixty-five-mile transit.

It was now summer, and the water level had dropped, making passage a more difficult operation, so the two men decided to minimize any potential hazards and joined the two rafts together before proceeding on. Successfully negotiating the rapids, the men completed the length of the river, passed into the St. Lawrence and, after another one hundred miles, arrived in Quebec City in late September. There, they decided to part ways and separate out their respective logs, an operation that resulted in some of Mix's wood floating downriver. While he was in the process of retrieving a seventy-foot oak and was out of sight, Adams directed his men to remove the markings Mix had cut into some of his logs and to include them with his own. They did so, but Mix later detected the larceny, and a spat of litigation broke out between the two men that dragged on for some years in Vermont courts.[47]

Guy Catlin (1782–1853), brother of Moses, both originally from Litchfield, Connecticut, also became extensively involved in the growing lake trade and played an important role in approaching times. Whether it involved any of the many timbers that Moses was accused of stealing in January 1805 is not known, but at the same moment Mix encountered his problems, Guy took command of a raft in St. John that had originated on the Lamoille River. From that point on, he experienced his own set of difficulties, including combating contrary winds that blew his endeavor about, damaging an oak timber crib, blowing him onto an island and causing a collision with a competing raft. In an open display of contempt for authority (and certainly not for the last time), as Catlin tried to untangle the mess on what was supposed to be a quiet Sabbath day, he explained, "There came an officer on board and forbid our doing anything more…which occasioned a dispute between him and me which was settled by one of the hands giving him a severe glazing." Hard feelings aside, the men were able to sort things out, and after finally arriving at their destination, Catlin, along with many others bringing so much wood to one place at one time, experienced unhappy, complex negotiations with savvy purchasers seeking to exploit an abundant market.[48] This particular venture might have been unpleasant for Guy, but the resourceful, well-connected Catlin brothers were by no means without success in future years.

Timber constituted but a part of this important trade, and while some were drifting lazily down the river, there were those—as evidenced by Moses Catlin's voracious appetite for the many hundreds of cartloads of Childs's valuable undergrowth—who refined voluminous amounts of wood ash left behind from burning so many limbs and unmarketable timber. It was a commodity providing an alternative to wheat as a form of ready currency to purchase goods or pay taxes and did not require the resources of a Catlin or a Mix. Neither did it require any particular expertise to create—albeit, there were the periodic unfortunate accidents, as when Watertown's Edward Whipple was killed in December 1807 by a falling frame in his potash works.[49]

Potash (potassium carbonate) and its close chemical neighbor, pearl ash (baking soda), were in great demand for their use in producing lye, gunpowder, soap, glass and paper and processing textiles (so-called fulling, which cleaned, shrank and softened cloth). Throughout this period, the English Industrial Revolution was in full operation, and in a country destitute of wood, having access to North American potash was no small matter, fiercely driving Vermont's production. Both forms of ash were created using a simple technology easily adaptable to a frontier setting. Suppliers of necessary equipment, such as boiling kettles, were readily available. Among them was Wait Rathburn, who had two operations working in Clarendon and Tinmouth, taking advantage of the output from local iron mines and allowing him to proudly announce in 1807 and 1808 that his furnaces were "now in full blast" with his wares on hand for sale.

In its manufacture, wood ash was first gathered from "culinary fires," or from those "designed to burn up the wood," and placed into a large container with holes in its bottom, resting atop a second, similar tub that acted as a gathering basin, tilted in one direction. The upper chamber was first filled with straw or hay, and then upward of a foot of ash was packed on top. Water was then poured over the ash, allowing for the lye to leach out and run into the gathering vessel below. The leachate was then boiled in kettles, leaving behind a dry, salty, brownish residue, now called potash, or black salts, which was then scraped out. Further refinement resulted in the production of pearl ash, a more valuable commodity used in the manufacture of pottery and china and even called for as an ingredient in New England "Election Cake," a colonial specialty reserved for those occasions.

The process required roughly thirty cords of wood in order to produce a ton of unwashed ashes, which were then refined down to three hundred pounds of ash, valued at between $10 and $25 by local merchants. Storing and transporting ash required large barrels able to hold upward of five hundred pounds each. The physical labor involved in just their production was also considerable, netting workmen a modest return, as evidenced by one 1809 transaction in Alburgh, when Lemuel Fales agreed to make six hundred barrels for Shadrack Bickford (who provided the necessary staves, headings, hoop poles, et cetera), netting him a mere $175, or twenty-nine cents each.[50]

Merchants collecting ash acted as middlemen and either sent out others to purchase it at farms or collected it from settlers carrying it to a central location in burlap bags. Many were engaged in such fashion, such as M. Jewett of Burlington, who in May 1808 offered cash for "any quantity of pot and pearl ashes," or Jonathan Smith in Randolph, who was willing to pay fifteen cents per bushel for dry house ashes. It is not difficult to appreciate the importance such a mundane article held for these businessmen when they could purchase bushels of it from farmers for mere pennies and then see it at the very top of the Boston exchange in February 1808, selling for $175 per ton—by far the most valuable commodity listed. And by June, it was selling for between $300 and $400 per ton, while in Liverpool it was going for $700.[51]

Ash was so important that resourceful individuals sought ways to artificially create an equivalent that did not rely on trees, generating significant attention from early chemists and politicians. In 1753, Boston's William Frobisher attempted to make a credible form of potash, but after lengthy disappointments in convincing officials of his success, he met with frustration in the end, losing £700 in the process.[52] In Philadelphia, Samuel Hopkins encountered greater success when, on July 31, 1790, he obtained the first patent issued by the U.S. government, signed by George Washington, for the manufacture of pot and pearl ash.[53] By 1793, New York authorities had developed such a reputation for the quality of their ashes that David Townsend, inspector of pot and pearl ashes in Massachusetts (Vermont created a similar position in 1790), lamenting the disrepute into which his state's ashes had fallen, sought to duplicate their experience by establishing definite, predicable criteria for their production. The result was his *Principles and Observations Applied to the Manufacture and Inspection of Pot and Pearl Ashes*, describing in great detail the most acceptable methods of production, including leeching, scorching, pearling, melting, assaying and the use of a furnace. He further noted that he was doing so because ashes "have for a long time been among the most valuable articles of manufacture and commerce in this part of our country" and that by establishing uniform standards, one could avoid the losses "sustained in transporting so heavy an article by land carriage, some hundreds of miles," only to later find it had been improperly prepared.[54] However, for those settlers on the Vermont frontier, such issues hardly mattered when there was such heavy demand; for them, it was simply enough to get the product into barrels and headed north.

Determining the extent of the ash trade with Montreal is problematic. Various figures exist allowing for reasoned extrapolations, but a true number is simply not possible in light of the extensive amount of criminal activity taking place. From Canadian customs records, the legitimate importation of potash for a one-year period between 1800 and 1801 shows that 3,549 barrels of the commodity were declared at St. John.[55] However, the evidence as recounted by observers reporting to newspapers (and as further revealed in numerous court cases of those actually caught and prosecuted, discussed later) shows beyond any doubt that many tens of thousands of barrels were moved north. It became a year-round endeavor, accomplished through the use of timber rafts and boats for three seasons and sleighs during the winter months. Accounts from January 1809 provide a striking contrast from what was taking place only a few years before. On the fourteenth, one account stated that no fewer than seven hundred sleighs traveled between Montreal and Middlebury, with those headed north carrying "provisions, potashes, &c."; while another reported seeing three hundred sleighs traveling daily, also loaded with pork; and a third recounted that during the preceding year, some 30,000 barrels of potash had been brought into Quebec.[56]

However, none of this activity took place without difficulty. One 1808 traveler witnessed the serious danger lurking on the frozen waters, leading him to caution others that "travelling on Lake Champlain, is, at all times, really dangerous; and I would not advise any one to attempt it, if it can be avoided." Dodging large fissures, as much as six feet wide and larger, *carioles*, or "clumsy, box-shaped" sleighs, pulled by two-horse teams (Canadians used a single horse) were steered the long distances across the lake between Montreal and Vermont towns. In anticipation of potential problems, teamsters looped a long rope around the horses' necks so that when they began to break through the ice and sink,

> *the driver, and those in the sleigh* [could] *get out, and catching hold of the ropes, pull them with all their force, which, in a very few seconds, strangles the horses and no sooner does this happen, than they rise in the water, float on one side, are drawn out on strong ice, the noose of the rope is loosened, and respiration recommences; in a few minutes the horses are on their feet, as much alive as ever. This operation has been known to be performed two, or three times a day, on the same horses; for, when the spring advances, the weak places in the Lake, become very numerous; and the people, whose business leads them often on it, frequently meet with accidents. They tell you that horses which are often on the lake* get so accustomed to being hanged, that they think nothing of it.[57]

Those successfully negotiating the hazardous trip had an immediate impact in Montreal upon their arrival. As one observer noted:

> *On market days, which are Thursday and Saturday, it is very difficult to pass the streets near the market, on account of the prodigious number of sleighs, filled with provisions, which crowd every space and avenue…Sleighs are coming in daily, and every house is so thronged with Americans, and others, who are continually coming in, that genteel boarding is very dear.*[58]

Clearly, a robust and active connection existed between those living on the shores of Lake Champlain and Montreal. Their trade had been consistent and predictable in the past, but now, in 1808, it became noticeably more frantic, assuming a desperate tone. Why had there been such a rapid increase in traffic in just a short time, an endeavor in which people were willing to risk their lives in order to achieve success? In answer, one must look elsewhere, to persons of national and international repute able to significantly impact the course of life on this far-off frontier, often with the mere flourish of a pen.

2

EMBARGO

A century earlier, Vermont had constituted little more than a highway for the invading French and their Indian allies as they challenged Massachusetts settlers during the course of the many years making up the wars of empire, those European-based disputes with such far-reaching impact. The lake and its feeding rivers, particularly the Onion, allowed them easy transit eastward to the Connecticut River, where they headed south, downriver, to conduct their depredations and then returned back with captives. Much had certainly changed politically in the intervening years, but the remoteness of northern Vermont continued to identify it in large measure as disconnected from the rest of the country. Prompted by the nation's doubling in size with the Louisiana Purchase four years earlier, in March 1807 the U.S. Senate directed Secretary of the Treasury Albert Gallatin (1761–1849) to prepare a plan for opening roads and canals, as well as making other public improvements, to remedy the problem.

On April 4, 1808, Gallatin forwarded to Congress his important *Report of the Secretary of the Treasury on the Subject of Public Roads and Canals*, prefacing it with an apology for the rushed manner attending its production and explaining that "time has not permitted to present the report in a more satisfactory form."[59] Gallatin need not have been concerned because it was well received, providing much detailed and useful information to policymakers greatly in need of his input and direction. While making many observations and recommendations to increase the efficiency of the country's quickly growing economy, Gallatin also addressed the attending benefits derived from better communications, a role in which government had an overriding responsibility:

> *The inconveniences, complaints, and perhaps dangers, which may result from a vast extent of territory, can not otherwise be radically removed, or prevented, than by opening speedy and easy communications through all its parts….No other single operation within the power of government can more effectually tend to strengthen and perpetuate that union, which secures external independence, domestic peace, and internal liberty.*[60]

In reaching such a sweeping conclusion, Gallatin relied on the assistance of steamboat inventor Robert Fulton, who had already developed substantial insights concerning the importance of better connections between the coast and the nation's interior regions.

Fulton did not disappoint in this regard and provided significant details describing the economic advantages and disadvantages that could be obtained. His analysis was extensive and wide ranging, including an estimate that while a single horse pulling a canal barge was capable of hauling twenty-five tons of weight, on land, a load of three tons required the efforts of four to five horses—meaning that the one animal pulling the barge was capable of performing the work of forty. In his descriptions of costs associated with hauling various commodities, Fulton estimated that transporting wood on land was not economically viable if it required covering a distance of more than twenty miles, an effort costing on average three dollars per cord, whereas over water, it dropped dramatically to twenty cents. Similarly, for potash, Fulton determined that it cost five dollars to haul one hundred pounds on land a distance of three hundred miles, while on water the cost fell to fifteen cents.[61] None of these cost-saving distinctions would have surprised anyone living on the frontier who possessed ready access to waterways to move their produce. But it was Fulton's further observations—those of a political bent—that brought the experience into a clearer light.

As Gallatin had done in noting the importance of the government's development of communications through the building of roads and canals, Fulton turned to

> *their effect in cementing the Union and extending the principles of confederate republican government. Numerous have been the speculations on the duration of our Union, and intrigues have been practiced to sever the western from the eastern States. The opinion endeavored to be inculcated*

was that the inhabitants behind the mountains were cut off from the market of the Atlantic States; that consequently they had a separate interest, and should use their resources to open a communication to a market of their own; that remote from the seat of government, they could not enjoy their portion of advantages arising from the Union, and that sooner or later they must separate and govern for themselves.[62]

His reference to "intrigues" seeking to separate states from the Union refers to the discontent that removed trans-Appalachian states were experiencing, resulting in calls for succession—a concern no doubt exacerbated by the recent machinations of Aaron Burr within the nation's interior that had only recently been resolved through his trial, and acquittal, for treason.

While Vermont had already passed through that particular phase years earlier with the Allens' overtures to Canada, its continued inaccessibility to those important Atlantic markets still posed the same concerns for Washington policymakers—specifically, that those on the northern border harbored perceptions that they were separate from the mass of their fellow citizens and the discord that might arise if not alleviated. It was a condition becoming ever more real with each passing day in the spring of 1808 and explains why Gallatin, who was simultaneously dealing with issues concerning the slave trade, the public debt, the mint and various land claims, was so busy—and apologetic—at the very moment he submitted his report to Congress. Even so, his workload was about to explode exponentially.

ENGLAND AND FRANCE RESUMED their belligerent differences once again in 1803, and just like a century earlier, it was a situation that brought on numerous difficulties for those living on the North American continent. For the British, control of the seas remained of paramount importance, necessitating close supervision and control of any shipping, regardless of nationality, that might benefit its enemies. While Jefferson sought to steer a difficult neutral course, by 1805, Britain continued to seize on American shipping and impress its sailors into service in a desperate measure to maintain its very survival. For Jefferson, who abhorred contention but also understood the ill effects these actions were taking on American prestige and neutrality, it became obvious he had to exert some form of affirmative action short of war, and he came to rest on economic sanctions.

The adoption of discriminatory trading practices to manipulate one's neutrality to gain an advantage during wartime was not a new concept, as the nation had aggressively utilized such efforts several times in the years leading up to the Revolution.[63] For America and its great natural resources contributing in substantial part to the Atlantic trading network, it was not difficult for Jefferson to imagine that denying far-off belligerents access to them would hasten an end to their disputes. However, for the suspect Republican Francophile Jefferson, any reliance on strategies perceived to favor that country over Britain, no matter how neutral a course he tried to follow, opened him up to vicious attacks by Federalists with continuing sympathies for the mother country. Europe's travails forced American politicians to revisit ideological battles dating back to the Revolution's end in which Federalists argued for a strong central government and military, as well as access to foreign markets, and rejected Jefferson's effeminate policies directed at internal development and reliance on domestic manufactures.

The division between the two factions further revealed the parochial view of Federalists, who considered themselves "the Fathers of the People"; Democrats assumed a more humbling mantle as "the Friends of the People." Federalists demanded the public's deference because of their elite status, made possible through their education and wealth, while egalitarian-inclined Democrats sought their opinions in the pursuit of equal rights and opportunities for the common man. In the process, vicious recriminations were exchanged between the two, frequently in violent ways, as one New York Democratic broadside shouted: "Every Shot's a Vote, and Every Vote Kills a Tory! Do your Duty, Republicans, Let your exertions this day Put down the Kings and Tyrants of Britain."[64] And when the events of August 1808 soon played out on a Vermont river, those philosophical differences, exacerbated by violent hyperbole, could not have been more evident.

Following the June 22, 1807 attack by the fifty-gun HMS *Leopard* on the American frigate USS *Chesapeake*, in which three American seamen were killed, their differences were temporarily set aside as national outrage rallied solidly around Jefferson, providing him with ample support and allowing him the opportunity to take aggressive action. However, with his parsimonious eye always on the nation's purse strings, all he could muster for the moment was a cautious, tentative response ineffectually ordering the protection of seacoast towns with gunboats and preparing for the federalization of 100,000 state militiamen—an effort that fell mainly on those living in the northern states, as the South sought to keep its resources close to home for fear of slave revolts.[65]

Jefferson then put into place his grand economic "experiment" seeking to indirectly affect foreign commerce by implementing an embargo prohibiting the departure from the nation's shores of any American shipping involved in international trade. As he later explained its purpose:

> *The embargo keeping at home our vessels, cargoes & seamen, saves us the necessity of making their capture the cause of immediate war: for if going to England, France had determined to take them; if to any other place, England was to take them. Till they return to some sense of moral duty therefore, we keep within ourselves.*[66]

On December 22, 1807, following only a few hours of debate, Congress agreed and passed the law, the first of four such efforts to come into existence.

Initially, the embargo was a defensive, one-sided affair placing a stranglehold on American trade goods, keeping them onshore, but later it included a countering effort as various non-importation acts restricted the arrival of certain foreign goods into the country. Most unfortunately, Jefferson's precipitate actions took place without giving full consideration to their possible outcome, including implementing any coherent enforcement provisions. This effectively brought about a fractured, piecemeal effort throwing the administration into a continuous state of responding reactively to circumstances as they arose and not in the affirmative manner one might expect. In the early days, at least, he considered it a "candid and liberal experiment," a form of "peaceful coercion," but as historian Gordon Wood concluded, it was "a very strange act," one that was "an act of self-immolation."[67] In fact, that is exactly what happened.

As a result, throughout 1808, when there was no real prospect of the country going to war and no clear enemy on whom to settle, people in northern Vermont became naturally confused by Jefferson's intentions, and discord rapidly arose. He had set in place a situation initially intended as protective of American interests but which quickly transitioned to an oppressive state with many unintended consequences. It would consume his attention for the duration of his second term, expiring the following year.

As he forged ahead, Jefferson naïvely believed the American people understood and appreciated his actions and would willingly comply and adapt to any ensuing hardships, a view shattered in large part by what took place in northern Vermont. For the recalcitrant minority not willing to submit to the embargo, he steadfastly maintained their challenges to authority warranted the use of force to bring them into compliance, allowing him to vindicate the unquestioned power of majority rule. Any failure to resort to force, in his eyes, resulted in arrogance, insult and chaos festering in its wake, and these were wholly unacceptable alternatives.[68] For the loyal and hardworking Secretary Gallatin, the next months required his full attention as he struggled to convey and make real Jefferson's idealistic vision among an exceedingly diverse population spread out over significantly differing geographic locations, each with its own unique economic expectations.

The importance of the work that Gallatin's Treasury Department—and, in particular, the Customs Service—provided the country at the time cannot be overstated:

> *As our young nation was on the verge of economic despair and in search of revenue, the First Congress passed and President George Washington signed into law the Tariff Act of July 4, 1789, which authorized the collection of duties on imported goods. This, the fifth act of the 1st Congress, established Customs and its ports of entry as the collector and protector of the revenue on July 31, 1789…*
>
> *[U]ntil the passage of the Federal Income Tax Act in 1913 Customs provided our federal government with its only source of revenue. During this time, the incoming revenue from Customs funded the purchases of Alaska and Florida, and the territories of Louisiana and Oregon. In addition, Customs collections built Washington, D.C., the U.S. military and naval academies, and many of the nation's lighthouses from the Great Lakes to the Gulf of Mexico. Most impressively, by 1835, Customs revenues alone reduced the national debt to zero.[69]*

Upon its creation, fifty-nine customs districts came into existence in eleven states, each manned by, minimally, a collector of revenue who, while often the only customs officer in a district, was later authorized to employ inspectors and deputies deemed necessary in his work. The collectors' positions were awarded through political patronage, and they remained in place on good behavior, a situation that changed in 1820, when specific four-year terms were implemented.

The primary responsibility of the collector was the inspection of goods arriving into the United States, relying on their value as declared by an importer and on which a duty was assessed and collected (changed in 1818 because of the obvious potential for abuse), as well as receiving bonds posted to secure their payment. In the early years, there was no uniform system for paying salaries, so compensation was derived principally from numerous fees assessed on "every entrance of a ship," "for every clearance of any ship," "for every permit," "for every post entry," "for every bond," "for every debenture," "for every bill of health" and "for every official document," as well as commissions for storing imported merchandise.[70] Clearly, it was a position affording an incumbent the possibility of accumulating substantial rewards.

The flow of information between Jefferson and his appointee collectors during this volatile time was direct, passing through only the ever capable Gallatin, thereby allowing the chief executive to remain aware of what was taking place in rapid fashion. Gallatin was a most fortunate choice for this position, and while not in total agreement with the implementation of the embargo's dictates, he was determined to make it as effective as possible as he dealt with the many demands that the various collectors up and down the coast and along the borders placed on him.

One of the principal challenges facing Gallatin concerned the lack of direction contained in the quickly drafted embargo's provisions, forcing his men to deal with rapidly evolving situations requiring definitive, mistake-free responses. Unforeseen complexities with enforcement arose, and by late 1808, Gallatin lamented that his subordinates were not always receiving the full guidance they deserved, requiring them to rely on their own discretion. Complaining to Congress, he reflected on the recent past:

> *It has been the uniform practice, from the establishment of the Government of the United States, to give positive instructions to the collectors respecting the execution of the laws, and which they were bound to obey, unless a different construction should be established by a legal decision. This indeed was essentially necessary, in order to secure an* [sic] *uniform construction and execution of the laws.*[71]

However, the vague embargo altered those expectations, and immediately following the explosive events in Vermont that brought those failures to light, Gallatin was forced to confide in James Madison, "I had rather encounter war itself than to display our impotence to enforce our laws."[72] Notwithstanding, on the whole, if not always in a timely manner, the more mundane enforcement decisions were decisively reached; reduced to writing, providing as much direction as the circumstances allowed; printed; and distributed to his subordinates by means of numerous circular letters which were, in turn, frequently published in local newspapers. It then became the collectors' responsibility to put them into action. The manner used, and the results obtained, were not always what those in Washington might have expected.

DR. JABEZ PENNIMAN (1764–1841), originally from Mendon, Massachusetts, had been living in Westminster, in southern Vermont, when Ethan Allen's widow, Francis Allen, arrived with her three children, Ethan, Hannibal and Frances, following Ethan's death in 1789. The two met, were married in 1793 and subsequently moved northward, living between Burlington, Colchester and Swanton in the next few years.[73] Penniman had land interests along the Onion River on Burlington's north side, and in the fall of 1798, he conveyed some of it to Captain Jonathan Ormsby, an individual destined to play an important role in events taking place in that same area in 1808.[74]

While in the process of raising their family, increased by four children of their own, it became clear that the executor of Ethan's estate, brother Ira, had engaged in suspicious land transactions in the Burlington area that interfered with Francis's dower rights, entitling her to one-third of her deceased husband's estate. By 1802, as evidenced by letters between the two families, significant discord had arisen, and on May 23, 1803, Penniman, suing on his and his wife's behalf, obtained a favorable $7,000 court award against Allen.[75]

The ensuing battle waged by Penniman in 1805 to execute on the judgment, in the case of *Jabez Penniman v. Silas Hathaway and Heman Allen*, brought to light an extraordinary situation revealing not only Allen's highly questionable land machinations but also the existence of suspect alliances between several local men, which continued on into later years. Ably represented by St. Albans attorney Asa Aldis, Penniman doggedly sought out evidence revealing that, through the use of schemes, trickery and deceit, many questionable land transfers had taken place in Burlington and surrounding communities in order to defeat the legitimate claims of creditors, as well as Francis's dower rights. Of particular note, it was revealed that businessman/timber merchant Moses Catlin was one of Allen's close confidants and had gone daily to the Burlington jail, where Allen had been incarcerated as part of the proceedings, to take personal responsibility for Allen's temporary release and to return him at the end of the day. While Catlin later denied participating in any illegal activity with Allen, his name became closely attached to a "secret trust" between the two that allowed additional fraud on Allen's creditors.[76]

The noose became increasingly uncomfortable for Allen, and from late April to early May 1803, as Penniman's suit proceeded against him, "on a Saturday night about 12 o'clock," as witness Thaddeus Tuttle recalled, nephew Heman Allen and Judge Silas Hathaway put into operation a scheme to aid his flight, beginning with Tuttle posting a bond for his release.

With that accomplished, through the efforts of brother-in-law Roger Enos, Allen was quietly conveyed to a waiting boat on Lake Champlain manned by Collins Lake, taken southward and deposited in the area of Fort George, New York. There, upon alighting, he tipped his friends and laughed that he had put one over on his creditors. Lake was first recruited for the effort by Hathaway, and when he expressed hesitancy at becoming involved and wondered aloud why some who seemed to be against the difficult Allen in the past were now willing to help him in escaping, the pragmatic judge told him that "the greatest enemies should be friends sometimes." Indeed, the dizzying relationships existing among these men, and many of their friends, as they both assisted and exploited each other were aptly described by attorney Aldis during the course of the lawsuit. In his estimation, their questionable actions taken to harm Francis were nothing more that attempts by men to "cloak themselves in that mantle of mystery which fraud delights to shroud itself."[77] This was certainly not the last time a court witnessed such behavior from Burlington's esteemed elites.

As Allen's fraudulent actions were becoming known, in March 1803, apparently not satisfied with incumbent David Russell, Jefferson removed him and named steadfast Republican Penniman in his place as the third collector for the District of Vermont. The customs building at the time was in South Hero, not far from Burlington, but Gallatin chose to relocate it some twenty-five miles northward, to remote Windmill Point, where, in July 1804, Penniman negotiated the purchase of a half acre of land from Amos Morrill for twenty-five dollars.[78] The sale was completed, but it does not appear that Penniman ever took up residency, hiring instead an assistant, Samuel Buel of Burlington, to do so. Penniman was also attending to family issues at the time, as he and Francis dealt with the persistent demands being placed on them by her daughter, Fanny, clamoring for permission to relocate to Montreal to complete her education and become more familiar with the Catholic religion. Those objections finally overcome, Fanny was allowed to move, and on September 29, 1808, she entered the nursing order of the Religious Hospitalers of St. Joseph at the Hotel Dieu, later becoming one of America's first nuns.[79]

Penniman's deputy, Samuel Buel (1766–1831), originally from Coventry, Connecticut, was the fifth child of Major Elias Buel, himself a prominent local figure serving in various capacities. After moving his family to Vermont, in 1780 Elias participated in founding the town of Coventry, served as an assistant judge in the Chittenden County Court in 1799 and 1801, was a member of the Council of Censors in 1799 and served four terms in the General Assembly.[80] As Samuel explained in later years when he sought to recover personal losses suffered during the War of 1812, upon Penniman's appointing him as deputy collector (which appears to have been done, in part, because of his father's connections and was a title Buel believed should more accurately be described as "acting collector"), he went to the Point, where he found the building housing the windmill in such disrepair that he spent his own money to make it habitable and to conduct business. He was successful in this effort, and the customhouse remained in continuous service for the next decade, with Buel in attendance, until the war; in the summer of 1813, it was "burnt and destroyed, by direction of a British officer, from the alleged reason that it had been occupied as a public office, and was presumed to be public property."[81] Until that happened, Buel remained a prominent figure in the area in the upcoming years, establishing himself even further when he leased two hundred acres of land on the Point in 1806.[82]

After customs inspectors in Boston, Philadelphia, New York and Baltimore filed petitions in 1805 seeking additional compensation because of excessive work and difficult living conditions in their crowded cities, Gallatin conducted a survey of the agency to ascertain exactly how many of them there actually were, the number of days they worked and their pay. In a return for the year 1804, the inquiry reveals that of the 320 men working nationwide, there was a single inspector in Vermont (presumably Buel) who worked a total of twenty-two days and received compensation at the minimum statutory rate of $2 per day or, in total, $44. Collectively, all of the inspectors received $129,608 in pay, a mere 1 percent of the Treasury's net receipts for that particular year.[83] While specific amounts of duties collected in Vermont are not clear, the number of penalties, forfeitures and fines realized indicate relatively little work being done in an enforcement capacity. Between 1794 and 1809, only three instances arose in which goods were seized in violation of revenue and navigation laws and thirty-seven occasions giving rise to some $3,500 in fines.[84] These numbers are noteworthy for their sheer paucity when compared with the staggering number of violations about to take place following the institution of Jefferson's embargo.

Trade on the lake was on the rise, with ten vessels of more than thirty tons' capacity plying the waters between Vermont, New York and Montreal in 1802. Yet increasing demand resulted in an additional two vessels by 1807, and then, following the embargo and up to 1814, a staggering sixteen more appeared on the scene, several owned by local businessman Gideon King, the so-called Admiral of the Lake.[85] In addition, there were many other vessels of lesser burden that are repeatedly described in customs records for the period, including the cutter *Youth* out of St. John, which, as early as

1804, was being captained by Master Joseph Jasper, a business associate of local merchant Guy Catlin. By the fall of 1808, Jasper was master of one of King's sloops, *Lady Washington*, a thirty-ton vessel built in 1795 in Burlington, and he remained active in the Montreal trade.[86]

With the increase in activity, Penniman decided in 1805 that, with Buel located many miles to the west on the Point, he needed an additional representative in Burlington, and on June 8, he appointed nineteen-year-old Nathan B. Haswell (1786–1855) as inspector for the port. Haswell, originally from Bennington, had been attending the University of Vermont at the time but was forced to leave his studies to enter into business following his father's loss of his own printing business and home because of fire.[87] Only days following his appointment, Haswell was signing authorizations allowing Jasper to transport passengers and various commodities (barrels of potash, lemon, oil and eggs).

Not satisfied with a single source of income, on March 25, 1806, Haswell entered into a business relationship with John M. Peaslee and established the Peaslee and Haswell trading firm, located on Burlington's Courthouse Square, immediately offering for sale "a handsome assortment of dry goods, groceries, crockery, hardware &c." The relationship continued on for the next several years. The two men also became involved in many transactions steered their way thanks to Haswell's role as inspector, storing the valuable potash seized by government officials during the embargo. The following year, the intrepid young man took it upon himself to obtain a vessel allowing him to inspect arriving and departing vessels and wrote to Penniman, "I have found it absolutely necessary for the safety of the revenue and my own convenience in attending on the same to procure a skiff," forwarding on an eighteen-dollar bill "not doubting but government will allow [it]." Penniman did not appear to be offended at all by Haswell's initiative, as he repeatedly relied on him for the more mundane and routine aspects of life, such as having his young associate ship to him needed plaster of Paris and, on at least two occasions, bringing lawsuits on his behalf.[88] Haswell's admirable abilities did not go unnoticed, and when the times brought large numbers of troops to town during the crisis of 1812, he was repeatedly called upon to assist the military in provisioning its many men.

The embargo now in existence, the onus for enforcement fell on these three men. Led by Penniman, the administrator, who was never personally involved with any of the day-to-day physical hardships, Buel and Haswell were continually faced with diverse challenges requiring rapid, direct intervention, and it took all they had to meet what was about to unfold.

Immediately following the *Chesapeake* incident, as in many other parts of the country, Vermonters rallied behind the national government, making known their abhorrence at the unprovoked attack and loss of life:

> *Notwithstanding our remote situation from the source of the late outrage upon our national sovereignty, this hardy race of Mountaineers are all alive to the general sensations of indignation and resentment, and will form a solid and powerful phalanx against a vulnerable point of poor deluded England: we venture to predict, that not a single soldier of Vermont will want to be drafted into the service now required…The bravery and patriotism of the united body of free men that cluster our mountains' sides are not to be questioned, & the finger of vengeance points* with the needle.[89]

The support continued on into the fall when, on November 4, 1807, the assembly sent a missive to Jefferson reiterating the state's resolve to stand behind him, approving of his actions taken to date:

> *It is the duty of every American to rally around the constituted authorities of his country and to support them with his life and fortune…And we do farther, for ourselves and our constituents declare that fearless of the dangers to which we may be exposed as a frontier state, we shall be ever ready to obey the call of our common country, whenever it shall be necessary either for the purposes of redress or vengeance.*[90]

Perhaps anticipating forthcoming hardships, a week later, the body decided to set an example for the rest of the state, agreeing that during its next session, it would forego foreign-made clothing, wearing instead "the manufactures of this or some other of this United States." For its efforts, Jefferson favorably responded, writing back that he deemed Vermont's support "highly gratifying to me."[91]

Vermonters could, at least for the time being, assume a façade of allegiance and loyalty simply because they were untouched by the embargo's provisions, which, because of its rushed passage, addressed shipping only on the coast and not on the unique land and lake frontier they possessed. That oversight allowed them the opportunity to take up lighthearted mockery of Jefferson's effort: "A wit observed a day or two since, that by reading the word Embargo backwards, it would make *O-grab-me!* It is thought that a great number will feel the influence of its *Grab!!*"[92] The jesting continued in the following months, with at least one newspaper leading off its reporting of the embargo with "Ograbme news," describing the exploits of "Ograbme evaders," while another spoke of customhouses where confiscated goods were stored as "Ograbmerooms."[93]

However, the importance of what was taking place suddenly took on a new and threatening face with the changing of the seasons just as loggers, employed during the winter months in the difficult labor of felling and pulling their timber out onto the ice in preparation for spring rafting trips into Canada, waited in anticipation for the melting, allowing them yet another profitable year. Suddenly, on March 12 the so-called Land Embargo (the third act in the series) went into effect, and it did to Vermont what all the states along the Atlantic coast had experienced in December. Now, there was absolutely no easy outlet whatsoever for all that wood, all of those many barrels of pot and pearl ash, the pork, wheat and the many other products of the earth they so heavily relied on for income. Transporting those goods elsewhere was simply not feasible, and now they faced the stark reality of a devastation they never before imagined.

SMUGGLING HAS A TIME-HONORED place in American history. In 1760, England was faced with increasing instances of illegal trading between its North American colonies and erstwhile enemy, France, via its West Indies possessions. The ties existing between these mercantile interests in the western Atlantic, present well before the outbreak of the Seven Years' War, were so strong that they survived even that event. Despite London's passing an embargo act prohibiting the colonies from any further trade with France, it continued on, forcing Prime Minister William Pitt to order provincial governors to take decisive action to stop it. Deeming it a "dangerous and ignominious trade," Pitt sought the most vigorous enforcement, bringing "all such heinous offenders…to the most exemplary and condign punishment," to stop "such flagitious practices."[94] It was a futile battle to try and win in the first place because of the tremendous complexities attending something as overwhelming as trade.

Jefferson's embargo prohibiting the outward flow of goods was simply the most draconian of actions taken at the time when other, less restrictive regulations were already in place affecting the arrival of merchandise into the country. The Non-importation Act of 1806 restricted the introduction of certain goods and merchandise—such as leather, silk, hemp, tin, brass, wool, glass, etc.—coming from England. As in Pitt's time, revenue officers monitored the ins and outs of this commerce while remaining alert for the presence of profit-seeking smugglers trying to exploit any conceivable failing on their part. Thus, it came to be that the most notorious smuggler was the one who not only exposed officials' weaknesses but also unabashedly put on display his own intent for gain, regardless of whether it was "acquired by any means, foul or fair."[95] But there were also other factors present that allowed for this to occur in the first place.

Communal acceptance of the presence of criminal activity in its midst also presented a most challenging situation for undermanned and outgunned authorities. A situation in which the constabulary was rendered essentially ineffective presented an unintended consequence resulting in the community assuming that smuggling was a "tolerated evil." Compounding the problem, locals' refusal to accept Jefferson's rationale for the embargo resulted in high levels of resentment, which, in turn, led to moral and material support being provided to lawbreakers.[96]

With their neighbors tolerating their activities, it is not difficult to appreciate that smugglers felt comfortable in taking yet more forceful actions against authorities, such as actively obstructing them when confronted and going so far as to actually raid customhouses to recover confiscated goods. As one smuggler explained in pragmatic fashion:

> *Before the war had been waged one year there were two furious parties in every frontier town—one the federalists who were always ready to aid and lend a helping hand to the smugglers—the other the republicans who were the government party and were always ready to turn out and help the officers. The consequence was that the smugglers were obliged to go in large parties so as to fight their way if found necessary and the business became somewhat lawful because they carried it on with a strong hand and might often makes right whether legal or not. Sometimes one party would take property belonging to the other and this again would be taken by a third party and in fact the only way that anything could be saved which had once been in the hands of the smugglers was to consume it or to keep it secreted.*[97]

The events taking place the summer of 1808 perplexed some and brought about much inner reflection in others. One writer understood the varying shades of guilt attached to the smuggler—that his actions were not subject to easy explanation:

> *Circumstances would extenuate or increase the guilt of the culprit. Is it a foreign government whose laws he infracts? Is it his own government, and*

that preposterous? Is he poor and needy? His crime is then less atrocious, and repentance might purchase exemption from punishment. But does he violate the laws of his own government? Is that government involved in difficulties? Is he rich and above the reach of want? The circumstances change the hue of his crime; it becomes black, atrocious and unpardonable.[98]

Yet for others, the effects were clear and not subject to such fine distinctions:

This offense is productive of various mischiefs to society. The public revenue is thereby lessened; the fair trader is injured; the nation impoverished; rival, and perhaps hostile, states are thereby enriched; and the persons guilty thereof, being hardened by a course of disobedience to, and defiance of, law, become at last so abandoned and daring, as not to hesitate at being guilty of the greatest offenses.[99]

But these were arguments and concerns for policymakers to resolve as the smugglers busied themselves with their more immediate, personal concerns.

As the embargo continued, and was later replaced by other restrictions on trade, smugglers repeatedly maneuvered to afford themselves opportunities to explain their suspicious criminal activity in an innocent manner. One creative Vermont initiative in the early days involved utilizing a hill standing on the border, and

on the top a slight building is erected in which barrels, pipes, and other articles, are deposited. The construction of the house is such, that on the removal of a stone or a piece of wood, the whole edifice with its contents immediately falls on the British territory, by which means, although apparently accidental, the laws are evaded and speculations to a large amount made by the execution of the scheme.[100]

A similar ploy involved driving animals:

Now suppose a man should drive a herd of hogs close up to the line of the United States, but not over, and a Canadian should accidently make his appearance just within the boundary of the British colony, with a basket of corn in his hand, and should cry Pig-Pig-Pig *and the whole drove should run over the line into Canada, and voluntarily place themselves under the government of the tyrant of the ocean. Would it or would it not be a breach of the Embargo law?*[101]

But even if these efforts successfully circumvented the possibility of a criminal prosecution, for those who were actually caught, it remained possible to find refuge within the vagaries of the law.

At the onset of the war in 1812, it became illegal to transport certain goods, those considered "munitions of war, or any articles of provision," from the United States to Canada in order to impede Britain's ability to prosecute its intentions. One of the most important articles the British required was beef, and on November 1, 1813, George Sheldon, of Sheldon, Vermont, drove "ten living fat oxen, ten living fat cows, ten living fat steers, & ten living fat heifers" across the line and was prosecuted in the U.S. Circuit Court in Rutland the following year. Admitting that he had actually taken the animals north, Sheldon's counsel argued that simply herding animals was not the same thing as transporting them, and therefore, his client was not guilty. A perplexed jury returned a special verdict reflecting its consternation as it tried to discern whether the cattle were properly "provisions & munitions of war," concluding that if they were, then the defendant was guilty, and if they were not, he was not guilty. The decision resulted in a finding of no guilt, and the matter was appealed to the U.S. Supreme Court, which agreed, concluding that, while indeed the cattle were prohibited from being exported, driving them as Sheldon had was not the same as the prohibited "transportation" envisioned by the law.[102]

Seeking to avoid going to such lengths, dodging the attentions of the inquisitive revenue officer constituted the first line of defense for the smuggler, and it required great imagination, an attribute present in the extreme on the frontier. Sam Buel had occasion to notice that female passengers traveling into Canada and returning only hours later appeared larger and raised the curiosity of inspectors:

> *These appearances have, no doubt, often attracted the attention of those whose duty it was to wait on those characters; and sometimes induced a sympathy which has prompted assistance for their relief; which act of duty and charity, has often been complained of, by those delicate ladies, as an impertinent trespass upon delicacy.*[103]

John Howe, a particularly clever smuggler, constructed a fake coffin, cutting a small window into the top and placing a papier-mâché head beneath it, made to look "as if it was in a state of putrefaction." Predictably, the box was then used to conceal contraband, and when confronted by inquisitive officials, they quickly backed off any further inquiry on observing the ominous-looking "head" of its occupant. On another occasion, when accompanied by a female friend and her two young boys as he transported contraband in a sleigh, Howe fed brandy to the youngsters, causing them to vomit. Telling a customs officer who had detained him that he thought the boys had the pox, the official quickly waved them off without further delay. At another time, he used a sleigh equipped with concealed compartments that allowed him to move his goods without being detected. Howe was not always successful, as he once made the unwise decision to bribe a customs officer at the Vermont border to allow him to pass, only to later be confronted by another officer made aware of the situation who confiscated his goods when he reached Troy, New York.[104]

These are only a very few of the more benign, comedic ways some smugglers tried to avoid detection, but there were certainly others who took it to a whole new level.

ONE OF THE MORE TRAGIC consequences of the embargo concerned Vermonters' sudden resort to violence in response to perceived threats to their livelihood, both real and imagined. It was an exceedingly visceral and reflexive reaction indicating the very real day-to-day reliance those living along the frontier placed on their closely guarded trade, now rendered illegal by Jefferson's dictates. But it was not just a protest by one section of society because many shared the same concern.

With the advance of lake trade and accompanying development and settlement along the waterfront, and into the interior, taking place, it was only natural that criminal activity increased. There were, of course, the expected petty crimes, those usually associated with the lower classes most inclined to retaliate physically against those trying to stop them and whose members provided, if not the means or intelligence to conduct more sophisticated offenses, then the strong backs that smuggling timber, potash and pork required. Accounts frequently concentrate on the base smuggler, the one who committed the actual offense, who was caught and then called to account. But while others, their co-conspirators, assumed a more silent presence as sponsors of that activity, little of their influence has been discussed in the historiography of this time.

Taking an expansive view of events occurring on and around Lake Champlain in 1808, it is an inescapable conclusion that several highly placed men within the community, those in respected positions, including merchants, traders, doctors, bankers, entrepreneurs and militia officers, silently aided and counseled smuggling activities, and their complicity in the pending tragic events cannot be ignored. If the financing of a single timber raft destined for the Quebec market is any indication of the degree to which these men depended on one another for success, then there was indeed a highly complex set of relationships present to ensure their mutual gain in other endeavors, even those touching on the illegal.[105] Certainly, Ira Allen's escape from Vermont revealed the existence of their close interdependence and willingness to coordinate among themselves to thwart the law.

Accordingly, when the embargo took effect and the outcome of their various negotiations, affecting, quite literally, their own solvency, threatened them with the possibility of occupying a debtor's prison cell, they conducted themselves in an even more nuanced manner, allowing them to extract maximum profit from activities that had suddenly, and without warning, become illegal. When faced with financial ruin, even the most honorable men, including those charged with enforcing the law and facing their own confused loyalties, will consider resorting to unacceptable measures. As government attorney Cornelius Peter Van Ness, a clear beneficiary of the unrest, explained in understatement when later called on to give account of his own questionable behavior, "Many things were out of the common course."[106] The challenges were indeed many, and they came to touch those of all rank.

These men of privilege straying from lawful conduct may not have had as direct reliance on the land that their underlings did, but they did have interests every bit as important and affecting their social standing. While many at the time sought to explain the criminal activity taking place as simply a battle between Democrats and Federalists, at its most basic level, it was the manifestation of self-interest as only money can make real. At least one newspaper sought to give explanation to this Vermont phenomenon, noting that these were

> *the* Green Mountain Yeomanry, *men who supported the measures of the present administration while those measures appeared to have the public good in view, and were authorized by the constitution; but who feel it no dereliction of patriotic duty to evade unwise, unnecessary, arbitrary and unconstitutional edicts; and to oppose despotic power, from whatever quarter it may come.*[107]

That aspersion reportedly originated within the Republican element against Federalists' interests, but it was an observation that applied to both political parties, as those involved in crimes sought to mask their involvement while simultaneously appearing to walk a lawful path. Their duplicitous conduct did not escape notice:

> *We are surprised and mortified at finding* New England men, *men of* steady habits, *resorting to…unreasonable means of redressing their wrongs. We fear that the short reign of democracy in Vermont has caused a degeneracy in the morals and principles of the people.*[108]

As events unfolded, the cracks in the veneer of seeming respectability became even more evident.

Those financiers of activities taking place on the lake had high stakes in all aspects of trade headed toward Canada, estimated to have increased a remarkable 31 percent between 1807 and 1808.[109] They not only financed the expensive timber rafts but also acted as middlemen in obtaining pot and pearl ash from hardworking settlers living in the interior and facilitated the transfer of goods headed south out of Quebec into Vermont during the years when non-importation acts prohibited their movement. Importantly, in the early months of the embargo, they assisted the illegal transfer of contraband northward and thereby assumed a level of complicity equivalent with the conduct of those men they employed.

Despite whatever difficulties they might have encountered, businessmen Guy and Moses Catlin took it in stride and persevered through these particularly difficult years. Whether it was timber and wood products going north or fur coming south through their connections with John Jacob Astor, the two men recognized and fully exploited every possible opportunity. The two arrived in Burlington following Moses's own successful litigation against Ira Allen in 1795 for his maladministration of Ethan Allen's estate in which his wife, just as in Francis Allen Penniman's case, had an interest. By 1800, the town was gaining prominence through its port activities, the establishment of a regional post office, a county courthouse and the University of Vermont. Allen's settlement outside town on the north side of the Onion River, located immediately adjacent to significant waterfalls, called the Colchester or Burlington Falls, was an important place for early development but was beginning to lose some of its luster, particularly with his sudden departure in 1803. So it was only natural that additional development took place on the other side of the river, closer to town, and that's where the two Catlins established their mercantile interests.

With their arrival, other businesses came to the area, and together with various workers' rough dwellings, it became known locally as Catlinsborough.

In October 1802, Moses petitioned with others for the imposition of local taxes to allow for the construction of a toll bridge at the falls, where a ferry operated, which was accomplished the following year. The bridge remained in operation for the immediate time, but in the spring of 1808, following heavy rains, officials were forced to condemn it as unsafe for passengers.[110] Just downriver from the Catlins, past the large pool at the base of the falls where yearly timber rafts were assembled, were the important intervale lands where the murders would take place months later.

A year following his Quebec rafting adventure, in November 1806, Guy Catlin entered into a business relationship with boat captain Joseph Jasper; they called themselves Catlin & Jasper, and their partnership lasted until December 1811. Because of his ready access to distant markets, Jasper dealt primarily with the actual shipping aspects of the business, while Catlin concerned himself with land-bound responsibilities. Setting up shop in the same locale as the recently established concern of Peaslee and Haswell, the two advertised their wares, explaining they had a wide variety of dry goods, hardware and spirits for sale at the "New Brick Store, Westside of Courthouse Square, Burlington."[111] Payment from customers was expected in the form of either "cash or country produce," which certainly included potash.

Business was so good that by early December 1807, the two decided it was time to move their operation to the falls and placed an order for "three or four hundred feet of clear seasoned clapboards" for their new building. They had recently purchased just over an acre of land that April, later expanding their interests in 1810 with the purchase of an additional two acres, together with more buildings. An October 1808 business invoice indicates that among the many other items offered for sale at their new location, there were no fewer than forty-two kegs of tobacco, four hogsheads of rum and various amounts of brandy and wine.[112] The presence of so much alcohol available from a single outlet indicates the importance the general population placed on it and the role it would play in the approaching murders.

There is also evidence of some discord involving the Catlins when, in January 1808, Moses became involved in a lawsuit against Sheriff Staniford seeking $30,000 for lost goods, apparently the result of a mishandled court judgment. Catlin succeeded in obtaining a guilty verdict, but his losses came in at only $107, plus minimal costs, which could not have instilled in him much respect for local authority.[113] Additionally, the brothers were under further financial pressure for two loans, totaling $800, that Daniel Farrand, president of the Burlington Exchange Company, made to them in September 1807, which they refused to pay despite repeated requests to do so. Farrand finally resorted to a lawsuit against them less than three weeks following the murders, indicating the uneasiness some within the business community felt toward the two men at that moment.[114]

Other merchants besides Guy Catlin also became complicit in the August murders, including Samuel Fitch, the principal of Samuel Fitch & Co. Fitch had previously been in a business relationship that broke up in 1805 but by 1807 was back in operation, offering various dry goods for sale and soliciting the purchase of salts of lye and pot and pearl ashes at his store on College Green.[115] Importantly, and particularly relevant to what occurred later, he was also involved in the illicit sale of alcohol. During the Supreme Court's January 1807 term, he was indicted for selling wine and "foreign distilled spirituous liquors" in illegal quantities—by the gallon, half gallon and quart—in the preceding months. He later pleaded guilty and paid a $10.00 fine and $9.25 in costs.[116] It is also noteworthy that he was not the only one involved in this activity, as the grand jury also indicted an additional fourteen individuals for similar conduct, including running unlicensed inns and taverns.

The consumption, or tippling, of spirituous liquors, also called ardent spirits (defined as that substance "obtained by distillation from fermented substances of any kind"), constituted one of the most troublesome societal issues in early nineteenth-century America.[117] These intensified, refined concoctions rendered through the distillation process resulted in the creation of cider brandy, potato and grain whiskey and maple and New England rum, which delivered heightened amounts of alcohol into one's system when only a small amount was consumed. Widely available from many outlets throughout the community, people, including minors, could easily obtain both large and small amounts depending on their particular wants. Whether dispensed from bottles or in individual portions drained from a nearby barrel, merchants made free, salted codfish available to further tease the drinker's thirst.

Though deemed a pernicious commodity condemned by Jefferson when it was provided to the Indian population, ardent spirits were widely tolerated throughout Vermont. There were more than two hundred distilleries, including Staniford's Burlington operation, present before the War of 1812 broke out, all contributing to the astonishing 28,720,000 gallons manufactured nationwide in that year alone. Two years earlier, a national census of stills had revealed that when imports were included, the number climbed to over 33,000,000 gallons, or an estimated—and staggering—4.5 gallons each year for every man, woman and child. If children and slaves are excluded, it climbs to 7 gallons for every man and woman, a figure likely further skewed by the man's reputation for being the largest imbiber. Many feared what was happening to the general population, and in 1815, the Greene and Delaware Moral Society lamented, "The thing has arrived to such a height that we are actually threatened with becoming a nation of drunkards."[118]

Alcoholism was indeed commonplace, with one estimate concluding that no less than one-third of a daily laborer's earnings was spent on spirituous liquors. Many engaged in so-called dram drinking, in which spirits were consumed at various times throughout the day, starting off with a glass first thing in the morning "to sharpen the appetite and give tone to the stomach." Then, as the day progressed and the drinker's appetite was adversely affected by the alcohol, he consumed yet more to ward off the discomfort. The habit knew no limits, and farmers began to pause in the hot mid-day summer sun to imbibe, while militia soldiers, through the expected courtesies from their commanders, did the same, all developing strong addictions that required constant feeding. In courtrooms, lawyers passed around bottles, and in churches, ministers took a drink "to help them preach," while the congregation did the same "to help them hear and understand."[119] And with so many thirsty consumers seeking satisfaction, there were many like Fitch and Catlin willing to hazard running afoul of the law in order to see them taken care of.

In January 1808, Fitch notified the public that those owing him money were to "make immediate payment, without further notice, or !!," and immediately following the murders, he further warned that payment was expected or he intended to file the necessary papers with an attorney for collection "without further notice."[120] The posting of such warnings was not unusual, but it does indicate that during these crucial times, Fitch experienced problems with income and might explain why a few short months later he went out of business.[121] Finally, a third businessman—identified as Reuben Harmon, who also operated a nearby dry goods store on Pearl Street, where he, too, offered to pay cash for potash—is reported to have provided counsel to the murderers.[122]

Immediately following the murders, authorities began a series of vigorous seizures on the lake, taking into custody fifteen vessels of varying configurations, together with over 340 barrels of potash destined for export. Court proceedings were instituted in the fall of 1808 against each of them, including their cargo, seeking their forfeiture to the government on the basis of being in violation of the embargo.[123] As a part of those matters, the public was provided notice of the proceedings by newspapers and postings in taverns and given an opportunity to appear in court to contest their forfeiture. Through an examination of those particular matters, additional light is shed on what the Burlington elite was up to, and it is reasonable to conclude that much more was taking place outside public scrutiny than they might have otherwise understood to be the case.

The condemnation proceedings took place on two levels, one examining any claims of innocence surrounding a particular boat, and the other looking at those concerning the potash. It was an easy thing for someone to say that, while they may have owned the ash, they had contracted with a boat owner to transport it to a location south of the border and that any seizure based on the belief that it was intended to go northward was something they had not agreed to, and any criminal culpability rested with the boat's captain. Accordingly, it is not surprising to see that, with the exception of a single boat, there were no claimants at all to any of the vessels, and they were condemned and forfeited to the government. Curiously, one case involving the *Dolphin*, owned by boating scion Gideon King, together with the sixty-six barrels of potash found on board, was quietly dismissed by the government in its entirety months after it was filed.

The one sloop that was claimed, the *Hope*, intercepted while illegally exporting tea the preceding May, became the subject of extensive litigation involving its owner, Abner Brigham, a tavern keeper from Dorchester, Lower Canada. Brigham claimed that the boat had originally been built in Whitehall, New York, and he took it to St. John, where it was taken apart and lengthened. Because its extensive reconfiguration essentially rendered it a different vessel, Brigham renamed it the *Governor Craig* and displayed the British flag in the belief that he could freely navigate the lake without restriction. In the end (despite an affidavit filed on his behalf by Moses Catlin), Brigham lost his case, but not before he threatened Penniman's counterpart that summer, Champlain district collector Melancthon Woolsey, that if he made any attempt to seize his boat, he "would make it a national question and hazard the consequences."[124] Challenges by foreigners to American authority aside, the more interesting questions arise when looking into the involvement of particular Burlington-area businessmen in the remaining cases.

Concerning the forfeiture of the many barrels of potash, four men came forward to claim an innocent ownership interest. Platt Rogers, of Vergennes, and Samuel S. Hawes, of Milton, both appear to have been of relatively modest means compared to the other two individuals. Each asserted his respective interests in only two cases, Rogers for fifty-one barrels, valued at $776, and Hawes for twenty-five barrels, valued at $621. Their matters proceeded to trial and ultimately met with unsuccessful conclusions, the court concluding that their protestations of innocence were "not true." That was not the end of their respective problems, as Rogers was subsequently sued for the return of a $2,000 loan made to him on January 9, 1808, which appears to have been the source of money he used to make his purchase of those seized fifty-one barrels. The conclusion of the suit is not stated, but it was no doubt delayed because Rogers fled the state. Similarly, Hawes found himself sued for debt, and his fate is not known since he also absconded.[125]

The results obtained by the other two individuals were distinctly different. John Curtis, of St. Albans, claimed an interest in eighty-nine barrels seized on two separate vessels, and Dr. Truman Powell, of Fairfax, asserted a claim for forty barrels taken from another two boats. Curtis possessed such sufficient means that he posted the bonds required for both Brigham and Rogers in their cases. As with Rogers and Hawes, their respective matters proceeded through the court system until 1812, when they ended. For Curtis, that constituted a simple dismissal by the government in one matter and a court finding of insufficient evidence in the second. In Powell's two cases, one was dismissed by the government and a default condemnation entered in the second, apparently because Powell had not deemed it of sufficient worth to pursue. Of the twenty barrels later returned to Powell in July 1809, several bore distinctive and indecipherable markings, such as E, WF N4 and N25, a fact consistent with the dozens of other barrels carefully identified by Buel and Haswell in their seizure papers. Their several descriptive columns reveal a bewildering array of letters, numbers and symbols ranging from the relatively simple to more bizarre combinations such as No8EDEDM+V#36, MxVx#45 and AxxB#12PJ. Clearly, one had to be intimately involved in this illicit trade to understand what any of this meant.[126]

Curtis drew attention as both a leading local merchant and because he was a director of the Vermont State Bank, newly formed in 1807. He shared that role with several others, including Chittenden County state's attorney William Harrington, a man destined to play a markedly different role in the future.[127] Circumstances eventually came full circle for Curtis when, in 1815, he was declared insolvent and jailed for debt based, in part, on his participation of a fraudulent land transaction involving Silas Hathaway, the individual Penniman had sued earlier for similar conduct.[128]

Truman Powell, described as a man "of large stature, powerful physique, and great energy of character," was one of the original nine corporators of the Third Medical Society in Vermont in 1804, the predecessor of the Vermont Medical Society (established in 1813), charged with screening qualified applicants seeking to become doctors. He practiced "Physic and Surgery," in the Fairfax and Essex areas, while also offering medical instruments, drugs and medicines for sale, and served as surgeon to the local militia.[129] In August 1806, he was sued for failing to pay a promissory note, and in November 1807, he was jailed with two others for failure to satisfy an $805 judgment rendered against them. They, in turn, instituted a suit seeking their release and a court order to halt Staniford's deputy, Seeley Bennett, from executing a lien on their property.[130]

In December 1807, Powell and six other men entered not-guilty pleas to an indictment charging them with disinterring Andrew Heauber's body in August 1806 for some undisclosed reason. Instances involving body snatchers, so-called resurrectionists and sack-'em-up men were not uncommon as a deprived medical community constantly sought access to forbidden cadavers to further its medical training. Efforts were frequently undertaken to have recently deceased individuals dug up or surreptitiously brought in from out of state, some preserved in full whiskey barrels. In one notorious instance taking place just over the border at Dartmouth College in New Hampshire in 1809, at least one faculty member and a number of students were implicated in such behavior in an event called an "Anatomy Riot." The charges against Powell and his associates were later dismissed by the Supreme Court following defense counsels' argument that the indictment was "vague, repugnant and nonsencical [sic]" because it alleged Heauber was buried in two different towns, agreeing that it was "insufficient."[131]

Dr. John Stoddard was also a St. Albans physician who became well known as a notorious smuggler and reportedly employed in that work the most infamous vessel plying the lake at the time, the *Black Snake*, the very first of the fifteen boats the government sought to forfeit in October 1808. Stoddard was also a creditor of another Burlington doctor, Daniel Coit, and publicly endorsed his "Dr. Coit's Family Pills" in 1806 but also brought debt-related proceedings against him at a later time, causing Coit to seek refuge from the legislature. He was successful in that effort when it passed a bill in 1809 giving him freedom from imprisonment from Stoddard's complaint, as well as in a similar suit brought against him by merchant Samuel Fitch.[132]

In sum, these court proceedings reveal the close business relationships these men had and give rise to reasonable inferences that they included owning boats engaged in illegal activity with which they in no way wanted to have their names associated as claimants. The nondescript, diminutive nature of many of those vessels the government seized as they transported contraband also explains why these men did not seek their return, as they proved of little value when later sold pursuant to court orders. The results of the forfeiture actions on the potash itself fell more harshly on those of lesser means, while the professional men escaped virtually untouched.

One has to question why those with money and status chose to participate in activities that could clearly be seen as illegal unless it was with some assurance that they would be able to distance themselves from it and not have their names publicly known. As for those more directly involved in trade, merchants such as Guy Catlin and Samuel Fitch, whose names never became tainted by what was about to take place, together with their many close-knit business connections, the facts clearly indicate that there was some degree of knowledge among many of them about the others' involvement in illegal activity, accompanied by an unspoken agreement not to talk should it become publicly known. And if the sponsors and counselors of that criminal activity were to remain unnamed, unchallenged and immune from punishment, then the public's disgust at what was about to take place had to fall on those of a lesser sort.

BEFORE THE EMBARGO SO radically altered the conditions for lawful business along the northern frontier, the most challenging affront to public safety came in the form of counterfeiting. Across the Northeast, ingenious individuals took advantage of the primitive, easily copied bank bills in circulation, including using fictitious names for seemingly legitimate financial institutions.[133] Their efforts were deemed a significant threat to the fragile economy then in the early stages of transitioning from one based on bartering to the creation of banks. Penalties could be significant, resulting in long periods of incarceration, while, conversely, those involved in egregious assaults leaving maimed victims writhing in pain received only minimal fines. The practice was so persuasive that one legislative committee observed "for many years, a very large proportion of the bills and coin in circulation was counterfeit. Of the criminal cases reported in 1808 from seven counties, there were sixty-three indictments specified for counterfeiting, or uttering base money."[134]

Of particular note was the manner in which large numbers of men assembled together to conduct this illicit activity, and it became a preferred method of operation in other criminal activity as well. For example, one 1805 account named four individuals in the Randolph area, "as abandoned a gang of counterfeiters as ever troubled this state," for passing a variety of bogus bills. They were charged, found guilty and sentenced to stand in the pillory for an hour, being whipped thirty-nine stripes and paying a $20.00 fine.[135] One of them was identified as being connected with the notorious Canadian forger Stephen Burroughs, "King of Counterfeiters" (formerly from Hanover, New Hampshire), whose gang of "profligate and unscrupled" men had begun operations just over the border in Lower Canada in 1803. They had such a dire impact in the state that nearby New York banks engaged the services of timber rafter Sam Mix, who, in January 1806, had just completed a successful prosecution against an individual on a complaint of defamation, receiving a $222.50 judgment. In a fascinating set of documents filed with the legislature during the next decade seeking compensation for his efforts, Mix explained what took place between the summer of 1806 and the winter of 1807 as he sought to infiltrate this particular operation, an effort that proved every bit as challenging as any rafting venture.[136]

The Canadians were first detected working in New York, and those banks affected attempted to halt their operations without success. When Mix learned the men had crossed over into Vermont, some apparently splitting off to create several other gangs, he approached the New York banks and agreed to work for them as their agent. He was to identify those involved and, whenever possible, gain their confidence and become part of their group, receiving an undetermined sum for his efforts. Over the course of eleven months, while spending significant amounts of his own money, Mix was highly successful and worked closely with several of the counterfeiters in the Rutland area, particularly in neighboring Shrewsbury. At one point, one of the counterfeiters was arrested, and in order to continue with his charade, Mix made the unwise decision to post bond on his behalf, ensuring his future appearance in court. Predictably, it ended with the arrestee's flight, and Mix became obligated to pay the bond.

The undercover work continued, and Mix remained in place passing information to authorities, allowing for several men's arrest and the seizure of substantial amounts of counterfeit money.[137] To maintain his appearance as an associate, as Mix later explained, "in order to be more useful in the suppression of those evils that threatened to become universal," he hired an associate to work with him. Unfortunately, because of the newcomer's "mistaken zeal & precipitancy," Mix ended up being personally subjected to "the humiliating & mortifying necessity of being arrested & submitting to ignominious treatment." The result was incarceration for him and then, continuing with the ruse, admitting his "guilt" and having judgments rendered against him in court. It all became too much for Mix, and he spoke confidentially with a Supreme Court judge aware of what he was doing who could tell him only that it was "too late to retrace his steps, but he must pursue the object he had undertaken."

Eventually, after meeting with much success, Mix ended his involvement and returned to private life, but not without having to endure further difficulties. First, the New York banks concluded that Vermont authorities had reaped such substantial benefits from Mix's efforts in removing so much counterfeit money from circulation, as well as swelling their coffers from the forfeiture of bond money posted by absconding offenders, that they should be the ones to pay for his work. Second, aside from the few dollars a Troy bank conferred on him, Mix was left with losses estimated at $708.67, had a criminal record and was liable for the bond he had posted earlier for the fleeing counterfeiter. Third, in August 1807, he found himself named as a defendant in a suit for refusing to pay for various services rendered to him in the recent past (horseshoeing, sleigh repairs, lodging, rum and many meals, several including "oysters and wine"), which appear to have been part of his undercover activities—albeit, Mix did have an inclination not to pay his bills, as when he was similarly sued in 1805 for refusing to settle his debts.[138] Despite the many hardships Mix encountered, it took many years, and many petitions to the assembly, before he obtained some relief, which, no doubt, left in him some lingering ill feeling toward those in authority.

Court records abound with examples of many others involved with counterfeiting. For example, farther to the north, in May and June 1807, Bradley Wilson in Milton and Moses Wilson (relationship unknown) in Shelburne were each indicted for engraving plates used to make fraudulent ten-dollar bills from the New York State Bank; they were arrested, charged and then set free on bonds guaranteed by several other individuals. By the following January, the two men had fled, and their bondsmen were obligated to pay the state treasurer. Richard Wheeler, of Swanton, took a more brazen approach and forged bank bills made payable to W.W. Van Ness, cousin of local attorney Cornelius Van Ness. Wheeler did not flee and was sentenced to stand one hour in the pillory, being whipped thirty-nine times and paying a $100 fine.[139]

In a single session of the Supreme Court, sitting in Orleans County in October 1807, eight men were sentenced for counterfeiting, with several receiving lengthy sentences that included hard labor. For John Johnson, a second-time offender, his involvement as a purported "cancer doctor" in the death of young Hannah Everts by putting an ounce of opium into a quart of spirits she consumed while in a delirious state, and whose defense in all of his cases rested on his being intoxicated himself, gained him the harshest penalty of seven years' hard labor. It certainly exceeded the one he received for Hannah's death, escaping a murder charge after being found guilty of manslaughter and receiving a sentence of standing one hour in the pillory and being whipped thirty-nine times.

Over the course of two hours late one afternoon in February 1808, Supreme Court chief judge Royall Tyler sentenced four more men for counterfeiting, one receiving a six-year term of hard labor, while an additional five had their cases continued, including one involving Timothy Blanchard. While records show that Blanchard was indeed indicted for passing counterfeit bills, additional documentation reveals he might have been pursuing the same course adopted by Sam Mix in allowing himself to be charged alongside others as part of a plan to infiltrate their operations. Those papers include attestations of others that Blanchard, who was apparently a militia captain, was engaged in lawful conduct at the time, possessing "a gaolor's determination to exterminate from society a set of men."

Those men included many coming from outside the state, continuing to demonstrate that it remained an attractive location to engage in illegal conduct. An October 20, 1808 petition for reimbursement for expenses filed by Israel Grovenor reveals that, over the course of the preceding three years, he, together with others, pursued many counterfeiters from Vermont and neighboring states, arresting them and seizing their bogus bills, prompting him to file a claim that he was entitled to some form of payment for his efforts. A sympathetic legislative committee agreed but limited the claim to $300, believing, as it had in Mix's case, that since banks in other states derived benefits from his work, they should also contribute. For Jabez Barnum, quickly deputized by an Addison County deputy sheriff in January 1808 to accompany him in rounding up counterfeiters roaming at large in New Haven, the foray resulted in his horse breaking a leg and having to be destroyed after the men were arrested, resulting in a claim of $65 for his loss. Regardless of any of their efforts, the state was able to reap a windfall of $7,000 that year because so many of those allowed free on bonds absconded, and the money was forfeited. For those based out of Quebec, their operations did not end until Canadian officials were able to finally arrest thirteen of them, three ending up in a Montreal jail, two fleeing to Vermont and the rest simply agreeing not to engage in such conduct again.[140]

Looking beyond the actions of counterfeiters and those involved in predictably petty crimes, Vermont's courts were a beehive of activity dealing with a staggering number of debt-related issues. Failure to make good on one's financial obligations constituted an overwhelming number of cases filed by creditors as they sought recourse from those unable, or unwilling, to pay what they owed. To more fully understand the underlying pressures and relationships of these individuals, and the many others with whom they interacted, modern-day students are fortunate to have access to a rich resource containing their various disputes within the Vermont State Archives—an experience that leaves one in awe of what they reveal. In box after box, there are literally hundreds of tightly bound, filthy stacks of folded papers concerning each of these many cases that have sat virtually untouched for two hundred years. The many stories they tell cannot possibly be recounted here, but for the representative few that were examined, a new world opens, providing a totally new perspective on what these frontier people were doing during this critical time in the state's history.

Of the many revelations, it is clear that the courts were extremely important to many in the business community. As one historian of Vermont's legal past notes, "It was law that created this state, and law that tamed it."[141] That was indeed the case, for the fact that merchants and bankers chose to sue one another is not necessarily surprising, but it is the frequency of times they did so that causes one to wonder at the underlying reasons. The names of the many litigants appear so often in the records that one is left with the impression that their going before a judge was as common an occurrence as acknowledging another's presence on the street.

The reason is simple. In an economy lacking a credible monetary system, dependent on bartering and agreements among gentlemen to pay their debts, as evidenced by their many book accounts and promissory notes, the failure of a single large debtor to make good on an obligation posed a significant problem. Not only was a particular creditor at risk, but also many others, including merchants, tradesmen, mechanics and farmers, all with their own interdependent relationships based on trusted reciprocity between themselves, relied on one another to fulfill their obligations in order to allow them to pay their own in turn. If one defaulted, then many suffered in consequence, and this explains their overriding preoccupation with punishing counterfeiters, who placed their fragile banking system at risk. It was a house of cards, threatening to fall apart if agreements were not fulfilled as promised, and it caused many to quickly resort to court action to obtain attachments against debtors and warrants for their arrest.

This, in turn, gave rise to yet another class of lawsuit, this time against debtors, and others, who posted bonds allowing for their release from the local jail with the promise of remaining available to address the underlying suit. And it was also not uncommon for sheriffs and their deputies to be further named as defendants for their own negligence in not properly completing court-approved orders, or executions, in creditors' favor. They were also sued for failing to keep prisoners within their custody who might, and frequently did, escape. The number of people incarcerated for debt during this particular time period is not known, but in the three years between 1827 and 1829, there were 4,091 individuals (approximately 1.5 percent of the population) jailed, and in one county alone, in 1829, there were 212 people locked up.[142] It is reasonable to assume that two decades earlier, during troublesome 1808, those numbers would not have been proportionately less and were probably even higher in light of the embargo's harm, resulting in several hundred people occupying the state's various local jails. It was not until 1834 that the state finally abandoned jailing female debtors; males were no longer jailed as of 1838.

There were also fundamental problems existing within the system itself in failing to administratively compensate government officials for executing their official acts, which resulted in their having to bring suits against the county for payment for services. Perhaps the most striking examples of such failures was when State's Attorney Harrington instituted suit against Sheriff Staniford for reimbursements while in the very midst of prosecuting those responsible for the August murders and when Staniford, in turn, went on to sue both his jailor and deputies for their own negligence. The possibilities presented in having so much litigation available to them were also important to several noteworthy lawyers, who not only represented the various parties but also became more personally involved, turning lawsuits into business opportunities by purchasing from plaintiffs their rights to sue others. The overriding zeal they displayed in pursing their individual interests cannot be overstated, as these pillars of the community aggressively engaged others in court.

The man primarily responsible for overseeing law enforcement, and the jail, in Chittenden County in 1808 was Daniel Staniford, who did not know it at the time but was then on a path that would quickly result in the end of his law enforcement career. While he appeared to be a highly conscientious public servant engaged in executing complex duties with limited competent resources at his disposal, the immediate circumstances proved unkind to him. As sheriff, an appointment made yearly by the legislature requiring him to post a $10,000 bond to ensure the performance of his duties, he exercised the traditional roles of serving court papers on parties, witnesses and others; seeing to the execution of judgments; and ensuring public peace. He had the authority to name deputies and a jailor, to execute searches and to call on the militia for assistance, while also being responsible for maintaining the county jail. The legislature supplemented those 1797 provisions in 1802, when it further authorized all county sheriffs to "occupy, improve or lease out…all apartments of jail-houses, which are not appropriated for the safe keeping of prisoners." Interestingly, the law further allowed county judges "to grant [a] license, to the occupier of any jail house…to keep a tavern, or house of publick entertainment, in the same."[143] So, incredibly, even jails became purveyors of insidious alcohol!

Staniford took his duties very seriously, and despite the strange circumstance of himself being incarcerated at the time for failure to pay a debt, in September 1807, he placed ads to employ four joiners to complete the construction of a "dwelling house" fronting on the jail, stating that "none need apply, but those who are capable and willing to do justice to their employer."[144] This concerned work being done on the new jail located on land the town had purchased for $100 from lake merchant Lyman King the preceding month, immediately to the north of Courthouse Square, where a number of businesses, including Guy Catlin and Samuel Fitch, were in operation. By December, as authorized by the legislature, Staniford advertised the house as available for rent, describing it as "a good stand for a tavern."[145] That month, Staniford named Elias Buel Jr., brother of deputy collector Sam Buel, as one of his deputies (sworn in on December 12), and he became the first tenant of the house. The residence later played an important role immediately following the murders, serving as a location to house prisoners and militia soldiers guarding the jail.[146]

Buel's tenure as deputy was not otherwise without its own problems. On May 30, 1808, Aaron Cooley was awarded a $33.89 judgment against Staniford for Buel's neglect in a case that later resulted in Staniford filing suit against Buel and two other men who signed jail bonds on Buel's behalf for reimbursement. Staniford was ultimately successful the following year in obtaining further damages and costs; however, the results of any recovery against Buel are unknown since he died in September, when the community was consumed in dealing with the murders and attending unrest.[147] For Staniford, there were additional challenges at the time, as he had recently filed suit in May against the people of Chittenden County for "fraudulently defrauding" him when the county clerk refused to comply with a court order that he be paid $40.00 for his recent work on the jail. He was ultimately successful in that effort and received an award of $56.38 during the court's September term.[148]

Other deputies working for Staniford at the time included Abiram Hurlburt, of Charlotte, and the perennially named Seeley Bennett, of Burlington, both having previously served and received their most recent appointments in December 1807. In light of the challenges Bennett posed to Staniford in the coming months, he ironically attested at the time of his reappointment that he did so with "perfect knowledge of your integrity & abilities," a statement he later came to question. Perhaps because of the increasing tensions brought on by the embargo, on April 18, 1808, Staniford appointed yet another deputy, Jacob Davis of Milton, who later survived the housecleaning taking place within the department following the December 1808 appointment of Heman Allen as the new sheriff.[149] However, even this most recent increase in manpower was not enough when, two weeks later, a counterfeiting prisoner was forcibly wrested from Bennett's custody by his compatriots, forcing Staniford to appoint yet additional deputies in the coming months.

Staniford also hired Benjamin Adams, of South Hero, as keeper of the Burlington jail, a position he held during the unrest and one he appears to have executed with some difficulty. The following February 1809, Staniford sued Adams for some undisclosed neglect, resulting in a sizeable $195.96 judgment rendered against him in the county court. Notably, when Adams decided to institute an appeal of that decision, none other than his notorious neighbor, rafter Colonel Sam Mix, agreed to act as surety.[150]

The responsibilities Staniford assumed in overseeing the jail were certainly not easy ones, particularly when even its definition was open to interpretation. The 1802 law allowed low-risk prisoners, such as those jailed for debt, to enjoy "the liberties of the jail-yard" upon their posting a bond guaranteeing their continued presence, subject to forfeiture should they escape.[151] On the evening of February 10, 1806, Darius Jacques did so in St. Albans, leaving the jail without permission. As part of later court proceedings (perhaps brought against those who had taken on the ill-conceived responsibility of bondsman for the absconding prisoner), sworn testimony was received from two witnesses residing alongside Jacques, describing their terms of incarceration. Jacques was already a person of some notoriety for having a horse and sleigh, carrying a quantity of furs and forty pounds of snuff, seized by customs officials at Alburgh in 1803 for violating revenue laws. He then went on to make an unsuccessful appeal of the matter to the Vermont Supreme Court, arguing that the collector had illegally delegated authority to a deputy to make such seizures.[152]

One of those prisoners providing information concerning Jacques's escape was Major Amos Morrill (presumably incarcerated for a debt-related matter), the man who had sold Penniman his land on Windmill Point two years previously, and the other was Alfred Hathaway. Morrill stated that when Jacques was brought to the jail the preceding November, there was no additional bedding available, and the two had shared a bed. He explained that while the structure housed both the jail and a school, the entire building was under the control of the sheriff and a jailer. The doors to the inmates' rooms do not appear to have been in any way reinforced, equipped only with "common latches & hitches," and were described as having been routinely left open during the day to allow prisoners to have access to both the jail proper and the adjoining school area. Hathaway related that he had seen Jacques go "several times to Col. Taylor's watering trough to wash and once in the knight [sic] time he went down on the green & several times out after wood and several times about twenty rods [outside]."[153]

The questioning also touched on the ludicrous issue of whether the sheriff actually intended the men to even remain in jail. When questioned about the fact that they could have escaped at any time of their choosing because of the open doors, Morrill explained, "In the day time they were, but in the nighttime I conceived the doors of the gaol room in which we slept to be locked, from the noise apparently occasioned by placing the bolt and turning the key." To further remove any insinuation that the sheriff did not take his responsibilities seriously, Morrill further related that, at one point, he heard the sheriff tell the prisoners that he could not trust them any longer and had to lock them up. In 1813, the legislature sought to remove any question concerning the extent a prisoner could be allowed "liberties of the jails," directing county judges to establish appropriate bounds, but none exceeding an area greater than four square miles.[154]

Despite the best of intentions, the Chittenden county jail remained a source of concern following the indictment of the structure in January 1808 for its many deficiencies, a situation that continued into the fall and contributed to Staniford's seemingly never-ending problems that year. Following his removal in December, the next month, the grand jury made its yearly inspection and once again concluded that "although neat and orderly kept, [it] is not in sufficient repair for the safe keeping of prisoners, that the lower room…is extremely unhealthy, unfit & unsafe for the confinement of criminals." In August, additional efforts were undertaken to bring water directly to the jail, at a cost of fifty dollars, for both the convenience of the family living there and the prisoners, as well as for fire protection. In 1818, the inspection made similar findings that the "gaol is sufficiently strong…if due care is used on the part of the keepers" but that the unacceptable accumulation of stagnating water in the lower level made the structure "insufficient." The following year, the grand jury's report deemed the cells "sufficiently strong" but also "too damp and unhealthy for want of air." The inspection also noted that the "weak" walls needed reinforcing, a condition that persisted into 1820, when the grand jury noted further that the "upper or debtors' room appeared insufficient to confine prisoners if a serious effort were made to break through."

By January 1821, the jail was in such bad condition that the grand jury concluded "no care or diligence of the sheriff or jailor, short of keeping a continual guard around the prison…will detain prisoners in this gaol, or unless they are chained and bound to the floor of the same," and recommended it be demolished. Only weeks later, on the evening of March 1, the building was destroyed by a fire believed to have started in a defective chimney. The current sheriff was then forced to rent a brick building from King in order to house debtors, and when the newly rebuilt jail was inspected in 1823, the grand jury found it acceptable. However, a return to bad habits was apparently too strong to resist; in 1825, the grand jury once again deemed the jail "insufficient."[155]

The possibility of falling victim to a creditor's suit and the appearance of a sheriff's deputy forcibly removing one to Burlington's jail instilled the greatest of fears in the law-abiding population, even with the liberties of the jail. As Stephen Smith of Shelburne made clear to the public in a December 2, 1807 article headed "To My Creditors," "In my last settlement I have disposed of every cent of the property I have earned with my hard labour the whole season past except the necessary provisions for my family; for which reason I shall be obliged to disappoint you." He said, "I owe about one hundred dollars in small debts, which with an addition of cost I never could pay; but must be dragged to the cold prison in Burlington and leave my poor family behind to suffer." He went on to assure his creditors that with their "indulgence in time I will pay you the utmost farthing, with use."[156] Smith related further that "the summer past, have paid rising of thirty dollars cost, upon less than twenty dollars original debt, which leaves me without provisions and very thinly clad." That a person could incur such substantial interest obligations on the unpaid balance of a debt, even a small one, particularly in these early days of the embargo, gives us pause to consider the ramifications for the common man in later days.

The presence of so many counterfeiters operating openly and the government's need to accommodate them prior to trial and then upon conviction, together with the burgeoning presence of debtors, forced the legislature to take action. Accordingly, right in the very midst of the early days of the embargo, it took on the dual challenges of creating banks while moving forward to build a secure facility to house the most serious offenders receiving long sentences. In mocking tone, wags quickly noted a "singular association" between the two interests: "The legislature of Vermont have increased the number of their banks, and ordered a state prison to be erected. Very well! For, more banks, more counterfeiters, and for more counterfeiters, more prison room will be wanted."[157]

Ironically, the legislature was convulsed at that very moment with the arrest of one of its own members, Abel Spencer of Rutland, for reportedly stealing thirty-one dollars in bank notes from three men. After taking Spencer into custody on November 9, 1807, rather than locking him up in the local jail, Deputy Sheriff Elijah Yemans allowed him to spend the night with two other representatives who promised to present him before the legislature the following day to answer the charge. However, Spencer was able to make good his escape at some point, thereby causing an investigation to be started not only against him but against the other two men as well for dereliction. Wasting no time in dealing with his "base crime," Spencer was expelled from the assembly the following day by a unanimous 149-member vote; the two bewildered representatives were not disciplined. It was not the end for Spencer, who remained at large and was again expelled in January 1808 from Mason Center Lodge, No. 6, in Rutland for "a flagrant violation of the principles of Masonry."

The day after Spencer's removal, lawmakers turned their eyes to the legal profession itself and passed a telling law, one providing great insights into the state of the profession at the time. In "An act to punish undue combinations, speculations, and unjust practices among attornies [sic] and pettifoggers," four devastating sections address several egregious practices, including making illegal agreements among attorneys seeking to keep others from engaging in law; entering their names in cases in which they were not retained by either plaintiff or defendant; excessive fees; and arrangements with sheriffs, deputy sheriffs and constables to delay certain executions in order to allow an attorney to gain an unfair advantage in a particular proceeding.[158] Clearly, even within the legal profession, there remained much room for improvement.

For his part, Governor Israel Smith recognized the rapidly deteriorating problem that counterfeiting posed, and in October, he admonished the assembly to look for guidance to the state's 1793 constitution, which provides:

> *To deter more effectually from the commission of crimes, by continued visible punishments of long duration, and to make sanguinary punishments less necessary, means ought to be provided for punishing by hard labor, those who shall be convicted of crimes not capital, whereby the criminal shall be employed for the benefit of the public, or for the reparation of injuries done to private persons: and all persons at proper times ought to be permitted to see them at their labor.*[159]

The call for a state prison to make these goals real was not a new one. People had now moved beyond the bizarre 1785 episode in Westminster when a debtor died in jail and officials refused to remove his body for fear of aiding in an escape. It was only as the body lay rotting that an imaginative sheriff found a way to convince townspeople that a nearby cemetery actually lay within jail bounds, allowing everyone to finally agree to remove and bury the poor man's remains.[160] Since then, several discussions were held at the legislative level between 1793 and 1804 concerning the creation of a state-run institution, but no final decisions were made.

In 1805, Staniford himself, together with Seeley Bennett and another individual, was among a few groups petitioning the legislature for permission to build the prison in Burlington, offering to do so for $28,000. Nothing further was done, but by the time counterfeiters brought about impending financial ruination, a new effort had been undertaken to address the threat they posed and the deteriorating condition of the county jails. As noted, two unlawful departures, or "gaol breaks," took place at Staniford's jail during the fall and winter of 1807–08, and the grand jury made wholly unsatisfactory findings concerning its condition, but he was by no means the only unfortunate. On October 30, 1807, recently sentenced counterfeiters in the Chelsea jail protested to the legislature that they "are nine in number and confined in a small room, with but two apertures for the admission of light and air, that their situation, owing to the noxious effluvia, and exhausted air…is almost insupportable to human nature." With their petition deemed of merit and changes ordered, only days later, every single one of them escaped. Rewards of $20 each were immediately posted, and two were quickly recaptured, including John Johnson, the two-time convicted counterfeiter also involved in murder. Incredibly, three weeks later, Johnson and five others escaped once again, and only a few days later, two more men departed. Then, an additional three jail breaks took place between March and September 1808 involving eight escapees, one of whom, Ezekiel Flanders, had been involved in a total of four breakouts.[161]

Further accounts describe yet more escapes, including four counterfeiters leaving from an unnamed Vermont jail in December 1807 who "got loose upon the world to join Burroughs and follow their old trade again." In fact, the notorious counterfeit leader himself escaped from a Montreal jail in January 1807, was recaptured in September and then made good yet another escape. At that same moment, his son, Edward, described as a "true chip off the old block," was arrested with another man, together with their counterfeit money, in Lebanon, New Hampshire, but they were also able to escape from authorities.

In May 1807, Abner Hayes, one of the counterfeit leaders from Shrewsbury, was arrested but absconded from a Rutland jail in July, his gait somewhat impeded by a "horse lock on his left ankle." In June 1808, four more counterfeiters escaped, a seemingly never-ending endeavor continuing on to, at least, 1811, when the local grand jury inspecting the facility determined it was made out of defective materials "totally unfit for any durable purpose," deeming it "a mere edifice of shreds and patches from repeated alterations and repairs." The grand jury condemned it further, finding that "cleanliness can never be introduced and a free circulation of wholesome air is prevented by the overwhelming exhalations of the loathsome place." So, it is not surprising that the jurors, as those examining the situation in Chelsea earlier, noted that "the prisoners, shocking to humanity, resemble the legitimate tenants of the mire, and not the inhabitants of civilized society." Clearly frustrated that similar warnings from prior grand juries had gone unheeded, they implored that something be done to correct the problems to vindicate "the honor and dignity of the County of Rutland."[162]

In July 1808, five more counterfeiters, housed on the second floor of the Danville jail, sawed through metal grating, lowered themselves to the ground with sheets and fled the area, believed to be headed to Canada, "from whence they can undertake new adventures, and again impose on the public with their nefarious trash." Their particular desires were apparently thwarted through the efforts of Caledonia sheriff Joseph Armington, who immediately sent out several men to track down and return the escapees, charging the state for not only their time but also for the use of horses and paying two other men $15.11 for "entertainment," likely a euphemism for ardent spirits. In one of the more imaginative escapes, two counterfeiters left their Townshend lockup, taking with them large quantities of their forged Canadian and Vermont handiwork. So many men were escaping that a virtual cottage industry arose in which citizens struck out on their own to recapture them and claim the rewards being put up.[163] Clearly, Vermont authorities had a substantial problem keeping dangerous men incarcerated, which could have instilled in the public at large only a general disdain for their ineffectiveness, put on display on a daily basis.

The diversity, tenacity and continuing challenges that many displayed toward any signs of authority remained of high concern, and the assembly moved rapidly ahead to fulfill Governor Smith's vision to site a new prison. Bids were solicited and several brought forward, including proposals from the Towns of Hartford and Windsor, as well as one from an individual living in that nest of counterfeiting activity, Shrewsbury, offering to provide fifty acres along the nearby Cold River for its building.[164] In the end, the residents of Windsor convinced commissioners that their town was the most appropriate location, and an acre of land close to the courthouse was donated, while inhabitants agreed to make five thousand tons of stone from nearby Mount Ascutney available, at their own expense, for its construction. That work began in the spring of 1808 with

> utmost vigor. The great number of workmen employed in hewing the stone, and the vast number of teams continually ascending and descending the mountain, presented a novel sight to the Vermonter. The corner stone…was drawn and laid with the utmost splendor. Hundreds, (not to say thousands), followed it in procession from the base of Ascutney attended by martial music. A large hackmatack tree was dug from its native soil and confined in an erect position on a car which was drawn by horses. On the top of the tree was suspended the flag of the United States. It was laid amid the roar of cannon, and the shouts of the spectators.[165]

The construction was not without controversy, as a public dispute broke out in August during the travails attending the murders in which allegations of favoritism and backroom political maneuvering were made. It began in July when "A Customer" questioned in a Montpelier newspaper article why Windsor had been chosen when residents in Middlebury were willing to build it at a lesser cost.[166] More letters began to appear, both in defense of and in opposition to the final choice, but it was one observation made by a writer that conveys the suspicions many appear to have had at the time with their politicians, those with their hands on the levers of power:

It is already time that the people of Vermont were made acquainted with the characters of some of those, to whom they entrusted their confidence. Their rights have long enough been the objects of bargain and sale—of venality and corruption. They have long enough been subject to the control of caucuses and secret councils.[167]

Notwithstanding those difficulties, work progressed steadily on the facility throughout the summer. The surrounding walls, "of hewn stone, and laid in lime…extend[ing] three feet below the surface of the earth, and…four feet in thickness at the base," climbed to their finished twenty-foot height. They enclosed the main, three-story building, eighty-five feet by thirty-six feet, also constructed with hewn stone and topped off by a belfry. It was destined to house 170 prisoners, scheduled to begin arriving the following year. They were to occupy the first two floors, while the third was reserved as a hospital for the sick.

In viewing the building from the outside, one could see that the first-floor windows were very small, with narrow openings, while those on the second were a little larger and those in the hospital larger still, with grating covering them. The building's exterior walls had attained their three-foot thickness, with eighteen-inch partitions between the rooms. Cell doors on the lowest level were constructed out of sheet and bar iron "firmly riveted together." An adjoining building to house the keepers and guards was also under construction, and its basement was destined to serve as the prison's "victualing room." A seventy-foot-deep well was dug and an aqueduct to a nearby mountain accomplished with great speed. Also included within the walls was a brick workshop where prisoners, in the early years, were expected to engage in "hard labor" making nails and weaving various fabrics.[168] Keeper Thomas Hewlet was appointed to oversee the facility, but unfortunately, he would not get out of there alive.

Following its near completion and opening in June 1809, and through the end of the year, twenty-four prisoners were admitted to begin serving their terms of hard labor. It is indicative of the seriousness of crime counterfeiting was considered at the time that fifteen of those arriving were sentenced for that particular offense, ordered to serve upward of ten years. Others had been sentenced for theft (two men for two and three years each), rape (one man for ten years) and horse stealing (three men for between five and seven years).

Of those first arrivals, twenty came from outside the state, and of the remaining four, three were Vermonters who received sentences of ten years for manslaughter, all involved in a single episode of devastating cruelty taking place the summer of 1808.[169]

GANGS ASSOCIATING WITH ONE another to counterfeit money or stage noteworthy jailbreaks were not the only examples of illegal activity involving numbers of men. The December 1807 term of the Vermont Supreme Court, sitting in Franklin County, discloses that it was dealing not only with Truman Powell's indictment for removing a dead body, two divorce cases and many more counterfeiting matters but also other instances in which several men were charged with rioting. Theophilus Morrill, of St. Albans, was the leader of two gangs assaulting two different men in February and March 1807. This was not the first time Morrill was involved in assaultive behavior, having already viciously beaten Silas Hathaway in 1805 with the assistance of two other men and received a modest twenty-dollar fine as a penalty. Earlier in that year, he was sued by his own attorney, who was seeking payment for representing him in an undisclosed criminal matter with others dating back to 1799.[170]

These more recent events concerned yet more of the same—specifically that Morrill and others did "beat, wound, & ill-treat" Jariah Lewis to the point where "his life was greatly despaired." But it was the second case that is the more noteworthy of the two. On that occasion, Morrill, together with four other men, including, importantly, Samuel I. Mott, also of St. Albans, did "unlawfully, riotously and routously beat, wound and ill-treat" a Zebulon Alger to the point where his life was also greatly endangered. However, that was not all, as the men were charged in a second count with rioting and disturbing the peace "for the space of one hour and more," causing "great terror and disturbances" to the public passing along a local highway.

While the Mott family name is closely associated with Alburgh's settlement years, and any connection between them and Samuel is obscure, records concerning him disclose that he was born around 1772 in Clinton, Dutchess County, New York; was six feet tall; and had dark brown hair, blue eyes and a light complexion. His name also appears in the 1800 grand list for the town (as does the name of Frederick Hoxie, another individual also coming to prominence), and he is listed along with several others, including Deputy Collector Sam Buel, in an October 1807 petition to the legislature seeking the establishment of a ferry connecting Alburgh with Highgate.[171]

On this occasion, Morrill, Mott and the others all appeared before the court on December 23. They either pleaded or were found guilty following trial and sentenced on Christmas Day, Morrill receiving a term of three months' imprisonment and the others paying small fines only. The several defendants appearing over those days included Amos Morrill Jr., who also had a history of engaging in assaults and had headed a group earlier in the month that caused serious injuries to Samuel Holton as they imprisoned him over a three-day period to extort money from him, using "swords, staves, and clubs" in their attack. Local attorney Cornelius Van Ness was also present in court and served as counsel to several of the men (he later represented Morrill in the suit brought against him by Jariah Lewis), including another matter in which his client reportedly imprisoned a man for thirty days and caused him significant injury.[172]

The Supreme Court's proceedings on this occasion are particularly instructive when considered in the context of the mayhem about to unfold months later during the summer. Clearly, gangs of men, both those involved in counterfeiting and those associating together to extract money or to vindicate some perceived slight, coursed freely over the countryside, all inevitably propelled by their ever-present ardent spirits. There was little stopping them from engaging in raucous behavior, and even when sentenced, the fines were very small when compared to the significant harm their victims suffered. In the case of the counterfeiters, their sentences reflected the more significant harm the court perceived they inflicted, and while Nicholas Duclos and Grant Wead (represented by Van Ness) were sentenced to stand only an hour in the pillory, be whipped thirty-nine stripes and pay a small fine, others, such as Silas Whiting, who possessed a single bogus bill, received five-year sentences of hard labor.

For Van Ness and the other local attorneys representing both plaintiffs and defendants, they were deeply involved in their respective clients' travails and had particular and intimate knowledge of who was responsible for the criminal conduct taking place. In sum, all of the participants knew one another in some fashion, and each took away from the experience some understanding of what the government was capable of extracting from them for their conduct. For the smugglers among them, there was certainly no evidence that they faced any type of meaningful sanction if they were ever to be caught. And even if they inflicted an injury on someone, the sentence was, in all likelihood, going to serve as only a minor inconvenience.

A final phenomenon that arose, no doubt exacerbated by the perceived lenient punishment they received, concerned the violent manner in which those opposed to enforcement efforts turned and actually went on the offensive against government agents. Not only choosing to pursue their livelihood regardless of legality, on many occasions, when they found their activities interrupted and their goods seized, smugglers carefully watched for any inattention by authorities to present itself. Should the opportunity arise, bands of men gathered together to forcibly take back, or "rescue," their property, providing numerous opportunities for physical injury to take place. To prevent any of that from happening, it was not unusual to see large numbers of people traveling together, presenting a formidable body and causing the most conscientious law enforcement officer to hesitate in trying to stop them. One report related that those along the border would "take their produce to market, in companies of twenty to thirty, and have resolved not to yield to any officers who may attempt to check their progress." In February 1808, just before the land embargo took effect, the roads near Swanton were literally blocked with great numbers of sleighs bearing lumber and produce northward, a situation that certainly presented challenges for the small number of customs officials.[173]

While many encounters took place between officials and smugglers in the next few years, in the early moments of the embargo, they were relatively benign, probing instances in which criminals tested the limits of the government's tolerance. In early January 1808, Collector Penniman wrote from Swanton to an unidentified individual who appears to have been either Buel, stationed out on Windmill Point, or Haswell in Burlington. One of the men apparently had occasion to take contraband into his custody, and Penniman wrote in warning:

> *I have been informed that means would be taken to get from your care part or all the property—the manner not known—I hope you will use due care and diligence and if you can suppose it possible have men placed secretly to watch…If anything of this kind should take place much blame would attach to us both.*[174]

The outcome of that particular incident is not known, but additional evidence of forceful, unlawful rescues was also taking place and did not involve customs officials.

In April, State's Attorney Harrington had been dealing with continuing counterfeiting matters and obtained indictments from the grand jury against an individual from nearby Huntington and a man from Lower Canada for forgery.[175] He also obtained an arrest warrant against Beriah Cleeland, from Underhill, for an undisclosed offense, probably fraud related. The warrant was then given to Deputy Seeley Bennett, who took Cleeland into custody on

May 3, at which point things began to quickly come apart for him. At some location in Underhill, as Bennett escorted Cleeland to jail, Joseph Hurlburt, Jonas Nye and Samuel Lewis all joined together and "with force and arms did aid and assist" in removing the man from Bennett's custody, allowing for his successful escape. Undeterred from any further criminal conduct, only three days later, Cleeland was at work forging bank bills to defraud the newly established Bank of Vermont, which resulted in yet more charges being filed against him by Harrington.[176]

For the time immediately preceding the intervention of national and international affairs into Vermont's circumstances, the state was experiencing an important moment as it sought to deal with external regional threats acting against its fragile monetary system. Gangs of counterfeiters, and those taking the law into their own hands, moved easily about, uninhibited by any kind of law enforcement measures. They moved back and forth across the border with Canada and between neighboring states as they conducted their business, and when intercepted, they forcibly sought to rescue friends who might be arrested or goods that were seized. Jails were wholly inadequate to the task, and the new state prison was designed in order to alleviate the many problems they, and the many debtors, presented. These were the big issues requiring correction, but now a more dire situation was about to arise, compounding a difficult set of circumstances into one that resulted in the deaths of innocent people.

3

INSURRECTION

Under extreme pressure, Thomas Jefferson would very much have appreciated the sentiment of such law-abiding Vermonters as Curtis Holgate, advertising in the difficult month of April 1808:

> *CASH. Paid for any quantity of potash…at eight dollars per hundred weight, delivered at his store on the lake shore in Alburgh, Vermont. It is requested that all potash brought may be secured in firm tight barrels, as we know not how long it will have to lie on hand before the Embargo may be taken off.*[177]

Holgate had no way of knowing precisely what was going on in other quarters at that moment as Washington authorities began communicating with Collector Penniman and Vermont representatives on an appropriate course of action in putting into place the draconian restrictions the land embargo imposed on the frontier. Had he known, he might very well have chosen not to waste his money on advertising but rather gird for the firestorm about to unfold.

When Penniman received a copy of the March mandate on April 1, he understood immediately what the sudden halt of local commerce with Quebec would mean if those many lumber rafts waiting for open water were suddenly halted in their journey. Many people were fully employed and staking their lives on success at that very moment in anticipation of the coming season, including seventeen-year-old Isaac Stow of Weybridge. He and his elder brother had been hard at work during the winter months dragging logs into the Otter Creek and forming them into two rafts in anticipation of floating them down to the lake. However, as they got underway on April 7, Isaac experienced some physical problem, jumped to shore and immediately "died in a fit." Also, up on the Onion, between Burlington and Colchester in the immediate vicinity of the falls near the Catlin and Jasper store, on the eighteenth, Jeff Brown and Nathan Post were both drowned as they worked on their logging concern.[178]

These were the types of operations—along with many others underway up and down the various rivers, all destined for the lake—that concerned Treasury secretary Gallatin very much. Accompanying the latest embargo notice, he specifically warned Penniman, "You will, of course, take particular notice of the section which forbids every species of exportation, whether in rafts, boats, sleighs, carts, by water or by land."[179] While the public was generally aware that Congress was considering such provisions, it had no way of knowing how they applied to it or how they would be implemented, affording Penniman time to make preparations to deal with those coming rafts and boats.

Seeking the assurances of others in his dire estimations, Penniman immediately consulted with two local men closely associated with those knowledgeable of criminal activity: attorneys Asa Aldis (1770–1847) and Cornelius Van Ness (1782–1852). Both men had extensive experience representing members of the various gangs in court when they were either charged with crimes or sued for their many assaults, and both had appeared before the Supreme Court the preceding December, when rioter Samuel I. Mott was present. Aldis had previously represented Penniman during the contentious proceedings concerning his wife's dower rights a few years earlier. He was originally from Franklin, Massachusetts; received his legal training in Rhode Island; and arrived in St. Albans in 1802. There, he found a small number of men involved with the law and quickly established himself as a highly capable practitioner (later becoming chief judge of the Supreme Court in 1815). He was a devout Republican and a firm believer in the embargo and nonintercourse laws, including their enforcement, making him part of a distinct minority within the Federalist, anti-embargo community.[180]

Van Ness certainly possessed the credentials of someone destined to achieve high rank. Described as "impetuous by nature, and somewhat rough and rude in his early years," Van Ness was the youngest of three sons of Peter Van Ness, first judge of the New York Court of Common Pleas. He came from his father's fine estate, also his birthplace, Lindenwald, in

Kinderhook, Columbia County, later the home of Martin Van Buren and the place where family friend Washington Irving penned some of his works. His elder brother, John, was also legally trained, elected to Congress in 1801 and appointed by Jefferson the following year as brigadier general of militia for Washington, D.C., where he eventually became mayor.[181]

Brother William was an attorney working in New York City, where he began his practice in 1800, allowing both Cornelius and Van Buren to apprentice for him prior to their own admissions to the bar. William was also a very close confidant of Aaron Burr and introduced Cornelius to him, a connection that led others to later label the three brothers as "Burrites." However distasteful Burr's later actions might have been, this did not deter President James Madison from appointing William as judge of the United States District Court for the Southern District of New York in 1810.

Burr developed such high regard for young Cornelius's abilities that in 1801 he recommended him as an assistant to an author working on an important account of John Adams's administration. That work behind him, after becoming an attorney in 1803, and only a week after marrying Rhoda Savage of Chatham on March 13, 1804, Van Ness took his first steps into local politics by shrewdly maneuvering one aspirant's name off the slate of candidates for governor that year and substituting Burr's name. However, those efforts quickly collapsed just months later when, in July, Burr, seconded by William Van Ness, killed Alexander Hamilton in a duel. The relations between the two families were so close that immediately after the duel, Burr fled to the home of uncle David P. Van Ness. Later that year, William came to Burr's defense and aggressively attacked the widespread disapproval being heaped on his friend. Their repeated demonstrations of strong devotion to the Republican cause served each of the Van Ness brothers particularly well in their coming battles with those seeking to advance Hamilton's Federalist legacy.[182]

After the death of their father in 1805, the three brothers acted jointly as executors of his estate, and the following year, perhaps sensing the absence of opportunity for the kind of advancement his older brothers experienced, Cornelius and Rhoda decided it was time to move on. There are no descriptions of why they chose the remote location of Grand Isle, Vermont, as their destination, but that's where they went, remaining for only six months before departing for St. Albans farther to the east. There, at 9:00 a.m. on December 17, 1806, Van Ness was sworn in by Chief Judge Jonathan Robinson as an attorney allowed to practice before the Vermont Supreme Court after taking the attorney's oath, an oath to support the U.S. Constitution and, lastly, an oath of allegiance to the State of Vermont.[183]

This was the beginning of a phenomenal career eclipsing any of his contemporaries as Van Ness shortly assumed important local positions within the federal government, becoming a state representative, chief judge of the Supreme Court (1821–23), governor (1823–26), minister to Spain (1829–39) and customs collector for the Port of New York (1844–45). Van Ness had arrived at a point in the state's history when it was uniquely vulnerable to the influences of an astute, charismatic individual such as himself and he was certainly not going to let the opportunity pass without fully exploiting it. However, none of this was possible until he had passed through the immediate challenges presented by the embargo, which, in turn, could not have happened without the critical support he received from Rhoda.

Van Ness has understandably received substantial positive reviews over the past two hundred years in acknowledgment of his rapid rise to fame, but there were certainly many blemishes present that past accounts have overlooked. He was a man of certain legal aptitude, voraciously driven by ambition, and despite being easy to sleight, petty, vindictive and prone to self-destruction, his peers saw attributes worthy of high recognition, ones certainly elevated because of his family and political connections and further attended by displays of kindness. The very first case he handled upon moving to St. Albans involved a widow seeking legal assistance to appeal an adverse ruling against her husband's estate rendered in the local court. Van Ness agreed to take the case, facing off against fellow attorney Asa Aldis, and he ultimately won. When he presented his bill of some thirty dollars, he wrote across its bottom, "I make a present to the widow and her fatherless children, as I have not the heart to exact it of them."[184] Certainly, the words appear sincere, but one questions their underlying truth when considered in the larger context of his recent arrival in town, which may have constituted only an attempt to make a good first impression, ingratiating himself into the legal community. Even a member of his own family had reason to question his intentions.

In 1849, Van Ness's son James penned a remarkable letter to a family friend providing intimate information about Van Ness that has not been fully incorporated into the historiography of this man and which explains more fully the sacrifices others made to allow his remarkable rise to power in the first place. James wrote immediately following what appears to have been a disagreeable encounter with his father during which he learned he would not be receiving an expected inheritance, one that Cornelius intended to bestow on his current wife, Madalena (née Allus), a woman from Madrid, whom James derisively identifies as the "Spanish harlot" and "Spanish milliner." First wife Rhoda accompanied Cornelius to Madrid at the time of his ministerial appointment but later died of cholera in 1834, after which he scandalously took up relations with Madalena (marrying her and concealing the fact for several years). He gained such disdain from President Andrew Jackson in the process that he found himself excluded from the Spanish mission as an embarrassment to the American legation.

In his letter recounting his father's difficulties, James took the time to explain to his friend the toll taken on the family, his mother in particular, and how they all suffered in these early years in Vermont as they watched their father's rise to fame. Rhoda was, he wrote,

> *a woman who toiled and struggled for half a life time to advance his interests and secure his success.*
>
> *For several years after his settlement in Vermont my mother did the entire cooking and washing of her family and up to the period of his departure for Spain she did much of her own housework, besides making her own and the clothes of her children. For the ten years previous to the departure of my father for Europe, he was insolvent, or so nearly so, that it was only prevented from being generally known by the wonderful energy, economy, and industry of my mother, who by her admirable management sustained her family and thus enabled this man to pursue his ambitious and political schemes...*
>
> *My mother's perseverance, economy and admirable management I have not told the half—and to know her true character, and her real merits and especially how she enabled my father to keep his head above water for years after his debts swelled to the amount of his property it is only necessary to ask any citizen of Vermont who ever heard her name, whether friend or foe, of the family. Her energy, her unceasing industry were in the mouths of all and to her are the children of this man indebted for having a house over their heads for the last five years of his residence at Burlington.*[185]

While Cornelius was rumored to have received an inheritance of some worth from his father's estate, this account indicates—and is certainly verified by the man's conduct—that in his early years in Vermont, Van Ness struggled to maintain an appearance of wealth that was not necessarily real. It also further confirms a strong predisposition toward accumulating fame and recognition, attributes that became evident at the time of the embargo and the War of 1812.

Van Ness's legal abilities were quickly recognized by local attorneys upon his arrival, and he became firmly involved in their affairs. He also returned to

Grand Isle during the March 1808 term to participate as a defense attorney in the first important criminal trial taking place in the newly established county court.[186] While unsuccessful in this matter, Van Ness had achieved sufficient credibility with Penniman to warrant consulting him about local conditions concerning enforcement of the land embargo.

Penniman explained the following month the reasoning for his meeting with Aldis and Van Ness:

> *When I* [received] *the last* [land] *embargo act I considered it my duty to state to the Secretary that a large number of men on the lake shore was* [sic] *deeply concerned in rafting timber for* [the] *Canadian market and that I had reason to believe that they would or would have the same exported and as I had little or no force wished him to give me particulars in relation to the same.*[187]

What the two attorneys told Penniman is not recorded, but the result clearly indicated a consensus among them that there was such significant local opposition to the embargo that it could not be easily subdued. Wasting no time, Penniman immediately penned a letter to Gallatin telling him of his meetings with the two men and their belief that such "conspiracy and combination" existed in the area that it was necessary to call for the militia to suppress it.[188] Certainly, such a suggestion was not unreasonable and constituted an accurate assessment of need in light of his very limited resources. But it was his unfortunate use of words insinuating the presence of sinister conspiracy and combinations, explosive terms bringing to mind the direst of situations, that propelled events to levels he could not have imagined.

Only a few days after their meeting, a curious situation arose involving Van Ness, which indicates that, despite whatever regard his fellow attorneys and Penniman might have had for him at the moment, there was at least one other individual living in this Federalist community not similarly enamored. On April 9, Van Ness chose to indulge himself and make known a particular grievance he suffered under, revealing, in the process, an unexpected petty side:

> *The person who has in the course of the winter past, stolen one of the cushions belonging to my chair, and who* need not flatter himself that he is unknown to me, *is hereby informed, that if the same is returned within a few days, without being injured, his name shall not be made public. But should this not be done, I am determined that he shall not escape*

the punishment due to such villainy. If it should be more agreeable to return the cushion at night, I wish it to be left on my stoop.[189]

Whether Van Ness was forced to take further action to vindicate this "villainy" is not known, but he clearly was not hesitant to assert himself even in the most trivial of matters.

As Penniman's assessment of the situation worked its way to Washington, news of the restrictive land embargo broke locally and immediately set off the anticipated protests. Pressure was already being applied to lake traffic when, two weeks earlier, Penniman had ordered Haswell that "no vessel can be permitted to go out of her port till the masters and owners have first given bonds for two hundred dollars on each ton." Then, in rapid succession, he quickly made known to all the course of action he had been directed to take, making available for publication a directive from Gallatin that presented for the first time the possibility that the government would resort to violence:

You are instructed by the President, that during the continuance of the embargo, whenever from the nature of the cargo of a vessel…there is reason to believe that she is actually destined for a foreign port, to stop her and refer the case to him through this department. Force may be used to detain them…Rafts as well as vessels must be prevented from proceeding to a foreign port, and for that purpose, one or two armed boats may, if necessary, be stationed near to the line, at the lower end of your district.[190]

With the government's warnings sounding, on April 16, Burlington residents assembled to consider what it all meant for them. High on their list of grievances was Washington's failure to recognize that they were the ones toiling so hard on this frontier and had only "begun to anticipate more prosperous days" working together with their Canadian counterparts, made possible because of the ease the connecting waters allowed. They were also concerned at the prospect of watching the loss of so much of the fruits of their labor, something they presciently predicted would result in difficulties of a different sort:

There was in the article of lumber, chiefly pine, on the banks of the rivers and waters of Lake Champlain, destined for Canada market, to the amount of four hundred thousand dollars, and a large amount in pot and pearl ashes, which by the prohibitions…become useless. It is not only a dead loss to the owners, but the evils arising to the country, generally, in not receiving the avails, are incalculable. It is easy to conceive that such a sacrifice must have immediately excited an alarm—must have roused all our sensibility—our anxieties, & filled us with gloomy apprehensions of what must unavoidably follow.[191]

Additional warnings were issued:

All excitement to industry and enterprise will cease; our farms will be neglected; our waving fields, whitened for the harvest will give place to their native briar and thistle; debtors of every description will be pressed for the payment of their debts; deprived of their only resources, and unable to pay, the utmost rigor of the law must follow; husbands and fathers, dragged from their afflicted wives, weeping over their half-starved offspring, must take up their dwelling in a loathsome prison; laudable ambition and enterprise will be succeeded by despondency, poverty, jealousy and despair.

Hyperbole notwithstanding, it really did not matter whether their fears were real, as the mere expression of shared anguish provides ample evidence of high levels of stress and emotion, responsible for propelling some to displays of extreme, untoward behavior.

Penniman remained constantly aware that tensions were on the rise, and he was not reluctant to put the public on continued notice that the government was not about to back down when faced with violations. Only days following Burlington's town meeting, in an article dated April 21, Penniman and his Champlain counterpart, Collector Woolsey, printed an additional, unequivocal caution:

All persons having property which was intended for exportation to Canada, whether lumber in rafts, or other merchandise, are informed that no such exportations can now be permitted.

The laws and instructions received by the undersigned Collectors, are such as require their utmost vigilance and exertion, in effecting the objects of the law; and while they lament the injury that will be sustained by some of their fellow citizens, they indulge a hope that no one will be so inconsiderate as to attempt a violation.

It is recommended, particularly to those concerned in rafts, that they lay them up in secure situations, and wait patiently, for relief in a legal way; but it is our duty, at the same time, to inform all concerned, that we are commanded to use force where reason and consideration are inadequate to restrain illegal acts.[192]

Absent from their warning was any description of the degree of force they were willing to use, but three days later, Woolsey made it clear to those working under him what he expected. In a most interesting notice to his deputies and inspectors, employing language indicating Penniman's concurrence, he instructed (emphasis in original):

> *If resistance is made, it is to be opposed, with discretion, but if necessary with force—for this purpose the secretary of the Treasury has directed us to arm—and deeply as it would be lamented, those arms and that force, must be applied, <u>even to extremity</u>...Temper and moderation in executing these duties are strongly recommended, but the loyalty of a true American knows no limits, and obedience to the laws he considers his first duty and his greatest ambition.* [193]

Statements indicating a willingness to resort to deadly force did not mean it would actually be employed because the resources available to the collectors were not only limited but also understandably indecisive when it came to actual confrontations. This is due to the unique closeness that naturally existed among those called to enforce the law—specifically, those many militiamen about to be activated who came from within the very same citizenry they were being ordered to subdue. Nonetheless, the stage had been set and the public put on notice that violations of the embargo would be dealt with severely.

AS PENNIMAN AND WOOLSEY prepared for the immediate future, Jefferson contemplated his next moves. History has been quick to condemn what he was about to do but also slow to fully consider the context of his actions in these highly unusual times when faced with allegations of conspiracies and combinations along the frontier. As troubling as Vermont's problems were, they constituted but a side issue when compared with his international concerns. The embargo raised many difficult issues for enforcement up and down the coast and across the north from Maine's Passamaquoddy Bay to New York's Lake Ontario, and it required a deft hand when trying to deprive Britain and France of America's resources while also ameliorating hardships on his fellow citizens. Compounding the problems, at that very moment, the country continued to debate the evils of a standing, or national, army as it persisted in relying on its outdated, traditional militia system. The result was that between the time he assumed office in 1801 until the end of his second term in 1809, Jefferson's administration, abetted by Congress, placed the country in a remarkably unprepared condition in the event of war.[194]

Even with the sudden and explosive increase in land afforded by the recent Louisiana Purchase (made possible by the work of customs officials), Jefferson still neglected to pursue any form of military presence to police its many miles of wilderness. Policy dictated a reactive, crisis-driven response that merely expanded and contracted the national army as events took place and forced continuing reliance on the timeworn militia system. The situation remained in place for the next one hundred years, providing for a distinctly unstable environment along Vermont's porous border in the summer of 1808. Nonetheless, the administration was successful in obtaining authorization for a temporary increase in the national effort, and by the end of 1808, there were 5,700 in the regular army, an increase of more than twice the number from 1807. This number increased to 7,000 in 1809.[195]

In deciding his most immediate course, Jefferson was constrained by the provisions of the Militia Act of 1795, which proscribed the limits of presidential authority in times of domestic discord:

> *Sec. 2…whenever the laws of the United States shall be opposed, or the execution thereof obstructed, in any state, by combinations too powerful to be suppressed by the ordinary course of judicial proceedings…it shall be lawful for the President…to call forth the militia of such state…as may be necessary to suppress such combinations, and to cause the laws to be duly executed.*
>
> *Sec. 3 That whenever it may be necessary* [to call out the militia], *the President shall forthwith, by proclamation, command such insurgents to disperse, and retire peaceably to their respective abodes, within a limited time.*[196]

The act also provided that any member of the militia ordered into service was required to serve for only a three-month period, a provision described as "an amazingly destructive limitation" remaining in effect until the opening days of the Civil War.[197] But for Jefferson, it was sufficient enough of a stop-gap measure that it allowed his administration to move forward with recruiting and assembling a national force to hurry to the northern border when the militia's term of service expired.

Therefore, in order for Jefferson to enforce the provisions of his embargo in these early days, he was forced to rely on the state's militia, but in order to do that, he had to make a finding, or a proclamation, that it was because of "combinations," or "insurgents," forcing him to do so. However, such a drastic move could create its own set of problems, ones familiar even to

George Washington. A decade earlier, in 1794, reports of substantial discord existing in western Pennsylvania had reached him, described as "filed by federal officials on the scene, who often magnified minor incidents," and involving challenges to the government's tax on spirits, the so-called Whiskey Rebellion. In response to Alexander Hamilton's coaxing him to crush any opposition to federal authority, as George III had done in sanctioning the use of force against colonists and Massachusetts governor James Bowdoin repeated during Shays' Rebellion in 1786, Washington proclaimed that an "open rebellion" existed, authorizing the use of force to subdue it, and called out thirteen thousand militiamen. The opposition had indeed been quelled, but he then faced a firestorm of protest from a Congress not about to accept his explanations that he had acted because of the purported existence of organized groups detrimental to federal interests. Many, believing they were being unfairly branded, were greatly offended by his statements, and his credibility was substantially undercut.[198] These are lessons that Jefferson would have been wise to fully consider before he acted.

With Penniman's inflammatory letter in hand, together with recommendations for action being made by Gallatin, on April 19, Jefferson spoke with Vermont's representatives to Congress, Senator Jonathan Robinson (who swore in Van Ness as an attorney) and Representative James Witherell. Right at this very moment, he was suffering under such tremendous strain that he wrote he was in "a state of almost total incapacity for business," and seeking the guidance of others was something he sorely needed to do.[199] Assuming a less aggressive approach than Penniman suggested, the two Vermonters explained to Jefferson that the problems he faced would disappear by May, after the snow melted, the water drained off toward the St. Lawrence and the rapids below St. John dropped, making the passage of rafts impossible. Jefferson then sought additional counsel from others and, refusing to concede any weakness exposing his administration to further condemnation, resolved it was time to "crush every example of forcible opposition to the law."[200]

However, Jefferson chose to proceed cautiously in escalating his response and ordered three things: 1) Gallatin was to instruct Penniman to equip and arm whatever vessels he believed necessary, manning them with appropriate personnel; 2) Secretary of State James Madison was to write to the U.S. marshal, instructing him to be ready to "aid in suppressing the insurrection or combination" should it prove too powerful for Penniman to handle; and 3) should the marshal require assistance, a separate proclamation was to be published and the militia called out, followed by a request that the governor become personally involved by going to wherever the unrest was occurring and providing assistance. He also decided it was necessary to begin constructing two gunboats on the south end of the lake, at Whitehall, New York.[201]

The proclamation Jefferson referred to then followed, and as for Washington, it constituted a singular act coming to consume much time, energy and emotion in the months ahead while also generating substantial, inflammatory resentment. Tracking the language contained in the Militia Act of 1795, Jefferson managed to both set out the requisite legal justification for calling out the militia while also rendering a scathing public indictment in condemnation of those living around Lake Champlain:

> *Whereas information has been received that sundry persons are combined, or combining and confederating together on Lake Champlain, and the country thereto adjacent, for the purposes of forming insurrections against the authority of the laws of the United States, for opposing the same and obstructing their execution, and that such combinations are too powerful to be suppressed by the ordinary course of judicial proceedings, or by the powers vested in the marshals by the laws of the United States.*
>
> *Now, therefore, to the end that the authority of the laws may be maintained, and that those concerned directly or indirectly in any insurrection or combination against the same, may be duly warned, I have issued this my proclamation, hereby commanding such insurgents, and all concerned in such combination, instantly and without delay to dispense and retire peaceably to their respective abodes; and I do hereby further require and command all officers having authority, civil or military, and all other persons, civil or military, who shall be found within the vicinage of such insurrections or combinations, to be aiding and assisting by all the means in their power, by the force of arms or otherwise, to quell and subdue such insurrections or combinations, to seize upon all those therein concerned who shall not instantly and without delay disperse and retire to their respective abodes, and to deliver them over to the civil authority of the place to be proceeded against according to law.*[202]

Based on a single letter from Penniman, accompanied by an unwavering view of his own correct course, Jefferson now unleashed consequences he could not recall. For a surprised Penniman, the action was out of all proportion to the level of threat that was posed. He wrote later, "I did not expect the President would have issued a proclamation" but rather "did expect that the Secretary would have ordered an adequate force if it was intended to carry the law into full effect."[203] With things now spinning out beyond Penniman's control, the execution of Jefferson's edict fell directly on Gallatin's shoulders, and the necessary papers were quickly drafted, signed and sent directly north via express rider.

As Penniman waited for further direction, those men warning him that they intended to continue with their rafting operations did so in blatant disregard of any potential punishment. Woolsey's April 24 instructions to his employees regarding the use of force also described how customs officers in New York and Vermont were to handle situations involving boats and rafts, with "each side to aid and assist the other with boats and men when called on for that purpose." For vessels, this included requiring bonds for double the value of them and their cargo and issuing limited clearances for departure to another district (not Canada), as well as prohibiting the unloading of any provisions to the north of the Champlain and Windmill Point offices in an effort to impede further smuggling. For rafts, Woolsey directed that

> *any which may appear below the Isle La Motte to be met by the boats, and ordered to make the first port of safety on either side that may be practical; if the raftsmen refuse, the senior officer of the boats on the service will take the command of such raft and endeavor to conduct it into port or anchored until it can be conducted in. If resistance is made, it is to be opposed.*[204]

As the two collectors fashioned rudimentary responses to their anticipated problems, in Washington, Gallatin succeeded in obtaining yet additional legal authority to assist them. On April 25, the last bill coming out of Congress on the last day of its latest session, the so-called Enforcement Act came into effect, directed toward the needs of those states located immediately adjacent to foreign territories. Under its provisions, no ship could depart to another country without the express permission of the president; collectors could seize merchandise suspected for export until the owner posted a bond attesting that it was destined for a domestic port; revenue cutters were authorized to stop, search and bring to port any vessel suspected of carrying goods destined for export; and customs officials could detain vessels resting in harbor suspected of illegal exporting activities.[205] In conveying these instructions, Gallatin further instructed Penniman that because of the great distance between Vermont and Washington, Jefferson had authorized him "to grant permissions in his name, which will put the navigation of the lake perfectly under your control."[206] Notably, these wide grants of authority certainly met, and often exceeded, anything Americans faced during times when British ships were blockading the Atlantic coast during the Revolutionary War.

Even with this well-intended guidance, officials were forced to rely on their own instincts to bring them into effect. One creative approach took place when Vermont customs officials simply traveled into Quebec, went to the St. John customhouse and asked for permission to inspect their books, a request that was predictably refused as "highly improper."[207] After Nathan Haswell took it upon himself to allow a British vessel (not affected by the embargo) to travel to Missisquoi Bay and it was later stopped by other officials, on May 2, he wrote to Penniman in a pique, believing he was being second guessed. Penniman immediately responded (on the same day that Beriah Cleeland's friends forcibly rescued him from the custody of Seeley Bennett) that this was not the case and explained that the vessel's captain had been detained "for making resistance when ordered to come into port" and not because of anything Haswell had done.[208] The incident serves as an example of both the sensitivity and perhaps suspicion beginning to creep into the relationships of officials, as well as one of the first indications that they were going to meet with resistance from tradesmen on the lake.

As these initial confrontations took place, an express rider bearing Jefferson's package finally arrived at the Rutland home of Republican governor Israel Smith, where, in the presence of at least one witness, it was quickly opened and read while the courier waited outside. While Jefferson's request that Smith personally travel to the place of unrest was discretionary, his first inclination was to immediately accompany the rider on his journey. However, as the witness described, the governor "was diverted from it by the advice of his friends. He was told that if there existed such a combination, he might meet with personal abuse; in addition to which, he would unavoidably lose his next election."[209]

Why Smith, an experienced politician who had ably served in Washington as both representative and senator for many years before defeating Federalist Isaac Tichenor for governor the preceding fall, ultimately chose to remove himself from the frontline is unknown. But it was, no doubt, to avoid a political catastrophe should he unsuccessfully penetrate into the heavily Federalist stronghold that Franklin County represented. His decision not to intercede ultimately proved a disaster for him personally, when he was defeated in his bid for a second term by Tichenor in the following months, but also for Vermont authority in general, which now assumed a role of secondary importance in the rising contest between federal interests and his own constituency. There is no evidence that Smith adopted Jefferson's recommendation that a graduated response be employed with the first intervention conducted by the U.S. marshal, and instead, he quickly ordered the militia into service.

In seeming coincidence, on the very same day that Rutland's three regiments of the Second Brigade, Second Division, were ordered to assemble for their required yearly muster the following month, Smith's directive reached General Levi House, commanding officer of the Third Division in St. Albans. Consequently, on May 4, House directed that a small detachment of about eighteen men under the command of Captain Heman Hopkins of the First Regiment, Third Brigade, proceed immediately to Windmill Point, where they were to coordinate with a detachment from the New York side to prevent the passage of lumber rafts.[210] As the local paper, the *St. Albans Advisor*, noted for that day:

> *There is now a heavy gale from the south, and the rafts being supplied with such a quantity of sail, that we think it hardly possible for human force to restrain their movements, till they pass the provincial line. We hope no serious consequences will arise from this conflict between the sovereignty of the United States, and the sovereignty of pecuniary want.*[211]

In an adjoining article, the paper published, for the first time and without comment, Jefferson's proclamation in its entirety.

Protestations from local residents questioning whether human effort could possibly avert the movement of rafts lingering near the border were quickly rejected by Penniman, who was preoccupied with closely assessing the quality of those militia troops arriving at the Point to assist him. In a letter written to Haswell from Swanton immediately following his return home, Penniman described his first impressions, but not without first expressing some dissatisfaction with his subordinate's handling of troops assigned to the Burlington area. The collector told him he "was much disappointed at not seeing you to be able to explain the measures pursued by the officers to prevent smuggling [*sic*] and violations of the laws and the cursed methods taken to evade them."[212] Either he had failed in the first instance to describe precisely the measures he expected Haswell to implement or was frustrated and giving vent to the young man's similar lack of a plan.

Regardless, Haswell had not been idle during this time, attending to a busy seven inspections of various vessels between April 14 and 29 in Burlington, exactly the same number he had conducted between July and

August the preceding year, when he documented the arrival of over 7,500 bushels of salt from Canada. His port responsibilities quickly diminished in the next month as the embargo took effect (only three days of inspecting work) but then increased to fifteen days in June, nine in July, dropped to three in August (when the murders occurred) and, finally, increased to five days in September toward the close of the season.[213] Concerning his other business interests at the moment, he and partner John Peaslee instituted a lawsuit on April 18 against an individual owing them money.[214] Then, Haswell had the extraordinary opportunity to purchase land at a tax sale because of the prior owner's failure to pay a one-cent-per-acre assessment levied by the legislature for construction of the new state prison. On April 7, he and another individual acquired two hundred acres of Burlington's so-called Undivided Land for a trifling $2.19, covering the assessed tax and costs—surely one of the more remarkable real estate transactions of the times.[215]

Penniman's disappointment in his young inspector aside, he continued in his letter to describe his frustrations with the militia's inability to maintain possession of rafts it had actually seized:

> All have been stopped and anchored in port beat by combinations of men from all quarters of this country and Canada. They have by force and stratagem been got off. No means or pains has [sic] been spared. All kinds of corruption has been practiced on these men, and no confidence can be placed in but few at Champlain and near the lines. These rafts have been lost for the want of sufficient and good help and I find it impossible to do the duty without.[216]

Penniman further explained that on one occasion, just before daybreak, two boats full of men removed a raft, including the guards standing watch on board, into their control and floated them all over the line into Canada. A second raft was taken by some thirty to fifty men who overpowered the guards, putting them into a cabin. Fortunately, other soldiers appeared, and many of the culprits, including several Canadians, were arrested and taken to the Plattsburgh jail. The rescued soldiers were found "very quietly sitting in the cabin, made easy by pay and fair promises no doubt." Another time, on a night when "men were seen walking…in all directions," others unsuccessfully tried to bribe another guard. What Penniman might not have been aware of at the time was the significant amount of coercion being used against the soldiers. The aggressiveness displayed by those many men forcing their way on board lightly guarded rafts in the darkness was something unparalleled in the experiences of these country militiamen. They were repeatedly threatened with death by these overwhelming forces should they interfere in any way and, understandably, simply chose to sit in unwelcome silence as they watched the rafts, and themselves, slowly and silently drift north over the line.[217]

On the New York side of the lake, Penniman continued in his letter, two vessels, seemingly without anyone on board, mysteriously drifted near the customs office and dropped anchor. Having rested there for some time, Collector Woolsey ordered a soldier to board one of them, but before he was able to do so, someone "slipped her cable," and aided by a southerly gale, it quickly drifted over the line into Canada. The second vessel was boarded, and 104 chests of tea were discovered. It was quickly taken into custody, "as intimation was given that a strong force would soon form to rescue her." Penniman concluded his letter, telling Haswell:

> *I have given you some faint sketches of the combinations and intrigues that has and is taking place at and near the lines—you can have no idea of it unless on the ground and saw the measures taken to disappoint the government.*

To the north, a Montreal paper was not at all hesitant to poke fun at the ineffectiveness of Penniman and his officers, noting on May 9 "that all the vigilance of the custom-house officers with an armed gunboat is required to enforce their embargo acts—and yet they are unable wholly to accomplish their purpose."[218]

Meanwhile, Hopkins and his men continued in their futile efforts, made all the more difficult by "hostile dispositions…manifested by many on both sides of the line, and determined at all hazards to export their ashes and other property…and in many instances actual force has been used."[219] There were those who complied with the law and landed their rafts on the lake's shores, which, in the Windmill Bay area, were reportedly "covered with produce." However, for those not so inclined, "repeatedly as many as twenty-five rafts went out, favored by the darkness and a strong south wind."[220] Their movements were so blatantly obvious that the public matter-of-factly took it all in as just another of the days' occurrences. One local resident recounted to a friend, "I returned home yesterday, soon after Mr. Enos came home with news that the raft had passed the lines, he also brought your horse."[221] Whether that particular raft was the one involved is not known, but at some point during this time, accounts relate that when two government sloops attempted to stop one, many men were killed and one wounded in an exchange of gunfire.[222] The report turned out to be exaggerated, as many were, but they do show that the government was indeed trying to address the problem, albeit with less than universal success.

To assist Hopkins with his efforts, another St. Albans detachment from the Third Brigade was ordered out, and Lieutenant John Whittemore led an additional twenty-five men to the Point. However, it remained a futile effort:

> *Several* [rafts] *have been brought to and boarded—they have, however, found means to liberate themselves, and not a raft, we understand, is now left in our waters. Taking advantage of the night, and a strong wind, those concerned in rafts, have evaded every exertion to molest them. On Saturday evening last, the wind being favorable, the then remaining rafts joined, making a surface, it is said, of about ten acres, carrying forty sail, made an expeditious and safe exit from the United States.*[223]

While the soldiers were unsuccessful in intercepting the sloop *Hope* (on its way to becoming Canadian merchant Abner Brigham's reconfigured *Governor Craig*) on May 15, on the twenty-fifth, Hopkins did stop a nondescript vessel, later identified as *Red Boat*, together with its cargo of twenty-five barrels of potash off the Point. Those efforts notwithstanding, an examination of the subsequent legal proceedings concerning this event, together with a number of others, gives rise to a serious question concerning the overall commitment of authorities in general in pursuing aggressive action by all possible means, as Woolsey and Penniman's dictates seemed to require.

On May 28, Gallatin addressed two letters to Jefferson at Monticello concerning the situation on the lake. In the first, he opined that "on Champlain I believe that everything that could be done has been done… [A]ll the evil which can accrue [there] is now at an end, and all we have to watch is our common coastal trade." Yet upon receiving additional correspondence from the north telling him that this was not correct, he was forced to backtrack, lamenting in his second letter that those efforts "have not been properly supported by the people," which had the effect of causing authorities, including local New York judge and friend to government Peter Sailly, to assume a cautious approach, suspecting they had been "afraid to act." Despite Gallatin's further observation that "I have, of course, written to the district attorney [Vermont's David Fay] to institute prosecutions, &c.," there was virtually no enforcement action being taken before any court whatsoever during these months. As for those who actually did reach a courtroom, Sailly lamented to Gallatin that even juries solicitous of the administration's Republican values refused to indict Canadians taken into custody, including those caught in the very act of forcibly rescuing and taking a raft across the line.[224]

The problem extended well beyond sympathetic juries failing to enforce the law. Immediately following the embargo taking effect in 1807, Massachusetts governor James Sullivan wrote to Jefferson and provided him with a dire warning:

> *I would not make the residue of your administration more anxious and troublesome than is necessary, but you are now in a critical situation... The machinations of the English party* [Federalists] *for some years past have filled our state judiciary with men who are determined to unite us again with Great Britain, ostensibly as an ally, but in reality as a dependent on her...our militia does well to be talked about, but cannot be depended on...Your judiciary of the United States are worse than ours in this district. Your attorneys, in some instances for the United States, would be completely on the side of Great Britain...The Federalists here openly avow that if war takes place England will send an army to the southern states to cause the blacks to cut their masters' throats. They talk of a division between the southern and northern states as a matter of course, and are openly forming a party to be united under the protection of a British standard. You will not believe this until it shall be too late. Nothing but an alteration in the judiciary can save us from destruction in this way.*[225]

Jefferson could be forgiven for asking if there was not a single aspect of American life that was not adversely affected by what the embargo had wrought, for now even the loyalties of federal judges and prosecutors were being called into question.

The public's willingness to accept the imposition of its constraints remained a delicate issue, and despite Woolsey's admonition to his men to take advantage of extreme measures if necessary, they continued to act with hesitancy and caution. One newspaper noted that authorities had taken "every means...to avoid prosecutions."[226] In fact, there were no cases filed in Vermont's federal courts (or fines levied) against any of those breaking the embargo's provisions until the precipitous murders in August, which finally jolted authorities on both the state and federal levels into action. Until that happened, encounters between soldiers, customs officials and smugglers continued, and without the necessary prosecutions following up, criminals remained emboldened to take yet more aggressive action.

While the St. Albans militia struggled on, farther to the south, an unusual event unfolded. On May 17, five men, guiding their wagons full of potash, passed through the town of Castleton, headed west toward the New York line. Taking to heart Jefferson's admonition for the public to become involved in stopping such trafficking, Matthew Anderson and two others armed themselves with axe and hoe handles and attempted to intercept them. The wagoners, "being too old birds to be catched by chaff," were unimpressed with their efforts and continued on their journey. Anderson, reportedly "infuriated with rage and the love of Liberty," then sought out all the authority he could find in the area to assist and met with much success. Responding to his summons were such noteworthy personages as General Isaac Clark, first judge of the county court; Robert Temple, justice of the peace and clerk of the Supreme Court; Clark's son-in-law, who was a member of the Governor's Council; A.W. Hyde, high sheriff of Rutland County; Captain David Sanford, in charge of the local artillery company; Roland Mallery, secretary to the governor and council; and several other individuals. The entourage was later derided as a "company of Embargoroons":

> *Then armed all both great and small,*
> *With clubs and bows and hatchets,*
> *The Indian King could never bring,*
> *An army that could match it.*[227]

Heading out in search of the wagons, the men reached Fair Haven, where they were joined by none other than their congressman, James Witherell, who had counseled Jefferson the preceding month in advance of the proclamation. There, they found the five "insurgents," who quickly handed over their goods and were jailed for the night. Their property was seized for later disposition.[228]

That same day, Gallatin warned the Philadelphia collector to take forceful action to detain suspected vessels in his port, explaining that the president intended to give "complete effect" in enforcing the embargo. In Vermont, Penniman wrote to Haswell that, from that time on, no vessels were allowed to depart the lake "without particular instructions from me."[229] Such heartfelt desires aside, as the month passed, it became clear that the St. Albans militia components were simply unable to stem the overwhelming flow of contraband and that other arrangements were required. As a Middlebury paper noted:

How is this law to be enforced? Answer—by calling out the militia. But suppose the militia detest it, can you prevail upon them to shoot their fellow-citizens for doing that, which (independently of this absurd and impolitic law) there appears no solid reason to say they should not do?... The administration, it seems, have no confidence in the militia of all this northern country; and we are in daily expectation of seeing militia marched from the southern part of this state, to teach these northern counties, at the point of a bayonet, the necessity of instant obedience.[230]

Certainly, a recent example of the local militia's unwillingness to enforce the law demonstrated why it could not be trusted. As an observer related:

The people, in the northern part of the state formed themselves into companies and carried their port, potash, &c. into Canada by force. And although twenty-five able bodied men were marshaled *on the plains of Swanton, and marched to the line, yet all would not do, they refused to fire upon their neighbors, were disbanded and sent home in disgrace.*[231]

However, any thought of calling in units from outside the immediate area to correct these deficiencies was not without its own difficulty, as it would not only call into disrepute the conduct of those initially responding but also question their all-important honor—a matter not to be trifled with.

In 1808, there were 17,931 men enrolled in the state's militia, an increase from the prior year's return of 16,436.[232] Spread out over four divisions, they were periodically brought together for local meetings to ensure their readiness, and once a year, a regional muster of all area components assembled for a few days of training. The men were told that they, not the government in Washington, were the nation's bulwark against outside enemies:

The unmilitary, feminine spirit of the federal government, has...operated to damp the spirit of every thing military and energetic. With more sense of military honor, and with more attachment to the reputation and safety of their country, the young men in many places, retain the spirit of their ancestors; take up the business with vigor and activity, and conduct it with propriety and honor.

The militia of Vermont are a body of brave, hardy, robust, and intrepid men. Trained up to hardship, labor, economy, and hunting, they have all the qualifications that tend to fit men for the military character. Discipline and actual service, transform them at once, into a body of excellent troops.[233]

In actuality, the level of that training, and any idealistic expression of their purported martial prowess, were assessments far removed from the wartime pressures their fathers experienced in the 1770s and '80s and had become so noticeably deficient in these more recent times that additional efforts were required to correct the problem.

In 1807, one of the state's first military training treatises was written by a commander within the Fourth Division, Montpelier's Lieutenant Colonel Larned Lamb (1768–1827). In *The Militia's Guide: Exhibiting a More Comprehensive Explanation...of the Posts and Duties of the Several Officers... Designed for the Instruction of a Young and Undisciplined Militia*, Lamb explained that his intended audience constituted the "young and undisciplined" men in Vermont's militia. He related that it was not his intention to replace, but rather to supplement, training brought about during the Revolution by General von Steuben in order to create "a more definite statement of the forms and evolutions of the military establishment in this government...As the military establishment...was designed, and is calculated for the use of an encampment, [and] a treatise similar to this has been much wanted." Over the course of one hundred pages, Lamb described in great detail the responsibilities of the various ranks in the context of a camp environment.[234] Unfortunately, none of his instruction touched on the larger issues of strategy and its implementation, limiting it to the more easily obtained goals that marching and drilling allowed.

While there was much that called the militia's capabilities into question, one of the more grievous examples of misplaced trust involved Attorney Aldis and his client, Collector Penniman. Aldis was one of those summoned to serve when the St. Albans contingencies were activated but had been able to hire convicted rioter Samuel I. Mott to serve as his substitute. It was an exceedingly strange arrangement, as Aldis must have known of Mott's vicious side from both his reputation and seeing him in court the preceding December, when he was charged with rioting and assaulting another man. Regardless, Aldis was reportedly so confident in the man's abilities that he paid him twenty dollars a month and boasted that "he had procured the man who could be depended on." Mott's name indeed appears on a roster of men under the command of Lieutenant Whittemore, and he might have been one of those first called to assist Hopkins and his men in their desperate work on the Point. Perhaps Aldis had arranged for Mott to provide him with inside information concerning any planned smuggling operations, but if so, the plan went quickly awry. Penniman was exempt from service because of his federal role;

nonetheless, he reportedly hired a second individual, Joshua Day, brother of the Franklin County sheriff, and paid him twelve dollars a month.[235]

As the effectiveness of those St. Albans units came under scrutiny, the services of these two men, called "confidential soldiers," together with several others, were discontinued when authorities decided to substitute them with other troops. Perhaps Mott and Day had seen more than they thought possible concerning the militia's ineffectiveness—or more likely, they were already part of the existing network breaking the law—and now decided the time was ripe for other pursuits:

> [I]*mmediately upon their discharge,* [they] *entered into the smuggling business,* and [Mott] *proposed to a man in St. Albans to engage in the business, informing him that he could make 1,000 dollars a month, as he calculated to have all the other smugglers apprehended, to have his boat armed, and then he could do the business of the lake.*[236]

The transition from militiaman to smuggler was not difficult for either man, and now they ventured out to participate in crimes neither could have envisioned at the time.

4

TIMBER RAFTS AND MILITIA MUTINY

B enjamin Pratt, of Rutland, entered into militia service in 1795, rose to the rank of captain by 1808 and was placed in charge of an infantry company in the Second Brigade's Third Regiment, Second Division, under the command of Brigadier General Caleb Hendee Jr. Following his upcoming service, Pratt was promoted to major and remained in the militia until the War of 1812, when he decided to seek a position with the U.S. Army. He was accepted and appointed first lieutenant of the Second Light Dragoon on March 12, 1812, resigning the following year. When he applied for his new role, Pratt provided a statement to army superiors briefly describing his prior service in the summer of 1808, of which he was clearly proud. Pratt wrote that he "had the honor to command a company of militia (in pursuance of orders from the President of the United States and was stationed at Windmill Point in concert with a detachment of regular troops) for the term of three months."[237] The regulars he referred to constituted one of the nation's first mobile artillery units ordered to Vermont as part of Jefferson's "temporary" increase in the national army, consisting of a sixteen-man detachment of soldiers from Springfield, Massachusetts, hauling two brass six-pounders and ammunition out to the Point.[238]

Pratt's immediate subordinate, Lieutenant Daniel Farrington (1773–1865), was a farmer from Pittsford who followed him into the army in April 1813; was promoted to captain and assigned to the Thirtieth Infantry; and served in the Pittsford and Plattsburgh areas during the war (discharged on June 15, 1815). When he was later granted a pension in 1832 (receiving $8.50 a month), Farrington was listed as an invalid, having served with the Vermont militia, indicating he became disabled in some fashion while serving in a state, rather than national, capacity.[239] After examining the events of 1808, the reason for Farrington's disability becomes clear and provides a brief window into the challenges he and Pratt, and their men, faced during their shared three months of service on Vermont's northern frontier.

When it became clear that the St. Albans men could not stem the problems they had been sent to resolve, Governor Smith turned to Hendee's division to provide the necessary substitutes and ordered 150 men into the fray. On May 24, Hendee issued orders to Pratt; the Second Regiment's commander, Captain Joel Harmon Jr.; and a detachment of cavalry from Captain John Ruggle's company to respond northward. Fortuitously, just before Pratt received his orders, he had traveled to the Whitehall area at the south end of the lake, where he observed a large raft of timber being assembled. Unknown to him at the time was the important role he was destined to play as it slowly progressed northward in the following days.[240] The three companies were placed under the overall command of Major Charles K. Williams, a Rutland attorney who later served as state representative, collector of customs, Supreme Court justice and governor.

Farrington's counterpart in Harmon's company was Lieutenant Alexander Miller (1776–1844), a respected businessman from Wallingford, located immediately south of Rutland. His father, Solomon, who had died the preceding year, had moved his family to the town from Williston and was involved in manufacturing agricultural implements, tanning and shoe making. Miller learned the blacksmith trade and moved on to produce tools, building a forge and blacksmith shop on the town's main thoroughfare that turned out hoes, axes, nails, et cetera. He continued the business for several years, and it has survived in various incarnations for over two hundred years, becoming the modern-day True Temper Hardware Company. His two brothers were also noteworthy individuals. Samuel was an important attorney in Middlebury and a founder of Middlebury College, and Solomon served in various legal capacities, including as clerk of the Chittenden County and Supreme Courts.[241]

Miller had served previously as his unit's orderly sergeant before being promoted to lieutenant in 1805. On that occasion, he and another individual also being promoted made arrangements to obtain two gilt swords from Jacob Houghton, a friend of Miller's from Troy, New York, who supplied him with the iron, steel and wire used in his tool-making business. Houghton went to great trouble in searching out and purchasing the correct accoutrements appropriate to their ranks and sent swords, costing thirteen dollars each, to Miller, telling him they were "very light, and with a little care, will always appear rich and elegant."[242]

It was apparently through Jacob's business, Robbins & Houghton, that Miller came to meet his associate's daughter, Lucretia Robbins (circa 1784–1839), sometime around 1802. Jacob possessed a ribald sense of humor and, in his various letters to Miller, made it a point to poke innocent fun of their mutual situations with the ladies. Writing to Miller in 1802, Jacob thought the only obstacle in Miller's pursuit of Lucretia seemed to be the fact that "you live too far in the country" and told him that "the subject of our correspondence is sensible, well-educated, elegant, kind, tender-hearted & compassionate: but…you know me, & you know my heart."[243]

After Miller received his sword, and while courting Lucretia, he received an invitation from another friend to join him in celebrating the New Year. The invitation addressed him as "a man of gallantry" and requested his attendance at a ball, where "we shall have something good for the stomach and perhaps for bachelors."[244] In the end, the festivities and miles separating Alexander and Lucretia proved no obstacle, and in 1807, the two were married. Fortunately, the ensuing correspondence between the two newlyweds the following year provides important insights into the challenges Miller was forced into as a most complex—and dangerous—situation unfolded along the border.

Miller first learned that his summer of 1808 was going to be disrupted on May 23, when he received a dispatch telling him he had been "appointed a lieut. of a company of infantry to be detached…for a military expedition." The following day, Hendee wrote to him directly ordering that he and his men "be immediately marched to the Office of the Collector of Revenue of the U.S. at Swanton." Cavalry commander Ruggles received similarly worded orders authorizing him to choose which officers he wanted to take with him. Sensitive that the deployment came at a time when farmers were needed in the fields, Hendee directed that in making his choices, Ruggles was to "use your best discretion in selecting men suitable for service and such as can best leave their homes at this season of the year."[245] As things turned out, it is unfortunate that Miller appears not to have had similar latitude in making these kinds of decisions.

Miller quickly made the necessary notifications to his fellows, those involved principally with farming spread out over Wallingford and in nearby Tinmouth and Danby. The other companies also went immediately to work assembling their men, as noted by a local newspaper:

It is now reduced to a melancholy fact that a set of unprincipled speculators *on and about Lake Champlain are determined to oppose and evade the embargo law, at all events. The interposition of a small detachment of the militia, which is now about to be made, we believe, will disperse these transgressors of our laws, and induce them to* return to their respective homes.[246]

On May 31, the entire assemblage set off from Rutland, as the paper proudly wrote, "to put a stop to the disgraceful Pot-ash and Lumber rebellion on Lake Champlain," but not without also noting it was "fearful that the opposers of the embargo law…have no disposition to quench but to kindle the fire of rebellion."[247] Such were the lofty expectations placed on these young men, some of whom never returned, while others were severely impacted by what they encountered.

A FULL EXPLANATION OF the various relationships among the many smugglers living along the border will probably never be known. Their relatively low positions within the community meant that little documentation about them was generated at the time, leaving frustratingly few clues for later generations attempting to reconstruct their involvement in crimes that summer. Nonetheless, they remained a boisterous, self-assured and loud lot when among their friends, claiming unity against the embargo, but when taken aside by authorities and removed from the presence of their brethren, some became willing to disclose things others would not have wanted told. However, until the government demonstrated it had some degree of control over the smuggling, those thinking of cooperating as witnesses remained in the background as events unfolded.

At the very moment the Rutland militia was assembling, and no doubt in direct response to that fact, smugglers dependent on their watercraft began to take steps to increase their firepower to ensure there were no interruptions with their lucrative work. Frederick Hoxie and his sons, John and Job, resided in the Alburgh area at least as early as 1800, when Hoxie's name appears alongside rioter Mott's in a town grand list.[248] Job's name later appears in a rare divorce proceeding before the Vermont Supreme Court, brought by his wife, Elizabeth, whom he married in May 1798. Not long after the events of 1808, she alleged that on February 15, 1811, Job "willfully deserted her, and has gone to parts unknown…leaving her without means of support," after having "treated her with intolerable severity." The court determined that her allegations were "fully proved" and granted the divorce.[249] What the Hoxie family's relationship was to a lumberman named Van Duysen is not known, but the fact that one existed became quite apparent in the next days as the raft that Benjamin Pratt saw in Whitehall moved north.

Another local family of renown in the smuggling business was the Taylors—specifically, the brothers John and Ezekiel. They, and their brother Reuben, arrived in Alburgh from the Schaghticoke, New York area and were distinguishable for being large, strong men. Reuben was well versed in boxing, deemed "a scientific pugilist," and had trained a local man in the art, resulting in a well-known slugfest taking place between him and one of the Hoxie clan.[250] Reuben is not reported to have been involved with the illegal activities taking place, but about his brothers' involvement, there is no doubt.

A third group of men also began to make an appearance at this time, one with its own familial relationships. Former rioter/militiaman and now smuggler Samuel I. Mott's name appears among them (as well as his being an associate of the Hoxies and Taylors), and it is this particular group, loosely headed by Mott's brother-in-law, Truman Mudget, that became responsible for the notorious murders taking place in August. Mudget was also the reported brother-in-law of Cyrus B. Dean, of Swanton, the man history has come to identify most closely with the incident. Importantly, the common link among all three of these groups was the boat *Black Snake*, which would lend its name to the notorious affair centering (wrongly) on Dean.

The *Black Snake* was the ideal smuggling boat. In its earlier days, it was built—and actually served in that purpose—as a ferry operating between Charlotte, Vermont, and Essex, New York. Described as forty feet in length and fourteen feet wide, with sides "straight and high" reaching down four and a half feet, it possessed a "sharp bow and square stern—a forecastle, but no cabin." When not being propelled by sail borne on its single mast, it could be maneuvered by fourteen oars, seven on a side, and guided by a removable rudder. The *Black Snake* was apparently never painted but rather smeared with black tar over its exterior. It was either the resulting appearance or the actual snake, called the racer because of its speed, that inspired the vessel's name. For those using it that summer, it was perfectly capable of transporting some one hundred barrels of potash at a time, and at five or six dollars per barrel, it is clear it could turn a meaningful profit to its owner.[251]

Some smugglers might have had the financial wherewithal to independently conduct their work, but many relied on others for employment, including merchants and speculators who were dependent on their rafts and potash completing their journeys to the north. Dr. John Stoddard of St. Albans, previously noted, was the reported owner of the *Black Snake* as it rode the lake's waters that summer. However, an examination of extant documents reveals that the vessel was the subject of a series of sale transactions at the time, indicating that Stoddard might have been in the process of conveying some, if not all, of his interest to others.

One account states that the boat belonged to John Taylor, while in another, Mudget had reportedly purchased it for $200 from the Taylors, and Mott was to become half owner with him at the completion of their murderous adventure in August.[252] A third version, an affidavit sworn to by Collector Penniman in August, provides yet additional information. Immediately following the murders, when the government finally sprang into action, Penniman sought arrest warrants for several individuals. These included John and Ezekiel Taylor and Frederick, John and Job Hoxie, together with a John Niles and Joseph Headon, for events taking place on various dates, including June 1, when the men, while in Alburgh, did

> *feloniously & wickedly commit the crime of High Treason by levying war against the United States…*[and] *did arm and equip a certain boat or bateau called the* Black Snake *for the purpose* [of] *resisting the authority of & making war against the government of the United States* [and] *did resist the authority of & levy war against the United States.*[253]

Unfortunately, the specific activities the men were involved in on that day are not described, nor is there information from other accounts giving additional insights. What is clear, though, is that seven men from two identifiable factions had gathered together at the very moment the government was increasing its presence on the border with the Rutland militia, had undertaken efforts to turn the *Black Snake* into a formidable opponent by arming and equipping it and then actually resisted efforts to stop them. Dr. Stoddard may very well have been in full possession of the vessel at that point, deciding only as the months passed and the difficulties attending a confrontation with authorities rose that it would be wise to sell it to those working it.

As the Rutland militia assembled, its St. Albans counterparts suddenly became noticeably more effective in their efforts, and over the course of three days, they were able to intervene in four separate smuggling attempts. First, on May 28, a sloop called the *Essex*, reportedly owned by "a Mr. Page of Middlebury," was intercepted without incident and taken to Windmill Point, where a search uncovered 157 barrels of ashes and 92 barrels of pork.

At midnight on the following day, Captain Hopkins and nine of his men were able to stop a bateau (a highly maneuverable flat-bottomed boat of shallow draft worked by oars), but only after firing three rounds in its direction and convincing its crew of six to turn themselves in. All of the men, determined to be from Plattsburgh, were taken into New York custody, and 25 barrels of potash were confiscated. On the thirtieth, Whittemore and his men proved highly effective as they took another bateau carrying a reported two tons of potash. But it was their second encounter that night that provides a deeper understanding of the challenges they were facing.

On that occasion, Whittemore was able, after firing two rounds, to forcibly stop a boat carrying nine barrels of ash. Its Canadian crew had been heading north following a visit to St. Albans Bay when they were discovered. However, the militiamen were stymied in any further attempt to detain them because they were unable to find a local magistrate to authorize their further confinement. It was then decided, reportedly by "the collector" (presumably Sam Buel), that the men should be released while their goods were detained. As Whittemore then learned, there were others on the north side of the border assembling together to prepare for a forcible retaking of their property.

While the outcome of that event appears to have resolved itself without further incident, a Bennington paper noted that the possibility of the use of force by the smugglers in their efforts "looks serious, for such an attack would be considered as a commencement of war."[254] In none of these incidents were the smugglers armed with guns; rather, they carried cudgels, or clubs—a situation that would ominously change with the arming of the *Black Snake*.

WITH HIS IMMEDIATE SUPERIOR, Captain Joel Harmon, then on furlough, responsibility for shepherding his Wallingford contingency northward fell to Miller, and by June 2, his and Benjamin Pratt's companies had reached East Middlebury. From there, they progressed up through Hinesburg, passed over the Onion River and arrived at their destination, Swanton Falls, on Sunday afternoon, June 5, with Miller suffering only a few blistered toes. There, he learned that he, together with some thirty of his men, would remain at that location assigned to watch for wagons heading north in violation of the embargo, while the rest of his men proceeded fifteen to twenty miles to the east with the same duties. Meanwhile, Pratt and Farrington and their men were ordered to march to Windmill Point.

Miller, who had anticipated running into opposition from citizens living north of Rutland, experienced an eye-opening march. As he explained to Lucretia:

> *The childish, whimsical stories reported in Wallingford about any opposition of their inhabitants is all false. The inhabitants here have as many stories about Rutland County and perhaps more than you can imagine. The inhabitants here, the thinking part, say when we get there it will all be peaceable times.*
>
> *The inhabitants north of Middlebury thought the troops were all a pack of vile Democrats selected for the purpose of insulting the inhabitants, but when they perceive our civility towards them they treat us with great respect.*[255]

For those in Middlebury witnessing the passing troops, their presence presented conflicting emotions, and some joked they were seeing "war in miniature," while others feared the opening of a civil war because of a law they resented, believing it could not be enforced.[256] In St. Albans, others noted that the Rutland men "appeared like good soldiers, obedient to the call of their country. They must suffer great personal sacrifices in point of property, in leaving their business at this busy season of the year."[257] However, Miller noted their presence was causing some unease in the northern community and told Lucretia that "the people here are extremely mortified to think that the government was unwilling to place any confidence in their troops and should send so far south for them, but they treat us very politely."[258]

For businessman Miller, responsible for continuing a tool-manufacturing operation and having to get in the necessary crops for his own needs while attending to those of his lonely wife, the timing of the callout could not have been worse. His departure from Lucretia was emotional, and she apologized for her performance at the time in letters immediately after he left, but she quickly regained her composure with the visits of friends. These included local militia officers of other companies remaining behind who assured her that her "commander in chief," as she teased him, was facing tasks that "will not be hard."[259] Miller was also fortunate to have the services of an attentive assistant named Aaron, who communicated through Lucretia, advising of the needs arising at home, while also responding to instructions concerning filling orders and collecting debts of the business and harvesting corn and hay.

Those challenges aside, it is clear that Miller was taking his responsibilities very seriously and, at least in the first days, fitting in well with his men. He wrote:

> *Our officers appear to be quite agreeable men & all appear to be quite friendly & what is more flattering to my pride I cannot consider myself*

the least amongst them. The troops are in high spirits & appear to be well pleased with their officers.[260]

However, it was not long before some of the troops began to question why they had been called out:

I am here a gentleman officer from the southward to be sure, but cannot answer the question when they ask me what Mr. Penniman wants of us…We set sentry nights to see if loaded wagons pass to Canada but see none…Our boys here think it odd we should come so far for nothing.[261]

Compounding Miller's problems was a lack of adequate provisions available to the troops, which would cause unrest in the near future.

As the highest-ranking officer at Swanton, and directed to coordinate his efforts with the civilian collector of customs, Miller immediately struck up a relationship with Penniman. For Miller, his initial assessment of the man was less than admirable:

Believe our collector is more skeart [sic] *than hurt or he intends to make a noise through the United States of his vigilance to execute the law and make himself popular. I should not think it at all surprising if he should keep constantly alarming the inhabitants with his petition to the governor for larger detachments as long as the embargo holds. I know of no service I, or my men, are here unless he wants us to guard his person for he has but few friends who wish to have him execute the law as he would if he had courage. I came away from home with a full determination to be neither a Federal or a Democrat but I cannot find scarcely a decent man here but is opposed to the present measures of government.*[262]

The following day, Miller wrote again, telling his wife that Penniman had confided in him that "he cannot prevent smuggling without detaining potash wherever he can find it." Moderating his initial estimation of the man, Miller wrote further, while also giving expression to the overriding significance of political party, that "Mr. Penniman is not so subtle as I expected to have found him, but is an affable, obliging man to me & appears to place more confidence in me that I thought he would in a Federalist."[263]

However, the arrival of the Rutland men had no discernible impact on lawbreakers, and the smuggling continued. "The Green Mountain Boy, we are told, as he trundles over the line his load of pot ashes, or his barrels of mess…and bone middlings, smacks his whip in the face of the collector without fear or let, molestation or remonstrance." A Montpelier newspaper provided additional, firsthand information:

> *Teams from New Hampshire and the eastern parts of Vermont, loaded with pearl ashes, are continually passing through this village on their way to Burlington. It is calculated that not less than one hundred tons of that article have passed within ten days. It is said there are troops in Burlington, ready to receive it, as soon as it arrives. When sufficiently laden they proceed to within a short distance of the line; there come to anchor; and continue in that situation for several days, apparently without any design; after which, they return empty to Burlington. What becomes of their cargoes is left to conjecture.*[264]

Then it warned:

> *Whatever may be the facts, respecting this business, it must be a subject of deep regret to every friend of his country, to observe that any of its laws are violated with impunity. Such conduct has a direct tendency to destroy all respect for government of our choice, and will, in its genuine operation, reduce the nation to a state of anarchy.*

Meeting around the time their militia was ordered to withdraw, St. Albans inhabitants assembled and prepared a memorial to send to Jefferson. He had initially, and naïvely, maintained that the people would willingly abide by the embargo's constraints without opposition, placing little concern on those who did not. In May, he wrote to a number of governors thanking them for their assistance and expressed his opinion concerning those pursuing an illegal course of conduct:

> *In that desire which you must feel, in common with all our worthy citizens, that inconvenience encountered cheerfully by them for the interests of their country, shall not be turned merely to the unlawful profits of the* most worthless part of society.[265]

For those along the border, worthless or not, they were having none of it. Repeating many of the arguments Burlington's residents had made in April, they took great umbrage and forcibly rejected any insinuation of insurrection's presence in their midst, bolding declaring themselves "TRUE and FAITHFUL CITIZENS" and calling on Jefferson to immediately remove the restrictions of the March land embargo. But in reaching that recommendation, they could not help but note their suspicions that their president had been led astray in his actions "in consequence of erroneous and unfounded representations, made, and transmitted…by some evil minded person or persons."[266]

Another writer expressed his own dismay at what was taking place, giving voice against those many deemed the most responsible for the community's discord—Penniman, Van Ness and Aldis—calling them Jefferson's "infuriated parasites" and "puny collectors." Disingenuously stating that "it is true our potash has been *stolen* from us *every night!* but we are not answerable for the theft of our neighbors," he then disparaged Jefferson himself, ridiculing any contention that he was "worthy" before moving on and calling Van Ness and Aldis "two violent and unprincipled Jacobin men" and blaming them for pressuring Governor Smith into summoning the Rutland militia. From specific information, the writer stated he had learned from someone intimately involved with their proceedings that the three Vermont men had consulted together and determined:

> The Administration would sink down under the imputation of inconsistency *should not a number of soldiers be stationed on our frontiers; which will have the* appearance *of keeping down rebellion at least, in order that the* immaculate [Jefferson] *should be thought to be correct in his proclamation.*[267]

Others also quickly concluded that "intrigue is the order of the day. The collector is blamed. It is said he has conveyed incorrect intelligence to government" and that the people had been "grossly libeled" in Jefferson's rush to judgment.[268] Deflecting all blame, recent troubles were attributed to those living outside Vermont who were simply using the state as a highway to get their goods from the south to the north: "Let the disgrace of insurrection rest on the infamous speculators, and not on the patriotic Green Mountain Boys."[269] Their adamant rejections of wrongdoing aside, the environment in which the Rutland militiamen found themselves was turning dangerous.

EVENTS QUICKENED, AND ON June 9, Major Williams issued urgent Battalion Orders from Swanton telling Miller to immediately detach three groups of men from his company, sending seven to St. Albans Bay, five to Georgia and eight to Hinesburg, assigned to a cavalry unit.[270] Their particular emergency is not identified, but much additional activity was afoot out on the water, including two substantial smuggling operations taking place the following day.

There are no diaries or accounts that describe the specifics of what occurred, but the timing of events leaves little doubt that the smuggling factions were communicating quite well with each other as they assessed the strengths and weaknesses of the militia contingencies gathered around the Point. As the soldiers' attention was drawn to the arrival of the large, conspicuous raft from Whitehall that Pratt had observed, other arrangements were being made among themselves to exploit both its fortuitous appearance and its militia weaknesses. Following their venture only a few days earlier, when they had armed the *Black Snake*, the Hoxies and Taylors met once again, and on June 10, they combined their forces at Alburgh, accompanied by a large body of men. Their particular purpose on that day was to ensure the transit of another large raft, one made up of "one hundred sticks of pine and one hundred sticks of oak timber," across the border to Caldwell Manor.[271]

From court documents filed after the August murders, it appears that the Hoxies and their associates manned this particular raft while the Taylors engaged in more serious efforts to support them. The specific involvement of the *Black Snake* is not described, but the Taylors appear to have possessed a credible array of weaponry to fend off any interference of militia forces brought to bear against the Hoxies as part of their joint effort. As the indictment later prepared against them alleging treason, or "levy[ing] war, insurrection and rebellion" against the government, states, they associated with at least twenty others armed with "guns, pistols, swords and pikes, and other warlike weapons" to accomplish their goal.[272] The specifics of their engagement with the soldiers are not described, but it appears that the raft was successfully taken north. However, the Hoxies did not remain there for long, quickly returning to Vermont to continue in their efforts.

During the trial of Frederick Hoxie and his sons taking place in October for their involvement in the following incident, a number of witnesses provided significant details describing what took place that have not been fully considered in past accounts of these days. Close examination of their testimony reveals the presence of a hierarchy within the smugglers' operations in which an individual of means was able to employ a number of men desperately in need of money, including at least one member of the Rutland militia, to thwart the government's efforts. This was achieved through the use of disinformation to first obtain their agreement to assist in what they believed was lawful conduct but then, when it was proving otherwise, resorting to bribery to convince them to continue on. Through this testimony, it becomes even more apparent that, beyond those who might be doing so simply to survive, there were area businessmen contributing to the lawlessness taking place—which eventually came to include murder.

As the Taylor and Hoxie raft passed north, farther to the south, overstretched authorities were at work dealing with the one from Whitehall. Pratt and his company had arrived on the Point by this time with orders to coordinate their efforts directly with Deputy Collector Buel in Penniman's absence. When Buel learned that the timber was then resting a few miles to the south at Isle la Mott, he ordered Pratt to take it into custody and "put it in some safe place." With some of his company stationed at other locations and the arrival of federal troops and their artillery still two weeks away, Pratt had only twelve men available and probably took most of them on the assignment—which might explain why the northbound raft was able to successfully pass by the few soldiers left behind.

The men, together with Buel, then proceeded to where the raft was moored along the island's shore and found it a formidable creation, two acres square in size and valued at $25,000, with masts and a rough shanty on its surface bearing a number of men bound for Canada.[273] Buel decided the most appropriate course was to read Jefferson's proclamation to the raftsmen, and after that was done, Pratt issued an ultimatum, telling them to either leave or "submit to orders." The men chose the latter. The owner, a man named Van Duysen, a reported "democrat," was also present and contested that "he wished the raft not to be taken away," fearing that if it was relocated to Windmill Point, "it was liable to be stove all to pieces by the first south wind." His concerns were dismissed, and the soldiers shepherded it the few miles back to the Point, where it was tied up in the adjacent bay, considered a secure location only a half mile from where the soldiers were stationed.[274] While several of Van Duysen's men were allowed to remain on board, he appears to have departed to set into motion the next series of events.

Josiah Edson was a wily smuggler with many connections, possessing an uncanny ability to remain on the periphery of important events and not drawing the government's ire to such a degree that it ever tried to prosecute him. As might be expected for someone in his position, possessing important inside information of the smugglers' intentions, agreements were later made between himself and authorities that he would not be held accountable for his actions if he cooperated in cases brought against them. Accordingly, his name appears in two contexts in these days, first as a participant on the Van Duysen raft and, weeks later, as an associate of the killers manning the *Black Snake*.

As the testimony at the Hoxie trial revealed, Edson, who was on board the raft at the time Pratt and his men took it, was the principal person Van Duysen immediately approached seeking assistance in arranging for its forcible retaking. His efforts over the next two days proved of great importance to his employer in both recruiting a force of sufficient strength and attaining the necessary tools to make the effort successful. To do this, he sought out others willing to assist and also traveled into New York State "to procure ammunition for this business." But there were also additional efforts being undertaken by some unidentified person(s) seeking to enlist the assistance of others actually serving within the government's ranks.

A payroll roster for the month ending June 30, 1808, lists Edmond Merrill of Clarendon, age unknown, as one of forty-eight privates serving under Pratt's command, receiving a total of $6.76. Others identified on accompanying papers as playing important roles at the time of the August murders include Lieutenant Farrington, Sergeant David Johnson, drummer Benjamin Johnson and fellow privates Ellis Drake, James Hays, Asa Marsh Jr., Alexander Walker and James White Jr.—two of whom would be lying dead a few short weeks later. Whether any of those others played a part in the retaking of Van Duysen's raft is not known, but it is certain that Merrill, further identified in the papers with the word "confined" next to his name, did participate and in a manner wholly inconsistent with his sworn duty.[275]

Before departing for Canada, where he planned to rejoin his raft after its crossing, Van Duysen left instructions with Edson and another man, Joseph Tinkham of Alburgh, to go into the countryside to locate a force willing to assist in the retaking, moving it around Windmill Point, into the channel and then over the border. The stories these "recruiters" passed on to anyone hesitant to join them was that the raft had been blown onto the shore, and their assistance was needed to refloat it. They said that Collector Penniman himself had agreed it was permissible and that he had given instructions to the soldiers to assist them. When Edson inquired of Tinkham what he should tell those he approached about payment for their services, he was told to use an "embargo trick," promising to divide the princely sum of $800 among the men for their efforts. In a telling indication of the desperate situation some were in, Edson recounted that "many of the men [said] that they would go through with the raft or lose their lives and it was agreed that if the men did not get the raft through they were to have nothing." That was the simple, pragmatic business proposition: payment for success and nothing for failure.

The recruiting took place over the next two days and was so successful that the many volunteers (estimated at more than sixty) were directed to two separate locations to coordinate their efforts: a barn owned by a man named Loupes and, not surprisingly, one owned by smuggler Samuel Mott, located only two miles from the Point. At Mott's place, a collection of twenty-five to thirty men gathered, and the discussion turned to the realities of the situation, including the fact that there were armed guards at the raft raising the concerns of some. To minimize them, they were told that if there was any firing, it would be with powder only, and no ball, and that it was being done as a "ruse" to give a false impression to any onlookers that they were actually trying to prevent its retaking.

The reason such a promise could be made was because by this time, somebody, perhaps a family member, a good friend or someone paying money, had succeeded in making contact with Private Merrill and gained his agreement to participate in the ruse, including his removing the lead shot from militia stores and providing it to the smugglers. The fact that Pratt's men were not otherwise fully equipped with ammunition at all times to meet an emergency indicates a lack of full appreciation of the dangers they were facing, an absence of trust in their possessing such items in the closeness of a camp situation or evidence of the government's continuing effort to avoid the possibility of any bloodshed taking place that would arouse the enmity of the local population. It is difficult to conclude that the reasoning was anything other than the latter, as Alexander Miller and his fellow officers in Swanton were instructing their men at the time "not to load their guns with anything but powder and if they do, to fire very low."[276] The militia's continuing reluctance to inflict physical harm appears to have been but an extension of the civil authorities' decision not to pursue criminal prosecutions in the courts for those actually caught.

Frederick Hoxie had returned from the prior rafting trip by this time and was present at Mott's barn. Edson seems to have known Hoxie well and testified that when Pratt's men first arrived in Alburgh, he heard Hoxie say "that any man who went on to the Point, his heart was in his arse and they had no business there and with a [illegible] & stick he could drive them all off." Hoxie continued in that vein on this occasion, appearing in the mostly unarmed crowd carrying his gun and ready to proceed. However, some of the men remained afraid and refused to go forward. Not dissuaded, the others marched out into the dark and down a road, where they met the second group of men coming from Loup's barn at the intersection of the road leading to the Point.

Now, their numbers had increased substantially, with over sixty men present, but they had only a reported thirteen or fourteen guns, twelve that were fit for use. A vote was taken, and Tinkham was chosen as their "captain." A discussion concerning a strategy for the raft's taking ensued. The options included actually subduing whatever guards might be in the area or attempting to remove the vessel quietly in the dark. After putting the matter to a second vote, the men wisely decided to take the latter course. Tinkham then ordered that those bearing arms were "not to fire a gun unless they were fired upon—and then to take good aim and if they killed three or four it would still them." He also told the men "who had no guns to get clubs or spike poles." Even then, the debating continued, as "some present said it was not lawful to take the raft, others said it was, some said they cared nothing about the law." Those willing to proceed did so, marching quietly on, and when they reached the water's edge, they could find no signs of any sentry.

It was an hour after the moon had risen, around midnight, that the men were able to separate the raft from the shore, rowing to a position where they could round the Point and proceed across the border a short distance away. Not long after they pushed off, Private Asa Hall, standing guard duty fifty rods away, testified:

> I heard a stick crack and some noise from the raft. I hailed the raft and received for answer, "come here and I will tell you." The next sentinel towards the Point then fired. The guard turned out. I was relieved and went to the guard house—our ammunition was chiefly gone. Some of the men were employed in running balls & in about an hour and half I went to the Point. There was noise and halloing on the raft so that it was said it would be of no use to hail the raft. We then fired. They returned the fire.

Merrill's treachery worked, and with the needed ammunition removed, it forced a lengthy delay on his fellows as they tried to melt, pour and extract from their molds the needed bullets as fast as possible.

The noise Hall heard coming from the raft, estimated to be a short twenty rods (approximately 330 feet) away, was the smugglers taunting the soldiers, calling out that they were "cowards and damned rascals." In response, the militiamen set off a volley, leading to a running exchange of gunfire from the raft that lasted for at least the next hour and a half. Merrill's obstructive actions, together with the shouting raftsmen, had turned this into a confrontation in which the government troops had clearly abandoned any hesitation in actually inflicting injury.

For Edson, what he witnessed from on board the raft was something to behold, estimating that during the exchange, "100 guns were fired from the raft, during which time the men on shore were plain to be seen" in the moonlight. The shots they were receiving caused men needing to reload to crouch down behind the shanty, itself "perforated in forty different places."[277] Between volleys, they rowed as quickly as they could, bending down as far as possible when they saw muzzle flashes from the shore, hoping to be out of the way before the bullets arrived from across the water.[278] For Asa Hall on shore, those shots that came toward the Point were every bit as lethal: "The balls from the raft struck the fence and the wind mill—one struck an apple tree and I felt the wind of one brush my handkerchief about my neck." When it became clear the raft was going to get around the Point and escape, Pratt ordered his men to cease-fire but to save one round apiece. Despite that order, at least one soldier reportedly "followed the raft down near the line and fired at the raft every once and a while."

Remarkably, nobody was injured during the fray, and as the men crossed over the line at daybreak, they fired off more rounds, but this time it was "for joy" at their success. Frederick Hoxie bragged that he had fired each of his two weapons between ten and fifteen times during the course of the mêlée. Once into Canada, they were rejoined by Van Duysen, who told them the promised $800 would arrive shortly and gave each $1 and a drink of grog. For his work in gathering up the volunteers, Edson received $18, while the others received an average of $14 and one shilling.

Under the heading "Dog Eat Dog," a Middlebury paper reported the incident shortly afterward:

> We hear from Alburgh, that an armed force of ninety men, in disguise, have taken the last raft on Lake Champlain (owned by a Democrat) and rowed it over the lines. It is said there was but little opposition. No lives lost. This is the first instance of force being opposed to the Embargo.[279]

The reporting was clearly not entirely accurate, for there was indeed a heated exchange between the two factions, and if the prior June 1 incident involving the Hoxies and Taylors reported in Penniman's August affidavit is true, it was not the first instance of force being used. But it was certainly the most blatant example to date of what the smugglers were capable of in their ability to attract large numbers of men and coordinate their actions— attributes that did not disappear anytime soon. It was also probably the last raft to make the transit, as the lake level was beginning to drop from its highs following the winter melt, making the rapids on the Richelieu River untenable. However, boats such as the *Black Snake* were able to continue on with their illicit trade, as was the unrepentant Fredrick Hoxie.

The government's demonstration that it no longer intended to restrain itself in using force caused the smugglers to reassess how they met that new challenge. Edson had personally witnessed Hoxie's refusal to be bound by the embargo following the Van Duysen raft incident and testified that

> *he had seen* [Hoxie] *with some others in a boat armed going into Canada with pot ashes…the object of those who run potashes into Canada was to run from any opposition and when the boat returned…that their orders were to run one way or the other as should but favor an escape, and if they could not get away to fight their way through.*[280]

The arming of the smugglers' boats did not escape the notice of the local militia, as Heman Hopkins noted their ominous appearance at the time, "for the purpose of conveying property into the Province of Canada."[281] The stakes were becoming even higher farther to the west, on Lake Ontario, where an individual employed by customs officials was "shot dead, when on the watch of those attempting to run property in [*sic*] the province. The coroner's inquest was *accidental death*. A solemn omen for American Custom House attendants."[282] But for now, Vermont officials had chosen to delay further action against those involved with Van Duysen, thereby allowing the situation to become even more explosive as the smugglers increasingly made clear their intention to "fight their way through." Charges of treason for their involvement with Van Duysen were later lodged against the Hoxie men and Tinkham, but the latter chose to flee the state and never answered for his actions.[283]

THE SAME DAY PRATT and his men were firing away at Van Duysen's raft, Alex Miller's Troy business associate, Jacob Houghton, wrote to him at his Swanton headquarters seeking information regarding the situation in the northwest part of the state. Miller was held in high regard by family and friends, with brother/court clerk Solomon boasting at the same moment that he was "a soldier in the service of his country to suppress the rebels" and fellow militia officer Thomas Towner confidently predicting his return home "richly laden with a cargo of military virtue & honor."[284] Those good thoughts aside, news from the frontier was confused for everyone, leaving the public unaware of exactly what the current situation was, asking if Vermont was indeed in a state of insurrection, as Jefferson proclaimed, or was it, as those in St. Albans professed, still loyal? Abandoning any display of frivolity concerning romantic pursuits, Houghton expressed the palpable underlying fears of many who relied on the Montreal trade and what the embargo's prohibitions meant for it, writing:

> *I feel that I have a claim upon you on account of our former acquaintance & friendship, but the anxiety of my friends here induces me to press the subject & ask you (if it is not too much) to write me once in each week during your service.* [285]

Miller's response is unknown, but he certainly had more pressing concerns at the moment.

The prior day, Miller had the unfortunate experience of learning that two of his soldiers, Privates Jesse Howard, of Wallingford, and Richard Shippee, of Danby, had left their Swanton Falls camp without authorization and were now considered deserters. Just two days following his confrontation with the Van Duysen raft, one of Benjamin Pratt's men had also deserted, but whereas that departure appears to have been an isolated event, Miller faced much more difficult prospects. [286]

One of the more urgent complaints Miller had to deal with concerned the condition of provisions provided to his men upon their arrival in Swanton. In 1814, he was called on to explain what had taken place, responding:

> *There was a general complaint among the soldiers that they were not fully supplied with their rations and that of the [illegible] which they received some was damaged & unfit for use. I saw some of the [illegible] which I considered as wholly unfit for use. Some of it was issued from a Mr. Blodget & some from David Page, Jr. I recollect making complaint to Mr. Page & received assurances from him that the soldiers should have better.* [287]

Miller continued to closely watch the local inhabitants and began to have a jaundiced view of their purportedly positive reception at the time of their arrival. Writing to Lucretia at that moment, he provided instructions for her to pass on to helper Aaron and told her about his own frustrations:

> *Tell our neighbors if they inquire the news, we are as much troubled with false reports here as at Wallingford. I find it next to impossible at once to*

learn the truth of stories. News from different parts, one day reports of men wounded, next close shots, none hurt, next it will be that only alarm guns are fired. The truth appears that the inhabitants want to only see what impression the troops have with such stories to know how far they can venture.[288]

Compounding his suspicions were the effects the recent treasonous conduct on the Point of fellow militiaman Merrill had on his men, together with the attractive option of deserting and their ceaseless, internal yearnings to return home to harvest crops ready for harvesting.

The demands on Miller continued, and even Lucretia added to them, writing on June 12 that a significant problem had arisen with a local family dependent on one of his men for support. He had reportedly refused to allow the man to stay at home and hire a substitute to take his place, and she wrote:

Husband, did you know what a difficult situation Mrs. Richmond is left in by Frederick's being taken from her[?] She is almost inconsolable thinking herself forsaken...she blamed you very much that you would not accept someone else...she knows not how they shall get along.[289]

Then, after reassuring him that she was handling their separation better than at first ("reason has resumed its reign on my mind and tears shall no more overcome me while reason is my guide"), Lucretia left him with a tender thought: "The sun has just retired beyond the western hill and was I blest with your company I should be delighted with a walk in the meadow for the blooming aspect which it wears is truly inviting."

Indulging in idyllic fantasy was not to last long, as Merrill's actions quickly became known outside the immediate area. A militia friend in Rutland wrote to Miller that he was "surprised to hear the news from Windmill Point." Commiserating with the difficulties he faced, the writer went on to caution him "to be very careful & extremely prudent and not be hasty nor rushed at anything that may happen. Men's lives are sweet & dear, more especially our own...but they ought not to [have] broken the laws. If they do they must abide the consequences."[290] His recommendation quickly became real when, on June 20, Miller was ordered to report to the Point on the twenty-eight, at 9:00 a.m., "to officiate as a member of a court martial" to determine Merrill's fate.[291] Still, the desertions continued, and the following day, fifer Nehemiah Rogers, of Salisbury, was listed among Miller's missing troops.[292]

The disdain that smuggler Frederick Hoxie held for those Rutland men on the Point (with their hearts in their arses and having no business being there) was a sentiment also widely shared by commanding officers within the St. Albans militia. Over the course of the next several weeks, a significant division became apparent within their ranks concerning whether an insurrection existed that warranted summoning the Rutland contingency to replace them, which also revealed a strong connection between some of those officers and the smugglers.

Clearly agreeing that an insurrection did, in fact, exist, one of these groups, made up of thirty-one officers, had no hesitancy in declaring that "*we do know* that the spirit of insurrection has existed. We do not hesitate to declare, that its existence has been proved by the most abandoned acts of the insurgents, in rising in large bodies, under arms, and attacking the troops." They further stated:

> *We have officers and soldiers among us, whose daily conduct and public declarations incontestably prove them unfit to be entrusted with the execution of the law; who boldly declare, that the officers of government dare not institute suits against the smugglers in this vicinity; and who express their joy, whenever the measures of the administration are thwarted, and even justify all the dastardly conduct of the violators of the law. And we do not hesitate to declare, that we have officers of high rank, who have been guilty of expressions respecting our relations with Great Britain, which ought to destroy the confidence of every true friend of his country in their patriotism.*[293]

They also explained that those with interests anathema to Jefferson's policies extended further to the local community, where some were reportedly willing to go so far as to kill the collector of revenue:

> *The constant and unceasing declarations of the lumber and potash merchants were they would arm, and run their property at all events. That if Mr. Penniman attempted to enforce the laws, his life would be short. That if military aid should be called, and the troops should kill a person in attempting to enforce the laws, the inhabitants would immediately RISE and drive them from their stations. In short, it was openly declared, that the inhabitants on Lake Champlain would never submit to the enforcement of the embargo law.*

The observations of this group of officers were clearly contrary to prior protestations advanced by their superiors that denied any complicity on their part and which they believed constituted

> *one series of high colored misrepresentations, or misstatements of fact, and the extravagant ravings of a foolhardy imagination. And we can discover nothing in the daily conduct and conversation of many of the officers, who signed that instrument, but a moral enmity to the operations of the embargo law, and the most deadly prejudice against every branch of the general and state governments.*

A second group of twelve soldiers similarly ventured to put their careers and community standing in jeopardy when they took unequivocal aim at any contention that an insurrection did not exist, blasting:

> *We denounce as a palpable falsehood; our troops have been wantonly fired upon in several instances, and by force of arms treasonable outrages have been committed…Why the officers of a brigade should be called together to declare that these outrages do not exist, or to excuse the authors from guilt, remains inexplicable. That bribery has been practiced on persons in the employ of the United States, about the Provincial line, in the recent struggle between law and anarchy, we have not a doubt.*[294]

To these men, evidence that such problems existed was so obvious that "every person in this vicinity…must be convinced, that stronger combinations and more powerful confederacies against our laws have never been witnessed since the establishment of the federal union." They went on to defend Penniman and further opined that their officers wanted "to scatter and diffuse the seeds of distrust against the Executive department, and proclaim puerile complaints, ridiculous in their nature, of insult and abuse."[295]

Even members of the public came to recognize the situation as it really existed when one wrote that "many attempts have been made by a set of designing men among us to induce the people to believe that no combinations and confederacies for the purpose of obstructing the execution of the embargo laws have existed on and about Lake Champlain."[296] Who were these "designing men" refusing to acknowledge the insidious presence of criminals in their midst?

The document causing the rupture within the St. Albans ranks, spilling out into the public arena, had been drawn up shortly after events taking place at Windmill Point. On June 17, a large gathering of the militia high command, headed by General House and which included the intrepid Captain Hopkins and Lieutenant Whittemore, assembled in Fairfield, a short distance from St. Albans and Swanton. Following the petition their civilian counterparts had signed earlier in the month, the men forcibly made known their resentment at any insinuation that they had failed in their duties. They contended that they had executed their orders "without a moment's delay…But, notwithstanding their ability and fidelity, as soldiers, they could not command the wind and waves, and consequently could not prevent the passage of rafts and potash into Canada."[297]

They went on, stating that Governor Smith's summoning the Rutland men to replace them, those "within the limits of this insulted brigade," did nothing more than create "little standing armies" in their midst. Further, it brought their reputations into ill-repute with "singular indignities [being] heaped on the meritorious soldiery of this brigade," thereby causing "our characters as men, and as soldiers, being thus wantonly traduced." It further resulted in their being "treated not only with contemptuous neglect, but with open, direct, and most degrading insult," prompting them to warn that "when the spirits of our militia are broken by unprovoked insult and abuse, if military force should be necessary standing armies must be established; and where their tents are pitched, liberty must quit the field." For them, any charge that insurrection or bribery existed was totally, wholly unfounded: "We consider them as the legitimate productions of a contemptible, yet dangerous policy, adopted and pursed by those, whose governing object is not the good of their country." However, for those living farther to the south in Bennington, hearing their protestations of innocence was singularly unimpressive and quickly dismissed: "The militia officers at the northward have published that they are not insurgents, but real patriots—Good!"[298]

There could not have been a more divergent interpretation of events taking place from a local standpoint. The dreaded proclamation and arrival of the Rutland troops were either an unwarranted attack on the honor of a worthy body of men, as the officers professed, or the visiting of a just result on a group whose leaders harbored treasonable inclinations against a government, as their subordinates alleged. They were not alone in their differences, as there were others who had simply taken their grievances out on one another through dueling, such as two marine officers assigned to the USS *Chesapeake*, involved the prior year's confrontation with the HMS *Leopard*, had done in May. Their disagreement concerned the evidence one of them gave against the other during a court-martial involving the event, resulting in their confrontation and one of them being wounded in the hip.[299] There is no indication of similar conduct in Vermont at the time, but blood was indeed drawn.

Even though some of the local St. Albans units had been replaced on the Point by Rutland men, they were still needed at other locations, and shortly after their Fairfield meeting, Whittemore and his men were reassigned eastward to the shores of Missisquoi Bay. On June 22, twelve of them were stationed at a depot guarding nine barrels of potash seized by customs officials, while the rest of the company had been sent some distance away. Whittemore describes what happened next:

> *About 2 o'clock in the morning of that day, about thirty men armed made an attack upon us, and secured the sentries, probably intending to take the potash while the soldiers were asleep. They required us to deliver up the property we had in store, or they would take it by violence, and expressed a determination to take it away at all events, and to kill every man in the garrison, unless the potash was surrendered. On our refusing to deliver it up, they commenced a fire upon us, which we returned. The fire was kept up on both sides, until our cartridges on hand were spent…when we were under the necessity of surrendering. They then took the nine barrels of potash, and carried it away into the Province, leaving most of their men as a guard over us, until the boat with the potash had got out of our reach.*
>
> *When the alarm was first given by the sentries, I attempted to go out of the door to relieve them, when one of the insurgents struck me with a gun across the breast, which knocked me back into the house. The sentries were then driven back into the house; we were fired upon in the barracks; while we were endeavoring to prevent them from entering the barracks, Sergt. Brigham, who was guarding the window, was fired upon by the insurgents, and severely wounded in the shoulder, by two balls, one of which is not yet extracted.[300]*

It is interesting to note that Whittemore, who only days earlier had been one of those disputing the existence of an insurrection, was now describing his attackers in precisely those terms. The disposition of the wounded Brigham is not recorded, but the event seems to have resulted in a lessening of confrontations for the time being, no doubt aided by authorities' continuing reluctance to take the contest directly into the smugglers' strongholds.

In the days following receipt of his orders to report to the Point on June 28 for Merrill's court-martial, Alex Miller was consumed by dealing with various minutiae concerning his company. He tried to arrange for some leave time to return to Wallingford but was unsuccessful and was further assigned by Williams as paymaster for all Rutland troops. He had indeed spoken with his drummer, Frederick Richmond, after receiving Lucretia's letter concerning Mrs. Richmond's hardships from his assignment. He explained to her that he was unable to release the man "without consent of my superior officers," having no knowledge of any such problems since Richmond himself "discovered no unwillingness to come. I did not know the condition of the family & we very much want him."[301]

In Burlington, the sixteen-man contingency of federal troops under the command of a Lieutenant Bennett finally arrived from Springfield, Massachusetts, on June 24 with their artillery and ammunition.[302] As Penniman was the only other federal presence able to securely store goods, their equipment was immediately turned over to him for safekeeping. A receipt signed by Nathan Haswell on that date describes an impressive array of military stores they had brought, including a cart bearing ammunition; "2 brass 6 pounder cannon with their carriages"; various implements needed to man them; two barrels of powder; "400 # musket ball"; "125 muskets, in five boxes, 25 in each"; one thousand flints; ten pounds of slow match; eighteen tents; six horse collars, et cetera.[303]

Penniman and Woolsey had recently arranged for two vessels, the sloop *Juno*, owned by Gideon King, and a schooner named *Beaver*, to transport necessary supplies over the entire lake for "the benefit of government." The following day, the men and their equipment were all loaded aboard one of these vessels and transported out to Windmill Point, where they joined Pratt and his few men. Their presence now significantly increased the government's firepower on the narrow waterway and surely sent a message to smugglers that they now faced more difficult prospects. Notwithstanding, and no doubt wishing to send their own message, later that very day, a group of smugglers came across the water from New York and stole the government's revenue cutter.[304] Also that evening, Whittemore and few of his St. Albans men, presumably at Missisquoi Bay, intercepted a bateaux loaded with twenty barrels of potash on its way over the line, meeting little or no opposition. And still, the mundane work of the customs men continued when Buel noted the arrival of 113 pounds of loaf sugar at the Point on June 28.[305]

Days later, Miller traveled from Swanton Falls to the Point, easily covering the twenty-odd miles to attend Merrill's court-martial. The affair lasted a single day, as the soldier readily acknowledged his guilt in removing the ammunition and turning it over to the men on Van Duysen's raft. While he also stated words to the effect that there were "others of his neighbors" involved, no further information was revealed about who they were. Never at a loss for words, the local paper passed its own judgment on the proceedings, snidely remarking that "our friends, at the south part of this state who are so fond of discrimination between the soldiery of that and this vicinity, we think need to blush and be silent."[306] The only indication of any penalty imposed on Merrill comes in a letter written to Miller the following month from a friend at home reporting that he had heard of "the most heinous crime of a soldier passed over with a small fine and a few days imprisonment." It does appear that Merrill did receive lenient treatment and was not dismissed from his duties, as Pratt's payroll records show that at the end of July, he remained in camp and received full pay alongside his fellow soldiers—$6.66 for the month.[307] Following his return to Swanton Falls, Miller submitted an invoice for his services and received payment of $3.75, or $1.25 for each of the three days he was gone.[308]

On July 3, the Taylors and Hoxies, accompanied as they had been on June 1 by Niles and Headon, struck once again. This time, it was in an area farther away from Windmill Point and the threatening federal artillery, to the south in North Hero. With frustratingly little detail, as he had previously done, Penniman swore out charges the following month, alleging high treason against each of the seven men, stating that they did "with force & arms feloniously & wickedly levy war against the United States of America by arming a certain boat or bateau & therewith resisted the authority of the United States."[309] While the instant vessel was not named, there is no reason to believe that the *Black Snake* was not involved once again. Meanwhile, on the St. Lawrence River two days earlier, a large raft of timber valued at $100,000 and carrying one hundred men had been struck by a tornado, totally destroying it and drowning ninety-seven of them.[310]

For Miller and his land-bound men, July's opening days portended only more pointless and boring watching and waiting, and he told Lucretia there was

> *little to do in our official capacity but detaching guards, placing* [sentries]…*all which everyone avoids that want to carry property to Canada which is no harder matter than to find where the guards are & then go some other road. We have been here in my opinion this time needlessly.*[311]

Miller further apologized to her for being away, explaining that duty intervened, and he felt obligated to remain because his "character is at stake." Also driving his interest was the fact that his superiors recognized him as one who would do "his duty to a punctilio." However, there were also benefits from his being away because, despite the harm it was doing to his business, it allowed him to make additional local contacts he hoped would be of assistance in the future. The service of all the Rutland men was also a source of pride to their friends at home, who toasted them at the July 4 celebrations in Sherburne: "The militia of Vermont in arms, on the shores of Lake Champlain: Vigilance to their officers, and watchfulness to their guards—may they never surrender to a smuggling poltroon enemy, till their steels are softened with fire, and their muskets stained with blood."[312] Unfortunately, any pride Miller and others might have felt was about to shatter.

This was also the time for haying and gathering in crops, something that Lucretia wrote about, telling Alex that helper Aaron had "hoed the corn twice…grass very good, he calculates to mow the clover the beginning of next week, the garden as good as anybodys." She was also having success in another endeavor, proudly telling him, "I have learnt to make cheese. I hope the embargo will be taken off by the time my cheese gets to be merchantable in the fall for I have made six very nice ones." News of the conditions the troops faced also filtered back home, and she warned him that she had heard something disquieting—that they "live so poorly they were some of them about to leave you and indeed some have come home [referring to the deserting Howard and Shippee] but Frederick Richmond writes those that behave well fare as well as they can expect." Miller himself acknowledged the pressures the men faced and told her that "at present our men are all so anxious to go home to haying."[313]

The company Miller commanded had a total of four corporals, including Ashur Blunt Jr. and Allen Vail, who, together with drummer Richmond and fifer Rogers, all received the same amount of pay per month ($7.33), indicating their comparable standing within the ranks. As such, they would have associated more closely with one another and possibly discussed what they planned to do during this time when nature called to them more loudly than duty. By early July, the company's third deserter, Rogers, had departed, while Richmond seems to have been reconciled to remaining at his post despite his wife's protestations that he return home.

However, on the evening before Miller wrote to Lucretia describing the men's desire to return to hay, Corporal Blunt took the opportunity to encourage "mutiny among the soldiers," and haying, in addition to their living conditions, was no doubt high on their list of grievances. Miller could not have anticipated the result, but the following day, his second corporal, Vail, together with thirteen privates from Clarendon, Danby, Middletown

Springs, Tinmouth, Wallingford and Wells, simply picked up and left. Three days later, yet another private departed, leaving Miller without a substantial part of his company. Blunt himself does not appear to have left and was probably taken immediately into custody for his actions, ones for which he later expressed deep regret, admitting his guilt after being charged with yet additional insubordinate acts.[314]

The cause of the men's departure was based on a number of things. Haying was certainly one of them, but Miller explained to Lucretia that it was also because of "small wages," in addition to "their property at home suffering," compounded by the local inhabitants making them "very uneasy." A storm had also recently passed through their hometowns, inflicting severe harm; "the roads and bridges were very much damaged, and many bridges torn away. All the bridges between Middletown and Poultney…were carried off, and some mills and mill dams received material damage," which may have contributed to their collective discomfort. Miller himself was anxious about the events and was requesting permission for a furlough, which Williams continued to deny because, as Miller wrote, "the eyes of everyone are upon him & he must oblige everyone to do his duty."[315]

Williams immediately wrote to a William Fox of Wallingford requesting his assistance in searching out the deserting troops at their homes and convincing them to return. Fox did exactly that and wrote to Miller that he met up with Vail and, between the two of them, had traveled to the men's homes in Danby, Tinmouth and Wallingford. While discussing with them their need to return immediately to their duty, the soldiers described other hardships they had been encountering, specifically "soap, candles, and such things the men say they have not had any since they have been there." While there does appear to have been a failure in supplying the infantry, a cavalry lieutenant accompanying them disagreed with their allegations, reporting that "the provisions are good and wholesome." Fox was successful in convincing the men to return, but only after promising them that they would not be punished, a condition Williams allowed him to bestow. Unaware of it at the time, their commander, Joel Harmon, had just issued a "Ninety Dollars Reward" notice to the public for their apprehension, or "five dollars for each, with all reasonable expenses." Fox also ominously warned Miller in his letter that the events of late had the effect of adding "new converts to Federalism"—yet more adherents to the British cause.[316]

Miller himself had also been having difficulty in fulfilling the conflicting demands of enforcing a Republican embargo while relying on troops inclined toward a Federalist philosophy. In walking this fine line, he also experienced an internal conflict, telling him he must appear Federalist to his men while demonstrating an inclination favorable to the administration. Senior officers and high-ranking civilians such as Penniman could openly avow the positive aspects of the embargo in support of their president, but a mid-level officer became a creature caught, essentially, between two worlds. Miller had previously indicated that he was aligned with the Federalists, but his men do not seem to have agreed, as revealed by one correspondent telling him what he heard while the deserters were at home:

> *One report that was circulated by the soldiers who came home to suck was that you had become as haughty and insolent as hell and that they believed (as they expressed it) that you was turning to be a d----d Democrat, which, if I had have believed, I should certainly have been prompted by curiosity to have risked my health on a journey to Swanton to have seen a part at least of the metamorphosing operation to have determined whether the tail and legs existed at any one period of the operation.*[317]

The writer also noted the suspicious favorable treatment accorded to Merrill for his treasonous conduct, and this, together with reports indicating "much property being taken which has all or nearly all been retaken" by the smugglers, raised questions of possible "treachery in the officers" ranks.

Certainly, there was no such thing taking place, but Miller was personally paying a toll for recent events. Following the desertions, and before the men's return, on July 18, 20 and 21, he made several purchases of alcohol—specifically, four quarts of highly alcoholic spirits, wine and rum (costing $1.92). Whether it was to share with those men remaining behind to ensure their continued support or was personally consumed is not known, but the company paymaster now became the victim of yet more abuse, this time at the hands of one of his own intoxicated privates, William Randall. The soldier reportedly said that "Miller received $200 a week more than his wages…Said Maj. Williams received more & Penniman more still," but when confronted, he responded that "he never said so or if he did he was drunk & that he had no reason to say or think so."

Regardless of the particular circumstance, Miller took no chances and sought out reassurances from his superiors that he remained in good standing. Accordingly, on July 22 and 25, Penniman and Williams each wrote out similar attestations in his support, with the collector stating (emphasis in original):

> *Whereas it is understood that certain reports are in circulation unfavorable to the military character of Lt. Miller, I do hereby certify that since his*

arrival at this station in the service of the United States his conduct has been prompt and directed in the support of the laws of his country, that he has strictly, fairly, and firmly attended to the instructions given him for which he deserves and receives my warmest <u>thanks</u> and <u>respect</u> both as an officer and a gentleman.[318]

The discomfort others may have had with Miller remained, and whether it was for these events, the degree and manner of his oversight of his men, embarrassment by his captain at the desertions or simply ill will between the two, only a couple of months later he sought outside counsel to determine why a divide had arisen between them. The issue appears to have been Miller's approaching Harmon for permission to train his men following their return home, and when he had not received any response, Harmon issued a "warning" against him. Miller then explained the situation to a fellow officer and was told in response that it was not his fault for failing to train when he had not received any orders to do so, further stating, "Your Capt. not conversing with you I think is an unheard of thing. At any rate, it is ungentleman like."[319] In any event, on July 23, Miller finally received permission from Williams to take a ten-day leave of absence, indicating that he was absent from the area at the time of the impending murders.[320]

The *Black Snake* and its crew continued on violating the embargo, and while Miller dealt with his desertions, and Pratt, working with the federal artillerists on the Point, monitored the passage onto the Richelieu River, they took advantage of that other water corridor to the east extending into Canada. On July 15, they transported a significant amount of potash, contained in forty barrels, up the east side of Alburgh and into Missisquoi Bay, landing it on Canadian shores.[321] This was, perhaps, the incident in which the boat was intercepted by a small contingent of government troops, commanded by Joseph Stannard, who was not able to take it into custody. However, other troops were not entirely without success at the time and seized between three and four hundred barrels of ash along the border.

In the meantime, a Maine newspaper lamented the ongoing counterfeiting problem it was experiencing ("would it not be well for government to punish everyone, detected in this villainy, with death?") and told of two Norwich, Vermont men recently apprehended for manufacturing "a spurious kind of indigo. It is so ingeniously made as to render it difficult by the appearance to be distinguishable from the genuine, but by analysis, it is found to be composed of clay, starch, charcoal, and indigo."[322] Clearly, opportunities for illegal conduct abounded, limited only by the imaginations of those so inclined in this environment devoid of effective enforcement. The benefits remained substantial, as a Bennington paper described the profits being derived by those acting in opposition to the embargo—specifically, the Federalists. After first giving an account of an eyewitness to the presence of "new roads [being] cut across the province line in every direction" for the smugglers' benefit, the paper excoriated them in the same manner that another had in belittling the Green Mountain Yeomanry for their two-faced protestations of innocence while violating the law:

> *Never were a people more industrious than the Federalists on our frontiers—their eyes are shut while dividing the golden proceeds of an excellent trip—all in* honest *speculation day and night; once in a while, to be sure, they rest an hour or two to tell the President how dreadfully the embargo distresses them—then to their smuggling again at a sweating rate. Never did a people bear* burthens *with such heroic fortitude—for they are actually grunting under the heavy pressure of cash. A parcel of federal officers some time since insisted on telling the people how patriotic and courageous they were; they made complaint of accusations against them; nobody had accused the officers, but doubtless they* [thought] *somebody might accuse them of something, and so they did exactly right by resenting it beforehand.*[323]

But Jefferson was not fooled by their duplicity, firmly of the opinion that "of the monarchial federalists I have no expectations. They are incurables, to be taken care of in a mad house, if necessary."[324]

Jefferson was beginning to understand the hardships his embargo imposed but also strongly cautioned against leniency in its enforcement or in efforts to ferret out suspicious activities of others used as "a cover for the crimes against their country which unprincipled adventurers are in the habit of committing." Now, together with the vigilant Gallatin, he vigorously advocated for the government to "harass the unprincipled agents," punishing as many of the smugglers as it could. But it also took a toll on him; Gordon Wood concludes that during this time, Jefferson was becoming "confused and sometimes desperate" in his obsession with the embargo's enforcement.

Jefferson was also loathe to consider the possibility of repeating recent history in New York. As described by Gallatin following a meeting he had with Governor Daniel Tompkins, "I had a long conference with the governor, and stated your reluctance to issue another proclamation declaring a part of this state in a state of insurrection. He felt the force of the observation."[325]

For the public, bewildered by the course of events, Jefferson's vision was increasingly being called into question:

> We have heard it asserted that Mr. Jefferson was a great mathematician, that he could calculate an eclipse by his head, without the use of figures—we cannot tell whether this is true or not, with regard to eclipses of the sun and moon, but he has most certainly given unequivocal proof that he can calculate and created an eclipse of the United States, which he has contrived to render visible, and almost total—and if he will now have the goodness to calculate its duration, or tell us when the period of political darkness will cease, he will confer a lasting benefit on our citizens, even if he were to leave it to future philosophers to investigate the causes, and explain the consequences, of this singular phenomenon.[326]

Unfortunately, even if Jefferson could have foretold what was about to take place, events had progressed so far and so fast that he would not have time to stop them.

COMPARED WITH THE PROBLEMS Alex Miller encountered, Benjamin Pratt's company on Windmill Point appears to have been relatively compliant during July, with only a single deserter, Sergeant James Houghton, listed as missing from his sixty-three-man company. Their monthly pay period ended on Sunday, the thirty-first, and the roll describes what each man received, ranging from $40.00 for Pratt down to $6.66 for each of the privates.[327] Since Paymaster Miller was on a leave of absence, somebody else assumed those duties, counted out each dollar and penny and looked each man in the eye as he passed it over, not realizing that this was the last time two of them would ever stand in that line again. They had only hours to live.

That same day, on the other side of the Alburgh peninsula, lumber raftsman Van Duysen's former employee, Josiah Edson, and six other armed men glided across the border, southbound out of Missisquoi Bay on their way to the Onion River to pick up another load of potash. The crew of the *Black Snake* had been most fortunate recently and experienced several successful runs into Canada as they openly dared anyone to try and stop them. Watching eyes noted their presence, and word was dispatched immediately to Penniman telling him of their return.

5

THE GANG FROM
THE NORTH

The name of William Chace Harrington (1756–1814) is ubiquitous
throughout these times, and he was perhaps the most noteworthy
individual participating in the many important, and mundane, events taking
place in the community. The simplistic description of him as "an able
strong-minded lawyer of the old school" hardly does justice to his many
unsung contributions to virtually every level of Burlington's population.[328]
The fortunate survival of one of his several account books, containing over
250 detail-filled pages identifying many names and dates and describing
matter-of-fact credits and debits, reveals the presence of a rich vibrancy
in the community not previously incorporated into its story. Because of
Harrington's close involvement with local affairs, as further detailed in
the town's "Records of Town Meetings," he also appears as one of the
principal individuals taking on the burdensome responsibility of assisting
the less fortunate. Spread out over the many pages of these documents, we
learn of not only his seemingly innumerable number of court cases but also
lists of virtually hundreds of transactions involving the purchase of goods
and materials for the less well off, offset by credits allowed for services they
provided in exchange.[329]

Harrington's personal history before his arrival in Vermont from
Connecticut following the war is obscure. His family first took up residency
just south of Burlington, in Shelburne, where the first census identifies him
as the head of a household occupied by three other individuals. In 1791,
while serving as a major in the Third Division of Militia as aide de camp to

General Ira Allen, he became Chittenden County's second state's attorney, holding that position until 1795. He moved to Burlington that year as one of the town's first settlers and worked as clerk during the original proprietors' meetings. Harrington then served for a distinguished period between 1798 and 1811 as state's attorney, during which time the 1800 census reveals his household increased to thirteen individuals.[330] He also served as town selectman between 1797 and 1800, 1804 and 1805, 1807 and 1808 and in 1811; as a representative to the General Assembly on five separate occasions; as a trustee of the University of Vermont between 1800 and 1810 (as treasurer for nine of those years); was one of the founding members of the First Society for Social and Public Worship in Burlington in 1805; and was a member of the Governor's Council between 1812 and 1814.

In 1807, Harrington described himself as possessing a modest estate consisting of a clock, a watch, two horses, three cows, one yoke of oxen, a house and eighty-two acres of improved land. In August, he took part in building Staniford's new jail and charged the town $35.40 for providing twenty-two pounds of nails, six thousand bricks and the use of a team for two days; the labor presumably came from individual(s) indebted to him. That same year, Harrington, together with Moses Catlin and five other men, became a justice of the peace, a position he held simultaneously with his position as state's attorney, which allowed him an expansive role in the approaching unrest, displaying the attributes of a "thorough-going Democrat" and "genuine disciple of the Jeffersonian school."[331] Notwithstanding later probate records revealing he actually possessed a substantial estate, Harrington maintained a modest lifestyle throughout his life, listing his possessions in 1813, the year before his death, as including an additional house, five acres and one more cow.

Burlington attracted many new arrivals in the opening years of the nineteenth century, many lacking either the means or ability that would allow them to succeed in a frontier environment, forcing the town to quickly recognize it needed to institute measures to control their burgeoning numbers. In November 1807, problems reached such crisis proportions that Harrington and fellow selectmen warned a town meeting to find a solution to deal with the "many lewd, idle and disorderly persons now in, and are continually coming [to town]…who not only disturb the peace, but have already occasioned great expense." Their proposed resolution concerned whether to build, purchase or hire a house of corrections, or workhouse, with appropriate personnel, "for the purpose of confining and setting to work the poor…and also all such vagrants, lewd, idle & disorderly persons as are or shall come to reside." After studying the matter closely, the town chose not to build any additional facility but to make use of the jail instead and appointed its overworked sheriff as overseer of the workhouse in addition to his other responsibilities.

Confining the indigent was not the only recourse available to them, as a revived 1801 law (lasting until 1817) also allowed officials to "warn out," or order to leave, those deemed unwelcome. By this time, the application of the distasteful provisions of New England's long-standing warning out process allowing for the forcible removal of people beyond the town's limits had evolved, providing for new, enlightened application. Now, it was a routine matter for new arrivals, regardless of their background, to receive such notices within their first year of residency simply as an administrative convenience to avoid having to provide for them at a later time should they become destitute or otherwise needful of community services. Should officials delay in serving the pro forma notice to beyond the one-year limitation, they automatically became entitled to make their claims, so conscientious selectmen always sought to make sure warnings were issued in a timely manner to avoid later claims of negligence. Even so, while the use of physical force was indeed rare, in 1812, Ebenezer Brown received three dollars from the town for "removing Noah Smith."

Taking full advantage of their authority, in 1804, selectmen ordered the constable to serve eleven individuals and families with their warnings, including Sally, "a negro woman," and her child, both residing at Sheriff Staniford's home. Between 1800 and 1820, the federal census reveals his household increased from four to eight persons, including two "slaves" and three others engaged in manufactures, presumably his distillery business. In March 1807, eighteen more individuals, many with families, including single women and men and "Edward Butler (a negro man), his wife & family," received their orders to depart. That December, Harrington and other selectmen ordered an additional four individuals and families to go. The following May 1808, another twenty-five received their orders, including the man who built Cyrus Dean's gallows later that fall—Content Hallock and his wife and family. The many orders continued on: thirty-one in 1809, twenty-three in 1810, seventeen in 1811, eleven in 1812 and over sixty in 1813, resulting in the denial of public benefits to well over two hundred new arrivals.[332]

Those duties aside, Harrington apparently found the courtroom a comfortable change. Of the many hundreds of cases filed during these times, few names, if any, appear more frequently than his, indicating the overriding importance that litigation provided for creditors requiring support in an economy largely dependent on debtors paying their obligations in a timely manner. But his involvement extended beyond mere representation of a particular party to his own suits for payment of amounts owed to him. He also pursued cases brought by others and obtained their particular interests, perhaps through a reduced purchase price or in satisfaction of a debt they might also have owed to him. The numerous cases and frequency of judgments rendered in his favor suggest he simply could not both remain in the courtroom and arrange for the collection of monies owed to him. Accordingly, he associated himself with Isaac Webb, Esquire, of Charlotte, who assisted in the suits and traveled about the county lodging the necessary executions he had obtained with town clerks and took in whatever money he could (his account book lists no fewer than 112 instances of the two working together between 1804 and 1811), for which Harrington paid him a moiety, or equal part of any recovery.

One of his earlier cases demonstrates his desire, despite disagreements with a client, to conduct himself in an ethically correct manner. It concerned an 1802 suit brought on behalf of a Colonel James Sawyer against "Seeley Bennett & his bail," indicating that Staniford's ever-present deputy had experienced his own particular problems at an earlier time. The records do not reveal the exact nature of the claim, but Harrington wrote to Sawyer, telling him that because a dispute had arisen between the two of them, he could no longer represent him. The two men appear to have served alongside each other in the militia, as Colonel Harrington assured his former client that "with respect to the business necessary to be performed in your official capacity that may arise out of my office, [it] will be continued as usual."[333]

The September 1805 term of court named Harrington as plaintiff in six separate matters. On December 4, he entered into an agreement with Daniel Barnes for the delivery of 152 bushels of "good dry clean winter wheat" on January 20, 1807. When Barnes and the wheat failed to appear that day, only three days later, in predicable fashion, Harrington initiated suit. That month, a particularly busy one, he brought an additional three suits, one naming Seeley Bennett again as defendant, against several individuals for having guaranteed the appearance of absconding prisoners and another in a debt-related matter.

Sheriff Staniford also appeared in court at the time, and the following month, he brought his own suit in one matter and, in turn, defended himself in no fewer than six other cases. These included various allegations, two brought by merchant Moses Catlin, of neglect in the execution of his duties for the failure to serve papers and faulty execution of judgments; frequently, the plaintiffs in these cases prevailed. Such allegations against Staniford had become more routine, and it does not appear that even prior suits, such as those in 1805 involving additional instances of neglect (service of papers and allowing seized cows to escape) and trespass (improper taking of a horse) against him had failed to remedy whatever deficient practices existed in his department. The unfortunate death of one of his children from dysentery in August 1806 no doubt added to his worries.[334]

While Harrington was frequently in court, in other instances he attempted to settle accounts through less formal means. Between 1804 and 1809, he represented George Deming in several matters (including one filed against customs inspector/trader Nathan Haswell and partner John Peaslee), which resulted in a disagreement over the amount Deming owed for Harrington's services. After receiving an unfavorable decision from two men chosen to resolve the dispute requiring him to pay Deming $59.63, Harrington made a revealing entry in his account book describing his philosophy toward those who sought to do him harm. He lashed out at "Deming's charges" against him as "the most extraordinary of any ever before exhibited, I think it my duty never to have any further deal with him. It however," he continued, "is my duty to treat him as a neighbor, but I cannot view him as an honest man, & as it becomes my duty not to injure or oppress him, my intention is to exercise all that charity which duty impels hoping that he will ere long see that a dishonest course will lead him & his family into many difficulties."

Harrington had a compassionate side that touched many less well off. He was solicitous of minorities and, as early as 1803 and continuing for the next several years, employed several members of the black community as laborers in varying capacities, beginning with Thomas Putnam, described in his accounts as a "negro of Burlington." Putnam and his unnamed wife received many goods paid for by Harrington in the next few years, offset by entries indicating work performed on his behalf. In October 1803, Harrington noted that they had moved into his house for an undisclosed period of time. The next year, he debited Putnam for having broken a hoe. In 1805, Harrington charged him for the cost of pasturing his cow on his land and eighty-four cents of a town tax paid on his behalf. Harrington frequently negotiated lengths of employment (usually seasonal), paying a specific amount of money in return. For Putnam in 1805, that included working for a seven-month period and receiving pay of eleven dollars a month, a situation the two repeated the following year. Harrington indicates that their relationship continued on through at least 1811, as Putnam continued to perform various services in exchange for the payment of various goods.

In May 1807, Harrington employed local black man John Miers, paying him ten dollars a month for five months ("if I like him"), while also obtaining the services of "Peter the Frenchman," probably the "woodchopper" identified in his journal; Peter and his wife had received their warning out notices in 1804. Of the several blacks identified, only Miers appears literate, signing his name with a flourish on one occasion when he and Harrington reconciled their accounts. Beginning in April 1807 and lasting through the coming troubled summer and on into 1809, Andrew Miers (relationship unknown) agreed to work for Harrington, also receiving ten dollars a month. One of Harrington's cryptic entries concerned a four-dollar expenditure made on his behalf in August 1808 "for our journey," and as events unfolded after the murders taking place that month, it may have referred to the two of them traveling to Rutland for court purposes. Harrington makes no indication of why, but in October, he paid thirty-one cents for a quart of cider spirits on behalf of "John Ceasor, negro of Burlington." He was also involved with several other white men at the time, and between November and April 1808, John Brigham worked on his Colchester Point property harvesting corn, potatoes, flax and firewood and taking care of his stock, while young Nehemiah Sutton moved in for an eight-month period and hacked out an impressive 108 rods (approximately 1,782 feet) of rail fencing.

Prince Robinson certainly stood out in the minority community, a partially blind man with a noticeable scar crossing his face and a limping gait that could not be ignored. Robinson, without a known birth date, had been taken from Africa before the war and sold into slavery somewhere on Long Island. When the war arrived, for the promise of freedom at its conclusion if he joined the army, he enlisted as a private in Captain John Waite's company, part of Green's "Black Regiment." Unfortunately, during a battle at Crumpond (Yorktown Heights, New York), where his company was "cut up and nearly destroyed," he suffered a disfiguring saber slashing that extended from his temple, over an eye (resulting in its blindness) and through one side of his nose. He was also injured by either a cutting sword or gunshot, leaving him limping on one leg and with one of his arms rendered useless. Though Robinson was severely injured, Jacob Sawyer, a white man from Rutland, took him up and carried him in his arms from the battlefield to camp, where he received aid, and after regaining some semblance of health, he transferred into a white regiment.

While serving on Long Island and before his wounding, Robinson met and married a woman named Ann. In 1840, described as being "one hundred years and upwards" old at the time, she sought pension benefits as the surviving spouse of an invalid veteran (Robinson died in 1830) and submitted an affidavit from acquaintance Jesse Gove, a Rutland attorney and clerk of the U.S. District Court in Vermont (1809–42). His signature, and Solomon Miller's in the state court files, appears on many court documents relating to the proceedings during this time. Gove recounted that Robinson told him of his military service, his wounding and that Ann, "spry & well looking," was present on one occasion. "I remember the question put to them, how she came to marry such a <u>lame</u> <u>negro</u> [emphasis in original], to which, the reply was, that they were married while Prince was in the Army and before he got hurt." Gove further related that Robinson was "extremely ignorant and illiterate" and that his physical condition only worsened over the years as he became totally blind and had to be led. However, Robinson's lack of sight does not appear to have slowed down the couple; they produced three children, moved to Rutland in 1795 and then on to Burlington, returned to Rutland in 1813 and finally settled in Cavendish.[335]

The eight-dollar-a-month invalid pension initially granted to Robinson appears to have been reduced to five dollars, and between 1806 and 1808, Harrington's records reveal that he aided Robinson in efforts to get that sum returned to its higher rate and in obtaining necessary goods on his behalf (corn, flour, potatoes, beef, pork, spirits, rum, cords of wood, boots), including paying small amounts of money to Thomas Putnam and John Miers, presumably for assisting their disabled friend. For his efforts, Harrington charged a very small sum of sixty-five cents (for "processing his money"). He reimbursed his expenses through Robinson's pension of thirty dollars every six months, paid to him by U.S. marshal John Willard.

Also appearing alongside those charges against the United States in October 1808 following the murders is the sum of $47.50 for services on the nation's behalf, which appear directly related to Harrington's involvement in the court proceedings that arose. His involvement with the black community for this time period concludes with entries made in 1810 and 1811 for "Mary Pempleton a negro woman of Burlington," whom he employed to do domestic chores, including "whitewashing my house, $1," who lived in his home with her rent offset by her labors.

Several women experiencing difficulties at the time also received assistance from Harrington in various ways, including on those days he dealt with the murders. In 1802, he represented Deborah Stone in her suit against Ethiel Stone for, as a legislative committee described it, "refusing to render her that justice to which she conceived herself entitled" upon her becoming pregnant. Deborah was jailed because she could not pay the costs associated with her unsuccessful initial claim against Ethiel and was forced to seek permission from the government in order to continue her suit; her request was denied.[336] Miss Betsy Currier's suit against Luc Johnson in 1809 did not result in any income for Harrington, who worked pro bono, noting she was "a poor girl & I give up my charges." In other cases, he assumed a dual role of not only defending women like Mary Pitcher but also acting on their behalf following the death of a spouse. In the case of Betsey Coit, who died in 1804, Harrington remained closely involved with the ongoing payments to maintain her young children, ending with an 1811 entry concerning daughter Nancy. He noted for a five-dollar payment, "'Tis best to be silent on this claim." Betsey Chapman nursed Jack Dagley, "a poor Dutch stranger," seeing to it that he received many quarts of wine for his well-being, all of which Harrington listed as charges against the town selectmen, on which board he served, as part of the community's responsibility to care for the poor, needy and destitute.

Other women came to work for him domestically over the years, with Rhoda Castle moving into his home in June 1803 for several weeks and then Betsey White in May 1809 (he paid her eighty-four cents a week). Harrington, by force of habit, would reckon even the smallest expense while ungrudgingly forgiving their payment. Betsey Chapman, with no resources of her own, continued to help Harrington and his family. In April 1810, he recognized "sundry services by her for my family in sickness and sundry bottles of beer during the time of her living in my house for which I do hereby give her a generous credit & do not intend to have her distracted for the balance due me."

In the fall of 1808, in the very midst of the upheaval brought on by the murders, Harrington's family contracted an illness that strained his ability to meet his civic, work and domestic responsibilities and which ultimately resulted in the death of his thirty-two-year-old wife, Roxselana. The victims of the illness—perhaps dysentery, which had carried away Staniford's son two years earlier and Cornelius Van Ness's son, Peter, on July 1—demanded care and attention. "The indisposition of his lady" prevented Harrington from meeting with Deputy Collector Nathan Haswell on one occasion during the trials, but he continued on with the work.[337] November and December entries in his account book describe payments to Betsey Harrington (relationship unknown) for "taking care with others of my sick family [for] 14 weeks" and to Thomas Pardo for assisting during a ten-day period with his son.

For Harrington, the foreboding presence of counterfeiters and smugglers on his doorstep did not prevent him from pursuing other legal interests at the same time. In December 1807 and January 1808, he instituted suits against no fewer than eight individuals for failure to repay debts owed to him. Between January and April 1808, he entered into at least four separate agreements with as many men for the repayment of money, all of which later devolved into inevitable suits for failure to meet their obligations. In March, he got involved with various aspects in settling the accounts of local doctor William Bostwick, who, with his wife and three children, rented a house from him. Bostwick had been returning to Burlington from Montreal over the ice in a loaded sleigh when the ice gave way on the Richelieu River, near St. John, and he drowned. Staniford also became involved with those particular proceedings and acted as a court-appointed commissioner, dealing with his estate and providing notice to creditors of Bostwick's insolvency.[338]

On April 27, around the time Woolsey issued instructions to revenue officers not to fear using force in their work, Harrington wrote from Burlington apologizing to a judge for his failure to appear at the Windsor circuit court. He explained, "My health will not admit of my going." A month later, he appeared in court representing a member of Alburgh's Mott family, Joseph, in suits involving the frequently named rioter Amos Morrill Jr. While the Rutland militia was marching northward, on May 28, he received a judgment against a Manassah Sawyer, of Charlotte, in a matter involving the trifling sum of $22.80. Harrington then obtained the appropriate paperwork from the court on June 2 permitting the sheriff to execute on that amount and turned the matter over to Staniford on June 20. On August 1, 1808, the very day that the crew of the *Black Snake* embarked on its deadly mission, Seeley Bennett was occupied in arresting Sawyer and putting him into the Burlington jail, where Sawyer was allowed liberty of the gaol after a friend, Nathaniel Newell, agreed to act as surety for his remaining on the premises. As events unfolded, matters within the jail itself became increasingly complicated with the presence of many prisoners and guarding soldiers, and on October 20, Sawyer escaped, leaving Newell automatically responsible for his bond, and as regularly happened in such cases, Harrington brought suit against him for payment.[339]

The relationship between Harrington, acting in his many and varied capacities, and Staniford, the sheriff, is complex. Harrington's account book reveals many instances of his involvement on Staniford's behalf between 1804 and 1814 in paying for goods, pasturing his horse, the use of a Burlington house and three acres of land between April 1808 and January 1811 and many lawsuits. These include not only those that concerned the defense of his client but also those in which he brought suit against him.

Their settling of accounts included amounts won or lost in court judgments but also fees that Harrington owed to Staniford for serving court papers, creating a confusing crediting and debiting of amounts owed to each other. This primitive legal system condoned an attorney's taking a position both for his client and then against him, yet the two men appear to have maintained an amicable relationship, as they understood these as strictly business necessities foisted on them by the unique economic situation existing at the time with minimal regard, if any, for potential conflicts of interest or as being ethically suspect. A further examination of Harrington's accounts also reveals the incongruous roles he played in these years as he interacted with people implicated in the murders, representing those such as merchant Samuel Fitch (in 1804) and militia officer Samuel Mix (in 1811).

Only four months after Harrington had defended Staniford before a jury, on June 30, 1808, he brought suit against him in yet another matter, alleging that his deputy, Abiram Hurlburt, had failed to execute on a judgment he received against two men the preceding February for debt. In the very midst of contending with the smuggling issue, Harrington served Staniford with papers on July 25, and the matter proceeded through the court simultaneously with the upcoming murder trials. In September, Harrington received a favorable result of $206.67 in damages, together with $9.31 in costs. Then, in two additional matters, on July 8 and 23, Harrington brought cases against four more men for bonds they signed on behalf of escaping prisoners. Staniford had the initial right to bring these actions but assigned them to Harrington, perhaps in recognition of Hurlburt's neglect and as an effort to offset the inevitable judgment that would be rendered against him. For Staniford, these months remained unkind, as he found himself a defendant in yet more suits (even one brought later by Alexander Miller's brother, court clerk Sol Miller) involving the escape of a prisoner and Deputy Bennett's reported failure to serve an execution and making a false entry onto a court document.[340]

Yet even with these suits coming precisely during these tragic times, Harrington continued to bring additional charges concerning his personal interests, and he put on an incredible display of versatility as he simultaneously became involved in his role as state's attorney and justice of the peace in dealing with the *Black Snake* murders. Perhaps it was because he headed a household requiring the care and feeding of twelve other individuals as his wife lay dying, or, compassion aside, perhaps it was because there were so many others depending on his fulfilling his own obligations, but he was propelled into these suits. Regardless, it is clear that despite one's station in life, William Harrington never let an opportunity for the vindication of an unwarranted harm, or personal gain, to pass him by.

WHEN THE VARIOUS TRIALS of the murderers took place over the course of the next few months, their attorneys sought to introduce evidence explaining their conduct because of other, unidentified individuals sponsoring their efforts. Calling them "the gang who came from the north," they argued that their clients were but "ignorant persons" who had received "their education in their country" and were deserving of having their lack of learning, intelligence and sophistication taken into account as they considered their cause. Prohibited by the court from pursuing such a defense, the attorneys were reduced to making veiled references to the presence of influential others, saying that the killers had been encouraged, "instigated," "courted and countenanced on all sides to do the deed." "Can you believe," one attorney argued, that these men "would have entered this village and killed men[?] Why is it so[?]"; he asked further, should "the men who stand at the head of the insurrection escape punishment[?]" and explained that the smugglers acted as they had because "they have been told that this law [the embargo] was unconstitutional, by men who could lead them whether they would."

That there were others who stood to gain, exhorting on and facilitating the smugglers with their illegal conduct, is beyond question, and even the government attorneys prosecuting the cases had to admit as much. David Fay, Vermont's federal district attorney who had come to Burlington to assist Harrington in the many cases, argued that the defendants should not be allowed to deflect their culpability. He told the court "that others are implicated may be true. But it can be of no advantage to the prisoners to have them discovered. And at any rate, it is to be hoped the grand jury will do their duty faithfully." Fay sought to keep the trials' focus on the defendants' specific conduct and not allow for the introduction of, from the state's perspective, irrelevant evidence, while at the same time keeping open the possibility that the grand jury would later pursue charges against anyone else involved in criminal activity.

Exactly who was pushing Truman Mudget, a purported militia officer and the leader of this gang arriving in the *Black Snake* from the north, on with his smuggling was never revealed. It might have been that he was working in an independent manner and simply associated himself with other groups of men as circumstances required. However, as events unfolded, it was clear that outside influences, those located closer to Burlington, contributed significantly to the approaching mayhem. Consistent with the timing of prior trips taking place in the opening days of June and July, Mudget and his men now embarked on their final voyage, bringing the two interests closer together.

On August 1, 1808, Mudget had a problem. He was apprehensive, worrying about the escalating tensions with government officials beginning to display less hesitancy to resort to violence than they had in the past, and accumulating adequate manpower to counter that threat was of concern to him. On this day, he was "slender of hands," as he explained to Elkinah Perkins when he appeared on his doorstop an hour before sunrise on Hogg Island, in Highgate, wearing his distinctive white hat and waking Perkins and his wife from their sleep. He had just successfully recruited local resident William Noaks and now insisted "very hard" of Perkins to join him and the others waiting down by the water's edge, sitting in the *Black Snake*. Perkins might have been hesitant at first, but after one of the crew told him, "Get in, it is time to be off," he agreed, settling in while also noting the ubiquitous presence of two gallons of rum.

The prior day, the crew had lost the services of informer Josiah Edson, who departed the boat when it reached Hogg Island on its southward journey from Canadian waters in Missisquoi Bay. Following his service on the Van Duysen raft, Edson became a member of the *Black Snake* crew in the interim and was involved in three smuggling trips northward carrying pot and pearl ash. Those facts, together with more detailed information concerning the actions of the Hoxies and Taylors, became known only in the days immediately following the murders when Edson voluntarily approached Buel at Windmill Point, telling him of his involvement with the smugglers and agreeing to provide information in exchange for not being prosecuted. He was immediately taken into custody and sent off with a military escort to Haswell's attention in Burlington to be turned over to Harrington for further debriefing. It is through close examination of his ensuing testimony, given before at least one grand jury and during several trials, together with that provided by two dozen additional witnesses, that these unfortunate events can be more fully understood.[341] It also reveals the difficult situation authorities were in at the time as they struggled to stay on top of events and desperately sought to accumulate valuable intelligence of the smugglers' intentions.

With the onus of enforcement falling squarely on Penniman's two deputies, coming at a time when there were no clear directions from Washington on how to do it, Buel and Haswell were forced to find creative ways to recruit reliable assistance and to then compensate these men. In June, Champlain's

Collector Woolsey hired no fewer than eight additional inspectors spread out along the lake corridor on the New York side, which may have influenced Buel's and Haswell's more immediate actions. Dr. James W. Wood was a respected Alburgh physician, having moved to the area around 1802, when he was involved in inoculating the local population for smallpox. In 1807, he was elected town representative to the legislature and also became an assistant judge in the Grand Isle Court, serving through 1808. It was during this time that Buel approached Wood, who, together with James M. Camp, also of Alburgh, agreed to act as inspectors under him. Eventually, after Buel instituted an unconventional method to compensate them, each man came to play an important role in his undermining, resulting in his dismissal from office. Before that unfortunate event occurred, Wood acted as a conduit of information to Buel, coming from at least one informant. As noted, Penniman had previously engaged the services of Joshua Day for the local militia. Day, upon his discharge, went immediately into the smuggling business with Samuel Mott. However, his purported participation in that activity gives every indication of being a ruse, and he was providing information directly to Wood, which presumably reached Buel.[342]

In Burlington, Haswell also recruited an individual to assist him in learning what was going on, explaining that, at the time,

> *we had many difficulties to encounter during the Embargo: learning that an illicit and smuggling business was carrying on in the neighborhood of Onion River, I requested a Mr. Asa Rice who lived on the Intervale (and who was a staunch friend of the government formerly from Bennington and brother of my father's wife)…to keep watch and give me notice of any smuggling boats come up the River.*[343]

The choice of Rice was indeed fortunate as he came to play an important role in approaching events on the Intervale.

Following his departure from Mudget, Edson became immediately involved with yet another smuggling operation being conducted a short distance to the south, in the area of Middle Hero, which involved, once again, the Taylors and Hoxies. As Mudget was moving his men to the south, these two other groups, made up of approximately a dozen men, assembled together to transport fifty barrels of potash, fifty barrels of pearl ash and fifty barrels of pork from Alburgh, past Windmill Point, ending in St. John. The specific unfolding of those events on August 1 is not identified, but in his affidavit filed in support of charges against John and Ezekiel Taylor; Frederick, John and Job Hoxie; and two others, Penniman alludes to violence taking place when the men "with force & arms feloniously commit[ted] the crime of High Treason against the United States by levying war against them."[344] Clearly, things were about to erupt on the lake, and while the final answer is unknown, a relevant question concerns the possibility that the Hoxie/Taylor and Mudget/Mott contingencies coordinated their efforts in some fashion in order to split up and disperse sparse militia resources, thereby increasing the chances of their individual successes.

Edson readily admitted that he was a crew member of the *Black Snake* on the last day of July (when the Rutland militiamen were receiving their monthly pay), and as they had done previously, the men were on their way to the Onion River/Burlington area to secure yet another load. When he boarded the boat in Canada, he found that in addition to Mudget there were five others, including Mott and Day, twenty-seven-year-old Cyrus B. Dean (Mott and Dean were Mudget's brothers-in-law), Slocum Clark and Captain Josiah Pease. A later description provided by Haswell of some of the men identified Mott as being "a stout dark complexioned person, about six feet high." Noaks was "about twenty three years of age, a stout man about five feet six inches high, light complexion, had on a mix [*sic*] home made short coat, tow cloth trousers and a wool hat." Clark was "six feet high, 22 years old, had on black homemade clothes with boots," and Pease was "of common size, had on a jean coat and pantaloons about thirty five years old." A description of Mudget made in 1810 following his escape from the Burlington jail for an unrelated murder stated that he was "about middling size, dark complexion, black eyes."[345] For their efforts, the crew members were to receive between ten and twelve dollars for each trip, while Mudget was entitled to between five and six dollars per barrel—a substantial amount of money when considering the many barrels the vessel was capable of hauling.

Edson further recounted that the boat always carried some form of armaments but that on this occasion they had been noticeably increased. Now, each of the men had a firearm, with Mudget possessing two. However, the amount of ammunition on board was severely lacking, as demonstrated by the presence of a mere ten bullets. To make up for that weakness, the men planned to travel to Mott's brother's home to procure yet another weapon, one of significantly larger capability. Also present were a number of clubs, estimated to be three feet in length; several poles tipped with spikes; and a large basket of stones, "each about as big as a man's fist." As Edson explained, "The poles I understood were to keep off the revenue boat and the clubs and stones to defend themselves," relating that those weapons were to "defend in case of close employment."

The atmosphere on the *Black Snake* was intense. Edson said "they expected to be attacked by the troops." Mudget displayed some degree of restraint in these early hours, directing the men that in the event of a confrontation, "no man [was] to fire unless they were fired on first by the Revenue, and if they were to wait the orders of the Capt. and if they did fire to fire straight as they could and if [the] Revenue boat came to them, to use their clubs first if they were overtaken." Regardless of any encounter, it was clear to all that their dangerous path might very well require them to fight their way back into Canada. As the day ended on that Sabbath, Edson departed for his next venture, the *Black Snake* crew settled in on the shore for the evening and the troops on Windmill Point rested.

THE FOLLOWING DAY, A Monday, as Mudget went about his recruiting and the Taylors and Hoxies ventured out to levy war against their country, Penniman made a personal appearance at Windmill Point. Word of the smugglers' southward passage had been conveyed to him, forcing him to make a quick decision on his next course of action. He could have simply traveled the short distance to Alexander Miller's militia contingency in Swanton to solicit its assistance, but for some reason—and one that no doubt was in recognition of the troubles Miller had recently faced with his many desertions—he chose to go to the west several miles to the Point for aid.

There, Penniman met with Lieutenant Farrington and discussed with him the fresh intelligence, including information that at that particular moment, as Farrington later testified, the *Black Snake* was "not sufficiently armed and therefore it was concluded she might be taken and no lives lost." From what source Penniman had gained this information is not identified, but as accurate as it might have been in the fact that there was a mere ten bullets on board at that time, it did not convey, or Farrington failed to further disclose in order to explain his conduct, the possibility of the crew obtaining additional firepower.

In order to conduct their work, some customs districts received the services of revenue cutters, each manned variously as the times dictated but which included at the height of tensions a captain, or master; not more than three lieutenants, or mates; and not more than seventy men (a situation particularly applicable to coast-based vessels subject to attachment to the navy). Additionally, the collector was allowed to employ open row and sailboats as needed to assist his inspectors. In 1799, Congress directed that these vessels bear a unique signal in the form of an ensign and pendant to convey to the public their authority to intercede with shipping in the enforcement of customs laws. Oliver Wolcott, then secretary of the treasury, designed an ensign with sixteen vertical stripes (indicating the number of states at the time), alternating red and white colors. The change in direction of the stripes to vertical distinguished it from the nation's flag and revealed that the vessel it was attached to belonged to a civil, and not military, branch of government. The flag's union bore the National Arms insignia, consisting of an American bald eagle grasping a bundle of arrows in one talon and an olive branch in the other.[346]

When particular occasions required it, the captain of such a vessel was authorized to use force to ensure compliance:

> [I]*n case any ship or vessel liable to seizure or examination shall not bring to, on being required, or being chased by any cutter or boat having displayed the pendant and ensign…, it shall be lawful for the captain…to fire at or into such vessel which shall not bring to, after such pendant and ensign shall be hoisted, and a gun shall have been fired by such cutter or boat as a signal.*[347]

When instances of assault, resistance, obstruction or hindrance of an officer occurred, the offender was subject to a $500 fine.[348] While that amount increased from the $200 mandated by a 1791 law, it is notable that there were no criminal provisions addressing instances in which a federal officer was killed while executing his duties.

Now, Penniman ordered Farrington to detach a sergeant and twelve men and to take the cutter *Fly* in pursuit to seize the *Black Snake* and any other vessels he had reason to believe were involved with smuggling. Witness testimony also disclosed that information was conveyed concerning a reward of $100 to the men should they succeed. As events later played out in a Burlington courtroom, each of these facts were recast in some fashion by defense attorneys to argue that the soldiers' actions constituted nothing more than a David versus Goliath situation. Turning the table on the government prosecutors, they forcibly contended that their smuggling clients were involuntarily put into a desperate situation requiring them to defend their property, which was being forcibly taken by others bent on obtaining a reward—men who were simply vicious "armed rioters."

Farrington obtained further instructions that should he encounter the smugglers, as the law dictated, he was "to hoist my flag, then to fire before her bow, then behind her stern and if she did not surrender, to level at her." As a further indication of their authority, the *Fly* bore a distinctive red rim, or bulwark, and Farrington himself wore a red tunic, or "regimental," that made him stand out and played a role in the coming challenge.

Farrington then prepared a list of twelve names from his roster and handed it to one of his four sergeants, David Johnson, ordering him to assemble the men, together with their arms and ammunition. In hindsight, however honorable Farrington might otherwise have been, he was fast approaching the most critical moment of his life and may not have been the best choice to lead the men. As he later explained, "I was determined from the first sailing out that there [be] no blood [shed] if it could be avoided." A witness encountering Farrington the following day had the impression that the lieutenant "appeared to be harmless & said he hoped not to hurt anyone." It was this peaceful, bloodless and timid approach in dealing with the smugglers that might have later raised the concerns of his immediate superior, Benjamin Pratt, who told Farrington's men upon their return to camp that "the lieutenant did not obey his orders."

For the rest of that day, the soldiers made their way to the south, passing around the southern tip of Alburgh's peninsula, or "tongue," and then headed back north. After reaching the area of Missisquoi Bay, they landed and spent the night, not far from where the crew of the *Black Snake* had departed earlier, on the west side of Hogg Island.

After the smugglers picked up Perkins earlier on that same day, they continued on to the south, arriving at the home of Peter Martin, at Martin's Bay, on the eastern shore of North Hero about sunrise. Unknown to either them or the militiamen, at the time they were separated from one another by only a few miles. These next events would significantly increase the smugglers' firepower. They remained at Martin's place until around noon, when they departed and traveled south along the eastern shores of North, Middle and South Hero until they reached the sandbar connecting the southern end of the island to the mainland just north of Burlington. Their destination for the moment was the home of Richard Mott, where brother Samuel said he intended to obtain a large gun, or blunderbuss. In a display of a man intending to protect his property (for he was to have half ownership with Mudget following the cruise), Mott told the crew that he wanted the weapon to be placed on the bow of the *Black Snake*, "which would give a fine rake if attacked" by any revenue boat trying to stop them.

They arrived at the sandbar after dark, and Mott, accompanied by Mudget, walked to Richard's home, returning a short time later carrying the weapon. They displayed it to the men, telling them that Mott had paid fifteen or sixteen dollars for it, and mounted it on the boat's bow. The gun certainly sent a message of devastation to anyone viewing it; measuring a formidable nine feet, four inches in overall length, the barrel itself constituted eight feet, two inches of it, with a jaw-dropping bore of one and one-quarter inches—a diameter midway between a two- and three-gauge caliber. The weapon was referred to variously as a wall gun, wall piece or blunderbuss and was later described by one of the soldiers witnessing its capabilities as a "common French arm." A 1750 French treatise provides additional information concerning these types of weapons, describing a typical one as "a kind of large fusil [formed by melting or casting], supported by an iron hook," used primarily "to fill up the battlements or loop-holes of ancient fortifications."[349] This versatile, albeit heavy and cumbersome, weapon could be called on as needed in quickly changing circumstances to defend various positions under attack by supporting it from above with a suspended hook or resting it on some convenient place, such as a window frame.

However, under the circumstances described by Mudget, it was more likely a so-called punt gun, commonly used in this pre-market hunting period to take down large numbers of water fowl with a single shot. There were already several gun makers working along the Connecticut River and around Lake Champlain at the time, capable of manufacturing such a flintlock weapon out of iron, attaching its large barrel to a shaped stock bound together with several metal bands. A gun of this configuration, weighing in the vicinity of seventy-five pounds, was commonly charged with two hands, cupped together, full of powder poured down the bore's opening, followed by some seven to eight one-ounce lead balls forced into place by a ramrod. For maximum devastation, a hunter could load as many as sixteen balls while using the same amount of powder.

The weapon was then mounted lengthwise in the center of a boat, or punt, perhaps supported by a swivel set into an oarlock, as the hunter crouched down alongside it to minimize his presence along a marshy shore. When birds landed, he quietly maneuvered his boat to an advantageous location before unleashing its charge, propelling the boat backward, while the shot traveled into and out of several of its victims before being spent, leaving dozens dead in its wake. The effect was every bit as devastating as that delivered by canister shell fired from a cannon in which many balls are set loose, making the big gun essentially a form of light artillery. Weapons in hand, the next challenge for the men was to find sufficient shot and powder to make them deadly.

Tuesday morning found the *Black Snake* moving south once again, passing around the neck of land stretching out into the lake north of Burlington (Colchester Point) and circling back, reaching the Onion River around sunrise. At one point, they came upon a Frenchman who sold them fish—possibly Peter the Frenchman, described in Harrington's account book. From there, they began their ascent of the river a few miles eastward, negotiating its several serpentine twists and turns until reaching the home of Magery Joy, located on the south side, a short distance from Burlington Village. There, the men glided onto the nearby landing, alighted and went up to the house, where they confronted its owner. Perhaps it was because Mott had already used the place on previous smuggling ventures that he felt entitled to comfortably demand of Joy that "they wanted to use my house," leaving the man, himself ill with "fever and ague," unable to object.

Meanwhile, the fourteen men of the *Fly* continued in their pursuit, reaching Martin's Bay that morning; they went on shore to eat their own breakfast. Farrington and Johnson then departed from the men and went to nearby Ensign Webb's tavern to inquire if the *Black Snake* had been seen, learning that the smugglers had had indeed gone south the day before, bound for the Onion River. Back on the beach, Peter Martin approached the resting soldiers and inquired what they were about. The testimony he provided at trial on behalf of the smugglers describing the ensuing conversation, countered by two soldiers also present who characterized it as "words of heat" passing between them, was not well received by those present, and he was subsequently "hooted" out of the courtroom.

Martin stated that upon learning of the soldiers' mission, "I told them that I was sorry to hear it as they would kill or be killed…and one soldier said he would not kill anyone, others said they would massacre the whole of them if they resisted." In a second trial, he further related that the soldiers "said they intend[ed] to take the *Snake* even to sacrifice of all the crew." One of those soldiers present at the time, Private James Hays, recounted otherwise:

> *I heard the conversation between the soldiers and Peter Martin. He asked us where we were going, we told him after the* Black Snake. *Some said we had got up before sunrise, he replied "if you meet the* Black Snake *some of you will go to bed before sunset." He inquired if we were going to fire, 5 or 6 of us said "if they fire on us we shall fire & kill them if we can," & then he said if we killed one man the people would rise and he would go & get a thousand men and kill all the men on the Point as it was a rascally thing and the soldiers were sent on to murder people.*[350]

A second soldier, Private Alexander Walker, also emphatically denied Martin's testimony, stating, "I did not hear any conversation of the kind" but that he did hear him make the same threats to rise up with a thousand people to kill everyone on the Point.

Hyperbole and contention aside, there is a portion of Martin's testimony that provides an important reference concerning the involvement of others in the smuggling who were not then on board the *Black Snake*. During his trial, Mott's defense attorney lamented the court's refusal to allow him to introduce testimony demonstrating the existence of these others, stating that "the father of the gentleman who opened this cause" had been prevented from appearing in court. The record does not disclose who this person was, but it appears to have been a reference to Truman Mudget's father, a fact alluded to when Martin testified that, upon hearing of the soldiers' purported threats, "I mentioned it to old Mudget and told him to send word to scuttle the boat and all disperse." Scuttle the boat? Send it to the bottom of the lake? These certainly appear to be the words of someone in a position of authority, indicating that Martin may have been in some decision-making role, capable of influencing the course the younger Mudget was taking. Or he may have been offering friendly, neighborly advice to a father, a man with influence over what his son was doing. Regardless, the soldiers' presence; their mission, no doubt embellished with allegations of massacre and destruction in mind; and their destination were now exposed. Word quickly went out and became known locally, then spread within the Burlington Federalist enclave on the Onion River and, finally, reached the *Black Snake* crew itself.

Upon leaving Martin's Bay, the *Fly* continued to hug the shore of the island in its southerly journey, and when it reached Middle Hero around noon, just as the smugglers were taking over Joy's home, the men saw someone on shore waving a white handkerchief at them. The identity of the man has never been revealed, but it was certainly someone aligned with Republican politics, favorably inclined toward the work that the soldiers were undertaking and also willing in this dangerous environment to provide important intelligence. Upon their meeting, the man confirmed for the soldiers that the *Black Snake* was indeed bound for the Onion River and provided them with the names of those on board. As Sergeant Johnson then related:

> He took leave and told us he would meet us again at the sand bar. We rowed to the sand bar and remained there all night expecting the **Black Snake** would come on. We met this man again at the sand bar and after some talk we were confirmed in the intelligence that the **Black Snake** had gone into Onion River.

But as the soldiers were gathering their information and considering their next move, they were, in turn, being closely watched by others.

In October 1811, Francis Ledgard, of Milton, signed a statement in support of a petition for a pardon he was seeking for his involvement in the upcoming events. In it, he made a number of important statements, many of which were corroborated by the testimony of other witnesses, concerning these hours that substantially reveal there were indeed others, including important community members, as defense attorneys had argued during the trials, involved in facilitating the coming mayhem.

Approximately twenty-three years of age at the time, described as five feet, nine inches tall, with a light complexion, dark brown hair and hazel eyes and originally from Litchfield, Connecticut, Ledgard was, on that very day, working for Joseph Phelps, Esquire, in the area of South Hero. He did not start out intending to do anything more than attend to his own personal interests but quickly became entangled with the smugglers. Since he had outstanding business with merchant Samuel Fitch, Ledgard decided on this day to go into Burlington to find him and settle his account. After heading out on horseback, he came to the sandbar, where he encountered militia colonel and timber raftsman Sam Mix, who told him he had seen the revenue boat pass by and that it was in pursuit of the *Black Snake*.

Mix presents an interesting figure in his role as both a militia commander and business entrepreneur. At that very moment, Silas Hathaway was actively pursuing him for the payment of over $1,000 for failing to fulfill an agreement the two entered into in 1803. It concerned hundreds of thousands of board feet of sawn lumber, cut into one- and two-inch widths, owned by Hathaway, which Mix agreed to transport to the Montreal market via rafts on the lake the next year. When Mix failed to pay money he owed for the transaction, Hathaway began to make demands on him, which later resulted in his obtaining a judgment against Mix in 1809.[351] With that particular matter hanging over him and its potentially devastating impact on his already stretched financial condition from pursuing counterfeiters, he was also a colonel in the local militia, a body of men whose allegiances had already been called into question.

As Ledgard later recounted of their explosive conversation, Mix told him:

If I would leave my horse and take a boat and go up Onion River and give the owner of the Black Snake *information, he would find me a boat and give me the sum of five dollars, and after many persuasive arguments I consented to go.*

He then told me to tell the company belonging to the Black Snake *to go down the river half a mile below their boat and lie in ambush for the revenue boat and fire upon them and kill every man without discrimination, and he would defend them at the expense of his whole regiment.*[352]

Further implicating himself, Mix indicated that he had firsthand knowledge of exactly what the crew of the *Black Snake* was up to—that it was en route to pick up its next load of potash from local merchants Catlin and Jasper at the falls. Also present at the time were Ledgard's employer, Phelps, and the man who had only hours earlier sold the big gun to Samuel Mott, brother Richard. This crucial information constitutes the first of several revelations that there were influential men personally participating, as well as coaxing others to commit serious offenses; this also shows the palpable fear becoming real for observers concerning the intentions of Farrington and his men, intentions that may have very well begun with the exhortations of Peter Martin.

Ledgard further explained in his petition at the time that he wanted the authorities to summon attorney Cornelius Van Ness to provide information he had personally told Ledgard, specifically that Van Ness himself was present with Penniman when Mix came seeking the very boat that Ledgard used in his mission. The result of his request to summon Van Ness is not known, but Mix did indeed provide him with a vessel. Ledgard then set out searching for the *Black Snake* crew. He related, "I then started and rowed about one mile and passed the Revenue Boat which had stopped under a point of the island known by the name of Halls Point where I understood they stayed all night." Ledgard ended his day when he reached the Onion River sometime between sunset and dark, rowing some distance up before turning in to await daylight.

MAGERY JOY DID NOT actually own the place he lived, occupying it as a tenant of local businessman Colonel Stephen Pearl, who owned both the house and lands adjacent to it. Joy appears to have been a recent arrival to the area since he, together with his wife and family, would be among twelve families receiving one of the routine warnings from the local constable the following January to depart. Pearl's land constituted a portion of a long, rectangular-shaped lot abutting the river extending to the southwest, identified as number 27 on a 1798 map of the town, first conveyed to Joseph Udell that same year. Pearl purchased it together with two other men, also in 1798, paying $400 to Daniel Baker, who bought it from Udell and four days later conveyed a portion of it to Thaddeus Tuttle, all indicating the presence of a robust land-trading network at the time. As noted earlier, Captain Jonathan Ormsby (1759–1808) lived just downriver from Joy and had purchased his property from Collector Penniman. In the years following the murders, Ormsby's surviving relatives sold off his lands—as did Penniman, with several of his own local lots, and Staniford and Moses Catlin, with theirs—to a local attorney quickly rising to fame, Cornelius Van Ness.[353]

These interval lands are low lying and subject to periodic flooding, making them attractive places for planting crops because of the fertile soil being laid down. Close to Joy's house were cornfields, some enclosed by fencing. This particular area is only a short distance from the village, located to the south on higher ground, and was connected directly to it by a rough road, faintly identified on the 1798 map. Farther to the east was another road connecting the town with the falls where Jasper and Catlin were located. The overall condition of that road (identified as the West Road to Milton) was certainly rough. Years later, in 1813, Burlington was unable to maintain that part of it extending from the lakeshore up to the College Green, and the grand jury returned an indictment resulting in the town being fined $600.00. The prior year, nearby Essex had shared a similar fate when it was indicted for failing to maintain a local road, described as being "very ruinous, very deep, broken and in great decay" and causing significant harm to horses, coaches, carts, carriages and the people and goods they bore.[354] In fact, in 1811 and 1812, Burlington paid out $52.50 to Ebenezer Cobb and an undisclosed sum to Samuel Bliss for the loss of their horses, "killed by the badness of our roads."

So it is very likely that the road connecting the town to the area of Joy's house was every bit as bad. Not indicated on any map was the presence of an intersecting road, probably not much more than a rutted trail, running parallel to the river, used by local farmers to gain access to their fields and not meant for general use. Between it and the river was a barrier of trees, including a stand of butternuts below Joy's, with thick undergrowth interrupted by brief openings that allowed periodic glimpses of the water. The growth provided such sufficient concealment that someone on the river would never detect the presence of anyone on shore. It was in this immediate area that these farmers and their helpers, including Ormsby, working for Asa Rice that day, and Peter Dils, on the north side of the river some eight to ten rods away (135 to 165 feet) in an area called the "Old Indian Fields," had the misfortune to become involved in, and witness, the events about to happen.

After the smugglers barged their way into Joy's home and cooked themselves breakfast, Mudget ordered them to retrieve their various weapons from the

Black Snake and to discharge them in preparation for cleaning. Perkins recalled that in addition to the big gun being present, there were "nine small guns, one had no lock," all taken up to the house. The men told Joy that "they were out shooting deer & ducks"; he watched them engage in target practice by shooting into a nearby stump and "afterwards cut out the balls" because of their scarcity. Stephen Pearl Lathrop, working in a nearby field with James Mackenzie, George Sheffield, James Pardo and one other man, saw the crew cooking their fish breakfast and heard the gunshots, including one that "was much louder than the others." He sent one of his helpers to turn over barley near Joy's place, and when he returned, the man reported that "there were men there with guns," leading Lathrop to conclude these were soldiers from the lines.

As the smugglers shot their weapons, one of the last people to participate in the upcoming events arrived at Joy's house, an individual who would have a devastating impact on everyone involved. David Sheffield, brother of laborer George Sheffield of South Hero, was seventeen years old at the time and a diminutive five feet, three inches tall with black hair and a dark complexion. While his aged, infirm and well-thought-of father later described him as having been "seduced by persons much older than himself" into taking part in their illegal activity, a close examination of the young man's immediate words and conduct belies any inference that he was overcome by the desires of others.[355] In fact, he harbored a very real and deep hatred for the display of any authority, and of all the participants that day, it was Sheffield's impetuous behavior that would turn what might have otherwise been an unpleasant, boisterous confrontation into one of extreme bloodshed.

As in Ledgard's case, Sheffield's contact with the smugglers appears to have been entirely fortuitous, with his arrival at Joy's simply out of curiosity. After all, the appearance of a renowned smuggling boat several miles up the Onion on the outskirts of Burlington, manned by several individuals firing their weapons, certainly drew attention. Sheffield watched the men and asked permission to fire one gun, to which they agreed. Then, upon unleashing a single shot from an unfamiliar weapon at a target some 125 feet away (coincidently, roughly the distance it took to shoot across the water), Sheffield was the only one to hit on or near the mark while the rest "made wild shots."

Witnesses recounted that it was during this time that Mudget said he had to make arrangements for his load of potash and engaged Sheffield in conversation, telling him "he must have 6 pounds more of that quick kind of powder." Quick powder is simply black powder ground down to a fine consistency, allowing for faster ignition within a weapon's firing chamber. Mudget further warned the young man "that they did not mean to be taken

& meant to fight their way back into Canada." Sheffield made a good impression on the leader and convinced him to let him become part of their company as cook, promising him he could obtain another weapon to assist them in their efforts, which he did.

Shortly after dusk, "two certain gentlemen" arrived at Joy's house bearing bad news and wanted to speak with Mudget. Their identities were never made known during the trials because of the court's refusal to allow such testimony, but Ledgard disclosed in his 1811 statement that Mudget told him the following day that local doctor Seth Cole was one of the men who came to him with news that the revenue boat was not far off. When the two men told the smugglers they would "not load the boat for it would be taken," they pointed out the big gun, and it appears to have made an impression.

One of the men took Mudget aside to speak with him, and when the conversation resumed in the presence of others, "one of these men said 'I will give you 10 gallons of rum to go and destroy the Revenuers.'" But when they were told that "we had but a trifle of ammunition, the gentlemen said they would furnish us with ammunition." However, some within the group began to hesitate at taking such drastic action, and informant Day, Pease and Perkins all expressed similar concerns that "it was not best to murder men" because "the weapons…were for the defense of the crew."

The news of the nearby revenue boat had an immediate effect on the smugglers' next actions. As Joy explained, "I understood they had intended to start with a load of potashes that night, but they now altered their plan." The men decided to put off any attempt to move that evening, and the following morning, Sheffield and Mott would proceed downriver to see if the report of the government boat's presence was true. In the meantime, Mudget and several others left with the two men to obtain the necessary ammunition and provisions. Sometime later, Mudget returned, as Perkins recounted, with "some powder, about a pound in a paper, and some lead, about 3 pounds which appeared to be part of a still's worm, and about a pound and ½ of pewter."

Alcohol production was never far from any activity, and the fortuitous arrival of a worm, a part of the internal workings of a still, now presented the men with an opportunity to make their needed shot. "We cut slugs out of the pewter which was half an inch in thickness. We tried to hammer them round, but [the] pewter was so brittle it would not hammer," Perkins explained. However, after loading the big gun with a quantity of powder sufficient to fill two cupped hands, three of the irregular slugs were forced down its barrel. The men then realized that they needed another method to arm the remaining weapons and decided to try to find a suitable mold able to cast rounds of varying diameter. When Sheffield told Mudget that he knew of one "at the next house which ran all sizes of bullets," Mudget and Noaks went out and returned shortly afterward carrying it in.

Noaks was then assigned to melt down the pounds of lead, casting the necessary bullets and loading the remaining guns. He readily took on the job and remained awake the entire night, showing Perkins the following morning "a handful out of his pocket and called them 'blue plumbs.'" The work was messy, and Joy complained that his spider (a straining utensil) and small skillet had been dirtied in the process, leaving Perkins to clean things up. Meanwhile, as Noaks loaded the remaining weapons with two balls each, Sheffield picked out those appropriately sized for his smaller-caliber weapon.

It was also necessary to package the loose gunpowder in some fashion so that it could be easily managed. To do so, Sheffield requested of Joy "that I should get papers to make cartridges," but he refused. "I would not let him have any," he said. How Sheffield dealt with that obstacle is not disclosed, but it does not appear to have interfered with the men's work the following day. In the meantime, the *Black Snake* was moved, as Mix had earlier advised Ledgard, to a safer location upriver behind a large island just below the falls and obstructed from view.

Word that a possible confrontation was about to take place spread throughout the area. Sometime that evening, an individual named Hall, accompanied by two other men—one named Cleveland, whom Perkins described as a man "who used to be a soldier at the lines," and another who was unidentified—arrived in a skiff, beaching it in the immediate area of Joy's landing. They joined the eight smugglers and Sheffield, creating a body of men quickly gaining in parity with the fourteen soldiers on the *Fly*. It had been a long day, and with the exception of the bullet-running Noaks, they all went to bed, spreading out on Joy's kitchen floor and in his nearby barn, where they also stored the big gun for the night.

The militiamen were then only hours from entering into a day that was going to require them to use great creativity and adaptability, together with a willingness to employ force if necessary. Whether they would do so, particularly when commanded by an officer not inclined to spill blood, remained a question. For the smugglers, while their plan to leave the area that night had gone awry, they quickly adapted and began to refocus their efforts. Not all were in agreement with the two "certain gentlemen" that they should kill the soldiers, but some were, and that meant all the difference in the world.

6

TRUE SMUGGLERS

Wednesday, August 3, 1808, constitutes one of the saddest and most tumultuous days in Vermont's history up to that time, the result of the violent collision of wide, disparate, irreconcilable interests meeting at one tragic moment of time on an otherwise quiet stretch of river. President Jefferson failed miserably to recognize the disproportionate impact his embargo inflicted on this remote northern frontier, naïvely believing that people eking out a living would simply fall into line and stop their important commercial activity with Canada. Compounding the problem, his lack of an effective enforcement mechanism left its vindication, for the immediate time at least, in the hands of a volunteer militia suffering its own internal divisions. People paid for these shortages with their lives, while others suffered the loss of community prestige and professional advancement. A fortunate few exploited and substantially benefited from those very same hardships.

However, some successes could be recorded for this particular day. In Alburgh, Penniman's men made a large seizure of sixty-eight barrels of potash found aboard a vessel, identified as "An Old Sloop" in court documents, intercepted on its way to Missisquoi Bay. For those pursuing more personal, and familiar, interests, such as State's Attorney Harrington, it started out as a day of no particular moment. The day before, he had paid Jeremiah Jordan $118.07 for work he and his men began in May (which continued for the rest of the summer) putting several tons of hay into his new barn, clearing and plowing fields, cleaning a spring and doing fence work. On this day, Harrington noted in his account book that $2.04 worth of pork was provided to the workers, and while there is no indication that disabled war pensioner Prince Robinson was also present, he, too, received three and three-quarters pounds of pork, being debited $0.47.

Harrington's accounts further reflect his continuing, longtime involvement with a Peter Dils, of Colchester, an important eyewitness to events taking place on that day. Their relationship dated back to at least 1799, with Harrington representing him over the ensuing years in several court cases, while also employing him for his own personal, farm-related needs. In June 1807, Dils received $100 from Harrington for "taking care of the produce and cultivation of the Colchester Interval for the term of two years at $50 a year," and on this particular day, he was employed doing the same thing—cutting hay, accompanied by his horse on the north side of the river—as events unfolded.

Two days before, Moses Catlin had brought suit in a Burlington court against smuggler Samuel I. Mott's rioting associate, Theophilus Morrill, as the bondsman of absconding prisoner Amos Morrill Jr., who disappeared to parts unknown from the St. Albans jail, while twenty-five-year-old brother Guy settled into his days-old marriage to Melinda Wadhams of Goshen, Connecticut, on July 25. Guy's business continued to thrive at the falls, advertising the next day, under the banner "Embargo," that it had "just received a handsome assortment of goods, which are embargoed for the want of purchasers…A few barrels of pork for sale." Credit was readily available to purchasers, including a number of sales posted to the account of cabinetmaker Justus Warner that month for "17 pair table buts," "2 gross screws" and "3 chest locks." In the following two months, he charged yet additional amounts for purchases of a gallon of brandy, sixteen and three-quarters pounds of cheese, gloves, more screws and $2.50 for goods provided to Nimrod, in all likelihood another of the several black men living in the community, employed by Warner in some manner. Predictably, all of those amounts went without being paid, and the firm later filed suit against Warner.[356] Simple and unimportant as these routine, trivial transactions might have been, any one of them certainly constituted a much better alternative to what those paddling on the Onion River faced that day as things began to fall terribly apart.

A WAVE OF COLD descended on the river at sunrise, sufficient enough to create a fog obstructing the view of anyone attempting to negotiate it. That was the immediate problem for Francis Ledgard as he resumed his rowing upstream to complete his errand for Sam Mix to warn the *Black Snake* crew of the soldiers' approach. He was more upbeat this morning and proud of his new idea, one he believed would result in their leaving without having to inflict the bloodshed Mix sought. Now, Ledgard thought that issuing dire threats to them instead would achieve the same result—a good thought, but not good enough.

The fog did indeed hinder Ledgard's vision, and he rowed up past Joy's landing, where the smugglers slept and Hall's boat rested on the shore, and then by the *Black Snake* hidden behind the island upstream, finally reaching the falls without seeing any of it. At this point, apparently because Mix had already disclosed the crew's destination, Ledgard walked up to Catlin and Jasper's business to try and find them. However, nobody was about because of the early hour, and not wanting to disturb anyone, Ledgard returned to his boat and went a short distance downriver to a nearby home. There, he learned the smugglers were at Joy's place and then headed back downriver to that location. When he reached the house, he found Mudget and delivered his message, telling him that "the Revenue boat was in pursuit of him and would be up the river before 12 o'clock and that he had better hide or sink his boat." It was then that Ledgard learned his warning had already been delivered the prior evening by Dr. Cole.

Ledgard also told Mudget he had come to speak with merchant Samuel Fitch to settle his account, and Mudget agreed to accompany him into town, but only after the two had "something to drink." The imbibing completed, the two men walked to Samuel Fitch & Co., located only a short distance to the south on the northeast corner of College Green. Fitch was present when they arrived, and they found his store stocked with a great quantity of goods for sale, including groceries, crockery and hardware, as well as "tickets in the Amoskeag Canal Lottery."[357] As Ledgard recalled, after Mudget told the merchant about the approaching revenue boat, "Mr. Fitch slapt [sic] me on the shoulder saying 'you shall be rewarded for what you have done. You are a good fellow.'"

Recall that the previous year, Fitch had been indicted for illegally selling spirits, was prosecuted by Harrington and had paid a ten-dollar fine, a lesson escaping him entirely on this day. Now, without a care, he offered spirits once again, freely dispensing yet more of the potent alcohol to the two men: "Mr. Fitch then drew a measure full of rum and invited us to drink." However, Fitch was remembered for his gracious hospitality in the following months when Harrington and the grand jury turned their attention to his actions, seeing to it that he was indicted once again for his illegal conduct. Fitch also took advantage of the meeting to dispense the prevailing local wisdom to Mudget, telling him that "every person would esteem him to be a coward if he gave up his boat without fighting for it." Ledgard said that he also told him that "the Embargo law was not constitutional, and that all the country would rise to defend him, besides many other things he told him which are too lengthy to mention." The two men finished their second round of drinks that morning and left.

The specific reason for the route the two men took upon leaving Fitch's store has never been described, but it appears that Mudget continued to look for additional ammunition beyond that provided to him the prior evening by the two "gentlemen." As Ledgard described their trip, they then proceeded to a store owned by Reuben Harmon, on Pearl Street, where they met up with the proprietor. Whether he provided more alcohol to the two on this occasion is not known, but it is certain that Harrington and the grand jury targeted him also alongside Fitch in the coming months with illegally selling spirits when he, too, was indicted for that offense. As Fitch had counseled, Ledgard recalled that Harmon also told Mudget "to fight for his boat and that the country were all ready to take up arms to defend the evaders of the embargo laws, and with many other arguments persuading him to fight for his boat." Nothing more took place, and the men set off once again.

Their route now returned them to the Catlinsborough locale at the falls, and when they reached his store, they found Guy Catlin in attendance. As with the other men, Mudget conveyed to Catlin the information Ledgard had brought, and it was so important to Catlin that he immediately took Mudget outside and spoke privately with him for the next half hour. Ledgard recounted that when they came back in, "Mr. Catlin gave Mudget a bag of powder [and] a piece of a lead still pipe weighing seven or eight pounds as near as I could judge." Now, Mudget had yet more of the powder and metal from another alcohol-producing still to form his musket balls, and he took it all up to leave. However, before doing so, Catlin further cautioned him to take the most extreme action possible to stop the government's actions, telling Mudget "to kill every man belonging to the Revenue boat and not let one escape alive to tell the news."

During their private conversation, Mudget might have told Catlin that some of his men had expressed a desire to take less drastic measures, as Catlin now turned to Ledgard and "said many things to me to persuade me to help Mudget to save his boat." Then, for the third time that morning, Catlin "drawed [sic] spirits and urged us to drink"; there is no indication that the invitation was declined. Whether Catlin was licensed to dispense alcohol is not known, but his name does not appear in Harrington's book as being indicted alongside Fitch and Harmon, indicating that he was one of those few fortunate enough to have their actions overlooked in the coming months.

With three bouts of hard drinking under their belts, the two men proceeded on with their journey, heading downriver toward the *Black Snake*. As they walked, Ledgard engaged Mudget in conversation and asked him "if he was determined to accept of their counsel and fight for his boat?" Martin, Mix, Cole, Fitch, Harmon and Catlin, a cross-section of a conflicted community, had all uniformly given expression to the prevailing Federalist views urging confrontation without compromise, accompanied by vague promises to support him if he did. He had also heard from members of his own crew expressing a contrary position—that to shoot militia troops going about their business was nothing more than murder—and he appears to have had, at least when not pressed by immediate circumstances, to have shared in that sentiment to some degree.

Mudget's response to Ledgard's inquiry indicates that he had been considering his situation for some time and was attempting to formulate an appropriate response, at least one his muddled, alcohol-affected mind could deduce at the moment. He had previously ordered his men to, if they encountered authorities, only return fire if fired upon, but now he made a further distinction that "he would not fight for his boat while it was empty, but when it was loaded with their [Catlin & Jasper's] property, he should fight for it at the expense of his life." Unfortunately, Mudget failed to make this distinction known to his men, whose only stake in the matter consisted of wanting to earn their paltry ten to twelve dollars if they successfully fought their way back into Canada. The two men continued on, and as they passed a nearby house, its owner observed Ledgard's intoxicated, sleepless state and offered him a bed to sleep in, which he gladly accepted.

Others also began to stir, as farmers walked about heading out to tend to their fields, and smugglers and soldiers continued to slowly emerge. Magery Joy was ill that morning, and after finding that the intruders were not going to have breakfast, he "went to Col. Pearl's in Burlington and he let me have some wine for a medicine." Joy remained away until late morning, arriving home around 11:00 a.m., just as the mayhem was in its final minutes.

When Ledgard first appeared that morning with his news, word immediately passed among the smugglers to gather up their arms, including the big gun, and to assemble downstream from Joy's at a stand of butternut trees to set up their ambush, just as Mix had counseled. While most of the men did as ordered, two of them did not, and their refusal to do so provides additional evidence of a division existing within the smugglers' ranks. Specifically, informant Day and Elkinah Perkins, recruited only the preceding day, were observed by Noaks to hesitate in responding, leading him to ask why. While the two men's answers are not noted, Noaks accused them of being "cowards and traitors," and indeed, a close examination of Day's conduct in particular reveals that he was in fact playing a dual role.

As Nathan Haswell's informant, Asa Rice, passed by Joy's house with a load of hay about nine o'clock that morning, he saw the smugglers and noted:

> *Some had guns in their hands, the big gun was placed on two blocks pointing* [down the river]. *There were three guns lying near the big gun. I saw Perkins by the big gun…Perkins asked me what I thought of that big gun. I asked him what they were going to do with it? He said "we hear a revenue boat is coming up after a boat they had and they were determined they should not go by that place."*

Rice warned the men that "if they fired one gun they would expose themselves to the law" and that "if they could get their boat away it was well, but not to use any firearms for I thought they had rendered themselves accountable already," and continued on his way.

When Lathrop passed the men on his way to work in the fields, he inquired who they were, and one called back that "they were true smugglers." He also saw their various weapons and recalled speaking with seven men who

> *invited me to drink and told me they had heard of the revenue boat coming up the river but they were prepared to meet them…They all said if the revenue boat came up they should sup sorrow. They had bullets in their pockets. They took them out in their hands and called them "blue pills."*

Other men issued additional threats and said that the soldiers "would never get out of the river alive." The men also told Lathrop that Sheffield and Mott had crossed over to the north side and gone downstream to see what the government boat was up to. There the band waited in ambush, drinking their rum and spirits, for events to unfold.

The absence of the *Black Snake* venturing out from the river and onto the lake during the night left the soldiers keeping watch at their post below the sandbar, wondering exactly what their prey was doing. Early that morning, after receiving additional assurances that the smugglers remained upriver, they crossed over to Colchester Point, where men working for Harrington were located, and ate their breakfast. There, they decided that Sergeant Johnson would strike out on foot overland toward the river to the south while Farrington steered the rest of his men around the Point to the river's entrance, where they would meet up. Not long after setting out, Johnson testified that he

> met a man, from whose conversation I learned that he took me for a smuggler; he asked me where I was going? I told him to the boat, he asked if we were after a load, I said I did not know whether we could get a load as I understood there were boats up the river. He said there were two. I said "is the Snake one?" He said "yes." I said "is she gone out?" He replied "No, if she had I should certainly have known it." He said there would be no difficulty in our getting a load…but that the Black Snake crew had obtained intelligence that the revenue boat was coming after them by a gentleman from Georgia [Ledgard] who went to them in a skiff early that morning.

Johnson managed to extract himself from the man by making evasive answers to the questions put to him and proceeded approximately two and a half miles, rejoining the *Fly* about a half mile up the river.

After Mott and Sheffield had separated from the others on their reconnaissance mission along the north shore, they split up with Mott staying on land while Sheffield found a canoe and set off paddling downstream. As the soldiers rowed their way in the opposite direction and turned one of the river's many bends, they saw Sheffield coming toward them. He immediately reversed direction. Believing him a spy, the men quickened their pursuit, losing sight of him as he turned a corner. They were hailed by an Indian calling to them from shore, and when they slackened their rowing, he shouted, "Canoe come down, see you, turn back!" They continued on, and after rounding yet another bend, they saw Sheffield land on the north shore, retrieve a gun and a pair of powder horns from within his boat and scurry up the slope out of sight.

In his efforts to divert the soldiers' attention away from his friends farther up and waiting on the opposite shore, Sheffield hastened to pass quickly upstream to get to them. As he did, he passed Dils on his horse, who called to him: "I asked him where he was going. He replied, 'Penniman's party is coming up the river.'" Immediately concerned at what meant, Dils told him, "David, don't be catched [*sic*] in any such business as this" but was quickly dismissed by the young man, who told him, "I know my own business…by God, we will plumb [*sic*] them when they come."

After Sheffield was out of sight, Dils saw Mott, a man he identified as Brigham (there is a strong possibility that this was John Brigham, employed by Harrington to do various farming chores in the area) and two other men, possibly those arriving on Hall's bateau the preceding evening, running past in the same direction. Upon Sheffield's arrival on the shore opposite the smugglers at the butternut trees, his brother, the laboring George present as one of the gathering spectators, paddled across and brought him back to his companions. When asked how bad the situation was, the winded Sheffield exaggerated and told them, "Bad enough, there is a boat coming with thirty men, twenty-six of them rowing." Informer/ex-militiaman Day then confirmed that the boat Sheffield had seen was painted red and immediately dismissed the claim, telling the men in confidence it was a "damned lie. I know the boat well. I think there can but ten men row."

More conversation ensued, and when the subject of Sheffield's marksmanship came up, someone pointed out that "though you are small, you can take good sight," offending the young man, who quickly responded, "By God, I can take as good sight as any of you" and offered to engage anyone in a shooting contest. Dismissing the challenge, and with Catlin's recently provided several pounds of lead pipe sitting there, someone noted the need for additional ammunition, requiring a different-sized mold for their weapons, and told Sheffield to go and retrieve another one. However, he refused, telling the men he had been "running all day & his feet were sore." What they did with the lead is not disclosed, but there was certainly time for Noaks to continue with melting and forming the shot they so desperately needed.

The men also decided that the slugs they had previously forced down the big gun were not sufficient for their needs and drew them out, replacing them with an impressive fifteen one-ounce balls. As they did so, another man drew out the single shot from his previously loaded musket and replaced it with five balls. There is no reason to believe that any of them had not rammed down the requisite "quick powder" Mudget provided, two handfuls in the case of the wall piece, to rapidly propel them when fired.

Mott and his companions then arrived on the opposite shore, and Elkinah Perkins brought them over in Hall's bateau. Mott confirmed the impending arrival of the soldiers, accurately telling the men there were fourteen soldiers on board and that one (Farrington) was wearing distinctive regimental clothing. The men then discussed the need to prepare themselves by removing all oars and sails from both Hall's bateau and the *Black Snake* resting some one thousand feet farther upriver. Additionally, they talked about where to specifically place the big gun and continued discussing the legitimacy of killing the soldiers should they decide to remain in ambush and protect Hall's boat. The men finally determined that "it is no small matter to kill men and have to flee our country. We did not come up in Hall's boat and it is foolish to fight for it."

Meanwhile, the soldiers on the *Fly* continued upstream, cautiously watching and looking for any signs of the smugglers, and upon reaching "old man Sheffield's place" (home of David and George), they came ashore for an hour and "took some refreshment." Now, despite the danger that should have put them on full alert, the soldiers halted in their mission to partake, as others upstream were doing, of their expected daily ration of spirits. The militia's consumption of alcohol was a well-accepted practice at the time, as commanders believed its daily intake allowed their men to better cope with the demands made on them. It was deemed "the staff of life" and considered so important that soldiers were thought better able to withstand hunger more readily than be denied their alcohol rations. When their British captors refused American soldiers alcohol during the War of 1812, many fell into a state of profound depression. As one of them lamented, they "felt the loss of their beloved stimulants, and their spirits sunk, and they had rather lie down and rot, and die, than exert themselves."[358]

While supplying the men with the destructive liquid was allowed to continue for another twenty years, it was not without the displeasure of the Vermont legislature. In 1821, a committee noted the ill effects it caused, brought about because of "an erroneous principle…long prevailed in the militia of this state, that their commissioned officers are bound, *in honor*, on all military occasions, to *treat* those, under their command, with *ardent spirits, and other expensive liquors*." By then, the practice had become so burdensome to supplying officers that many resigned their commissions.[359] However, those were problems for the future to resolve, and for now, the men of the *Fly* drank and then pushed off on their journey.

After commencing their rowing, and when they were one and a half miles below Joy's place, they heard a man calling to them from shore. This time, it was informant Day, who had left the others, deciding that this was an appropriate time to make contact with the soldiers out of sight of the smugglers. However, Day was not alone; Mudget accompanied him, and the two must have discussed Ledgard's strategy of issuing dire threats of harm in hope that the soldiers would abandon their quest. Day might have also confided in Mudget, who had already expressed a desire to pursue a bloodless response, that he had a prior relationship with Sam Buel's deputy,

Dr. James Wood, and that if they should find him on board the revenue boat, they would attempt to speak with him to explain their business.

When Day called out, he asked if Dr. Wood was on board. When the soldiers asked what he wanted with Wood, Day called back that he had "special business" with him. According to trial transcripts of Sergeant Johnson's testimony, the men responded (strikes in original), "We told him we ~~had nothing to do with~~ did not know Dr. Wood that day." Johnson further stated that he recognized Day from their time together in the militia (his name does not appear on the Rutland militia role at that time) and, no doubt surprised to see him there, called out, "Day, is that you?" Finding their first attempt in making a subtle approach not possible, Day changed tactics and asked, "Are you going up the river after the *Black Snake*, are you?" Johnson told him they were, and Day called back that they would not find it but that "we should find something more terrible than the *Black Snake* for there were thirty men armed." Undismayed, Johnson immediately called to his men, "Boys, row on!" as Day and Mudget turned and bolted upriver.

While the soldiers pulled on their oars, the two men made it back to the butternut grove and told the others what they had seen. It must have been a boisterous meeting, as they began to argue over whether to remain in that location or to move farther upstream. Farmer Lathrop watched the proceedings and overheard their conversation, testifying that "some of the company were very noisy. Mudget requested them to be silent, saying they would be heard by the revenue boat crew and those who talked the loudest would be the first to cow out." They finally decided to move their things upriver and to move the *Black Snake* from its hiding place behind the island to the south shore. They retrieved their guns and ammunition; Cyrus Dean picked up the big gun, and Mott carried the ramrod. They quickly departed, heading up the nearby road running parallel to the river, leaving Day behind to further threaten the soldiers.

Not long afterward, the *Fly* appeared and pulled onto Joy's landing next to Hall's bateau. Day was standing nearby and asked if they intended to take the boat. Farrington asked if he was the owner, and Day told him, "I have the care of her and while I have, I own her." As the lieutenant and Johnson stepped into the boat, Farrington explained to him that he had orders to seize all boats believed to be involved in smuggling and would tend to her once they returned back downriver. They then queried Day about where the *Black Snake* was located, and in an attempt to divert their attention, he told them it had left the river the preceding evening. Day also revealed just how much information the smugglers had learned of the soldiers' recent movements when he told them it had gone over the sandbar they were encamped near and that that they must have seen it. Johnson accepted none of the falsity and told Day he knew this was untrue because Day was one of its crew; if it had indeed departed, he would have been on it. Day continued in his denials and repeated his threats, telling the men, "If I did own the property, I would fight until every man was killed before I gave it up." Then he left.

Shortly afterward, bystander Asa Rice decided that this was a good time for him to make contact with the soldiers to tell them what he knew; however, it was not without some hesitancy. Johnson was the only officer present when he arrived, but Farrington joined them shortly afterward upon his return from Joy's home. Rice was not familiar with the men, and while he initially thought that Farrington was Captain Hopkins from St. Albans, he remained evasive when asked his name, explaining, "I did not tell him at first because I was afraid there were so many people about to be [identified as] the informer." However, when the red-coated lieutenant assured him that Johnson was his sergeant, Rice told them that the *Black Snake* rested on the river's edge above Joy's house.

Peter Dils continued to observe the proceedings from his vantage point on the opposite shore and witnessed the meeting between the soldiers and Day at Joy's. He also saw the sudden departure of "8 men running up to where the *Black Snake* lay" following their decision to abandon their position, causing him to also move upstream. In doing so, he found that the island that had obstructed Ledgard's view of the boat earlier in the morning did the same to his ability to see across the river, but by moving just above its head, he was able to look over and continue watching. Rice was also present, having returned up the rough road following his meeting with the troops, accompanied by neighbor Jonathan Ormsby, and the two men watched "a number of these men...running up with their guns." Lathrop also saw the men as they repositioned themselves and observed that they carried "guns in their hands," prompting him and his farming friends to linger in the area to see what might happen.

The boat that Sam Mix had provided Ledgard for his errand was also beached near the *Black Snake*, and one of the crew ran to where Ledgard was sleeping off his intoxicated state to tell him the troops were about to seize it. Unconcerned because it was not his boat, Ledgard simply told the man that he did not care and tried to return to his sleep, only to be reawakened and advised that he had better get down to the river to see what was happening. Ledgard then explains in his statement:

I went up towards where the Black Snake *lay and Mudget came running from Joy's house and overtook me with two guns. He gave me one of them which had no lock on it. I asked him what he was determined to do? He told me he meant to scare them out of the taking of it if he could, if not, they might take it.*

Even now, Mudget continued to exhibit hesitancy in escalating the matter further, believing that threats were sufficient to make the troops turn back, and he intended to maintain that course for the immediate time. For bystander Ormsby, the whole scene was disgusting, and witness James Pardo heard him telling Ledgard as he passed by that "every one of the *Black Snake* crew would be taken and he hoped they would."

The soldiers finally reached a point just below the falls that blocked any further advance, and after rounding a bend, there it was—forty feet in length, black tarred, absent sails, oars, rudder and its expected shipment of potash, the notorious talk of the lake, the *Black Snake*, was attached by a rope to nearby bushes. Just before their arrival, the smugglers had been getting into their boat when Mudget saw the soldiers approaching and told his men to continue boarding for "they do not look like revenue men." Had Farrington failed to display the important customs service ensign and pendant flag signaling his authority to detain and seize suspect vessels, as he had been previously instructed, leading Mudget to such a conclusion? Had he held back from making an ostentatious display of authority as he and his men penetrated into this heavily Federalist enclave, sensitive to the possibility of a violent reaction from the local populace? Was this the order that Captain Pratt said Farrington had disobeyed? Regardless, for the more discerning Mott, Mudget's order made no sense, and he immediately pulled Mudget out and scurried up the slope with the others, leaving him behind.

As the soldiers arrived, Mudget stood on shore, a few feet away from his prized possession, with a musket on his shoulder and called out that they should not land, and if they did so, it was "at the peril of our lives." Farrington responded that he had orders to take the boat, and as Johnson steered the *Fly* to a position between it and the shore, Mudget stepped back and continued with his threats: "I swear by God, I will blow the first man's brains out who lays hands on her." Someone called out to him that it was a free country and they had a right to land where they wanted, and the two officers, together with Private James Hays, stepped on board the *Black Snake*. As they did so, Mudget threatened them again, this time raising his gun as though he intended to fire, but instead, he turned and went up the embankment. Mudget's movements at that moment were never seriously called into question because of the readily recognizable white hat he wore and the spyglass he carried. As Johnson followed him in his climb, his eyes came to rest on an ominous sight: "As I looked up I saw Mott with the large gun resting in the crotch of a small tree pointing over the *Black Snake* where the lieutenant and I were. Mudget came to the left side of Mott and they talked." The substance of their conversation is not known, but Mott held his fire as the troops continued with their business.

Farrington then called up to Mudget and Mott asking where the sails, oars and rudder were located, and when told, unsurprisingly, that they did not know, he ordered some of his men to make a search of the area and for Johnson to retrieve an oar from Ledgard's nearby boat. They did find the sails but were unsuccessful in locating any other equipment. Ledgard was present by this time and took immediate offense at the seizure. He told the lieutenant he had no business taking his property, to which Farrington replied with words to the effect that he had a right to take what he saw fit.

Ledgard wrote in his statement that he called Farrington a coward and "told him if he would take a musket, I would take another and step one side and decide the business and not expose the men for we were both men of honor." Farrington "then clasped his hand over his breast and told me if I had a desire to fire there was a mark for me." In a second accounting of the event, Hays testified that he had heard Mudget similarly call out to Farrington, "We are both men of honor, you are a lieutenant, I am a major. Let us fight a duel and save the lives of our men!" He then threatened further, "I will lay your honor low and have your heart's blood before you get out of the river." The heated exchanges were so loud that Dils on the opposite shore and the farmers lingering out of sight on the road could hear them.

Now, Farrington had a fateful decision to make. He could simply take his quarry and return downriver or he could leave a guard with it and take the rest of his men and go after those so boldly challenging the government's authority. From the information conveyed to him previously, he certainly knew there were several others lurking in the area out of sight. As Farrington later testified, "I at first thought it my duty to go on shore and apprehend the men who were in arms, but I was determined from the first sailing out to shed no blood if it could be avoided and so I thought." He then ordered Johnson to remove six oars from the *Fly* and to take six men and board the rudderless *Black Snake*, thereby splitting his available force in half in the face of an opponent of unknown capability.

At this point, Mudget became increasingly concerned and shouted out to his concealed compatriots, "Come on boys, parade yourselves, you are all cowards, they are going to carry the boat off!" Then, two or three armed men, including Cyrus Dean, made themselves known, stepping out and coming down from their hiding places in the bushes. Hays cut the line connecting the boat to shore and joined Farrington and one other soldier on the *Fly*. The remaining four soldiers were ordered to go onto the nearby road as a "flanking party" and to walk downriver, keeping pace with the two boats as they descended. At Mudget's repeated urging, two more armed men stepped out from their hiding places as the situation took an ominous turn.

When the two boats pushed off and began their descent, Ledgard continued with his threats and "called out in a Methodist's tone of voice," warning Farrington: "Lieutenant, prepare to meet your God, your blood shall be spilt before you get out of the river." However, Mudget was apparently ready to concede his loss and told his men "they have got the boat, let us let them alone" as he prepared to walk back down the road. Their captain's refusal to go on the offensive and take action beyond threatening words became too much for some now being forced to abandon this, their second ambush site. Farmer Lathrop was nearby and overheard Dean and Mott talking, the former stating, "We will not go with them. They are damned cowards." Mott responded in agreement: "I will go home. I will have nothing more to do with them." However, the two moved off together to talk privately, and when they returned, Lathrop heard Dean say to Mott, "If you have a mind to be crooked, I can be as crooked as you." Mott then moved off, going down the road, while Dean stayed behind telling Lathrop that brother-in-law Mudget "was a damned coward, he wished he was burnt to death, he wished he was scorched with wet powder so as not quite to kill him."

With his goal now in hand, and having probably raised his ensign and pendant flag by now, if not done previously, it is reasonable to conclude that Farrington had inadvertently conveyed to the smugglers some degree of hesitancy on the soldiers' part during their encounter. For now, not only were Dean and Mott scheming, but Ledgard also recalled hearing one of the other men counseling his friends, "Let us go down the river and give them a start."

So BEGAN A CURIOUS progression walking downstream, keeping apace of the descending *Fly* and *Black Snake*. Four soldiers—Walker, Hays and two others—proceeded back the several hundred feet toward Joy's place in the accompaniment of four of the smugglers, Mudget, Sheffield, Ledgard and one other man. During their time together, Walker related that Mudget kept up his dire threats, telling them:

> *If the lieutenant proceeded down the river he would take his heart's blood, that he would not hurt the soldiers unless they stood by the lieutenant, but if they did there would be more than three or four gallons of blood spilt, that the soldiers would all be killed for they had thirty armed men at the mouth of the river.*

Several farmers trailed along behind them, curious if something more than shouting might take place. For the experienced Ormsby, it was all too much, and he turned to Rice and told him the smugglers were "cowards and I do not believe anything will be done."

During their walk together, Rice spoke with David Sheffield and asked him what he planned to do with the gun he was carrying. "I am going to hunt ducks and pigeons and I have a right to carry it," the young man replied, prompting Rice to caution him "to lay it by but he insisted he had a right to carry it where he pleased." Sheffield also warned him that "they have got the boat but you will see they never will ever get out of the river with her." Rice responded that the young man should put down his gun: "I fear there is going to be mischief and if you have mind to be a spectator [you] had better not carry a gun." Dismissing the caution, Sheffield simply told him, "I have a right to carry a gun." The farmers also heard more threats going out to the soldiers, telling them they would never leave the river alive and calling Farrington "a red-coated rascal." Taking it all in, Farrington called back from the *Fly* that he had taken the boat according to his orders and again offered himself up as a target: "If you intend to fire, here I set as a mark." Nobody fired.

The most troublesome of those on shore were the remaining smugglers lingering behind, trying to stay out of sight of the four soldiers and others in front of them. Perkins, who had previously held back from participating, was one, and he carried the cumbersome big gun in his arms with difficulty. Farmer Oliver Root was nearby and heard him ask Mott to help him carry it. With disdain, Mott replied that "it was a hard case [that] one man could not carry a gun," taking it from him and putting it on his shoulder. No longer willing to stand by and watch as their seized boat and all the moneymaking opportunities it represented drifted out of reach, the men began to discuss taking more affirmative action, those that their leader farther down the road would have no say in. And as the farmers continued to linger nearby and refused to go away, the smugglers turned and threatened to fire on them as well.

Upon reaching the area of Joy's house, Ledgard, who had been walking with the group in front, rejoined his trailing comrades and, for the first time, learned that something untoward was in the air:

> *Slocum Clark looked round on Jonathan Ormsby saying "Damn your blood, what are you following us for?" Ormsby said, "to see what you are going about." Slocum Clark then made this reply, "if you do not quit our company I will blow your brains out for the first man." I then saw that the company belonging to the* Black Snake *were determined upon some plan that I knew not of, and I then made this reply, "if this is what you are going about, I shall go no farther with you."*

Three-quarters of an hour had passed since the *Black Snake* was taken by the soldiers, and events now began to unfold in rapid succession as the two boats came into sight, nearing an opening in the woods several hundred feet below Joy's house, where the walking soldiers and smugglers parted ways. James Prado saw that Dean was carrying the great gun at the time but that Mott took it from him and said he was going to go and hunt partridges, dropping down the embankment toward the river.

At first, it was all quiet, and Farrington out on the water believed nothing more would take place than the back-and-forth shouting he had been party to, so he called to his men on the road to return and reboard the *Fly*. As the four soldiers began their descent to the river's edge, several of the following smugglers, without any direction from Mudget, also stepped off the road and down the bank. In re-creating what took place, Asa Rice testified that during this time, he counted a total of twelve smugglers bearing arms, in addition to the big gun—a number consistent with the several men making up the *Black Snake* crew, increased by the four who had arrived the preceding evening on Hall's boat. However, not all of them were in agreement with how things were going, and Day (who never left Joy's landing after the first meeting), Perkins, Ledgard and Pease all chose to withdraw from further involvement and became bystanders. Whether Rice's count included them is not known. Regardless, from the farmers' perspective, nothing more was going to take place, so several of them returned to their fields. Ormsby was so unconcerned at the moment that he told Rice if he had any business to take care of across the river, now was a good time to do so and to ask Farrington to take him over, to which the lieutenant agreed.

The four soldiers and Rice joined Farrington in the *Fly* at the water's edge and began their short crossing using the two remaining oars. Just as they neared the north shore, without warning, a single shot rang out from the bushes and splashed down between the two boats. When one of his men prepared to fire back, Farrington continued in his desire not to shed blood and told him not to because the smugglers were only trying "to terrify us." Hearing the report in the nearby fields, Lathrop turned to Pardo and observed, "It is nothing. One is afraid and another is scared. Come let us go to our work." However, it was the next commotion that brought them all running back.

The soldiers continued in their rowing, and when they reached the north shore, another shot rang out, this time striking the boat's stern, passing cleanly through and missing Farrington's legs by only inches. His repeated offers to serve as the smugglers' target had now become very real. Rice then scrambled out, pushed the *Fly* back out into the stream and went up the slope unharmed. Then, a third volley of several guns was unleashed but struck the water closer to the trailing *Black Snake*.

Now determined he had no alternative but to take these men into custody, Farrington made a fateful decision, ordering the two boats to the south shore and quickly instructing twenty-year-old Private Ellis Drake to take the *Fly*'s helm. Originally from Sharon, Massachusetts, Drake was the son of Revolutionary War soldier Melzar Drake and was residing in Clarendon when his company was mobilized.[360] After rising from his seat and beginning to position himself at the stern, another shot rang out. Elkinah Perkins, who was doing his best to remain apart from the fray, testified that upon hearing the first shots, he ran down the road and encountered Sheffield, who immediately accused him of being a coward for remaining apart from the others. Perkins then watched the young man as "he drawed [*sic*] his piece up and took as deliberate aim at the boat as if he was going to shoot a duck. He fired & said 'I took good aim.'" As Asa Rice described a conversation he later had with him, "Sheffield said their mark was fixed—they intended to kill the lieutenant."

Whether it was Sheffield's bullet or one of his fellows also firing around this time is not known, but one of the shots now sped across the water, a solid piece of ore propelled by "quick powder," both so freely provided only hours before along with alcohol, by those esteemed Burlington elites. Viciously ripping into Drake's forehead, the grand jury determined that the ball had struck him "in and upon the left temple…a little above the left eye," burrowing in and leaving a one-inch-wide channel penetrating almost entirely through his skull, finally stopping when it reached four inches in depth. Witness Peter Dils, along with others, examined Drake's body shortly afterward and concluded that there were two balls "so close together that we thought there was but one" and had "no doubt that the balls came from one gun." Asa Rice agreed, stating, "I thought at first it was made with one bullet, but on examining his hat I could see distinctly there were two." The distinction was irrelevant to Drake, for his death was instantaneous.[361]

As the young soldier's lifeless body suddenly fell, Sergeant Johnson on the *Black Snake* turned and saw it brush against the flagstaff attached to the *Fly*'s stern, causing the "colours" to fall and his hat to drop into the water. From his vantage point on the north shore, Rice heard one of the smugglers call out (strikes in transcript), "Damn them, ~~they~~ we have ~~struck their flag~~ knocked their colors down"—an apparent reference to the ensign and pendant. Farrington immediately called out that "they have killed Drake," and as he moved to examine the man's wound, Johnson rose up with his own gun to return fire. However, Farrington ordered him, "Do not fire, row to the south shore," which he was able to accomplish in his rudderless boat, landing a couple hundred feet farther downstream. Johnson then ordered his men out of the *Black Snake* and up the embankment toward the nearby road, which Farrington immediately countermanded, forbidding them from moving from where they were.

On the *Fly*, Farrington took up the tiller and turned the bow from the downstream direction it had drifted and pointed it toward the south shore as yet more shots were fired at him. Company drummer Benjamin Johnson was one of those rowing at the time, and he looked toward the shore in time to see a man later identified as Cyrus Dean taking aim at their boat. "He seemed not to like the place, he went to another and pointed his gun at us again, he then removed to a third place, pointed his gun at us and fired, the ball split my oar and knocked it overboard." Fearing more injuries, Farrington told the six soldiers that there was nothing they could do at that moment and ordered them to lie down. He then took up the last oar and began to paddle, first on one side and then on the other, continuing to move toward the shore.

By this time, some of the returning farmers had arrived, including a frustrated Jonathan Ormsby, clearly upset with Farrington's failure to bring the matter to an end earlier by taking the smugglers into custody. Ormsby was by far the most senior and experienced militia officer present on the Intervale that day; unfortunately, he was also without any authority to command any of the soldiers' movements. The forty-nine-year-old captain had served during the Revolutionary War under the command of his father, the respected Major Gideon Ormsby, in Ira Allen's Regiment of Militia, a unit that potash investor Dr. Truman Powell was also enlisted in. Ormsby's service included responding to a number of alarms taking place during the war, and in 1782, he was sergeant in a company of men ordered to respond to Windham County, in southern Vermont, to assist the sheriff in suppressing violent rioting. The unrest was the result of ongoing disputes between Vermont and New York authorities over land claims and the disturbing inclination of some residents to rebel against Vermont's exercise of power over them. General Ethan Allen himself was dispatched to confront the trouble in September, and with Ormsby in attendance, he was able to cow the insurrectionists into submission, employing dire threats of harm if they did not desist in their demonstrations.

Ormsby also had significant attachment to these particular lands. As noted, he had first acquired them from Penniman in 1798, watched as his household increased to nine individuals by 1800 and became immersed in litigation (represented by the ever-present Harrington) in 1802, when he and his father were sued by Ira Allen on behalf of Ethan's estate as a part of the ongoing, tangled land mess the Allen family made of so many of the local land transactions.[362] Now, the no-nonsense professional was forced to look on as a junior officer, fourteen years younger than himself and facing the most significant challenge of his life, attempted to deal with these drunken outsiders intruding into his peaceful world. As Ormsby stood by watching the rowing Farrington trying to reach shore, he called out, "Why do you not land and seize these men who are violating the laws of their country?" Not having much more to say, Farrington could only reply, "We are coming as fast as we can."

Meanwhile, Lathrop observed David Sheffield come crashing out from the heavy undergrowth without his gun and confronted him: "I said, 'In God's name David what have you been doing?'" Sheffield responded, "I have not killed a man. I have not fired." When asked where his weapon was, he said that he had thrown it away, "that they should not say I fired." Lathrop asked if his gun had been loaded, and he said that it had not, and when Lathrop told him he had seen him loading it, Sheffield replied, "You don't want to hurt me Pearl, do you?" Lathrop then ran off, arriving at the river in time to see Farrington rowing as fast as he could toward shore, while Sheffield sped off toward Joy's house.

When Joy returned home about eleven o'clock that morning following his visit to town and getting his wine from his landlord, he heard a great roar of gunfire (describing it as a "battle") coming from the area below his house. Suddenly, Sheffield appeared and began to solicit his assistance to support an alibi, telling Joy, "I was to work for you." Joy refused to have anything to do with the ruse, explaining that Sheffield "wanted to screen himself that way and I told him I could not lie for him."

By now, Farrington had finally reached the south shore, and together with some of his men, he climbed the embankment, gaining access to the nearby road. Informer Joshua Day continued in his role as observer and was also on the road with Ormsby watching as the soldiers began to position themselves when James Hays, recognizing him as soldier turned smuggler, raised his gun and fired. But it failed to discharge. Ormsby called to Hays that Day appeared to be a friend, and when Day claimed he had not taken part in any of the shooting, he lowered his weapon. When Day was asked by defense counsel at the trial, in an attempt to portray the soldiers as aggressors, whether it appeared as though they were intending "to take the *Snake*'s crew," his experienced eye told him otherwise, and he explained that "they appeared to be in defense with their guns."

For Mudget, the next moments were ones of great conflict. Despite whatever hopes he had to avoid it, his repeated, vociferous threats to draw blood had finally become real, and now he witnessed what he had sown as the soldiers prepared to take on him and his men. Farmer Root was one of those who came running in response to the firing, and he encountered Mudget, also running toward it. Mudget again warned the bystanders to go away, and when Root asked why, he was told, "We do not want you to be witnesses against us." Continuing on toward his men, Mudget, wearing his distinctive white hat, began frantically waving his arms and continued to do so for a reported five minutes, yelling, "For God's sake, fire no more!" and telling them that a man had been killed.

For Ormsby, it was essential that Farrington take immediate action, even if all of his men had not climbed up to the road, and Hays heard the experienced captain telling the lieutenant that the men responsible for the shooting were hiding in nearby bushes, and "we had best surround them and take them as quick as possible." Farrington then approached Hays seeking a cartridge to prime his gun and said, "Follow me, we will see where they are." The men began their advance, walking in proximity to one another, Farrington wearing his conspicuous red tunic, with Ormsby and privates Asa Marsh, of Rutland, and Hays to his left and Sergeant Johnson on his right, while Walker followed immediately behind and the others nearby.

As the men moved out, Walker watched as Mott, located some 150 feet ahead of them, suddenly bolted across the road in front of them carrying the big gun. This was the third time that morning that Mott was forced to reposition himself, and it was to be the last. Witnesses then observed as he quickly lifted the weapon with Dean's assistance, himself also recognizable by his distinguishing velvet coat (also worn during the trial), and rested its eight-foot barrel on a corner fencepost, prompting Hays to call out that they were about to fire. Mott hesitated, and Dean, clearly concerned that additional soldiers were quickly arriving, shouted to him, "Fire, why don't you fire? They will all be upon us, they are coming up the bank!"

None of the soldiers had been allowed to fire a single shot that morning, losing a comrade in consequence and more in the offing. Now, Mott's great gun, an extraordinary weapon designed to cut a devastating swath through an enemy in battle or dozens of waterfowl with a single shot, roared out, and fifteen heavy one-ounce balls, together with a quantity of buckshot, exited its one-and-a-quarter-inch bore, barely managing to spread out as it covered the short distance to the soldiers. The wounds inflicted on the men all indicate that if Mott was intending to center his shot on the conspicuous, red-coated Farrington, he failed; instead, he had moved slightly to the right, centering on Ormsby, walking just to Farrington's left. It might also have been that Mott did not miss his target at all but intentionally made the intrusive, obstinate captain the center of his blast.

When the shot arrived, it sliced directly into Ormsby, inflicting devastating injuries described in an inquest taking place immediately following the incident: "one of which bullets entered his [left] breast a little above the pit of his stomach, one entered the lower part of the abdomen near the center, one entered his right thigh near the groin, and one passed through his right wrist." Other court documents relate further that the wounds penetrated to a "depth of four inches and the breadth of one inch."[363] Upon being struck, Benjamin Johnson heard Ormsby cry out, "Lord have mercy, I am a dead man!" Indeed, he was.

Asa Marsh, just to Ormsby's left, was struck by a combination of ball and buckshot. Two "bullets entered the right breast near the center, one buckshot entered the right shoulder, one bullet passed through the flesh of the side under the right arm, and one buckshot grazed the right arm," the first wound penetrating to a depth of four inches and one inch in breadth. A nearby soldier witnessed Marsh falling to the ground, where he "gasped for breath once or twice, but could not speak and instantly died."

Farrington was also hit, described by attending physician Dr. John Pomeroy on his behalf in his 1832 pension application as sustaining "three wounds—one slight wound on the right shoulder—one in the center of the forehead, which grazed the skull and took off a piece of the skull—the other a bullet wound (as were the others) through the left arm, near the shoulder, the ball struck the bone, but did not break it"; the one hitting him in the head fell from his hat and into the hand of a soldier assisting him. Another physician, Joel Green, providing aid to Farrington for the next six months (after the wounded soldier testified at trial and returned home to Pittsford because there was no hospital in Burlington), further related that his wounds "were very severe & came near proving fatal."

Viewing his injuries, nearby Private Hays called out to Farrington, asking "if he was killed, but he said he was wounded." When Sergeant Johnson raised his gun to shoot back, Farrington once again directed him not to, ordering, "Don't fire, take hold of my hand, I am wounded." Johnson immediately turned to attend to his bleeding friend: "I saw the blood run down his face. I turned my eyes and saw Asa Marsh on the ground bleeding, and someone said 'they have killed Marsh,' he lay six or eight feet from me. Soon after I saw Capt. Ormsby lying dead."

At the same time the great gun roared, several other weapons fired, estimated by Dils from across the river to number between eleven and twelve. While Mudget had been so actively engaged in trying to get his men to cease fire, other witnesses stated that they recognized him—again, mainly because of his white hat—as one of those also taking part. This was an issue hotly contested at his trial when defense attorneys argued that there was at least one other person wearing a similarly colored hat and that Mudget had not fired. The smugglers then let out in celebration, taking off their hats and waving them while shouting out a loud huzzah. For the nearby farmers, their fright was so great that their first inclination was to immediately jump over a nearby fence and flee into a cornfield.

Witnessing the carnage he had just wrought, Mott immediately set off in escape. He took the big gun and began running up the road, where he ran into Perkins. "Have you fired that gun?" he asked, and Mott told him, "Yes, I have." Perkins asked if he was going to fire it again, and Mott responded that he would have, "if I had the ram rod, but I have left it where the *Snake* lay." Mott's actions were clearly unacceptable to Perkins, for, as he explained to a jury, their orders from Mudget had included that they not fire unless they had been fired upon. He then watched as Mott "throwed [*sic*] the gun off of his shoulder and went towards Joy's." There, Mott ran into Joy, who related that he saw the smuggler run into the house, "took a glass of water…he appeared to be out of breath. He was in his shirtsleeves. I asked him what he had been about? He replied, 'Don't say a word.' Took his coat and hurried away across the cornfield." For the frightened Perkins, it was all too much, and he, together with nearby Day and Pease, decided to lay down his weapon, leaning it against some trees, ceasing any appearance of opposition.

On the other side of the river, after getting out of the *Fly* and witnessing Drake's death, Rice immediately turned and ran several hundred feet up the north shore to where he could wade back across and return to the site of the confrontation. As he did so, he, too, witnessed Mott "running very fast," fleeing toward Joy's house. Shortly afterward, he met yet another smuggler, believed to be Josiah Pease, following behind Mott going in the same direction. Pease told him that three men had been killed and another wounded. "I asked him who they were? He replied, 'Your neighbor, Captain Somebody.' I said 'Ormsby?' & he replied, 'yes.'" Rice then continued on to the scene.

Francis Ledgard remained behind after learning that the smugglers had other things in mind than making threats, and when he heard the first reports of gunfire, he immediately sought to distance himself further, going upriver to his boat and leaving his own gun at Joy's house when he passed by. When he finally reached the boat:

> *Then came a man to me and desired me to carry him across the river and as we were crossing the river the man told me he fired the big gun and how many he had killed he did not know. We crossed the river. He then sat down and asked me to pull off his boots, which I did and left him there.*

Since his arrival earlier in the morning, Ledgard had had minimal involvement with Mott, not even learning his name at the time, and it was not until shortly thereafter, after he had walked to David Sheffield's father's home and spoken with the elderly man, that he actually learned it was indeed Mott he had helped. Ledgard remained at Sheffield's until others came and took him into custody, binding him up in some fashion. He remained in this state until he could explain to them what he knew; he was then unbound and transported into Burlington, where he was lodged in the upper room of Staniford's jail.

AT THE MURDER SCENE, people began to stir from the stunning events they had just witnessed. While Sergeant Johnson and the nearby farmers moved quickly to round up what smugglers they could, two of them were unaccounted for: triggerman Samuel Mott and Captain Josiah Pease. Now, events were clearly out of their control, and as the soldiers had questions about the extent of their own authority and how to proceed, they decided to send Asa Rice into Burlington to find someone able to direct them. Farrington's wounds caused Rice great concern, and he ordered Johnson to go immediately to find medical aid. But before leaving, Rice went down to the water's edge and called over to Dils on the opposite shore. "Neighbor," he called, "get your canoe and come over here, [there] are three men lay dead on the ground and our neighbor Ormsby is one." Dils rushed over and took control of his dead friend's body, laying him out reverently, washing away what he could of the carnage, examining him and ultimately concluding he had been struck by five balls rather than the four an inquest later determined. Even if the number was not accurate, the big gun's shot had struck the three men with an approximate 66 percent effectiveness—certainly a respectable performance under the circumstances.

Official Burlington exploded upon Rice's arrival in town with the devastating news. After telling his employer and relative Deputy Collector Haswell what had happened, Haswell mounted his "fleet horse saddled and bridled" and "immediately proceeded to the scene of action," covering the distance in short order. Upon arriving, accompanied by Rice, and finding that Mott had escaped, all attention turned to his associate, Cyrus Dean, standing near some bushes a short distance from the bodies. Haswell observed that he appeared intoxicated and asked Dean how he came to be at that place. Displaying his own disdain at what was taking place, Dean responded that he came by way of his own feet and questioned Haswell's authority to apprehend him. Haswell was having none of it and ordered that Dean be taken. He resisted. As Haswell explained, "He was getting the better of me in the scuffle and had drawn from his bosom a large shoe makers knife," causing him to call out to Rice, "a strong athletic man," for assistance. Rice further described what happened:

> Dean wanted to know by what authority I went to lay hands on him, he closed with me, took the lock of me and threw me down, but he soon after said he would go with others. He was led to Joy's; when we came there he was tied but he contrived to get loose, jumped out of the window and ran towards the woods. I was one of those who ran after him. When I came up with him he kicked me. We brought him back.

In the meantime, Johnson arrived with local doctor Mathew Cole, who presumably tended to Farrington before moving on to his more garish task.

Observing Marsh and Ormsby laid out on the ground, Cole noted their mortal wounds and simply concluded that "they were both dead when I saw them."

Following his own wounding, Farrington was bandaged with handkerchiefs around his head and another about his arm, described as being "all bloodied," but he was able to begin making his own way up the road. As he did, he met farmer Lathrop and told him, "They have wounded me, I do not know but mortally, but I do not mind that, but they have killed two of my men and one of your neighbors, and I am sorry for what is to follow." Day and Sheffield were also nearby and told the lieutenant that "they did not fire, nor ever expected the rest would."

At some point during the confusion immediately following Johnson's detaining of the smugglers, William Noaks and Slocum Clark escaped, probably while Dean scrambled out the window in his unsuccessful bid for freedom. As described in court documents later that month, the two men "were not apprehended," and while the record does not specifically state whether they ever answered for their conduct, one tantalizing entry indicates that they were not forgotten. A brief note in the Supreme Court's records while it was in session in Franklin County in December 1808 stated that officials sought reimbursement for work done in the matter entitled "Inquisition on the Bodies of Noaks, Clark, Vanhorn & Blake."[364] Those particular records concerning proceedings conducted to inquire into the circumstances of their deaths have not survived. However, the naming of the two escapees side by side in a single proceeding so shortly after the event indicates that some form of undisclosed retribution was indeed visited on them. Modern-day students of these times can only wonder if someone with views favorable to the government might have quietly succeeded in reaching out and extracting some degree of retribution to right the unsatisfactory results unfolding in the next weeks.

David Russell (the collector Jefferson had removed upon Penniman's appointment) was a local justice of the peace and had the necessary authority to order others held in detention for wrongdoing. He arrived during this time, having ridden "with speed" upon hearing of the murders. Seeing Dean and learning he was a member of the *Black Snake* crew, he "ordered him into the custody of Sgt. Johnson, to be safely guarded with others, until warrants could be made out for their commitment." Once that was done, "warrants were soon made out, the prisoners taken into custody by a civil officer, and by him secured in the gaol at Burlington the same day."[365]

As that was taking place, local attorney Charles Adams, who had also come to the scene, observed the tied-up David Sheffield. The soldiers had apparently searched the area for weapons involved in the mêlée and were able to find some, but they were also hearing Sheffield's persistent claims of innocence. Adams testified:

> *I unbound him. He went to show where the guns were found. I kept him in my sight. He told me he knew where some of the guns were. We found four which were loaded. We drew charges, one had three balls, one two & one one & one was loaded so hard I could not draw the charge.*

Clearly, the smugglers had been frantically firing, reloading with multiple rounds, firing and again reloading when everything finally quieted. With the culprits now in custody and the soldiers turning to guarding the nearby boats, Russell and arriving fellow justices of the peace William Harrington and George Robinson decided to immediately convene official proceedings at the very scene of the murders.

However, before the civilian justices could proceed with their work, they were confronted by a legal technicality, one of such moment that it remains an issue even in recent times. This concerns the interplay of state and federal authority in the execution of their respective interests as they attempt to simultaneously address the same problem—in this case, the vindication of federal customs and state murder laws. In the end, one of them takes precedence while the other assumes a secondary role, and it can, at times, foster significant ill will between the participants. For these Vermonters in the early years of statehood, with virtually no experience involving a federal hierarchy, the embargo clearly presented a new set of challenges.

For the state justices, their most immediate concern was the capture of the escaping smugglers at a moment when no sheriff was present or, in the alternative, a federal revenue collector on whom to call for assistance. Penniman was at his home in Swanton, and Staniford's location is not known, a fact later attested to by Haswell when he explained that he became involved with the state investigation only at the request of "several gentlemen" because "the sheriff, the afternoon the unfortunate affair took place, was absent." Staniford was no doubt not far off, probably out serving his many court papers, but not having a state official with the necessary authority to immediately close in on the escapees forced the justices to prevail on federal official Haswell. As Russell explained (emphasis in original):

> *We, with others, thought it proper that measures should be <u>instantly</u> taken to apprehend the culprits; and, as Mr. Nathan B. Haswell was the*

customhouse officer in this place, it was thought best for him to undertake that task, which he did, on being requested, undertake.[366]

Haswell did not disappoint them, and after securing Dean and seeing to the needs of others, he immediately dashed off, returning to town to compose a hasty advertisement notifying the public of the affair: "100 DOLLARS REWARD, the above Reward is hereby offered for the apprehension of Samuel I. Mott." Haswell wrote this at the top of the notice, first providing a physical description of the man and then explaining he had been involved in smuggling and "the wanton murder of two men employed in the service of the government of the United States and one private citizen." He then announced a fifty-dollar reward for the apprehension of Noaks, Pease and Clark, together with their physical descriptions, and sent the notice to the local paper for immediate publication.

The murders mark an important milestone in the government's response to the illegal activity taking place that summer, severely jolting it from its previous hands-off attitude for fear of raising the ire of the population to one of forceful action. Whatever additional instructions state officials made at the time is not known, but records reveal that an aggressive policy was quickly instituted in which others involved in smuggling, regardless of whether they were present at the murders, should now receive the government's undivided attention.

With Staniford still absent, Haswell began to deploy a number of men in the search, including Seeley Bennett, Luther Moore, Zenas Washburn and Daniel Woodward. Bennett assumed the role of an express rider and went immediately to Windmill Point with the news to preclude any escape via water, later seeking $19.53 for his, and his horse's, efforts during the next four days. One invoice of that day ($4.50) also shows that James Cummings, together with three other men, was successful in "taking Ledgard, [Frederick] Hoxey, Headen & others, & bringin [*sic*] them forward to gaol." The fact that Hoxie and Headon—whose illegal conduct, along with that of the two Taylors, had taken place the preceding June 1 and 10, July 3 and August 1 (and which also involved the use of the *Black Snake*)—clearly shows the wider net the government now cast and that their prior conduct was going to receive the attention it deserved. Continuing in that effort, the very next day, John Taylor himself, a resident of Quebec, was discovered in Burlington and taken into custody, an effort apparently meeting with some difficulty. As Taylor alleged in a lawsuit he filed in November against Penniman (only hours after the federal trial described later had ended), it was the collector himself who "beat and wounded, imprisoned and evilly treated and kept and detained him…in prison for a long time" on that day.[367]

Pease did not remain at large for long and was taken into custody on Hogg Island by members of Alexander Miller's Rutland contingency, delivering him to the jail the following day. Asa Bulkley, of Sheldon, fervently took up Mott's pursuit, as he later explained when he submitted his bill for services: "Your Petitioner animated with the love of justice & his country at the risque [sic] of his person pursued said Mott about twenty miles into the Province of Canada, apprehended him & caused him to be committed to the public gaol in Burlington." Clearly, issues concerning the lawful and orderly extradition of criminals from foreign soil to the United States were in their infancy and deemed irrelevant under the current emergency. Bulkley's expenses for the seven-day adventure amounted to $125.79, which included his hiring of a skiff and oarsmen, riding in a stage, the use of horses and "cash paid for assistance, $75.00."[368]

Staniford did arrive to assist at some point and became concerned at the many prisoners' rapid arrival to his new jail; the *Black Snake* crew's Mudget, Sheffield, Dean, Ledgard, Day and Perkins, joined by Frederick Hoxie and at least one Taylor, then followed by Mott and Pease, created an extremely volatile situation. So many dangerous smugglers responsible for so many of the problems of the past few months, all associated with one another in one form or another and housed under one roof, constituted a most dangerous situation for his understaffed jailor and stretched deputies. Pursuant to law, he immediately called on militia officials for assistance, and ten soldiers under the command of Captain Justus Warner, First Company of Infantry, First Regiment, Second Brigade, Third Division, responded.

Recall from earlier that Warner (another of Harrington's many clients) had allowed a number of charges on his account with Catlin & Jasper during this month, which he later refused to pay, resulting in the business suing him. It is reasonable to conclude that Warner might have chosen not to pay his bill, not because of any want of ability, but rather because he quickly came to learn in these moments of Guy Catlin's involvement with the smugglers. In any event, Warner's men remained at the jail for only eight days until a system was put into place allowing for various companies, each made up of some thirty soldiers, to rotate in and out over the next several months, guarding and transporting the prisoners to and from court.

Until the many soldiers were able to fashion some means for their own accommodation and maintenance, the initial burden fell on Staniford to see that those needs were met. Accordingly, he looked to the house recently added to the jail, rented months earlier by Deputy Elias Buel, as a place to feed the men. The intrusion did not rest well with Buel, who later petitioned the state legislature for reimbursement because he had "expended much money in repairing said house, and fitting it for use," only to then suffer "great injury of his furniture and other property" because of the soldiers.[369]

Buel's complaint was for another day, and whether he liked it or not, on August 3 he became actively engaged providing support to the arriving soldiers. On that evening, he fed them supper (charging $1.67 total), a "pint of rum for guard on duty," another for an unidentified recipient and some candles. The following day, he provided the guarding soldiers two quarts of rum, as well as several other pint distributions, a pint of spirits, more candles and food. Even one of Warner's soldiers, Private John Youngman, was able to turn a profit providing bread and lodging to the various militia units during their stay, later reimbursed by Haswell. As Staniford subsequently detailed for the legislature when he sought reimbursement of his expenses, the demands the soldiers placed on him were huge: 235 weeks of board (each week constituting one soldier's feeding); an impressive 137 gallons of gin, together with rum and brandy; ninety pounds of candles; powder; flints; salt; lime; paper; blankets; building a shanty for the prisoners; blacksmith Johnson's bill for putting on and taking off the prisoners' iron shackles at various times; and boarding horses.[370]

Back on the Intervale, justice of the peace and state's attorney William Harrington must have experienced some degree of shock and, certainly, anger. Viewing the body of his former client lying on the ground, an esteemed war veteran and captain riddled with shot torn viciously through him, Harrington now faced the monumental task of sorting through all of the evidence and seeing to it that those responsible for Ormsby's and the two soldiers' deaths paid the price. In his usual, highly competent and thorough manner, Harrington dispatched an express rider on a seven-day assignment to head directly to the home of Chief Judge Royall Tyler (1757–1826), of the Supreme Court of Judicature, located more than one hundred miles to the south in Newfane, to deliver the news and then proceed with whatever orders the judge might make. As Tyler later explained to a grand jury appearing before him:

> *When, in consequence of this melancholy event we received the application from your respectable states attorney we did not hesitate immediately to suspend the business of the Eastern Circuit and to convene this special sessions of the court conceiving that mere decisions on civil contract inferior*

in magnitude and importance to the inquiry into the murder of our fallen citizens and the peace of this highly valued section of the state.[371]

Now, the local justices' attention turned to getting to the bottom of what happened.

With the three bodies lying before them, Harrington and Russell quickly put into operation the 1797 law concerning "the mode of taking inquisition on the body of a person found dead, by casualty or violence." This required them to assemble fifteen local residents to view the deceased and to decide "whether he died of felony, or of mischance or accident; and if of felony, whether of his own, or of another; and if of the felony of another, who were principals, and who were accessories, with what instrument he was struck, or wounded, and so of all prevailing circumstances."[372] Fifteen men were immediately summoned to the scene, including, among them, fellow justice of the peace Robinson, Elias Buel and the man who had taken Ledgard into custody, James Cummings; for their efforts, each was allowed fifty cents in compensation. Then, over the course of the remainder of that day and concluding on the following, witnesses were called and examined in the presence of the bodies concerning their knowledge of events. At their conclusion, the men unanimously agreed on the circumstances surrounding the deaths of Ormsby and Marsh; their particular findings regarding Drake do not appear in the records. Unsurprisingly, they determined that the two had died because of bullets shot into their bodies by the wall piece fired by Samuel Mott and that the men of the *Black Snake* crew had assisted him.

Asa Rice remained available throughout this time to assist the judges, including keeping watch over the dead as they conducted their business. Between August 3 and 4, he, together with David Hoare and one of Warner's men, Private Barnabus Hoose, stayed with the bodies attending to their safekeeping as further preparations were made. Hoose's fellow private, Thomas Pardo, and two others named Price and McMasters dug the necessary two graves for the deceased soldiers, while John Smith provided two coffins (costing $5.00). Judge Russell arranged for burial shrouds and purchased ten yards of India cotton, two cotton balls and a handkerchief, all used as winding sheets. To quench the thirst of everyone involved, he also provided the requisite five quarts of rum, while other "refreshments" were administered by A. Crane. To further dignify the proceedings, three yards of crepe and two red cords were also purchased, perhaps used to decorate the two soldiers' coffins. Because these state militia officers were in the employ of the federal government conducting national business at the time, Haswell, on behalf of the Revenue Service, arranged to repay all these expenses, including his own charge of $5.00, totaling $36.21.[373]

Upon completion of the inquests on August 4, Warner and those men not otherwise engaged with guard duty escorted the three bodies into Burlington and took them to the courthouse, where they were laid out. Word of the murders spread quickly, and a large number of people from the town and surrounding communities gathered that morning to hear Rutland's Reverend Dr. Samuel Williams deliver "an appropriate and pathetic discourse." Williams had arrived in Burlington in 1805 upon the formation of the First Society by Harrington and others and, according to Harrington's account book, was being paid $400 a year to preach to the community (closely noting he had delivered twenty-two sermons between his start on October 20, 1805, and March 16, 1806). Following his sermon, the bodies were escorted, with "martial honor," to the graveyard, followed by a procession nearly a half mile long.[374]

Later that day, with the causes of death now established, Harrington and Russell took the next step and convened themselves as a Court of Inquiry to determine what charges should be instituted. They received testimony from an additional twelve witnesses. As a result, Harrington filed the first of many court documents, a complaint and warrant for murder, against all eight members of the *Black Snake* crew and ordered them held for further proceedings.

And while the drunken "gang from the north" had succeeded beyond anyone's imagination in making its threats to spill gallons of the soldiers' "heart's blood" a reality, one can reasonably ask where were the threatening hordes rising up to protect the gang, as previously promised by the removed, but certainly not disinterested, local professionals only hours before?

THE REMOVAL OF THE smugglers from river to jail hardly quieted the government's most immediate concerns about the possibility of further violence. Now, it turned to the question of what to do with the most insidious and potent symbol of all that was wrong: the *Black Snake* itself. As discussed later, the boat did remain in existence until, at least, the following spring, when it was sold pursuant to court order. But for the present time, it constituted a volatile rallying point for those emboldened by the murders to try and forcibly retake it, a very real possibility of the times. There are no records describing exactly what was done with it in the interim, but there are cryptic references providing some clues.

As Nathan Haswell went about settling the various claims made against the government for services provided by the local community, he sent Penniman a letter referring to them and advising that, at that moment, he was forced to make an urgent trip to New York because of business partner Peaslee's ill health. One of the claims he mentioned concerned his own "for supplying the party who took the *Black Snake* with liquors &c. and other hands conceived necessary to employ." While he may have been referring to Farrington and his men at the onset of the encounter, the context of employing additional people in some vague role "conceived necessary" indicates that there was something else going on.[375]

Bates Turner was one of two attorneys representing Mott at trial and had occasion to make a lengthy closing argument to the jury describing the defense's interpretation of the evidence introduced against his client. In one of his many attacks on the government's case, he argued that authorities acted in a secretive, unilateral and illegal manner in their pursuit of his client and crew. There is no specific testimony available to describe what he was referring to, but he asked the jury to recall the "evidence by the Customs House officer, that the boat was to be sunk in the lake. That it should not be a bone of contention, only [illegible] to sink it in the lake, without judge or jury." His contention that the government had a prior plan to simply sink the boat, and its troublesome crew, somewhere out of the sight of lawful authority and thereby be done with the problem was an attractive one, as he went on to remind them of what the authorities should have known: "there is to be a trial on this business." He then asked a curious question, "What has become of this boat?"

Turner then weaved into his argument a sweeping condemnation of the government, stating that, because "the Constitution and the laws of God & man protected this boat from being sunk," if it had acted illegally at some point after it was seized, then it "makes everything wrong that was done before." What was it that authorities did after taking the boat that now made all of its prior conduct illegal? They buried it!

As Turner argued, "Why, if government can bribe their officers to go and take our boats and hide them in the sand, what will become of all our property? And you must by your acquittal of the prisoner to [*sic*] prevent our property from being hid in the sand." He then asked, "Where are these men to look for their property after they are hung?" While one can question the underlying logic of Turner's argument, placing the large and imposing *Black Snake* in some location out of sight for the immediate time certainly made sense. Any effort to keep a constant watch over the boat would entail a large expenditure of time and money, and simply taking it to some remote location, digging a hole and burying it seems most logical, legal and hardly constituting an excuse for the killing of three people.

There were other compelling forces in play at the moment. Immediately before Mott's trial began in late August, his second attorney, Amos Marsh, sought to continue the proceedings because, he argued, "the agitation of the public mind" was so extensive, his client could not get a fair trial. Unfortunately, the relevant single page contained in the record describing his contention is torn in half, and some important information is missing. However, words such as "Federalists...an opportunity to bring forward... [ot]hers more guilty" all point toward the defense's underlying belief that the murders "could not have been done without [the] instigation of some persons [i.e., Federalists]." Indeed, they were not the only ones believing that was the case.

Two days after the murders, on August 5, the local paper, the *Vermont Centinel*, published the first news under the heading "Melancholy Event" and provided a general description of what took place without assigning any blame, hoping "that all opinion will be suspended." In the soldiers' hometown, the *Rutland Herald* repeated the article, but under a banner blasting out "OUR CITIZENS MURDERED BY POTASH RUNNERS!" However, for Sergeant David Johnson, who barely survived the event unscathed, it was not a time for condemnation: "Gratitude will never suffer me to forget the kind and benevolent treatment of the people of Burlington towards my wounded lieutenant, myself, and surviving fellow soldiers, and for the respect paid to the remains of our bleeding companions." But people talked, and they had opinions, as Marsh told the jury, "You may have heard in bar rooms...that if we do not hang some people murders will encrease [*sic*]." Others immediately took up invective pen and freely engaged in long discourses assigning fault and blame, some looking directly at those who committed the killings, while others made vague references, without naming names, to the hidden forces backing their actions. Some even blamed the collector himself—"The men died like fools; they were sent here by Penniman to steal an empty boat"—while another hoped "to God Penniman will be hung for it."

While some lamented that it was simply an absence of shared communal virtue, others viewed the deaths as political statements: "If they were republicans who were killed, he was glad of it." Still, another saw it from a wholly different perspective, describing Mott and Day as Republicans themselves and the killings a case of "democrat kill democrat...[and] we rejoice that no federalist has been guilty of staining his hands in blood and infamy." For the Democrats, news of the murders "had not been 3 hours in this town before federalists were heard to say, 'All is well; government had no right to seize the boat.' *Tories* appear in all garbs but the right one—they are perched behind the merchant's desk—they are among the knights of the green bag—they turn up their noses in the walls of all our colleges—they are advocating British insults and murders, and domestic insurrection and havoc in every corner." In fact, a political price was paid when Governor Smith was replaced that September by Federalist Isaac Tichenor as the position then rotated between the two parties for the next several years. Even that event did not escape condemnation, with allegations of "aristocratic lawyers, those leeches who have sucked from the people their vital subsistence," having now been put into power.[376]

However, it was those several references to the participation of unnamed others managing to escape punishment that reveals the existence of an ugly underside within the community, the presence of those others managing to evade exposure. It is not necessary to simply accept accomplice Francis Ledgard's 1811 statement at face value that Mix, Cole, Fitch, Harmon and Catlin had participated by counseling mayhem and supplying its tools. There was additional information to conclude that was the case, as one observer of Cyrus Dean's trial noted concerning the meetings taking place between the smugglers and "certain gentlemen" on the night before the killings. He related that "the names of those two persons were suppressed by the court, but they were so well described by the witnesses that but little doubt remained as to their identity."[377]

One particularly noteworthy handbill bearing three black coffins across its top was circulated and further assigned blame to those "principal merchants [who] furnished the insurgents with powder and ball, for the express purpose of performing this bloody work." The papers made repeated, veiled references to the existence of these individuals, and one St. Albans contributor, calling himself A TRUE AMERICAN, reasonably asked (emphasis in original):

> *Would it not be an insult on common sense to say that 10 or 11 men would go armed and equipped in the most warlike manner, from the Province line to Burlington, a distance of 40 miles, declaring and proclaiming as they went, their determination to resist the authority of government and to kill the first man who should attempt to molest them; and when within a mile of one of the largest towns in Vermont commenced a fire upon the troops*

of the United States, and killed a part of them; if they had not been countenanced and encouraged by a considerable number of individuals in this state, and were not fully impressed with the belief that they would be supported and protected! These are serious considerations. For the honor of my country, for the honor of human nature, I wish to God it were not so. But facts are stubborn things…

In the year '76, he that held correspondence with and gave aid to our enemies was demanded as a tory and a traitor, and was of course despised by every friend to his country. In the year 1808, does he who spends a great part of his time in abusing and defaming our government for the purpose of assisting a foreign enemy! and who gives aid and countenance to a set of assassins deserve a better fate?[378]

It is interesting to further consider the Burlington paper's handling of the first news of the murders. Immediately following the article describing the event was information concerning Pease's arrest, the seizure of the previously mentioned sixty-nine barrels of potash, that authorization had been obtained for the construction of two gunboats on Lake Champlain (to be built locally) and the appearance of Haswell's reward notice for the four escaped smugglers. However, in between these articles was the curious placement of news of Guy Catlin's marriage on July 25, followed immediately by the Catlin & Jasper advertisement boldly proclaiming "EMBARGO," describing the recent arrival of goods "embargoed for the want of purchasers." There might be some innocent, wholly fortuitous explanation for why the editor chose to combine these dissimilar pieces of information in this manner, but one can reasonably question why a supposedly responsible merchant should have his name (in two contexts) directly interwoven with news of the murders unless it was being done, perhaps, in some backhanded, quiet acknowledgement of his removed participation. Interestingly, maybe in an effort to lower their profile, the firm did not run another advertisement until the following November.

However, even further compounding their complicity, Catlin and Fitch took immediate steps to stem the flow of incriminating information that might implicate them further. As Ledgard recalled on the day following his imprisonment:

Between the break of day and sunrise there came a man to the door of the prison and called to me and handed me a half pint of rum. He told me Mr. Catling [sic] and Mr. Fitch had sent him to me to agree with me to keep what they had said and done as a secret and they would give me two hundred dollars and help me to get clear on trial. I told him if they would perform on their part, I would keep it as a secret.

Ledgard did indeed keep the matter quiet for the immediate time, but it proved to be an ill-advised agreement on his part.

For those professionals in opposition to the embargo's goals, the murders represented a new reality requiring them to maintain an air of respectability, not dirtying their hands, as they considered their next moves. In their shared connivance, these pillars of the community composing the "Green Mountain Yeomanry," people who professed allegiance to authority when it suited them but conveniently turned in opposition when it conflicted with their personal interests, were simply two-faced, duplicitous, unindicted co-conspirators. Their involvement and escape from public scrutiny and punishment constitutes one of the more tragic results from this most melancholy event. And for the sacrificial few actually caught, the consequences of their actions became quickly known—in unexpected ways.

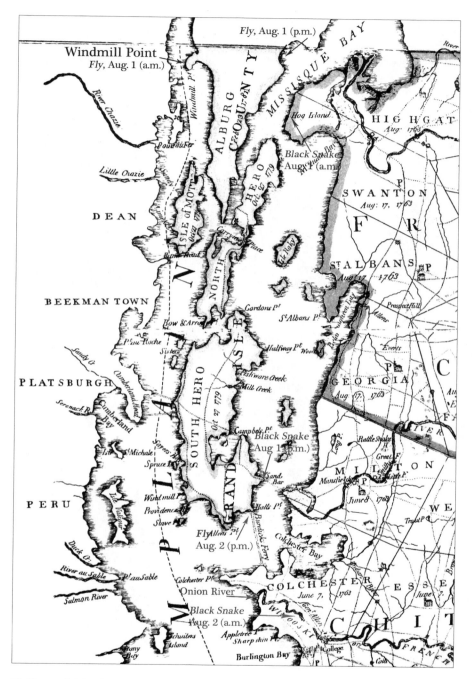

"A Correct Map of the State of Vermont" (1810), with a timeline of the *Black Snake* pursuit. *Map courtesy of Special Collections, University of Vermont.*

Modern-day re-creations of period potash barrels. *Courtesy of Lake Champlain Maritime Museum.*

Opposite, top: Log raft on Lake Champlain. This was a common way of transporting forest products to the Canadian market in the early nineteenth century. *Courtesy of Lake Champlain Maritime Museum.*

Opposite, bottom: Cornelius Peter Van Ness (1782–1852). *Courtesy of Special Collections, University of Vermont.*

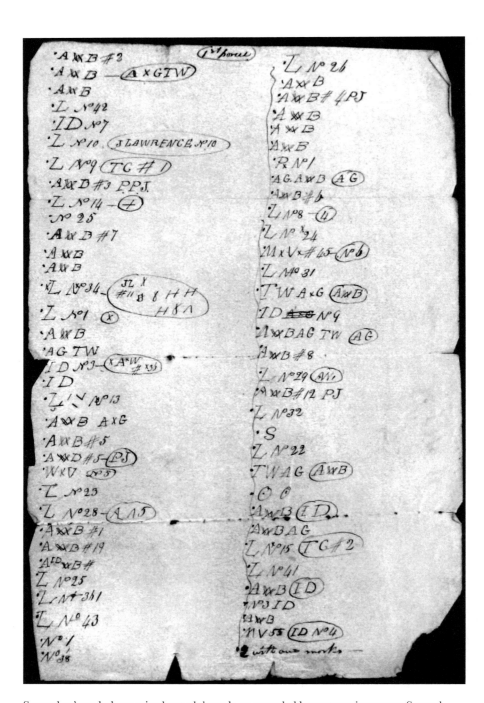

Smugglers' symbols on seized potash barrels, as recorded by customs inspectors Samuel Buel or Nathan Haswell. *Courtesy of Special Collections, University of Vermont.*

A portion of the July 31, 1808 Rutland militia payroll (three days before the murders) naming Farrington, Drake and Marsh (the last two are not visible). *Courtesy Vermont Historical Society, Barre.*

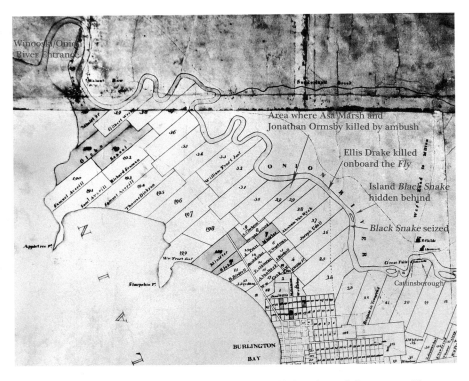

A portion of "A Correct Map of Burlington" (1810), with locations of the events taking place on August 3, 1808. *Map courtesy of Special Collections, University of Vermont.*

TO THE PEOPLE OF VERMONT.

FELLOW CITIZENS,

IT IS DONE! The cup of guilt is full! Treason, rebellion and murder ftalk abroad at noon-day! Our land has been ftained with the blood of our citizens, acting in defence of the government and laws of our country. By whom? A foreign foe? No: but, (horrid to relate!) by the bloody hands of domeftic traitors.

Capt. JONATHAN ORMSBY, a refpectable farmer, belonging to Burlington; Mr. ELLIS DRAKE and Mr. ASA MARSH, two refpectable young men, belonging to Capt. Pratt's company of militia, ftationed at Windmill Point, were all killed at Burlington, on Wednefday the 3d inftant, about noon, in a moft wanton and barbarous manner, by a party of infurgents, employed in fmuggling potafh into Canada, in violation of the laws. The Collector detached Lieut. Farrington, a fergeant and twelve men, in purfuit of a boat, which had gone up Onion river after a load of potafh.— The Lieutenant found the boat and took poffeffion of her, notwithftanding the infurgents threatened to blow out his brains if he attempted to meddle with her. The Lieutenant dropped down the river, with the cutter and the boat he had taken, about half a mile; when the infurgents fired upon him and killed Drake. The Lieutenant then ordered both boats to be rowed on fhore, near the place whence the fire proceeded: he landed with his men, and afcended the bank of the river,— immediately the infurgents difcharged a large gun, called a wall-piece, the barrel of which is eight feet in length, and was loaded with fixteen ounce balls, and fome buck fhot— which carried inftant death to Captain Ormfby and Mr. Marfh, feverely wounded the Lieutenant in the head, the left arm, and flightly wounded him in the right fhoulder. Capt. Ormfby had been laboring in his field during the forenoon, near the fatal fpot, was on his return to dinner, had juft reached the place where the government troops entered the road, when the murderous difcharge took place, which, at the fame inftant, fent two fouls companions into eternity.

If any thing can add to the horror of this, too horrid fcene, it is the obfervation of certain federal characters of the vicinity, who even lay claim to the name of high refpectability, tending to fcreen the affaffins, and throw the whole weight of guilt on the part of the government.——Says one, *The men were fent here by Penniman to fteal an empty boat, and died like fools*—Says another, *I hope to God Penniman will be hung for it*—Says another, *I fhould care but little about it, if I did not fear it would influence the enfuing election*—Says another, on hearing of the melancholy event, *I am glad of it, they are republicans who are killed.*——Such was the current of expreffion which poured from the mouths of federalifm, while the blood was ftill gufhing from the weltering bodies of our countrymen, murdered by federal hands at mid-day, within the boundaries of that town which boafts itfelf of being the ftrong hold of federalifm, and fome of whofe principal merchants furnifhed the infurgents with powder and ball, for the exprefs purpofe of performing this bloody work.

The federalifts now begin to lengthen their faces, and pretend to feel regret for the tranfaction; but their hypocritical tears will not avail them. This horrid deed has been done by their procurement; they are partners in the guilt of the perpetrators, and they are accountable to their country and their God, for all the blood that has been fhed.

When a large body of men, and more efpecially thofe in the higher walks of life, who arrogate to themfelves all the virtue, all the talents, and all the religion of the country, combine together for the purpofe of oppofing the laws of their country; when they openly and publicly, by printing and fpeaking, treat the government and the officers of the government, from the Prefident of the United States down to the loweft executive officer, with abufe, ridicule and contempt; when they trample on the laws of their country, by daily exciting, both by precept and example, the violation of thofe laws by force and arms; when they exult at the fuccefs of the infurgents in every act of treafon they commit; when they

bid defiance to government, and threaten the officers with affaffination if they attempt to do their duty; when with more than favage barbarity they exult over the bleeding bodies of our murdered citizens; and when they even infult the faithful foldier while oppreffed with grief at the lofs of his beloved comrades:— then is the cup of guilt full; then is it time TO ROUSE IN DEFENCE OF YOUR COUNTRY AND YOUR LIVES.

This is no ordinary conteft. It is not a fimple queftion, who fhall be governor and councillors; but it is a ftruggle for the exiftence of your government, for the protection of thofe rights purchafed with the blood of your fathers; and for the protection of your lives. Should that faction whofe hands are ftill reeking with the blood of your brethren, come into power, what have you to expect? If they have done thefe things in the face of law, in the face of authority, what will they do when clothed with power? This bloody fcene is but an opening wedge to the meafures they would purfue. The tragedy of Roberfpierre would be reacted in the United States; and every diftinguifhed character, who is a friend to his country, might expect to be facrificed to the malice of an unprincipled and vindictive faction.

Fellow citizens, on you depends the fate of your country—by your fuffrages at the approaching election, you will decide, whether you deferve the name of freemen; whether you are worthy of your fathers; whether you will defend the government of your country, and protect your wives, your children, and your own lives; or whether you will tamely give up your dear bought rights, and fubmit your necks to the axe of the guilotine.

By fupporting our prefent patriotic governor and councillors, you will perpetuate the exiftence of our government, and tranfmit to pofterity the bleffings we now enjoy.

By neglecting to attend the poll, or by voting for the federal ticket, you will entail on your country all the horrors of flavery, oppreffion and murder.

MONITOR.

"To the People of Vermont" broadside describing the murders. *Courtesy of Vermont Historical Society, Barre.*

An 1808 architectural rendering of the Vermont State Prison in Windsor (opened in 1809). *Courtesy of the Vermont State Archives and Records Administration.*

An 1817 rendering of the pine tree on Burlington's Court House Square, where two smugglers/murderers were whipped. *From* Child's Gazetteer of Chittenden County, *1882.*

Next page: The August 9, 1808 Jabez Penniman affidavit describing smuggling on Lake Champlain involving the *Black Snake*. *Courtesy of National Archives and Records Administration, Boston, Massachusetts.*

State of Vermont   Jabez Penniman of Swanton in the
Chittenden County   County of Franklin & State of Vermont
comes before William C. Harrington Esquire
Justice of the Peace within for said Chittenden County and on his
oath complainant makes & says, that John Taylor, Ezekiel Taylor, Frederick
Hoxie, John Hoxie & Job Hoxie, John Niles all of Alburgh in the
County of Grand Isle & State aforesaid & Joseph Headen of Highgate
in the County of Franklin & State aforesaid all owing allegiance to the
United States, did with force and arms on the 1st day of June 1808
at Alburgh in said County of Grand Isle & State of Vermont as this
as this complainant has reason to believe, & verily does believe
feloniously & wickedly commit the crime of High Treason by
levying war against the United States of America, in as much
as the said John Taylor, Ezekiel Taylor, Frederick Hoxie, John
Hoxie, Job. Hoxie, John Niles & Joseph Headen did arm and
equip a certain boat or batteau called the Black Snake, for the
purpose resisting the authority of & making war against the
Government of the United States & that the said John Taylor
Ezekiel Taylor, Frederick Hoxie, John Hoxie, Job Hoxie
John Niles & Joseph Headen did resist the authority of a levy
war against the United States of America, all which is
against the peace & dignity of the United States of America
and whereas afterwards, to wit, on the third day of July 1808
at North Hero in the County of Grand Isle aforesaid the said
John Taylor, Ezekiel Taylor, Frederick Hoxie, John Hoxie, Job
Hoxie, John Niles, & Joseph Headen did with force & arms
feloniously & wickedly levy war against the United States of
America by arming a certain boat or batteau & therewith
resisting the authority of the United States and making war
against them. And whereas also afterwards to wit, on the first
day of August 1808 at Middle Hero in the County of Grand Isle
aforesaid the said John Taylor Ezekiel Taylor, Frederick Hoxie
John Hoxie, Job. Hoxie, John Niles, & Joseph Headen did with
force & arms feloniously commit the crime of High Treason
against the United States of America by levying war against
them, all which is against the peace & dignity of the said United
States —

This complaint exhibited   Jabez Penniman
to me this 9th day of August   of Swanton State of Vermont
1808. Wm C. Harrington Jus. Peace

CRIMINAL TRIALS AND SUING FOR COWS

William Harrington was an absolutely driven man these days. Nothing in his life came close to the myriad challenges now before him, and they required that he employ every bit of knowledge, creativity and perseverance he possessed to deal with the eight men involved with the killings and seven others accused of committing high treason. As he told the first jury he appeared before in Mott's trial later that month, this was "one of the most important trials ever had." Indeed, there were few in the country's history that could compare; certainly, Vermont had never seen anything like it.

Despite the mysterious illness plaguing his family during these months, Harrington was not about to let anyone take his place, and as dozens of soldiers quickly arrived in town, he started to assemble a variety of resources to prepare the many cases for their respective trials. The magnitude of what he faced was starkly demonstrated when he issued a staggering eighty subpoenas to many witnesses, ranging from soldiers on Windmill Point to civilians living in New York, across northern Vermont and eighty miles down to Rutland. Each one required the assistance of Staniford, who, in turn, called on the services of no fewer than seven deputies to make arduous trips by horse and boat, search out the witnesses and, when found, read out the document to them telling them where and when they were required to appear.

Realizing the practical legal challenges he faced, Harrington also sought out the assistance of other attorneys. One was David Fay (1761–1827), the federal government's attorney for the District of Vermont. Originally from Hardwick, Massachusetts, Fay arrived in Bennington at age five and served as a young fifer in Captain Samuel Robinson's company at the Battle of Bennington in 1777. He remained in the militia in the years immediately after the war and served in the same call-up of militia troops that deceased Jonathan Ormsby had participated in during the 1782 riots in Windham County.[379]

Fay, together with Ormsby and Judge Russell, was also an early member of the North Star Lodge of the Free and Accepted Masons, founded in 1785 in Manchester pursuant to authority granted to it by Boston's grand master, Paul Revere. This was the second such lodge in Vermont and one of the most important of the several coming into existence during these years. By 1808, twenty-eight of them were spread out over the state (bearing such memorable names as Olive Branch, Golden Rule, Rainbow and Cement), collectively serving as vital gathering places for many of those being pulled into these more recent events. Nathan Haswell eventually became the state's grand master during the crucial anti-Masonic period between 1829 and 1846. It was a time when Masonry might otherwise have perished but for his admirable "wisdom, courage, self-sacrifice and infinite patience," earning him widespread approbation as one of the greatest Masons in nineteenth-century America. Even as those in Burlington frantically sought to unravel what took place on the Intervale the day of the murders, Masons unaware of the tragedy continued with their routine, meeting at Chelsea's Washington Lodge (where Matthew Gray was expelled for "gross, immoral, unmasonic conduct"), at Hiram Lodge in Pawlet and then at North Star Lodge in Rutland the following day. These times eventually became so widely unsettling that even within the Masons' ranks, many were expelled, suspended or rejected, swelling to dozens of names by 1813.[380]

Democrat Fay became a member of the bar in 1794 and served as Bennington County state's attorney for the following two years. Between 1799 and 1806, he was a member of the Council of Censors and was named by Jefferson in 1801 to become the state's United States attorney. The timely occasion of the murderers' trials served only to further enhance his reputation, elevating him to become a judge on the Supreme Court the following year; he would remain in that role until 1812. Just weeks before the tragedy, Fay, a colonel of militia, stood before more than two hundred Bennington Republicans and read out the Declaration of Independence. Two weeks later, he probably attended the anniversary of the Bennington Battle on August 16 and raised a glass to each of the seventeen toasts made, one addressed to "Our murdered brethren, ORMSBY, MARSH AND DRAKE," asking, "Is not the hand of federalism in all this?"[381]

The trials also served as an important milestone in the career of local attorney Cornelius Van Ness, who could always look back on them as the beginning of his meteoric rise to power. Considered by Federalists as one of Jefferson's "infuriated parasites," Aaron Burr's friend and a thorough Democrat, Van Ness, and mentor Asa Aldis, advised Penniman in April with such persuasive counsel that the president issued his egregious proclamation announcing an insurrection and setting off such widespread discord. At some point in the next couple months, following the death of his son, Van Ness moved his family out of St. Albans and into Burlington, where Harrington sought his assistance with the crisis. Van Ness was also amply rewarded when, at age twenty-seven, he later became the United States attorney for Vermont, making him one of the youngest to serve in that important role in the nineteenth century. Together, the two colonels and Van Ness coordinated their various efforts to bring to bear as many of the state and federal resources they could against the murdering smugglers. Unfortunately, but unsurprisingly in this fractured political world, the results they obtained were nothing any of them could have imagined.

On Windmill Point, Sam Buel remained at his post and sent periodic letters to Haswell in Burlington advising him of the status of the arrests and the flow of witnesses passing through to Burlington. On August 5, Job and John Hoxie were taken into custody at some nearby location, and Buel sent the *Beaver* to forward them on, with Lieutenant Bennett providing the necessary guard. With their father already in custody, the two sons agreed to cooperate with authorities, as Buel explained:

> *I expect that you have some of the principal insurgents (Taylor and others with you). I should advise that then* [sic] *be suffered to have any communication with them. They (the Hoxies) appear willing to make disclosures that may be useful, which I think they will do if not sought upon by others.*[382]

Buel also sent along a number of recently seized barrels of potash, directing Haswell to record their many unique symbols and then store them. Invoices for this time reveal that Haswell was earning a respectable amount of money in his dual capacity as inspector and John Peaslee's business partner. For "storing, watching, guarding" and transporting eighty-two barrels between August 10 and the following March 9, Haswell received $113.75, and for ninety-seven barrels, $235.75.[383] Three days later, Buel's deputy inspector and smuggler Day's contact, Judge/Dr. Wood, made the trip to Burlington bearing a letter of introduction from Buel to "Friend Haswell," explaining that he "goes on behalf of the U. States to bear testimony against the insurgents with you" and asking that he be accommodated.

On August 12, the customs men seized a pirogue (a flat-bottomed boat) off Windmill Point carrying the fifty-one barrels of potash that Platt Rogers later unsuccessfully sought to recover. The boat received its cargo at Willsborough, New York, but failed to stop and declare its load before being intercepted. In sending those barrels on to Haswell for storage, Buel requested that he again record their unique markings but then went on to make an important observation concerning those sponsoring the smuggling and possibly escaping punishment. "I hear with much satisfaction of your exertions in support of the laws and hope the judiciary powers may effect something to purpose," he wrote, "but apprehend that the nerves of mischief will not be exposed as they ought from the art and systems they have used to screen themselves." To get to the bottom of it, Buel next suggested that Haswell speak with Penniman and consider summoning Judge Peter Sailly to testify about information he had concerning the Taylors, whom he believed had been "instrumental in arming" the smugglers.[384]

Originally from France, Sailly (1754–1826) arrived in the United States in 1785 and took up residency in Plattsburgh, served in numerous local capacities, became a major in the militia and then a county judge and member of the state assembly, was elected to the U.S. House of Representatives and, between 1809 and his death, worked as collector of customs for the Champlain district. In 1807, he was tapped by officials to travel covertly into Canada to assess and send back reports relating British military and civilian attitudes toward the United States as tensions between the two countries rose.[385] Importantly, in 1811, he became Buel's father-in-law and played a role in the early stages of his son-in-law's coming legal woes.

Many novel issues became immediately apparent to the attorneys sorting through the various cases, including the need to take action beyond criminal prosecutions to also forfeiting the boats and potash. There were federal statutes that applied to obstructing revenue officers in their work (a $200 fine), but none addressing their murder, thereby necessitating Harrington's resorting to using the state court to prosecute the *Black Snake* crew. However, in light of the larger size and geographical scope of the smuggling operations undertaken by the Taylor and Hoxie groups, it made more sense to the attorneys to consider using federal law to prosecute them. Unfortunately, beyond the toothless penalties allowed by the embargo's provisions, there were no laws specifically dealing with their particular conduct, and Fay was forced to look elsewhere for guidance.

In this case, that involved examining the circumstances surrounding Van Ness family friend the notorious Aaron Burr.

Burr's trial for high treason was well known and had been closely followed by the public when it took place only a year earlier in the U.S. Circuit Court overseeing Virginia and North Carolina, with Supreme Court chief justice John Marshall presiding in his role as a circuit court judge. The case was an uphill battle for the government from the very start and involved numerous, unsettled legal issues surfacing in an environment with little precedence. Only two cases, those stemming from the 1794 Whiskey Rebellion and a 1798 matter involving tax resister John Fries applied in the federal arena, none of which provided Fay with the necessary legal backing to wage an effective prosecution of the smugglers for treason. Notwithstanding, as far as concerned Jefferson, who without hesitation accused Burr of engaging in treasonous conduct—firing on public officials and forcibly rescuing seized contraband—it "may not be an insurrection in the popular sense of the word, but being arrayed in war-like manner, actually committing acts of war, and persevering systematically in defiance of the public authority, brings it… fully within the legal definition of an insurrection."[386] Jefferson's exhortations aside, Burr's subsequent acquittal for treason did not bode well for Fay, who chose to push on anyway, believing that the smugglers' underlying conduct would serve as adequate basis to at least file charges and then see what might auger for a different result in the context of the Vermont frontier.

For the time being, in order to allow Fay to arrange for a federal prosecution for treason, a capital offense requiring the presence of a U.S. Supreme Court justice, the attorneys decided that Harrington, in his role as justice of the peace, would conduct the necessary hearings to hold the second group of men in custody. Accordingly, for the second time, between August 10 and 13, he sat as a Court of Inquiry using Penniman's August 9 allegations that the Taylors and Hoxies, Niles and Headon had committed high treason by levying war against the United States. Each man pleaded not guilty, and after receiving testimony from many witnesses, Harrington bound over all but Niles and Headon (charges dismissed) for trial in the U.S. Circuit Court in Rutland on October 3. It was during these particular proceedings conducted before Harrington that Van Ness's name first becomes associated with the government's interests when he "recognized" (guaranteed) the prosecution against the men in the sum of fifty dollars.[387]

The turmoil running rampant through the Burlington community during these days had virtually no effect on the inhabitants' long-standing tradition of bringing lawsuits against one another. In a dizzying display of both devotion to duty, and a refusal to put self-interest behind them, several prominent men continued to pursue one another in their quest for gain. On the day immediately following the soldiers' funerals, Harrington instituted suit against Addison County jail keeper Azariah Painter, accusing him of allowing one Jabez Fitch to escape custody, thereby denying him the opportunity to recover a $40.69 judgment. Two weeks later, only days before the start of the most important trial in the state's history and of his career, he filed yet two more cases, accusing five men of failing to pay him money they owed. He was by no means alone, as on the very day the hearing began on his allegations against the smugglers, Penniman himself instituted his own suit against two men for failing to return a cow he had loaned to them three years earlier. He was also in the middle of another suit at that moment, one in which he alleged he had been forcibly ejected from a 103-acre tract of land he owned on the Onion River.[388]

For the Catlin brothers, as suspicions of Guy's complicity became known, the two previously described suits brought by banker Daniel Farrand were filed against them on August 21. A week later, Moses went on the offensive and instituted his own case against Staniford for failure to pay a $98.20 note; it was also the very moment that Staniford allowed John Fay, Esquire, free on bond in a case involving claimant Moses, which served as the basis for him to file yet another suit against him the following January.[389] Even as Staniford and others working with him diligently executed their duties in these hectic days, officials controlling the county's purse strings refused to reimburse them for their expenses, resulting in yet more burdens for the courts when they later filed additional suits for payment the following February. Even Deputy Seeley Bennett was involved, filing his own suit in the midst of the first trials on August 26 against two men owing him money for a debt.[390]

Staniford's workload was ceaseless as officials moved the many cases forward in lightning fashion, no doubt a situation driven not by any concerns of a constitutional right to a speedy trial but to quell community unrest as quickly as possible. Not only were he and his men searching out Harrington's dozens of witnesses, but they were also executing court orders issued on August 15 that required them to go to eighteen surrounding towns to find that same number of individuals to serve on a grand jury (commencing days later on August 23 at 11:00 a.m.) and fifteen others for a petit, or trial, jury (starting on August 25 at 8:00 a.m.). The timing of their required appearances, separated by only two days, leaves little doubt that authorities urgently rushed to move the proceedings directly from any findings the grand jury made straight into a trial—certainly an unheard-of circumstance in the modern world.

None of this was easy work, and it was done quickly, as Ephraim Hurlburt explained, "Sheriff Staniford requested me to assist in the service of the venire, as he observed the time allowed for service was so short and he and his deputies so much engaged." The work required them to travel to the many towns identified by the court, find the particular town clerk and then, through a random drawing, select the name of a local resident to serve, search him out and then tell him where and when he was required to appear.

The process did not go without incident, as the intrepid Seeley Bennett found out when he arrived at the Williston clerk's office to find a grand juror. Current law required that the drawing be done in the presence of the clerk or, in his absence, one of the town's selectmen. While the clerk was indeed absent on his arrival, Bennett found a piece of paper bearing two names separated by a partial tear between them and a note from the clerk that these were the town's authorized representatives allowed to serve on a grand jury. Needing to continue quickly with his work, and in the presence of the clerk's wife, Bennett separated the names and placed the two pieces of paper in a box, covered it with his handkerchief and picked out the name of Truman Chittenden, Esquire. Bennett's deviation from the law by not doing so in the presence of a selectman later served as a basis for defense attorneys to argue that the verdict involving their client, Cyrus Dean, should be put aside. However, the Supreme Court disagreed for various reasons and determined that "this misconduct of the officer" was insufficient grounds to do so. The work for all Staniford's men was onerous, as his bill to the legislature for $142 (including the costs for candles and "sweeping & cleaning Court House, $1.00") reveals.[391]

ALEXANDER MILLER RETURNED to his Swanton post by early August and, even if not present for the events suddenly erupting around him, in time to experience yet another instance of insubordination. Once again, Ashur Blunt, the man who had counseled mutiny to his fellow soldiers a month earlier, took it upon himself to inflict more discord. On August 13, he refused to obey unspecified orders and, as he wrote out in his confession from the guardhouse, used "disrespectful language against my superior officers" while also "endeavoring to make uneasiness and…breeding contention among the soldiers," leading him to ask for forgiveness.[392] The disposition of any charges against him is not stated.

As part of his continuing correspondence with his wife, Miller described for Lucretia the toxic political atmosphere in Burlington the day before the grand jury was scheduled to meet and told her that "the demo[crats] have undertaken to lie down the Federalist." He believed the approaching trials would be used "as a weapon by the demos. They begin to say the Republican lawyers volunteer their services in favor of the state & because some of the lawyers engaged on the side for the criminals happen to be Federalists they say hard things against them and personal[ly] abuse them." But in the end, he thought it was all politics, telling her that when the upcoming election was over, "I hope there will be less said and less to say."

Miller also told her he had seen the men awaiting trial:

> *They appear to be very indifferent about life or death & in fact they are a gang of fellows that have two* [sic] *long escaped justice. If their* [sic] *is any of them hung (which in my opinion it ain't possible for them all to escape), their* [sic] *will be few to mourn for them & if more had their desserts that are on the lines of this same class, they would share their fate. They are retchedly* [sic] *frightened & I believe there will be no more arming at present against governments.*[393]

Jefferson had learned of the murders, and the prospect of the men's execution was of concern to him. Writing to Gallatin the following month, he opined, "If all of these people are convicted, there will be too many to be punished with death," expressing hope that "they will send me full statements of every man's case, that the most guilty may be marked as examples, and the less so suffer long imprisonment under reprieves from time to time."[394] However, any thought of having a Washington official involved in the unfolding execution of the law was unthinkable, and Jefferson, along with the rest of the country, simply had to wait to see what would happen next.

The three-month call-up for the Rutland men was about to expire, and Miller spent part of the last two weeks in August traveling to Middlebury on Penniman's behalf. There, he picked up an impressive $4,000 in cash, as well as more than $2,000 in Bank of Middlebury notes, and returned it to Swanton for the collector's use in paying the federal government's many bills. Acting in his role of paymaster, he paid wages to Williams's men, and on the twenty-ninth, he paid $1 to a local man for keeping his horse.[395]

All of the Rutland men had returned home by the beginning of September, and while several companies continued to serve in various roles in the next few years, Miller soon encountered problems with his commanders. The reasons for their dissatisfactions are not clear, but the various desertions and ensuing embarrassment they caused might have been at their heart. There is also evidence that political affiliations were in play as Federalists came into power that fall and were determined to cleanse the ranks of anyone not sympathetic to their cause. One senses from Miller's many letters that, despite his protestations of being within their ranks, it was with lackluster enthusiasm—a factor that may have led those deserting soldiers into their protests. Notwithstanding, in September 1809, he was promoted to captain of the Tenth Company of Infantry, only to learn a year later that he was not destined for any further promotion, setting off a long, tortuous period of correspondence and leading to his resignation from the ranks in September 1811.

Following his return home, in March 1809, Miller expressed a desire to move his growing farm implement business northward to the Burlington area and to make an unidentified "purchase at the Fary [sic]," a reference to the developing ferry trade taking place across the lake. As one correspondent enthusiastically wrote back, "In my opinion, it is the best plan for your business in the country, Mr. Catlin [Moses?] is quite anxious & will give any chance you might ask."[396] However, Miller did not pursue the idea and remained in Wallingford, returning to his role as town librarian and serving as selectman for eight years and as town representative to the assembly for one year. He died in 1844.

As preparations for the trials continued and more potash was seized, court documents reveal a bizarre turn of events concerning an August 20 encounter with the sloop *Dolphin* somewhere out on the water. Forfeiture papers show that sixty-six barrels of ash, each bearing their distinctive, curious symbols, were found on board, and they and the vessel all became part of forfeiture proceedings in the district court in Rutland. Strangely, U.S. attorney Fay stated in his papers that Penniman and his men were responsible for the seizure, thereby justifying suit being brought in Vermont. However, it took until the following May, after much work had been done by claimant Jared McGraw and his attorneys, for Fay to notify the court that, because the items "were seized by the collector of Champlain district…the United States will not prosecute that suit or libel any further."[397] It is strange to see such a fundamental error of this nature taking place, even in the early days of the law. However, because it was one of several such cases filed at the same time, it might simply have been innocent confusion or miscommunication between the revenue men and their prosecutor. Even so, it was no doubt an embarrassment.

The same day, government officials received a substantial boost to their efforts when smuggler Josiah Edson approached them with information that he could tie together and explain much of what had been taking place in the preceding months. When Buel sent the man on to Haswell's attention in Burlington under military guard, he explained, "I have arrested [Edson] who has been active in mischief in this vicinity and is well acquainted with the actors and movers of the drama." Buel further wrote that "he has come forward of his own accord to disclose the knowledge he has of the criminality of Taylors, Hoxies, &c. and perhaps some others who have not as yet been called in question." When Edson expressed some hesitancy toward providing cooperation because of "the injury it may do the feelings of his connections," Buel related that he had "given him assurance of every indulgence and attention which he may be entitled and which will depend much on his frankness and sincerity."[398] The timing of Edson's coming forward could not have been more fortuitous, as the proceedings were just about to begin.

CHIEF JUDGE ROYALL TYLER'S extraordinary decision to suspend all normal court operations now brought him and his two associate judges, Theophilus Harrington and Jonas Galusha, into town not only to supervise the biggest trial in Vermont history at the time but also to do so in an atmosphere dripping with faction. Additional pressure on the court concerned its need to return to the demands of litigants in other parts of the state forced to delay their already scheduled hearings so that this emergency could be dealt with.

Boston-born and bred, a 1776 Harvard graduate and the frustrated and denied fiancé of John and Abigail Adams's daughter, Nabby, Tyler served during both the Revolutionary War and as aide to General William Shepard during Shays' Rebellion. During the latter, Tyler made his initial foray into the Vermont wilderness in pursuit of fleeing protestors, only to suffer the indignity of having Adam Wheeler, one of the captured leaders, forcibly retaken out of his custody by sympathetic Yorkers. Tyler became a member of the Massachusetts bar in 1780, and following his settling in Vermont in 1791, he served as Windham County state's attorney between 1794 and 1801, when he became an assistant judge of the Supreme Court. In 1807, he was named chief judge, continuing in that role until 1813.[399] An inveterate, eclectic author, he wrote many literary works, including what is considered America's first play, *The Contrast*, in 1787. For the town's 1799 Fourth of July celebrations, Tyler penned a "Convivial Song" espousing the fruits of American freedoms, those represented and guaranteed by Vermonters, stating in part:

> *Here's to Vermont State, boys,*
> *And all her manly rustic joys,*
>
> *Here's to Vermont State, boys,*
> *Columbia's Brave defender;*
>
> *For while our pines ascend on high,*
> *And while our mountains mock the sky,*
>
> *Our Independence, Liberty,*
> *We will never surrender.*[400]

Several years removed from those words of unity, Tyler now faced the daunting challenge of conducting unbiased and fair trials in an atmosphere portending no such thing.

Only twenty days after the murders, with courthouse floors swept and candles lit as needed, the eighteen members of the grand jury assembled and were sworn in at 11:00 a.m. on Tuesday, August 23, remaining in town for the next nine days conducting their business. In only two days, the fifteen petit jurors were to arrive, but they could do nothing without the necessary indictment returned by a grand jury, and it was to that body that the court now turned its attention. Clearly mindful of the difficulties before him, Tyler addressed the men concerning the reasons for their gathering, one occasioned by the "awful and melancholy" murders staining their "happy land…with human gore" as "the voice of the blood of our brethren crieth from the ground." He admonished them to act as unbiased judges of the evidence, turning aside outside influences: "Let not therefore your acquaintance or friendship for the deceased, the tears of the widow, the lamentations of the fatherless or the distress of surviving relatives affect you."

Realizing that he could not let the fact that politics was very much part of the public's discussion in assigning blame for the incident, Tyler warned, "If in some hours of levity any of you have thought that the primary laws of society, those made for the preservation of human life, ought on this occasion to be relaxed and be accommodated to certain supposed exigencies of the times, purify yourselves also from these prejudices." He told the men to let their oaths be their guides, and the matter was then turned over to

Harrington to shepherd them through their work, but only after he sought, and received, permission to have Fay and Van Ness assist him.

The presence of these two men for the next several weeks was certainly a necessity as Harrington began to negotiate a complicated path that included so many smugglers, soldiers and witnesses (some remaining in town only a few days and others as long as twenty-six days), all present in a community closely watching their every move. For Van Ness, the assignment brought on additional responsibilities, diverting his attention from some of his pending cases. These included an important suit he had begun a week earlier on behalf of local judge Jonathan Janes against St. Albans militia general Levi House for his purported defamation of the judge; another involved the theft of fifty thousand bricks, one concerned the theft of a yoke of ox and still another was a complicated mortgage matter involving the perennially named Silas Hathaway and Heman Allen.[401]

By the time Harrington began introducing witnesses to the grand jury for questioning, he had prepared two important documents to guide the course of the prosecutions. The indictments he used described the smugglers' involvement in two separate acts: Drake's killing on the river and Ormsby's and Marsh's on the roadway. The most compelling, and outrageous, of the two concerned the death of local resident Ormsby, and that's where the grand jury concentrated its first efforts.

Over the course of the next three days, the jury received testimony from many individuals, finally concluding on August 26 that there was sufficient evidence to warrant trials, and Foreman Abel Cooper, of Richmond, signed the requisite "A True Bill" on the front of the matter now known as *State of Vermont v. Samuel I. Mott, William Noaks, Slocum Clark, Truman Mudget, Cyrus B. Dean, Josiah Peas, David Sheffield & Francis Ledgard.* Agreeing with Harrington's description of the killings, the eighteen jurors determined that the defendants had "feloniously, willfully, and of their malice prepense [premeditated]…[made] an assault" on Ormsby and Marsh, resulting in their murders. Specifically, it determined that Mott had pulled the trigger sending the many "leaden bullets" into their bodies, causing their devastating and mortal wounds, and that the others were similarly responsible for "aiding, helping, abetting, comforting, assisting, and maintaining" him in his deadly work.

As the grand jury's work continued for the next several days, Harrington lost no time in immediately filing the first indictment with the court, allowing for the next round of proceedings to get underway. It is clear that he was proceeding at a breakneck pace, and in choosing not to wait any longer for the grand jury to finish its work, he demonstrated that efficiency and the stressful demands being placed on scarce resources were of secondary concern in the pursuit of expediency. In this era when the criminal law, with its attending procedural rights for defendants and the mechanics of conducting complex trials, remained undeveloped, Harrington exploited every opportunity possible to demonstrate to the community that the government possessed sufficient teeth to quickly quell the nefarious work of people such as these killers. Unfortunately, in his and the court's haste, these particular proceedings proved to be fatally flawed.

Meanwhile, out on Windmill Point, the pressures brought by authorities began to have an effect when forty pieces of leather were discovered lying on the shore, apparently surreptitiously deposited by an unknown vessel seeking to avoid being caught with undeclared cargo. Ironically, it was Inspector Buel himself who ended up owning the goods a year later after he successfully outbid others (paying fifty-five dollars) at a court-ordered public auction of the forfeited goods based on a proceeding brought by Fay (who received twelve dollars for his efforts).[402] It later proved a purchase he wished he had never made.

As much as the government attorneys might have wanted to move the case forward immediately, the law provided that no arraignment could be held until at least twenty-four hours after the return of an indictment, at which time Harrington was required to provide a copy to each defendant (charging the state eight dollars for his labors).[403] Accordingly, the following day, a Saturday, Mott, Dean, Ledgard and Pease were all brought into court, where they entered not guilty pleas and put themselves "on the country," or demanded separate jury trials. When Tyler inquired how he planned to proceed from that point, Harrington advised that he wanted to begin with Mott's trial and then move on to Dean's, and the parties were ordered to return in forty-eight hours' time to begin.

On Monday morning, as previously noted, Mott's two attorneys, Marsh and Turner, made their request that his trial be continued because of the "agitation of the public mind" making a fair trial impossible, also adding their protestations that others—those Federalists—were responsible for the actions of the "ignorant" smugglers. While period accounts do not disclose his participation, trial records further reveal that attorney Asa Aldis was also present and argued on Mott's behalf. Aldis joined in with Marsh and Turner and reiterated that this discord did "not arise from the transaction itself, but from the political agitation"; he also expressed his fear that "the public agitation will affect the judiciary." Their requests were denied, and then "David Sheffield, the boy, was arraigned and pled not guilty and on the same morning Truman Mudget was arraigned & pled not guilty," whereupon the court adjourned until later that afternoon.

Upon reconvening, University of Vermont president Reverend Daniel Clarke Sanders (1768–1850) appeared to bless the proceedings, doing so through an address to the "the Throne of Grace" in a manner described as "an able, pertinent and pathetic prayer."[404] Jury selection immediately ensued, and following defense challenges to several of the jurors and questions about the sheriff's authority to seat talisman (community members chosen at random) in their stead and then questions about some of their partiality, a jury was finally chosen.

Harrington now rose, and after reminding the men that this was "one of the most important trials ever had," he named several of the witnesses and their expected testimony. Then, over the course of the next two days, some twenty individuals were called to describe their personal involvement with Mott in smuggling (Edson and Perkins), as well as civilians who had personally seen him on the Intervale (Lathrop, Joy and Dils) and soldiers witnessing the events of August 3 (Johnson, Walker and Hays; Farrington was still convalescing).

The proceedings were not without incident, as evidenced when Peter Martins was "hooted" out of the courtroom and when Lathrop's testimony was interrupted just as he told of his conversation with David Sheffield, claiming the young man said he possessed his gun in order to shoot ducks and pigeons. As the court notes explain, "Here it was suggested this witness had not been sworn. He was sworn. Court: 'on the oath you have now taken, is what you have just related the truth?' Answer: 'It is.'" Unfortunately, this was not the last occasion of the court's neglect. On Tuesday morning, Private Hays was allowed to leave the room "on account of sickness" after having gotten only as far as identifying himself, but he returned later in the day to complete his testimony. That afternoon, the public had its first exposure to the big gun when it was brought into the courtroom, and Lathrop identified it as "the gun I saw the prisoner fire."

After the government finished presenting its case, the defense called seven witnesses and questioned them about a single matter: the purported bounty offered for the capture of the *Black Snake*. In their attempts to portray the soldiers as a reckless band of mercenaries set loose to rampage across the countryside in their quest for financial gain, the witnesses were each asked about statements the soldiers made about receiving a reward for their efforts. There were some indications that Sergeant Johnson mentioned a reward, but none of the testimony appears to have been particularly damaging to the government's case.

It was at this time that information arose concerning Farrington's conduct during the fray. During his questioning, Alexander Walker was asked about the soldiers' orders to fire on the smugglers, and when Harrington cross-examined him, he explained, "I never knew of any orders to fire. After the affair I was in Burlington and some people were blackguarding me and said we had orders not to fire. I told them what Capt. Pratt said, when we returned to the lines, that the Lt. did not obey his orders." When faced with the volleys of lead being aimed in their direction on the river and Sergeant Johnson's attempt to return fire, Farrington's honorable, though misplaced, order not to do so might have been the source of Pratt's dissatisfaction with his subordinate's conduct. Or perhaps it was his failure to have consistently displayed the important ensign and pendant flag of the customs service. The receipt of testimony then ended.

According to terse entries in the margin of the court's record, U.S. attorney David Fay rose to present the government's case at "10 minutes past 3...concluded 25 after 4 o'clock." During this time, he summarized the evidence, demonstrating that Mott had intended to fire the big gun now sitting in the courtroom and to kill Ormsby and Marsh. In reaching their decision, he told the jury they were not "to consider the tears of the wife & children of Capt. Ormsby or the distress of the surviving relatives. Nor should you place yourselves in the situation of the prisoner, but stand as candid men before God & Man & so deliver your verdict." Then, the defense attorneys had their opportunity.

The press reported shortly after the trial nothing of what Mott's attorneys said, summarizing their efforts as being "true to their client, and with much ingenuity [they] availed themselves of every circumstance in his favor," adding that Bates Turner was the first to speak. He began at "half past 4, court adjourned half past 6."[405] The news account did not relate why the proceedings were halted at that time, but the record reveals it was at Turner's request because he had worked himself into such a state that he "felt so indisposed in body he could not proceed." Indeed, the court's notes also reflect that during this two-hour summation, followed by another four hours the next morning and then an additional "2 hours and 6" minutes' argument by attorney Marsh, the court and jury were witness to one of the more remarkable displays of creative and ingenious lawyering taking place in Vermont's early legal history.

Both of the attorneys realized they faced a difficult prospect in convincing the jury that their client had not pulled the trigger. The evidence that he had done so was overwhelming, and any attempt to argue to the contrary was destined for failure. In the alternative, they sought to demonstrate that his conduct did not fall within the scope of the law warranting a death sentence. Specifically, they argued that he did not commit murder because he did not act with malice against Ormsby and Marsh; therefore, he was guilty only of manslaughter, which would allow him to live. As Turner pleaded:

> *If you will find him guilty* [of manslaughter], *he is sent to be whipped 100 lashes, then put in the pillory…for people to see him and the state are* [sic] *now building a state's prison, that people may go and look at his poor, mangled back through the grates. Better than to hang him up a few minutes & put him in the ground. Would not the flogging, and pillory, and 10 years imprisonment, is not that worse than hanging?…Should you bring in your verdict against him* [for murder], *he would perhaps be sent into Eternity by next week before you leave this ground.*[406]

It was a logical decision given the circumstances, and the next several hours were devoted to obtaining that end.

Turner opened by telling the jury that Mott's life was in its hands: "It is a solemn business, is it not, to inquire whether he shall be continued a member of his family or committed to the silent manners of the dead?" He then observed that while "some think a lawyer is an unprincipled person," he was not one of them and intended to strictly argue the facts, as bad as they might be. After making references to biblical murders (Cain and Abel, David and Uriah), Paul's persecution of the Jews, trials under Roman law and numerous British trials, Turner distinguished Mott's case from all of those. In a wide-ranging attack on the government's case, Turner argued that Mott was ignorant and unschooled, he was confused by the piecemeal way the embargo had been implemented, Jefferson's proclamation that an insurrection existed did not make sense and the law was not only unconstitutional but also not God's law.

Interwoven with these arguments were others, familiar to those living centuries later, concerning a man's right to defend his own property, the right to be free from searches and seizure and the right to bear arms. Directly taking on the government's purported authority to enforce the embargo's provisions, Turner relied on the law of equity, arguing that before it could do so, it must "come with pure hands," showing that it was doing so error free. What right did the government have to order that the boat be sunk out on the lake without due process, or by what authority did it act in burying it in the sand, out of sight from its owners, after it had been seized? "Had the collector a right to offer a reward? Was it not holding out a temptation to murder?" he asked. Even when faced with the coming militiamen, Turner argued that Mott had acted reasonably and without malice:

> But they came, this gang came on shore with their arms & kept their property. One snapped his gun at these men [Hays's unsuccessful firing at Day]. The prisoner knew that these men were bribed by an agent of government to murder. Their guns presented at him. Was he not compelled by the laws of God and man to fight to defend himself? Was this a cool and deliberate murder? If I had been there, I should have fired further off, but he discovered the firmness of a soldier to let them come so near to him.

They had a right to recapture wrongly taken goods, Turner argued. They had warned the soldiers not to do it, and then they had taken reasonable measures to stop them by first firing into the water. He also acknowledged that as they employed "as little force as possible," somebody fired into the boat and killed a soldier, but Mott was not on trial for that murder, implicitly telling them to put it out of their minds.

Turner also acknowledged that even if the embargo law was constitutional, the jury should construe it very narrowly and determine whether the government closely followed it. In a tantalizing reference to the unique customs flag that was supposed to be displayed, he asked them to "see if they had an ensign and pendant, see what you cannot see." Unfortunately, the testimony remains unclear about whether Farrington ever hoisted the flag, and Turner's invitation to inquire if he had indicates that he did not, which might also explain Benjamin Pratt's displeasure toward Farrington's actions.

At one point, Turner perceived that the court was becoming restless with his arguments and told the jury, "I should produce more authorities, but the impatience of the Court & my own ill health prevent [it]." However, Judge Tyler immediately corrected him, stating, "Mr. Turner, the court are not impatient. They request you to conceal nothing which may operate for the benefit of your client." He finally ended and warned the jury of its own humanity, stating that the jurors, too, would one day be judged:

> Remember you are to see another day, [but] if you should find this man guilty you may see him hung up before tomorrow night and perhaps six more in the course of the week. But the time is approaching when you will appear before another tribunal. It will be no excuse that you have been persuaded by reason.

Amos Marsh then took up Mott's defense, ending two hours later in blazing fashion.

Marsh went further than his co-counsel in arguing that the jury had to find that malice existed in Mott's mind, that it could not be an emotion felt generally but must rise to the level of hatred directed specifically at the person killed. Ignoring the fact that Mott had immediately fled the scene after the murders, Marsh asked if hatred was present in the smugglers' minds when some of them had joined in helping the wounded. Was it hatred when the smugglers told the soldiers not to take their property, to stand off, and issued orders among themselves to avoid firing whenever possible? Was there hatred when others, including "influential people," had told them to defend their property? "They have been told from every quarter this was right," Marsh argued. "They saw property passing from the whole line of this state and the whole of St. Lawrence, but how did these people feel, why stop this little outlet. Government must be wrong." Without specifying the incident, he asked why a raft of lumber had been allowed to go north unmolested. Why was the government acting inconsistently? Confusion over the embargo's provisions removed any inference of malice, he said.

Marsh even went so far as to equate the smugglers with heroes, saying that "these men are like the soldiers of Washington, many a brave man has been sacrificed to party spirit," and told the jury that "they did not come in the night, they lay in the face of the most populace city for days. They were offered gallons of rum to do it. Did this look like malice? They [were] courted and countenanced on all sides to do the deed." He also took the government to task while interjecting some personal invective, asking whether it had "come to this, that our revenue office can send little standing armies about the country," and if so, "I would pass the line and abandon the country." He further contended that only officers of the revenue service had the authority to enforce the customs laws and not militia soldiers and that they had no authority to cut the rope connecting the *Black Snake* to the shore (an act that would have brought justifiable, deadly retaliation in other societies, he said) and asked where the pendant and flag were.

Marsh then made an unwise choice, straying away from the evidence and venturing into areas that were not his to go. He had been lamenting over what was taking place in town with the arrival of the soldiers, saying, "I never saw before an armed force round a prison, for fear there was not virtue enough to guard them," when he slipped and brought up "the rapidity of this trial." Why was it taking place so quickly, he asked? Then he answered, "The court have forced us on to trial because they knew that if time allowed for the popular [passion] to cool, these men would be acquitted." The arguments may have been long and arduous, but Tyler had heard enough, as the record reflects, "The court here called Mr. Marsh to order [and] assured him this imputation they would not bear." Then Tyler warned him in no uncertain terms, "For while the people have confidence in me to honor me with this seat, this Court shall not be insulted. I shall think it my duty to order you to prison for a contempt of court." Recognizing his error, Marsh quickly backed down, "made some apology and closed."

But that was not the end of it. State's Attorney Harrington then stood up and made his own displeasure known, both in manner and terms the court had withheld:

> *Sir, I have manifestly exercised great patience in hearing you and your associate sedulous to search for everything in favor of your client. But at the same time, I do not sit here [to] bear insult & while the citizens of Vermont have confidence in me to place me on this bench, this Court shall not be insulted in my person. For if you persist in charging this Court with having brought on this trial for the purpose of pursuing the conviction of the prisoner, I shall order you to prison, and consider sir, it is easier for me to say than to do this.*

One can only wonder at Marsh's mortification and how his blunder might have affected the jury. None of the exchange was reported in the press, but it did note that Harrington, "in a cool, candid dispassionate manner, then made the closing plea in the behalf of the government."[407] The case was turned over to the jury at 11:00 p.m., and an hour later, it predictably returned guilty verdicts for Mott's murder of Ormsby and Marsh.

ONLY HOURS LATER, WITH the start of the new day of Friday, September 2, the proceedings rushed on without delay. As Mott's trial was unfolding, two days earlier the grand jury had completed its work concerning Drake's murder and filed its second indictment in the matter of *State of Vermont v. David Sheffield, Francis Ledgard, Truman Mudget, William Noaks, Slocum Clark, Cyrus B. Dean, Josiah Pease & Joshua Day*, alleging Sheffield's responsibility for discharging the gun that killed him and the others as his aiders and abettors. Because Van Ness was never reported to have been involved with Mott's trial, it appears he was elsewhere in the courthouse at the time, shepherding witnesses before the grand jury. This was the formal end to the grand jury's work, but before disbanding, it did something extraordinary. The pressures within the community were clearly building, and fully aware of the unrest surrounding the jury as accusations and blame were exchanged between Federalists and Republicans and the magnitude of what it was doing pressed in, the eighteen men deemed it necessary to enter the fray with their own assessment. As their findings were characterized in the press:

> *The Grand Jury…voted an address to the citizens of Vermont, in which they refute the falsehoods which had been circulated by the hirelings of the administration, against the Federal inhabitants of Burlington, and its vicinity. The address thus concludes: "And with pleasure we assert, that from our own observations, and every information we could collect, the respectable inhabitants of Burlington and its vicinity, have throughout the late unhappy transaction, manifested every disposition to support and enforce the laws of their country, and bring the offenders to justice."*[408]

Unfortunately, as well intentioned as their protestations might have been, there is no evidence whatsoever indicating that they ever received any testimony describing the involvement of some of their well-esteemed community leaders. Now, their duty discharged, they were allowed to return home.

As Harrington had earlier promised the court, now he intended to proceed against the man assisting the murdering Mott: Cyrus Dean. Immediately following the return of the second indictment, only Dean and Sheffield were arraigned, and both entered not-guilty pleas. Perhaps not wanting to divert the next jury's attention to the circumstances of Drake's murder, Harrington chose to proceed against Dean for his involvement in the deaths of Ormsby and Marsh. With his knowledgeable attorneys, Amos Marsh and Bates Turner (no doubt still fuming at the speed of the proceedings), at his side, Dean told the court that he was ready to proceed with his case.

This time, Van Ness joined Harrington and Fay in representing the government as a long day of jury selection got underway. It was a process not without incident, as Harrington later lamented: "It is painful to find that party spirit in this part of the United States has already assumed an alarming attitude. Have we not seen…measures taken and pursued by the prisoners' counsel to sweep every republican juror from the panel by peremptory challenge? Have we not repeatedly heard this question, 'Is such a juror a republican or a federalist?' If the former he must not sit, if the latter he will answer our purpose."[409] Interestingly, one of the potential jurors summoned to the courthouse was a cousin of the wounded Farrington, who was predictably excused. In fact, so many of their names were struck from the list that the court ordered an entirely new panel to appear the following day—surely more work for an already overworked sheriff's department.

On Saturday, a jury was finally chosen, and trial began immediately. Harrington made the government's opening statement, and the balance of the day was taken up with extensive testimony from nine witnesses, with the introduction of the big gun and the many poles and stones seized from the *Black Snake* to ward off the soldiers placed into evidence. The day ended immediately following Elkinah Perkins's explanation that the crew understood that Mudget owned the vessel, having purchased it from the Taylors for $200, and that Mott was to become half owner at the conclusion of their most recent trip. Tyler then adjourned the court until 8:00 a.m. Monday and ordered Dean back to jail, while the jury was sequestered and sent into the care of an overseeing officer.

The testimony adduced during Mott's trial was repeated when trial resumed at the start of the new week. The underlying information remained unchanged, as did the defense attorney's attacks on the government's witnesses attempting to portray them as aggressors and reward-seeking opportunists. The only additional noteworthy testimony came from Lieutenant Farrington, who had regained sufficient strength to allow him to attend. While his information did not deviate from what his fellow soldiers had testified to, the appearance of the wounded man must have had a profound effect on anyone present in the courtroom. The receipt of evidence closed following his testimony, and this time Van Ness represented the government in making its closing argument, followed, once again, by the two defense attorneys. The record does not disclose what any of the men said at this point, but there is no reason to believe that, aside from the possibility that Marsh chose to avoid any aspersions on the court's motives to rush the trials, it differed much from what Mott's jury heard.

Because Dean's trial resulted in the imposition of the state's first execution by hanging, its proceedings were the subject of intense scrutiny in the coming months. The record fails to disclose what the court told the jury was the correct legal standard in determining his guilt, but subsequent correspondence from Tyler to an inquisitive state legislature does provide some information. His personal opinion of Dean was certainly not good; he considered him the "most daring and reckless" of all the smugglers who went on trial—an interesting observation when one recalls that it was Tyler himself who had seen, and sentenced, triggerman Mott the preceding December for his involvement in a riot.[410]

Notwithstanding this, Tyler's description of the available options appears correct, as he explained, "The main point of the prisoner's defense went to insist that he was, if guilty in any degree, guilty of manslaughter. [The law] was repeatedly read to the petit jury," whereupon it was instructed that it could return a manslaughter verdict if the evidence to support the murder charge was insufficient. He also told the lawmakers that, "in their several charges," the judges had not only defined murder but also had "expressly informed" the jury that in cases of justifiable homicide it could also find the defendant guilty of the lesser crime of manslaughter.[411] For the legally trained Tyler, having two lay judges at his side (the last to serve in that capacity) must have been of some concern, but he was gracious enough in later summarizing their contributions during this time: "Brothers Harrington and Galusha have given me substantial support. Judge Galusha's maiden charge will do him honor in print, and Judge Harrington forced principles upon the most ignorant in his peculiar, energetic way."[412] In the end, between the three of them, it appears they adequately fulfilled their obligation to provide an essentially correct interpretation of the applicable law.

The case was then turned over to the jury for its consideration, and at two o'clock the following morning, it returned. As the record describes what happened next, the jury was asked:

> *Clerk: Gentlemen of the jury, are you agreed in your verdict?*
> *Jury: Agreed.*
> *Clerk: Who shall say for you?*
> *Jury: Our Foreman.*
> *Clerk: Who is your Foreman?*
> *Jury: John Brown* [of Williston].
> *Clerk: Mr. Foreman, look upon the Prisoner at the bar. Cyrus B. Dean, look at the Foreman of the jury. How say you, Mr. Foreman, is the Prisoner at the bar guilty of the charges in the Indictment, or not guilty?*
> *Foreman: GUILTY.*

With the second culprit now convicted and the court no doubt wishing to press on, it had to vacate the building for the balance of the day to allow the town's freemen to assemble at one o'clock that afternoon for yearly state elections. The community now had an opportunity to make its own interests known and, in a clear rejection of Republican influence, handily endorsed Federalist Tichenor to replace Israel Smith as governor by a vote of 185 to 52, while in the smuggling stronghold of Alburgh, it was by a resounding 120 to 8.[413]

The third person with the most criminal responsibility was seventeen-year-old marksman David Sheffield, and his trial on the second indictment for the murder of boatman Ellis Drake got underway immediately the following day. The names of his attorneys are not disclosed, but there is no reason to believe they did not include, once again, the indefatigable Turner and Marsh. In one of the court's more unusual decisions, perhaps indicating its continuing course to move the proceedings along, the entire jury panel from Dean's trial was summoned to appear again. The reason the court was willing to utilize the same jury was because Sheffield's case was based on a new indictment, with new charges, and there was no reason to believe Dean's jurors should not remain—certainly a situation that could never occur in the modern day. Even when one of the talisman, Jirah Isham, openly declared for all to hear that "these men ought not to be condemned," Tyler ruled that because he had not expressed any bias directly toward Sheffield himself, he had to be seated. A second talisman, nineteen-year-old Ethan Allen Jr., expressed similar sentiments, and Tyler ruled as before, but Harrington then stepped in and moved to exclude both of them, which was granted. In the end, seven of the twelve men who had found Dean guilty of murder were seated.

The trial lasted until Friday, when Sheffield was found guilty of the lesser crime of manslaughter, perhaps an understandable result when one considers the amount of lead passing over the water toward the *Fly* around the same time he fired. His age no doubt also played a factor, as the prospect of seeing a teenager swinging at the end of a rope was something neither political persuasion could have countenanced. But the question remains: why was a man who had shouted for another to fire a weapon guilty of murder while another, who actually did fire, was guilty of a lesser crime. It is one of those unfathomable mysteries that will probably never be answered.

At this point, the trials ended. Three men were found guilty for their various roles in the killings of three others, and the court needed to end its special session and resume its circuit duties. The decision to delay the remaining trials and move on raised its own set of problems as the state continued to accumulate yet more debt in the interim, paying out a respectable $2,298.28 for maintaining and securing the jail guarded by the many soldiers over the course of the next several months.[414] But before the court could depart town, there was still the matter of imposing sentences on the three convicts.

Immediately following the conclusion of Sheffield's trial, Mott's attorneys sought to set aside the jury's verdict in his case, alleging several reasons for doing so. Of the seven allegations, five had to do with the manner in which the grand and petit jurors were chosen, Staniford's and one of the juror's purported biases toward him and the seating of a juror who was not a freeholder but a British subject. However, the remaining two contentions rose above the others.

The fourth reason, the attorneys alleged, concerned the petit jury's deliberations conducted without proper oversight, as they stated, "without being committed to the charge of any officer to attend them." This was not the first time the court had failed in its oversight of the most important trial in the state's history, having previously failed to swear in a witness and having had to correct that error mid-testimony. Now, in its haste, it had neglected to have a sworn officer attend to the sequestered jury, forcing Tyler to acknowledge that fact and put aside Mott's conviction; days of testimony demonstrating his clear responsibility for killing two men were now discarded, and he was held for retrial to take place the following January. History will never know the answer for the fifth reason alleged by defense counsel because the verdict had already been set aside, but it is tantalizing to wonder why, as they alleged, Mott "was not suffered to be heard in his defense."[415] Again, it is one of those circumstances that would never occur in the modern age and demonstrates the nascent state of the criminal law at this time. As bizarre as Mott's case was, a most peculiar ending remained for the following January.

The following day, Bates and Turner sought to repeat their success by filing similar motions on behalf of the other two defendants. They were able to overturn Sheffield's verdict for undisclosed reasons, and he, together with Mudget, Pease and Ledgard, was ordered held awaiting trial in January. Harrington dismissed all charges against informer Day, and the absconding Noaks and Clark remained at large. For the last man, a very different result was about to unfold.

CYRUS DEAN, A "MOST daring and reckless" man, according to the chief judge, now stood before the court to hear its decisions on his attorney's motions. The reason does not appear within the record, but Turner's name is not listed on any documents, and this part of the proceedings fell on Marsh and Vergennes attorney David Edmonds to handle the seven arguments Marsh filed, while the government was represented by U.S. attorney David Fay. Harrington's name is curiously not listed at the time, and he might been attending to the needs of his ill family and dying wife. None of the issues that Dean's attorneys now raised had been addressed in either of the two previous sentences because the court had found alternative grounds on which to decide. Now, it determined it was possible to avoid deciding on four of them because defense counsel had either withdrawn them or there was no evidence to support them.

The remaining three reasons concerned the authority of a deputy to summon jurors, the manner in which it was done and the fact that one of the grand jurors, John Tharp of Charlotte, was a natural-born subject of Great Britain and not a Vermont freeholder. Easily deciding that the first two issues did not present sufficient reasons for voiding the verdict, the court moved to the last, finding that it was "a question of primary magnitude and importance." However, after observing that the town of Ryegate was owned primarily by Scottish adventurers sending others to settle their Vermont lands who were deserving of the right to sit on local grand juries even if they were not freeholders, and that the U.S. Constitution did not prohibit them from doing so, the court determined that Tharp's participation was not illegal.

All eyes then fell on the defendant as Solomon Miller inquired, "Cyrus B. Dean, have you ought to say why the Court should not proceed to render the sentence of the law against you?" It was all a formality, as the trial's end was a foregone conclusion, and all his attorneys asked at this point was that his execution be scheduled when the General Assembly gathered, indicating that an appeal to that body was forthcoming. Then,

> *after some preparatory remarks, the Court sentenced the prisoner to be taken to the place of public execution on Friday, the 28th day of October, 1808, then and there, between the hours of 10 o'clock in the forenoon and three o'clock in the afternoon, to BE HUNG BY THE NECK UNTIL HE IS DEAD.*

Miller wrote out an order that Dean be taken to the Burlington jail to await his execution, and his attorneys pondered their next moves.

No execution could take place until the governor and his council had an opportunity to review the proceedings and issue a final order allowing it to go forward. In the meantime, Marsh and Turner began a tortuous, unchartered journey seeking the assembly's agreement that the jury's verdict should be overturned. Their petition to the legislature did not—indeed, could not—take issue with the overwhelming evidence of Dean's complicity, stating, "Tho' deeply sensible that his conduct has been highly reprehensible, yet feels himself innocent of the crime of murder"; rather, it concentrated on the legality of the proceedings and the toxic environment in which they took place.[416] First, they made an ineffectual argument that the Supreme Court did not have the authority to hold a special session. Second, they asserted that since Dean had been indicted as an accessory to Ormsby's and Marsh's murders and Mott as principal, and since Mott had then had his verdict overturned, Dean could not suffer punishment until Mott's case was decided on retrial—and only then, if Mott was found guilty. While these were certainly creative legal arguments, neither seems to have been particularly convincing. However, it was their remaining contentions that reveal what was really taking place in the courtroom.

In setting the stage for the legislature's consideration, the attorneys pointed out that the horror of the murders, or "transactions," as they were repeatedly referred to, were of such magnitude that the jury could never be divested of "passion and prejudice." Contributing to their discomfort was the fact that Dean's trial took place on the very eve of a fractious election when "the newspapers were full of inflammatory speeches relative to the transaction imputing the facts to different parties alternately, even while the trial was progressing." The atmosphere in the courtroom itself was so wretchedly bad (recall that Peter Martin was hooted out of the room), they argued, and "the blood of all was warm, if not hot" such that "cool investigation of the principals on which the cause rested could not be found." Hyperbole aside, these few words reveal much more than what a disinterested review of the transcripts can ever show. They tell us that in less than three weeks after the murders, and over the course of a short fourteen days, the Supreme Court rushed three of the most important cases in the state's history through grand jury and trial proceedings, involving dozens of witnesses, to inconsistent conclusions. Tyler's protestations aside, Turner's complaints that the court had pushed these cases to a resolution much too strongly rings true. These were compelling arguments, but there were more.

As Turner and Marsh had argued to the jury, the public did not appreciate what it was that Jefferson was trying to do with the embargo; its "nature, intent & effect" were simply not understood. How, then, could a person be found guilty of committing murder with malice, with intent, if he did not even understand what the underlying law meant in the first place? Then, in recognizing the impact that such an allegation might have on their political audience, they made veiled reference to the misguided contributions made by professionals within the community—that "misinformation has led to measures which had a direct tendency to raise the passions." Finally, they reasonably argued that in this unique economic climate, it was appropriate to exercise a degree of compassion and that the "merciful infliction of penalties insured by an infringement of a new law which apparently curtails the natural & accustomed rights of citizens is productive of the greatest good." When one considers the failures of the other two trials, their appeal must also have implicitly conveyed a message that Dean, an accomplice to murder, was likewise the victim of a flawed system deserving of higher review. Regardless, their overall message was reasonable under the circumstances and was transmitted straightaway to Montpelier to be filed with the assembly for its consideration upon its reconvening following the election. In the meantime, much more work remained.

8

THE "BANEFUL INFLUENCE OF LEADING DEMAGOGUES"

U.S. attorney David Fay lost no time bringing the remaining smugglers to count in his arena. Just as the extraordinary circumstances had called the Vermont Supreme Court into special session, now the United States Circuit Court for the District of Vermont was asked to quickly assemble to conduct yet another trial of great importance, one every bit as consequential as those taking place on the state level. This time, the accusations involved not murder but treason and levying war against the country, and it required calling on the jurisdiction that only a circuit court could provide when capital crimes were committed against the United States. For these proceedings, those sitting in judgment included not only the state's district court judge, Elijah Paine, but also a member of the U.S. Supreme Court, Associate Justice Brockholst Livingston, assigned to the circuit that included Vermont. Requiring a Supreme Court justice to participate in such onerous duties continued for many years and was only abandoned in 1869, when full-time circuit court judges were appointed.

In only two days' time following Dean's sentencing, Fay quickly made his way southward sixty-five miles to Rutland, where he met with the court clerk, Cephas Smith Jr. Fay advised Smith that he wanted to make arrangements to present evidence to a grand jury in Rutland in three weeks and provided him with the names of many individuals to summon for testimony. Between those proceedings and the upcoming trial itself, Fay subpoenaed some sixty people from all over northern Vermont and New York, including not only some of those recently participating in Dean's trial but also many others whose names arose during the investigations in one way or another. This was clearly going to be a major inconvenience for all involved, and Fay left nothing to chance as he continued in the same aggressive manner he and Harrington had taken in the state cases. The only question that remained was: would the law provide him with a favorable result?

Just as Staniford executed his difficult duties in searching out the many state witnesses, now U.S. marshal John Willard and his deputies received a similar assignment. This time, they were armed with papers issued in the name of Supreme Court chief justice John Marshall, bearing a dire warning for the recipient: "You are hereby commanded that laying aside all business & excuse," ordering them to appear in Rutland on Monday, October 3, "as witnesses on the part of the government." Fay cast a wide net, and among the many summoned were Guy Catlin's business partner, Joseph Jasper; Colonel Sam Mix; Sheriff Daniel Staniford; Samuel Mott's rioting associate, Theophilus Morrill; smugglers Joshua Day, Josiah Edson and Elkinah Perkins; and militiamen from St. Albans and Rutland, John Whittemore, Benjamin Pratt and Asa Hall. The members of the grand jury summoned to meet on that day, and remaining in session for the next six days, consisted of eighteen men coming from surrounding towns, those very locations that had contributed so many men to the militia contingencies going north a few short months prior, coming from Castleton, Clarendon, Pittsford, Poultney, Rutland and Tinmouth.[417]

Things might have quieted on the lake for the moment, but local citizens remained very concerned for their well-being, displaying little faith in the possibility of outside help arriving to protect them. On October 18, residents in Caledonia County (whose sheriff and high bailiff had absconded to Canada the preceding year) petitioned the assembly for permission to establish an independent company of artillery to supplement their militia. Two days later, on the lakeshore itself, many in Orwell sought similar approval to form a company of grenadiers. The following year, residents living farther inland, in Groton, demanded ("in our Republican Government we claim equality as our Right and privilege") that the legislature impose a three-cent-per-acre tax on the town to pay for improved roads to replace their primitive "paths as we ourselves make," which extended several miles "through swamps, windfalls, &c." Refusing to accept any denial of their petition, they reminded their representatives that "as remote as we live from inhabitants, we are compelled to bear arms in defense of our country or take the effects of the law."[418]

On the New York side, Champlain deputy inspector David Mayo demonstrated the continuing influence that smugglers were having in

September when goods were forcibly retaken from his custody on several occasions. Trying to avoid any suspicion of malfeasance on his part, Mayo published a notice lamenting that, "notwithstanding my endeavors, a large quantity of tobacco, stored in my barn, was rescued by persons unknown to me, for which I have been accused of bribery and treachery." On another occasion, he reported, "While gone to Montpelier, on important business, a quantity of tea was in the same manner rescued." He also shed additional light on the participation of respected community members in smuggling, revealing that attempts at bribery had been made: "Gold has been offered to me in handfuls at different times and by respectable characters," which he protested he had rejected.[419]

Communications between Mayo's supervisor, Collector Woolsey and Haswell in Burlington that month also reveal the latter's soliciting business to store New York's seized ashes. Haswell assured Woolsey that those "heretofore sent me remain unmolested; I hardly think the smugglers will dare to come this distance to steal property." He added that he would "endeavor to take the best possible charge of them." Woolsey was unable to agree at the moment because he lacked any way to transport them across the lake, but the offer was certainly attractive because, he confessed, "the smugglers have stolen seventy-odd barrels of what I had in Plattsburgh." It was a most difficult activity to curtail he said, because "altho [sic] every exertion has been made, we obtain no intelligence." He also told Haswell he had just seized some cargo from Joseph Jasper's sloop *Lady Washington* because the captain unloaded it illegally and failed to report to officials as required.[420] Whether Jasper had received his subpoena to appear in the Rutland court at the time is not known.

William Harrington remained as active as ever throughout September. Benjamin Adams required representation in several suits, including one brought against him by Moses Catlin, for which Adams paid by "taking morgages [sic]" for claims Harrington had against the notorious Sam Mix. Samuel Atherton also needed assistance in two suits, one concerning potash claimant Truman Powell, while Captain Abel Turner called for help in yet another case, and Hezekiah Barnes retained him to recover $7.18 in a suit brought against the Congregational Society. On September 26, Harrington continued in his unremitting fashion and obtained a judgment against Sheriff Staniford for $206.67 for unspecified reasons; Staniford successfully appealed to the Supreme Court in its next January term. Staniford's deputy, Elias Buel, died unexpectedly in Waterbury on the seventeenth, and on October 1, Staniford appointed Thomas Brownson, of Richmond, in his place. Ironically, Buel's father, Major Elias Buel, ran a local inn at the time, illegally selling wines and spirits without a license, and was indicted by the grand jury the following January.

Moses Catlin signed a petition on September 25 in support of John and James Winans to obtain an exclusive thirty-year right to navigate a steamboat on the lake, and an undated entry in brother Guy's notebook contains a tantalizing reminder to himself to "Call on Capt. Pratt for the gun." One can only wonder what this complicit man had in mind. Was he trying to get evidence that might link him to the murders and remove it from the government's custody before it could be used against him? Or was it in reference to some other gun being held by the Rutland militiaman?[421] Meanwhile, on twenty-ninth, Jabez Penniman's stepdaughter, Fanny Allen, finally entered into her long-sought religious training at Montreal's Hotel Dieu in preparation of becoming a nun.

Proceedings before the U.S. Circuit Court in Rutland began on October 3, and they did not bode well for the prosecution. Recall that five people were being held awaiting the filing of federal charges—Frederick Hoxie, his two sons and the two Taylors. Immediately following the murders, Penniman instituted charges with Harrington alleging that they were all responsible for several smuggling incidents, and all were taken into custody based on his assertions. Now, weeks later, and after having time to reflect further on what evidence there was to support charges against them, Fay came to a different conclusion. This does not mean that any of the conduct alleged by Penniman was untrue or did not happen, but rather, it constitutes a pragmatic assessment of whether he could assemble the needed proof to convince a jury, particularly in this divisive atmosphere, that the men were indeed guilty of some form of criminal conduct. It was not an easy task.

Rather than look to Penniman's allegations, Fay focused on the June 10 incident in which twenty men illegally floated a raft of some two hundred logs into Canada, targeting the two Taylors with responsibility. He then looked at the June 13 forcible retaking of the large raft from Benjamin Pratt's company at Windmill Bay by dozens of men in which the Hoxies and Joseph Tinkam participated as reason to bring a second set of charges. Accordingly, he drafted two indictments, one for each set of men, alleging that their actions constituted, murder notwithstanding, the most egregious conduct known to man, the so-called king of crimes: high treason.[422]

Treason's long and rich history dates back to 1351, when Parliament deemed the times so fraught with danger that Edward III's person, and his immediate family, deserved protection from those inclined to "compass," or plan, any of their deaths and those levying war against him or giving aid and comfort to his enemies. The law assumed a varied application over the ensuing centuries, taking on added importance for America's first settlers, located so far from the seat of government, who sought out creative ways to discern its ominous presence. By the time of the Revolutionary War, treason was being applied in instances never imagined centuries earlier, including conspiracy, sedition and in varying interpretations of what levying war exactly meant. Many ran afoul of authorities when they engaged in such innocuous activities as questioning the king's prerogative or in seeking the redress of grievances, resulting in so many abuses that the revolutionaries decided a change was necessary when it came time to draft the Constitution in 1787.[423]

Article III, section 3(1) of the U.S. Constitution provides:

> *Treason against the United States shall consist only in levying War against them, or, in adhering to their Enemies, giving them Aid and Comfort. No Person shall be convicted of Treason unless on the Testimony of two Witnesses to the same overt act, or on Confession in open Court.*

The 1793 Vermont Constitution's equivalent simply provides that "no person ought in any case, or in any time, to be declared guilty of treason, or felony, by the Legislature." Interestingly, a 1797 state law was in effect that specifically addressed treason (punishable by death) but for some reason was not utilized by the attorneys, who deemed the federal provision the only viable option. The timing of the Taylor and Hoxie matters came precisely at a moment when federal law was still addressing the nature of one's conduct falling within the Constitution's proscription of "levying war." For the drafters of the Constitution, and the few cases brought in the ensuing years, it became increasingly clear that such violations could be found only in the most restrictive of instances—certainly, a lesson learned just a year earlier upon Aaron Burr's acquittal for his own purported treasonous conduct. Now, it was going to require more than simply firing weapons at government officials in order to find treason's presence, and David Fay was about to learn that in quick order.

With no discernible evidence that either John or Ezekiel Taylor had ever taken the bold, affirmative step of levying war against the United States, Fay drafted indictments against each alleging that they had, but through constructive means. In other words, what he could not prove directly, he sought to do indirectly by asking the grand jury to find that war had been waged through their assembling together with other men in an armed manner. It was a creative use of the law to allege that they, "with force and arms, unlawfully, falsely, maliciously, and traitorously…[did] compass, imagine, and intend to raise and levy war, insurrection and rebellion," but it was futile. In winnowing through the testimony of sixteen witnesses, the grand jury assessed the allegations and, after comparing them to the law, determined that Fay had failed in his effort. On Saturday, October 8, Foreman William Jenkins, of Rutland, simply wrote on the indictment, "This bill not found."

The Taylors' two Burlington attorneys, Daniel Farrand and Samuel Hitchcock (respectively, one of the town's overseers of the poor and treasurer that year), immediately sought the men's release from custody, and the court agreed, allowing each to "go at large whither he will." John Taylor waited only a short time to file his lawsuit against Penniman for injuries he had allegedly received at the time of his arrest. Undismayed by the grand jury's rejection of the charge, the following May, Fay successfully obtained two indictments against the Taylors, not for treason, but for committing a lesser crime—that of violating the embargo's provisions against goods moving northward. Both John Taylor's lawsuit and the government's second attempt to hold them accountable failed because the two men fled the state, returning to Canada, resulting in Farrand's dismissal of his client's claim and the withdrawal of arrest warrants because, as deputy U.S. marshal Luther Barnard attested, he had "made diligent search throughout the District" but could not find them. Notwithstanding, efforts were made once again in 1810 to arrest them but met with similar results.[424]

The cases against Frederick Hoxie, his two sons and Joseph Tinkham were another matter. This time, the grand jury agreed that they had levied war when they assembled their large body of men, fired on the militia and obstructed Penniman in his duties. Four indictments (using the same language found in Burr's indictment) were approved, and an arrest warrant was issued for Tinkham. He was never located, despite searches for him at the time by the U.S. marshal, and then again in 1810, and he ultimately escaped any punishment. With the indictments now filed, the court determined it was impossible to conduct the trials in far-off Grand Isle County, where the offenses took place, and instead ordered a special session be held in Burlington, beginning on October 27. Recognizing the difficulty before it in trying to obtain an unbiased jury, the court further ordered that a staggering forty-eight men be summoned from Grand Isle, Chittenden and Franklin Counties as potential candidates.

On October 10, the government began its first significant forfeiture proceedings in many years by filing papers in the district court naming the *Black Snake* and *A Sloop & Sixty Eight Barrels of Potashes* as contraband used in criminal activity, all subject to sale and the proceeds being divided according to law. Very little had ever been done in this regard, and these cases constituted a wholly new experience for everyone involved. Indeed, the overall workload of this particular court appears to have been quite modest. Up until the *Black Snake* papers were filed, there had been only three instances, beginning in 1794, when the government brought such actions in Vermont. Presided over by Judge Paine (1757–1842; Harvard 1781), the court's most recent work consisted of convening for a single day in July, in Cornelius Lynde's Williamstown home, for what appears to have been a civil jury trial.[425]

Both the configuration and workload of Vermont's federal courts were cause for concern for policymakers. Later in the month, no doubt relying on the difficulties the circuit court itself noted in conducting the Hoxie trial, the legislature made attempts to put pressure on the state's national representatives to reassign the circuit court from its duties in Rutland and Windsor and move it to Montpelier. The principal contention concerned the hardships those living in the north encountered in having to travel to the south to resolve their cases. The effort failed but was revived again in 1826, utilizing arguments that looked closely at what these courts actually did in the years immediately after 1808.

Considerable efforts were made to analyze the volume and nature of the cases, where the litigants came from and the cost and benefits to the government, but none provided such pointed observations as those made by one legislator. For this observer, "he would state it as a fact" that the greatest part of the district court's business in these years "was the condemnation of, sometimes a sleigh, sometimes a horse and sometimes a sleigh and horse &c." and that the "whole business was done in three hours" time. Concerning the number of suits instituted, he could not recall a single one "that had been entered within four years except the one of the Postmaster General against the Mount Holly Post-master [in Rutland County] in which he claimed 38 cents." Of the 120 prosecutions actually brought by the government between 1815 and 1825, an incredible 73 of them, or 61 percent, resulted in acquittal, dismissal or were discontinued with costs charged against them.[426] Certainly, Judge Paine did not find the workload particularly onerous, as he assumed additional duties, becoming Williamstown's postmaster between 1815 and 1842 while setting aside time to raise fifteen thousand Merino sheep.[427] Despite their high standing in the legal world, Vermont's federal courts during these years constituted a substantially less than formidable presence in any matters in which it was called upon to participate.

At the same time, the embargo's provisions the courts were asked to enforce continually revealed their inadequacies. Jefferson remained aloof in dealing with their problems, leaving them to Gallatin to resolve as he expressed his rage at what was unfolding: "I did not expect a crop of so sudden and rank growth of fraud, and open opposition by force could have grown up in the United States." He may have hoped the Vermont smugglers would receive some degree of leniency for the murders, but he also believed it "so important in example to crush these audacious proceedings, and to make the offenders feel the consequences of individuals daring to oppose a law by force, that no effort should be spared to compass this object." But for the long-suffering Gallatin, much more was required before that could happen; Congress had to enact the laws necessary to put teeth into the embargo's amorphous prohibitions. The inadequacies remained throughout the summer and fall of 1808, and in November, Gallatin lamented to the Senate that "every degree of opposition to the laws which falls short of treason is now, with but few exceptions, an offense undefined and unprovided for by the laws of the United States; whence it follows that such offenses remain unpunished."[428]

And this was the conundrum that Vermont's United States attorney faced at the moment: whether to bring the draconian charge of treason, virtually the only one available to him, against the three Hoxies or to simply turn away and let them go. In short, this was a most tenuous case, and it remained only for it to play out in a Burlington courtroom.

DAILY LIFE CONTINUED WITH   Seeley Bennett's seemingly never-ending neglect inflicting yet additional harm on Staniford's reputation. On October 10, 1808, he received court papers requiring him to seize property, but with the press of other more important business, he failed to do so, resulting in a suit being brought against the two officers the following January. Within the jail itself, debtor Manassah Sawyer was being held on one of Harrington's judgments and escaped on the twentieth, probably aided by the confusion present with so many prisoners and soldiers involved in the more important proceedings; unsurprisingly, Sawyer's escape led to another lawsuit.

Enforcement actions continued on the lake, and on October 22, 1808, Penniman's men made an interesting seizure in Alburgh. Only days earlier, they had impounded the reconfigured sloop *Hope*, captained by the recalcitrant Abner Brigham, the Canadian owner seeking to ignite a "national question" over revenue officers' authority. Court records do not provide any details into the circumstances, but forfeiture papers filed by Fay only days later reveal that a long canoe and three bateaus, called the *Bat*, the *Coffin* and the *Mudget*, were taken, while in a second action, a fifth vessel carrying three barrels and a hogshead of potashes was seized; no persons were named in any of the cases. It is an interesting mystery how these boats came to obtain their names, and one wonders at their possibly being used in some fashion in the murders' aftermath. While the potash was later sold at public auction (for forty-five dollars, as Fay also extracted his twelve-dollar fee), when the U.S. marshal sought to levy against the vessels, his return to the court states that "[Penniman had] never shown me" the boats, thereby making any sale impossible.[429] This was yet another curious turn of events, and one wonders why the government would institute extensive court proceedings, incurring unnecessary costs, only to later decide not to participate in them.

It took more than a month after his trial, but ten days before their client's execution, Dean's attorneys' petition first appears in the legislative records, revealing that on October 18, it was read and then referred to a committee of three men for further consideration. The inclinations of those considering his fate were starkly opposed to any thoughts of leniency. The preceding day, the assembly had gone into session and heard an address from newly elected Governor Tichenor calling on the people to obey the hated embargo dictates, despite "the stain upon [their] character…in consequence of the conduct of a few." He also made reference to the prison under construction, "a matter of much importance," asking the representatives to inquire into its progress. He also asked them to consider revising the criminal laws, "especially those dealing with high crimes and misdemeanors," to ensure that "modes and degrees of punishment" were adequate to deal with them.

Disputing several points, the minority Republican response could only agree with Tichenor's dismay at the presence of the recent opposition displayed against government's authority, made possible by the actions of a "few avaricious, self-interested, and designing men." These were people, they protested, "destitute of patriotism as to attempt, for the acquisition of wealth or some more reprehensible object, not only by fraud but in open defiance to the laws, to defeat their wholesome provisions, or by their treasonable opposition…deprive their dutiful brethren of life and expose themselves to an ignominious and untimely death."[430] Clearly, this was a body united in seeing that anyone involved with the recent troubles, whether for murder or treason, faced a severe penalty. In fact, on this very day, Content Hallock,

Israel Williams, James Tyler and William Hinkson were hard at work completing Dean's gallows, making his coffin and digging his grave.

Upon receiving the condemned man's petition, one of the committee's members was chosen to meet with the Supreme Court judges to "request of them, a copy of the proceedings…or any such evidence relating to said trial, as may be in their power to communicate." Since there was no published account, arrangements were made for Burlington printer Samuel Mills to gather the necessary information. Only four days later, he produced a forty-eight-page document for the committee's use, entitled *The Trial of Cyrus B. Dean, for the Murder of Jonathan Ormsby and Asa Marsh, before the Supreme Court of Judicature of the State of Vermont, at Their Special Sessions, Begun and Holden at Burlington, Chittenden County, on the 23rd of August, A.D. 1808.* Because the case was of such paramount importance to the public, it was also made immediately available as advertised on October 21 for sale at the Burlington Bookstore and, days later, at Mills & White, in Middlebury, costing twenty-five cents.[431]

When the assembly met again on Monday, October 24, the very first order of business concerned the Supreme Court's charge to the jury (not described in Mills' account), indicating that there were continuing questions in that regard. Following further inquiry of the court, and in rapid fashion, only hours later, Tyler responded, telling them that it had repeatedly instructed the jury members on the law of murder and that it was their prerogative to find guilt for the lesser crime of manslaughter if they thought proper. With Dean's execution looming only days later, the legislators were determined to move forward with all due haste and allowed the three-man committee to depart its chamber to confer further on the court's report. They returned shortly afterward, reporting that they had met with Dean's attorneys, considered a number of exhibits, as well as the Supreme Court's response, and ultimately concluded that the petition "ought not to be granted." Still wanting to hear more, the assembly invited Marsh and Turner out onto the main floor to argue whether the committee's report should be accepted, instructing them to "confine their remarks" to the pertinent issues. The two attorneys were probably taken aback by the prospect of standing before the entire state legislature at that moment, and Marsh quickly requested their indulgence to allow them to delay until the following day to prepare their remarks, which was granted.

Following their convening at nine o'clock the next morning and considering some routine business, the assembly returned to the troublesome Dean case and listened to his two attorneys. The record frustratingly does not provide any account of what they said beyond their having "delivered their arguments in support of his petition and against the acceptance" of the committee's recommendation. After they finished, the matter was discussed further, and they adjourned.

Only hours later, the first of three important votes took place. The first concerned whether to refuse accepting the committee's report in opposition to the petition, and after one member demanded that each of the representative's decisions be recorded and a lengthy vote undertaken, the matter was "negative," 112 to 79. On the question of whether to allow Dean a new trial, the result was the same, voted down 166 to 18. When one representative proposed that Dean be allowed to bring a bill seeking a reprieve of his execution until the last Friday in February 1809, the matter successfully passed, 118 to 66, and was referred to a committee for drafting. The bill was quickly put together, and the following morning, only forty-eight hours before the scheduled execution, the assembly quickly approved the wording and sent it off to the governor and council for their consideration.[432]

The assembly's every move was being closely monitored during these few days, and not knowing Dean's fate caused great stresses within Burlington, particularly for those guarding the many prisoners at the county jail. The challenges presented to the soldiers were apparently so severe that others had to be called in. As Staniford later attested, he had been "obliged to augment the guard in order to prevent the destruction of the jail and the escape of Dean," which required him to "personally attend as well as my deputies the whole night and day."[433]

Now, the delicate matter rested with Tichenor and his select council, and they immediately took up the new bill at 9:00 a.m. on October 27. The preceding day, Royall Tyler had appeared before them and was sworn in once again as chief judge for the next year, and now they had to consider an appropriate ending for the most important trial in his and the state's history. There were apparently a number of issues raised during their discussion, and while they ultimately concurred with the reprieve in general, they, too, wanted to see things expedited while also taking up questions relating to Chittenden County sheriff Staniford.

For Dean, the reprieve had limited success, and by a vote of seven to six, his execution date was delayed not to February but for only two weeks to the "second Friday of November." Whatever the hardworking, faithful Republican sheriff had done in the preceding months, it was not universally appreciated, for when the execution order was rewritten, it was addressed to "the said Sheriff of Chittenden County for the time being, or the High Bailiff, acting as such" to carry out, indicating that Staniford was not long for his current position.[434]

AT THE VERY MOMENT the legislature met in Montpelier, Supreme Court justice Livingston and District Court judge Paine convened the matters of the *United States v. Frederick Hoxie, Job Hoxie, and John Hoxie* in the Burlington courthouse. Also present were U.S. attorney Fay, U.S. marshal Willard, Clerk Smith, crier Stephen Conant, defense attorneys Farrand and Hitchcock and forty-eight potential jurors that marshals had tracked down from twelve surrounding towns. There does not appear to have been any substantive work done that day other than to discuss logistics and planning how the trial would proceed. All were ordered to return at 11:00 a.m. the following day, and the court issued an order requiring Staniford to produce the three defendants at that time.

For the next two days, lasting well into Saturday evening, the parties began the difficult work of questioning and winnowing out unacceptable jurors from the many seated before them. As with the state cases, individual trials were planned, Frederick Hoxie's first and his two sons' following immediately afterward. Very little information remains telling what took place at the time, but one piece of paper buried in the court's files bears words familiar to anyone ever attending modern-day jury selection: "Are you any way related to the prisoner?" and "Have you ever formed or delivered an opinion as to the guilt or innocence of the prisoner, or that he ought to be punished?" While the proceedings appear to have been contentious, with virtually every potential juror having the word "challenged" entered next to his name, a jury was finally selected, and all members were ordered to return in two days' time, on Monday, October 31, at 10:00 a.m.

Trial began as William Harrington made the government's opening statement. Why Fay chose to allow his fellow colonel that privileged opportunity is not known, but he reserved for himself the job of making the necessary argument of the prisoner's guilt at the trial's close. There is no indication that Van Ness ever participated in these proceedings, having been elected a justice of the peace for St. Albans by the legislature only days earlier—a curious circumstance for someone not residing in the town who was then living in Burlington.[435] The specific testimony that followed in this important trial was never recorded verbatim, but at some point afterward, defense attorney Farrand took time to write out a seven-page document describing his recollections, modestly stating at its conclusion that "from my minutes and memory I think it is substantially correct." It is from his notes that we are able to piece together, as previously described, the merging of the various parties as they sought to retake the Van Duysen raft seized by Benjamin Pratt and his men on June 10 and their violent confrontation in the late night hours three days later, when dozens of armed men retook it, engaging in a long exchange of gunfire with the soldiers.

While Fay summoned many dozens of witnesses to testify before the grand jury, Farrand's notes indicate that only eight were called at trial. As he had provided crucial evidence against *Black Snake* defendants in the first trials, Josiah Edson continued to cooperate with authorities and appeared as its first witness. He explained how he became associated with the raft and was employed by Van Duysen in finding men, who included Frederick Hoxie, willing to undertake the dangerous work of its retaking. Benjamin Pratt and Asa Hall told how they seized it at Buel's direction and of their efforts to moor it in Windmill Bay, while other witnesses took the stand, some implicating Hoxie directly in firing at the soldiers and others providing circumstantial evidence of his involvement.

Following the government's close of its testimony, Farrand and Hitchcock had an important decision to make. Asking themselves if the evidence they had heard rose to a level of proving their client had levied war against the United States, the issue was whether they should respond with their own countering evidence. When the court inquired how they wished to proceed, they responded that "they had several witnesses, but should decline taking up the time of the Court" because, in a devastating, off-handed dismissal of the government's case that the jury could not have ignored, "they conceived it wholly unnecessary."[436] The proceedings then moved on to closing arguments; Fay went first, followed by the two defense attorneys and then Fay in conclusion.

It now fell to Justice Livingston to explain the law of treason to the jury as it considered the evidence, doing so after rising and making a "profoundly eloquent address" to them in a "clear, concise, energetic" manner. Brockholst Livingston (1757–1823), son of a New Jersey governor, had served as an officer during the Revolutionary War, graduated from the College of New Jersey (Princeton) in 1774 and read law in 1783, whereupon he opened a private practice in New York City, remaining there until 1802, when he was named an associate justice of New York's Supreme Court of Judicature. He held that position until 1807, when Jefferson appointed him to the Supreme Court, also taking on the role of Vermont's circuit court judge only months earlier, in March 1808. When in Washington and under the sway of the formidable John Marshall, Livingston kept his judicial opinions consistent with the prevailing winds and did not strike out in independent fashion. Even so, when his circuit court duties might have afforded him some degree of freedom, he resisted invitations to expand the law's reach beyond strict conformist interpretations, an attitude he openly adopted in these important proceedings.[437]

It was late in the day when Livingston asked the jury's indulgence, telling it that he would not take the time to once again read the indictment as he had earlier that morning or to recount the undisputed testimony. His role, he told jury members, was to explain the legal concept of treason in the context of levying war against the United States, what it was and what it was not. Livingston then read out a seventeen-page charge, carefully crafted to include a devastating indictment of his own against the government's case while also sheepishly contending that he was being fair to the process, leaving the ultimate decision to the jury.

Belying his own feelings, at one point Livingston felt it necessary to make an apology, pointedly taking a jab at the paucity of the government's evidence, saying he could not "help thinking that the District Attorney must have been greatly deceived in the information which was given him, of the prisoner's conduct…[as] the proofs on trial have fallen very far short of his expectations, or that you would never have been put to the trouble of deciding on this case." That being the situation, Livingston continued, "But as…he seems seriously and sincerely to believe treason has been committed, the Court has thought it a duty to state to you its opinions, most explicitly, the other way."[438] It was a performance that probably left the two defense attorneys smiling in relief in their decision not to introduce any evidence as they sat back and watched Fay's case crumble before his eyes.

Livingston had little trouble summarizing existing treason law simply because there was little to rely on. There had been so few instances when the government sought to hold anyone accountable for the 1787 Constitution's prohibition that this was virgin territory for judicial interpretations, and his ruling in this case was going to provide important precedent for future generations considering its application. Certainly, a history of British and colonial abuses finding treason present even in the mere questioning of royal prerogative, together with the intention of the Constitution's drafters that it be narrowly restricted in its application, provided an important foundation to drive a stake through any interpretation seeking a wider application, such as what Fay was trying to do in this case.

To levy war was a most serious thing, and for Livingston, it meant armed men joined together to overthrow government's authority. Yes, treason might have existed in the Whiskey and Fries Rebellions (which, the judge noted, resulted in pardons) when men sought to directly obstruct the enforcement of acts of Congress, but did it exist when men simply gathered together to pursue personal gain? Hoxie's case involved an event of a private nature, he said, with no further violence contemplated than to seize a single raft a short distance from Canada, float it over the line, turn it over and then return to the United States, "not at the head of an army, but peaceably and quietly, each man to his own home."

And what of their arms? How can ten or twelve muskets, he asked, "so very small and despicable," constitute force equivalent to levying war? To the contrary, it was "scarcely competent to the reduction of a single family," he said. How could the government seriously contend that such an opposition "so feeble, so transitory, so free from every traitorous intention, so destitute of every appearance of war, and so evidently calculated for the sole purpose of private gain, was making war against the United States?" Ridiculing the government's contention that Hoxie had done so, Livingston said his behavior was "hardly a resemblance; and yet, you are seriously expected to condemn [him] as a traitor." Why did the government bring this case in the first place and not pursue other, more appropriate laws, such as those dealing with impeding the law or the forcible rescue of seized goods? Just exactly how was the jury to decide otherwise when told by a U.S. Supreme Court justice that "not an instance can be found in England, during a period of several hundred years, which have elapsed since the statute of treasons, in which an act like the present, was determined to be treason"? This was a total condemnation of the government's case, and it lay shredded for all to see.

Livingston finally concluded about 11:00 p.m., telling the jury that in expressing his opinions, he felt no other motive than "a desire to assist you in coming to a correct result on a point which, to the honor of this state, has never before been a subject of public discussion within it." There was certainly no doubt what his interpretation of a correct result was, and it took the twelve men only a "few moments" to decide and return to the courtroom, telling the judge that the defendant was not guilty. Now, Frederick Hoxie heard the same refreshing words his friends, the Taylors, had recently heard, as the court ordered his release to "go at large whither he will."[439]

It had been a long day, and the court went into recess until 9:00 a.m. the following morning, when Fay, recognizing the severe beating he had just taken, immediately moved to dismiss the remaining charges against Job and

John Hoxie, which was granted, and they were ordered freed to join their father. While it had been a victory for the two defense attorneys, Fay was not about to let the men to go unchallenged, and as he would do with the Taylors, the following May, he successfully obtained indictments against the three Hoxies for, as Livingston had suggested, the lesser crime of violating the embargo's provisions on June 10 while ignoring their conduct in retaking Van Duysen's raft on the thirteenth. But just as the Taylors had evaded any future arrest by fleeing, the Hoxies also absconded, eventually arriving in the wilds north of Detroit, in Macomb County, Michigan.

Fay also filed the necessary paperwork to begin twelve additional forfeiture cases the government had been holding in abeyance as the trials unfolded, which consumed yet additional court time the following May with varying degrees of success. The only ones profiting from the wreckage of these most recent proceedings appear to have been those working to bring them about in the first place (Fay and Harrington) and those assisting them (Staniford, Willard and Smith), all submitting their respective bills and running up costs approaching $200. Even so, when it was time for Judge Paine to make the final authorization for the distributions in 1811, he certified that "there was reasonable cause" warranting the government's prosecutions.[440] It was a bit of a complicit, face-saving measure, for one has to wonder at the possibility of the government's further embarrassment if he found otherwise, as Justice Livingston had so strongly inferred.

Content Hallock and his men had finished Cyrus Dean's scaffolding by now, and those waiting in anticipation of the spectacle began to assemble for the November 11 event. Earlier in the month, Harrington had been involved with Captain Silas Billings and Mason Benona Bishop (who received his own pro forma warning to depart town in two months' time), compensating them for stone work they had done at the university and also paying Billings for building a fence "round my new orchard," while debiting Bishop thirty-seven cents for a quart of cider brandy. On the seventh, he and potash claimant/ merchant John Curtis were each awarded sums of money by the legislature for their work as directors of the Vermont State Bank, and the mysterious illness striking his family carried off wife Roxselana four days after Dean's execution, on the fifteenth.

Nathan Haswell was duly conducting port work inspecting the *Mars* on the fourth (bearing twelve barrels of seized potash at the direction of Sam Buel out on Windmill Point for him to store) and the *Jupiter* on the ninth.

In Washington, Jefferson's "State of the Nation" address on November 8 explained that he had ordered federal troops into service to replace those militia troops on the "northern frontier which offered peculiar facilities for evasion" of the embargo. In Montpelier, the legislature could not be bothered further with Dean and was fully engaged with many other issues, including accounting for newly gathered taxes assessed for the state prison; inquiring into costs for its construction and oversight of its administration (conducted by so-called Visitors); passing "An Act Providing for the Regulation of the State Prison, and Altering the Punishment of Crimes"; and publishing disciplinary rules for the state militia.

Counterfeiting continued to be perhaps the most troublesome crime of the day, and representatives remained uninterested in any delay in transferring those already convicted out of the state's insecure local jails and into the prison as soon as possible. As Dean was hanged by his neck, they urged Tichenor to warn Canadian officials immediately to the north "to remove and disperse...that band of counterfeiters, which infests the southern borders thereof, and are constantly preying upon the property of the good citizens of this and the United States." But even that logical, well-intentioned effort could not escape a subsequent political firestorm after Captain Josiah Dunham submitted a ninety-one-dollar claim for twenty-six days of work in carrying their request to Quebec governor James Henry Craig. When Dunham returned with the unhappy news that Craig believed himself unable to stem the problem, Tichenor was faced with allegations that his "special agent," as his opponents called Dunham, was on a secret mission attempting to obtain Canadian assistance to separate Vermont from the Union.[441] Certainly, nothing could have been further from the truth, but it is clear that the times remained highly contentious.

It had been exactly thirty years since the last state-sanctioned hanging took place, and Dean's promised to be a well-attended event. David Redding's death at the hands of Ethan Allen in 1778 in Bennington, one of highly questionable legal validity, was the last in Vermont's experience, taking place when there was no legally recognized state, only a confused, contested frontier struggling for national recognition. Hanging was frequently used by those committing suicide and also seems to have been utilized by those administering their own particular brand of justice. In 1810, State's Attorney Harrington inquired of an associate in Shelburne to look into a report that burglar John Content, who survived the incident, "was actually hung...by the neck after Isham's store was broken [into]." Harrington requested that an accounting be obtained from Content describing "the name of the persons who put the rope round his neck, the place where & the name of the persons present at the transaction." The outcome of that inquiry is not disclosed, but death by public hanging did continue following Dean's execution. After the arrival of federal troops when Burlington was declared a military post in 1812, on June 11, 1813, Private Peter Baily was one of some 32 soldiers from throughout the army strung up that year (up from just 3 in 1812 and climbing to 146 in 1814) following his guilty plea to deserting. That event was witnessed by "a great number of citizens," who watched as his lifeless body was then placed into a coffin and lowered into a grave dug immediately below to receive him.[442]

Precisely at twelve o'clock that afternoon, Dean was marched out of Staniford's jail several hundred feet to the south and into the courthouse. Period newspaper accounts report that some 10,000 people had gathered to witness the event, but the roughly 1,600-person population of the town (18,000 countywide) calls that number into question; the entire populations of Albany, New York, and Providence, Rhode Island, in 1810 were, respectively, 10,762 and 10,071.[443] Regardless, the numbers were impressive (no doubt in recognition of the murder of their esteemed Captain Jonathan Ormsby), and certainly the courthouse was standing room only as they crowded together to hear Charlotte's Reverend Truman Baldwin deliver a "solemn and appropriate discourse."

From there, Dean was taken outside, turned right and marched back the way he had come. If he looked just to his left, about one hundred feet out onto the Courthouse Square, he would have seen the tall, eighty-foot pine tree reserved for those receiving court-imposed whipping punishments, such as those his associates would receive in the future. He was probably not much interested as he passed by Lyman King's Tavern located immediately adjacent to the courthouse or the stores surrounding the square—those occupied by Ebenezer Englesby, Elnathan Keyes, Samuel Hitchcock, King's sail-loft, Lemeuel Page's shoe shop, Howard's Tavern, Moses Jewett's saddle shop, Lewis Curtis's jewelry shop or the firm of Peaslee and Haswell, many of whom likely chose to close up shop for the next couple hours to witness the spectacle.[444] From there, the procession continued on to Pearl Street, where it made a left for a short distance before turning right onto a little-used lane to a knoll with second-growth pine, not too far from Staniford's home and where Hallock and his men had erected their gallows.

The precise location of the execution is not known, as Burlington's burial practices for the immediate time were haphazardly administered, with many plots located about the town. In 1813, a committee determined that the burying grounds at the falls were "so much filled up with graves which are placed in such irregular form" that standard practices had to be instituted. Changes were made, and for "the burying ground north of the village," plots were specifically laid out and strict rules instituted limiting the land's use to interring bodies and recording their names with the town clerk. Additionally, a portion of the land was set aside for "strangers, people of color & poor persons."[445] Eventually, many of these period families, regardless of social, economic or political ilk, came to rest here next to one another at Elmwood Cemetery.

This was certainly a serious occasion, but one wag responsible for the December entry in *Franklin's Legacy; or, the New York & Vermont Almanack, for the Year of our Lord 1808* took the opportunity to share a joke at a condemned man's expense. After being escorted to the place of execution, the soon-to-be-departed turned and asked his executioner "if he had any commands where he was going?" In reply, the man thanked him for the civility of his question under the circumstances but said that "he believed he must trouble him with a line!" And "at that instant clapped the halter about his neck."[446]

On this occasion, Dean's parting assumed a wholly different atmosphere. As eyewitnesses described, "When Dean arrived at the gallows, he asked for some tobacco; after receiving it, he ascended the scaffold without the least appearance of remorse, fear, or serious reflection, and took his stand upon the staging." Then, he called out to the crowd to see if "a certain witness, who testified against him on his trial," was present, professing that what this man said about him was "absolutely false" and that he "wished to see the witness to tell him what he thought of him: 'He was the cause…of my coming to this.'" Nobody appears to have responded, but Dean was probably referring to witness Stephen Pearl Lathrop, who had provided damaging testimony against many of the smugglers, including Dean's alleged admonition to Mott to "fire, why don't you fire." Dean then looked at Staniford standing nearby and asked him directly if he had ever said that he intended to hang the prisoners without the benefit of a judge or jury, laughing so loudly that many could hear him.[447]

Staniford never answered Dean, telling him instead that he had a minute to live, and the condemned man responded that he "was innocent of the crime alleged against him," concluding, "That ends my story." Then "he kicked his hat into his grave, spit upon his coffin, and pulled the cap over his eyes" and "was swung off about three o'clock." As far as his outward behavior was concerned, the newspaper wrote that "he exhibited to the last, a degree of careless unconcern, that perhaps was never equaled, and which seemed to suppress those emotions which such a shocking spectacle is calculated to excite."[448] If the disposition of Dean's remains was anything like Private Baily's, then he was immediately placed into his $4.25 burial clothes, then into his $2.00 coffin and lowered down into his $2.00 grave.

FOR STANIFORD, THE EFFECTS of the execution were long-lasting. Two years later, in 1810, and continuing on for some time, his claims to the legislature for reimbursement of expenses were delayed and repeatedly referred from one committee to another for decision. In explaining the costs incurred for this "painfull [sic] and disagreeable" task, as well as in the time beforehand, his list included $300.00 for conducting the execution itself, $40.00 for paying four deputies for six days' work and $20.00 for guards, accompanied by an eye-popping $51.75 bill from the blacksmith, "who furnished and assisted in putting upon the said prisoners the necessary implements of confinement." Some of those expenses were finally repaid, but troubles associated with his department continued, even after Heman Allen was named the new sheriff at the beginning of the following month.

On December 9, 1808, now out of office, Staniford appeared in court once again and filed suit against the county (defended by Harrington) for reimbursement of eighty-four dollars for "diverse labors and services" associated with renovations at the jail, and then, only weeks later, he brought an incredible claim against Seeley Bennett. Alleging that his deputy had committed "neglect, non-feasance, misfeasance & malfeasance," court documents detail a staggering seventeen instances (again, defended by Harrington) in which Bennett reportedly failed in his duties, thereby rendering Staniford, as his employer, liable to the many plaintiffs. Jailor Benjamin Adams was also sued by Staniford in February 1809 for neglect in his maintenance of the gaol. Debt pursued Staniford, and in 1812, he wrote to one owing him money, pleading for repayment, telling him he only "wish[ed] to do as I would be done by." By 1815, his troubles had so compounded that he sought from the legislature, and received, a bill in his favor, entitled "An Act Exempting the Body of Daniel Staniford from Arrest & Imprisonment," in an effort to free himself from the possibility of jail while putting his financial affairs in order.[449]

Seeking to distance himself from the problems of his predecessor, Allen promptly replaced several of Staniford's men and appointed Jacob Davis, Lyman Woorster, Herman Lowry and Roger Enos in their stead. He also put local notable John Johnson into the role of keeper of the jail. But even Allen was not immune from controversy when, only months later, on the evening of April 19, 1809, while continuing to guard the various smugglers in his custody, Thomas Green Jr., "with force and arms," broke into the jail and somehow successfully liberated "Thomas Green the elder" from confinement. The effect was immediate, and forceful, as Harrington quickly obtained an arrest warrant for the young man, and six deputies responded, arresting him the following day.[450]

The impact of Dean's hanging appears to have been a significant one on the community in the next weeks, as evidenced by what took place in the trials of his associates in early January 1809. Convening once again in special session, the Supreme Court met in Burlington on January 3, continuing its work until the fourteenth, when it concluded the four matters involving Mott, Mudget, Ledgard and Sheffield. Harrington and Van Ness represented the state (Fay had no involvement in these proceedings), while a bevy of local attorneys—Daniel Chipman, Elnathan Keyes, Amos Marsh and Bates Turner—were all involved with one or more of the defendants.

Mott's trial proceeded first, and as bizarre as his first might have been, the result on this occasion was even stranger. When the jury returned to the courtroom at midnight on January 7 with its verdict that, despite overwhelming evidence that he had murdered Ormsby and Marsh by discharging the devastating rounds from the nine-foot wall piece that ripped into their bodies, he was guilty only of manslaughter. A U.S. Army officer witnessing the proceedings called it "a most astonishing fact that politics will have such an influence over a jury…when it was proved to the satisfaction of everyone present" that Mott had fired the weapon a full three-quarters of an hour after the soldiers had seized the *Black Snake*, a "fact not even denied" by his attorneys.[451] Without a doubt, premeditation had been proven, but for whatever reason, it was rejected by the jury.

The specific order of the remaining trials is not clear, but the results remained frustratingly and consistently unsatisfactory. For David Sheffield, the jury once again rejected any finding that he had murdered boatman Ellis Drake, ruling instead that he, too, committed only manslaughter. Mudget's trial, which began on Wednesday morning, January 11, saw the state's case against the crew's captain for the murders of Ormsby and Marsh severely damaged through the testimony of several witnesses, who claimed he was not the only person wearing a white hat during the confrontation, insinuating that others had been mistaken in identifying him as responsible. In the end, the jury was unable to reach a decision, and the case was dropped. But he remained in custody until 1810 to face the indictment charging him with aiding in Drake's killing; for unexplained reasons, that case was also dismissed. Whether it was part of the Drake proceedings or a second murder is not described, but on May 25, 1810, Mudget is named on the local front page as being held on a charge of murder but having, along with two other felons, escaped from Johnson's jail.[452]

However, it was the trial of Francis Ledgard for his aiding in Drake's death on the water that appears the most contentious of them all, at least in the behind-the-scenes actions, which involved several individuals. Recall that immediately following his arrest, and while resting in the local jail, Ledgard was approached by someone on behalf of merchants Catlin and Fitch seeking assurance that he would remain quiet. He was to agree not to tell what they "had said and done," for which he was to receive $200 in payment. As Ledgard explained in his 1811 statement, he kept his part of the bargain up to this point but found he needed money to pay his attorneys and sent his brother, Charles, to Fitch to provide him with $50. Apparently seeing that they had nothing to fear from anything Ledgard might say, Fitch provided "one dollar only, which was on Coos Bank" (indicating it was worthless counterfeit). Ledgard immediately understood the message being sent—"that they had some other plan in contemplation to stop my mouth"—and on the second day of trial, he decided to explosively reveal to all the machinations of those esteemed others and show exactly what their involvement was in the murders.

Ledgard planned to call two witnesses with firsthand information able to describe his involvement with Sam Mix, Sam Fitch, Guy Catlin and Reuben Harmon, ardent Federalists counseling violence against the militia soldiers and providing the necessary ammunition to do so. Ledgard explained, "I called Barney Hoos and Mr. Haswell into court determining to prove all that was in my power for they were knowing the many circumstances that I have mentioned." Hoos (or Barnabus Hoose, as he is also identified in other papers) was a local militia soldier who had stood guard over the murdered bodies and testified at Mudget's trial that he had gone down to the river early that morning and seen Ledgard speaking with Mudget. What his specific information was that Ledgard believed would exonerate him is not revealed, but Haswell's involvement is somewhat clearer.

As noted, Ledgard also wanted the court to order attorney Van Ness to testify about the meeting he had witnessed when Mix came to Penniman demanding the use of the boat that was shortly thereafter provided to Ledgard to take up the river to find and warn the *Black Snake* crew. It is possible that Deputy Collector Haswell was also present at the time and could have provided similar information and that's why Ledgard wanted to call him as a witness. However, what he did not realize was the effect his plan would have on his unsuspecting attorneys.

At first, Ledgard's intentions were not clear, so "Daniel Chipman, being one of my council [*sic*], asked me what I intended to prove by these evidences?" When Ledgard told him what he had in mind, the attorney immediately "flew in[to] a passion and told me that he would not have them examined," his reason being "there was enough proven against me already to hang me." However, his second attorney, Bates Turner, provided a more moderate suggestion than his Federalist co-counsel and agreed that the witnesses should be examined. Certainly, Ledgard's part in warning the smugglers and then becoming so intoxicated that he fell asleep and arose only to warn Farrington off from taking his boat hardly constituted conduct warranting his execution. With a division between the attorneys becoming apparent, the court immediately adjourned, and upon reconvening, the attorneys sought additional time and permission to take Ledgard outside the courtroom for further discussions, which was granted.

Then a most unusual meeting took place at a nearby house. There, Ledgard met with not only Chipman and Turner but also Prosecutor Van Ness. Chipman told him he should "give up my cause to manslaughter," pleading guilty to that lesser charge, and avoid the potential of being found guilty of the hanging offense of murder. However, that was not the opinion of the other two: "Van Ness said if the cause was his to handle he should not give it up [and] so said Bates Turner." Ledgard maintained his refusal to enter a guilty plea, and they all returned to the courtroom, where the attorneys continued in their discussions. Again, the men obtained permission to take their client out to talk with him further.

In this next meeting, Chipman and Marsh were joined by Keyes and told him he was "ignorant of the law and if [illegible] trial I should certainly be hanged for my cause was much worse than Motts and, in short, they would not assist me if I would not give up my cause to manslaughter"—indeed, this was highly suspect counsel revealing a concerted attempt by these attorneys to shield others from being exposed. By this time, Ledgard had been worn down, and as he recounted, he agreed to plead guilty to manslaughter with the understanding that he would not receive any sentence of more than one year's imprisonment. Notwithstanding his decision, Turner reportedly came to him afterward and told him "he believed my counsel had been hired to get me convicted by those men," referring to Catlin, Fitch and Jasper. While this is his first reference to the involvement of Catlin's business associate Joseph Jasper, the fact that he was willing to identify him together with the others indicates his name was also before the public as yet another of those business leaders backing the violent actions taken.

On Saturday, January 14, Mott, Sheffield and Ledgard, all found guilty of manslaughter, appeared before the court to hear Judge Tyler sentence them. Just two weeks earlier, Tyler had presided over the trial of Nancy Blackmore, a single mother who delivered a bastard child the preceding July and allegedly promptly drowned it, for which she was found not guilty. He also sentenced three other men for their involvement in counterfeiting taking place in September, handing out seven-year sentences for hard labor to each, accompanied by a fine of a single dollar.[453]

Now, for killing Ormsby and Marsh, Mott was sentenced to "sit in the pillory one hour," between noon and 4:00 p.m. on January 17, and then "to be taken from there to the publick whipping post and there whipped fifty stripes on his naked back," after which he was to be "confined to hard labor for a term of ten years" and to pay costs of $150.07. Sheffield's and Ledgard's involvement in Drake's killing brought each of them the same sentence, except Sheffield was ordered to pay $115.84 in costs, and Ledgard escaped any whipping.

As ordered, three days later, Sheriff Allen took each of them from their jail cells out onto the Courthouse Square and there "set" each in the pillory for an hour and whipped Mott and Sheffield, returning them back to confinement. Had they inflicted only serious bodily injury on their victims rather than death, it is unlikely that any of the men would have received anything more than a small fine. That was the result when the court later sentenced two men for separate incidents in which one viciously assaulted another man with a hatchet, inflicting serious bodily injury, and received a fifty-dollar fine, and another was ordered to pay forty dollars for plunging a pitchfork numerous times into a man, taking him to the point of near death.[454]

What explains the change that had taken place allowing for someone such as Samuel Mott to escape the death penalty imposed on Cyrus Dean, the man who had only exhorted him to fire off the fatal shot? The community had initially been horrified at the three murders and quickly gathered together to bury the dead and put the main culprits on trial, but then familiar political spirit returned. The recent elections had decisively rejected Republican leanings, and hometown Federalists were on the ascent. During Dean's trial in September, Harrington had lamented the presence of party spirit as defense counsel repeatedly attempted to remove Republicans from juries, and now, months later, the divisions continued. As Mott's second trial concluded, Harrington sent Judge Tyler a draft of what he proposed to say during his closing argument, admitting that because he was "apt in many instances to have my feelings too warm & pursue some points too far," he requested the judge to "lop off" all those parts he deemed unimportant. Harrington was being careful because, he explained, "I should feel sorry to see any of my observations in print that are not well founded. Too much caution cannot be used when party spirit rages as what it now does."[455]

Later in the year, "SPECTATOR," writing as one "thoroughly acquainted" with the machinations witnessed during the recent trials, similarly concluded that the different results obtained in the Dean and Mott trials were political.[456] After noting the court's refusal to allow testimony concerning the two local businessmen assisting the smugglers, whom everyone already suspected, he described efforts taken to undermine the respected sheriff. Whereas Staniford, an acknowledged "friend to government," had conducted himself appropriately in summoning reputable jurors for the first trials (where Mott was found guilty), his replacement, Heman Allen, coming from the local hotbed of Federalism at the falls, suspiciously packed the next juries with prejudiced men of similar persuasion.

SPECTATOR further lamented Staniford's fall from grace, brought about by a constant, revolving series of men going to Montpelier and lobbying in Allen's favor as his replacement. They reportedly met with members of the new council, a body packed with "aristocratic lawyers, those leeches who have sucked from the people their vital subsistence." Staniford's removal, compounded by Mott's surviving and Dean's death, made no sense, leading the writer to bemoan that lives should be held at the mercy of this "baneful influence of leading demagogues." But Staniford was not the only one paying a political price, as Solomon Miller, fifteen-year veteran and respected clerk of the Supreme and County Courts, and the one who had presumably failed to administer the oath to the officer overseeing the jury in Mott's first trial, was summarily dismissed from his position. It was a move so disapproved by members of the local bar that they entered a formal resolution in opposition, ascribing it to yet more political maneuvering.[457]

There is no indication that the grand jury ever pursued the course Fay suggested at the opening of Mott's first trial when registering his opposition to any delay—that it investigate the men exhorting and facilitating the work of the murderers—but it did look into their violating liquor laws. In 1807, merchant Sam Fitch was one of at least fifteen others indicted by Harrington for the illegal sale of spirits, paying a $10.00 fine. The indictment charging him reveals that he was not only selling wine and spirits without a license but doing so in gallon, half-gallon and quart quantities drained out of larger casks.[458] The activity continued unabated, and immediately following the most recent trials, Harrington once again sought to curtail the illegal sales. In February 1809, he worked with the grand jury to institute twenty-one indictments, fifteen against taverns and six involving individual retailers. Unsurprisingly, Fitch was once again named, but this time he was joined by fellow merchant Reuben Harmon, allowing Harrington to charge the county $21.29 each for his efforts. Whether this aggressive action was the cause of it is unclear, but months later, during the September term, the number of indictments for illegal sales fell substantially, to eleven.[459]

Was this the best Harrington could do to bring those backing the smugglers to account? With the reported complicity of Catlin, Mix, Fitch and others ripe for further inquiry, none of it appears to have ever been pursued. If it was considered, the pragmatic side of the state's attorney perhaps told him that the prevailing political winds would not allow for any kind of forceful government action against them. First, it would require a grand jury willing to find grounds to bring a criminal prosecution and then a unanimous trial jury to actually convict—certainly an insurmountable task under the circumstances. It is enlightening to consider what the latest grand jury said when it disbanded on January 9, 1809. In words similar to those used by the grand jury concluding its work the preceding September, an "Address" to the public explained that while it had found violations of law "in respect to licenses and roads," "after diligent enquiry" there was "no cause of complaint" warranting charges in other matters (involving Catlin and the others?) being filed in the Supreme Court. To this body, the recent murders, described as an "accidental and melancholy event," were the responsibility of "strangers" arriving in their community, and they simply chose to ignore the complicity of those living among them.[460]

Harrington was certainly not one to enter into a contest he could not be reasonably assured to win, and from that point on, the matter was dropped. While none of the businessmen, who certainly must have been the subject of continued, secret whispers, suffered punishment, they succeeded in maintaining some degree of respectability when town freemen gathered to decide who was to serve in various capacities. Each of their names is present in the town records for the years immediately following as being elected to serve as jurors, haywards (overseers of fences and hedges), surveyors of highways, fence viewers and listers. And ironically, William Harrington's name also appears alongside theirs as selectman, engaged in his usual service of administering to the poor and on school districting issues.

9

VANNESSED

C hristmas Day 1808 brought a reflective Thomas Jefferson to consider what he had wrought these past months: "I feel extreme regret that an effort, made on motives which all mankind must approve, has failed in an object so much desired. I spared nothing to promote it."[461] Chastened and thoroughly frustrated, though unbent and unrepentant, his grand experiment was finally repealed on March 4, 1809, at the very moment James Madison assumed the presidency. In its stead, Congress did away with the onerous embargo's prohibitions, substituting various nonintercourse and non-importation acts, showing further that it meant business through the implementation of draconian enforcement provisions in its ongoing, futile aim to decisively affect the warring British and French contest. However, its efforts remained ineffective, and with no end in sight, in June 1812, Madison was forced to declare war against Britain.

For Vermonters, situated literally within sight of the enemy, between the violence of 1808 and the war's final end in 1815, these years remained starkly unsettling, causing many to lament their situation. For the smugglers among them, notwithstanding the continuing arrival of federal troops replacing state militia units, their presence did little to stop any inclination to continue on with their illicit trade to the north, viewing the soldiers as nothing more than a mere nuisance to go around. At the same time, for others, these times represented a moment ripe for the exploitation of lucrative opportunities falling into their laps, ones that the presence of a competent authority might otherwise have prevented.

Burlington's port inspector for the past four years, Nathan Haswell, had seen enough, and a month following the disappointing trials, on February 19, 1909 (one week after Abraham Lincoln's birth), he tendered his resignation to Penniman. Explaining his reasons, Haswell told him he could no longer work in that capacity, as it was "incompatible with my feelings," expressing the hope that Penniman recognized he had tried to discharge his duties "with fidelity, and, I hope, your satisfaction." He appears to have become disillusioned with the job's demands at least by the preceding November, when he had an unfortunate encounter with militia soldiers while executing his duties.

The sloop *Essex* had duly arrived in port one Sunday afternoon to have its cargo inspected before proceeding on as the law required. However, before Haswell was able to do so, a contingent of militia boarded at the direction of the local commander and demanded the master's papers for its own inspection. As Haswell arrived alongside, he "received several threats" from the soldiers if he attempted to board, but not one easily put off, Haswell quickly bounded on deck and immediately instructed the vessel's master to report only to himself and to allow no one to remain on board unless he approved. Additional delay ensued as the inspector and militia continued in their dispute, but no violence took place. The principal harm was to Haswell's honor; he quickly penned a letter to Penniman demanding an investigation because of his "feeling my authority [was] trampled upon, my integrity called in question." Writing to "Friend Buel" on Windmill Point at the same time, Haswell solicited his input and asked what he would have done. Only days earlier, possibly recognizing the profits that Haswell and business partner Peaslee were making in supplying troops stationed on the Point, Buel had written to him suggesting that he would like to be included in their work. What Haswell thought of the proposal is not known, but in this most recent letter, he explained that he felt himself "injured and insulted" at the soldiers' actions. Clearly upset that he, who had accepted the hazardous job of seizing and storing contraband on the government's behalf when others would not risk it, was forced "to meet with such treatment," he concluded it "is an abuse which I cannot put up with."[462]

Neither Penniman's nor Buel's responses are known, but the distasteful encounter with the militia commander remained a source of contention. Haswell wrote to Penniman a month before resigning that while he did not believe goods stored in his custody were in any danger, if the militia wanted to place a guard over them, he would not stand in the way. The discomfort that federal inspector Haswell was experiencing with state officials is representative of the inherent power struggle taking place when two governmental entities seek to simultaneously enforce their respective interests, and it was a problem that did not disappear.

Following his resignation, and while storing goods for Penniman, on March 8, 1809, a militia officer visited Haswell's business with a state court order taking custody of eighty-three barrels of potash seized on August 10, immediately following the murders. The order, a so-called writ of replevin, allowed for a creditor to obtain the return of unlawfully held goods, and when the officer walked into his cellar, literally laying the writ on the barrels, Haswell immediately sought advice concerning an appropriate response. Local attorneys told him not to resist but to contact Penniman to obtain a court order charging the soldier with trespassing.

While the results of that encounter are not recorded, on April 22, Penniman wrote to Haswell and told him what action to take in the future. Based on a recently received directive coming straight from Secretary Gallatin, he related, "I have received instructions…not to let any property be taken from me which is libeled and to resist an officer, even with force, as the laws of the United States would at once be prostrated to the state judiciary," and accordingly, "You will prevent any more being taken in any form."[463] In these highly volatile times, with international and local problems pressing in on them, the best Washington could do was to instruct those working to enforce the country's interests to actually take up arms and physically resist state officials to vindicate federal law. It was an extraordinary situation.

For Harrington and those working alongside him on town issues, it was all they could do to corral the continuing transient problem as issues of whether to build a house of correction to confine the poor and the maintenance of roads appeared yet again during their March 20 town meeting. Extensive discussions concerning the mundane, domestic problems remained the community's primary concerns, and in 1810, much work was done to address horses, swine, sheep and rams running at large. The state of their financial affairs finally came to a head when an 1811 review of the town's accounts, dating back to 1805, brought the sad conclusion that it was "considerably in debt" and that the dismal state of recordkeeping, described as "irregular and unintelligible," made it impossible for a reviewing committee to make "even a rational conjecture" of its true financial condition. Specifically refusing to condemn any of the selectmen serving up to that time (which included Harrington), the committee decided it needed more help to get to the bottom of the problem.[464] So for these particular times, while Washington railed at the interference of state agents, and as local officials dealt with their own, in comparison, petty problems, it is not surprising that neither Dean's execution nor the sentencing of his associates to whipping and ten-year terms of imprisonment had little effect on those still inclined to engage in criminal conduct.

The unidentified, and disgusted, U.S. Army officer witnessing Mott's second trial in January 1809 described what he saw at the time as uninhibited smugglers blatantly continued on with their trade: "Immense quantities of produce of every description, find their way into Canada every day; on a fair calculation, 100 loads per day for 15 days past, have gone into Canada, through Swanton." They were "a desperate set of fellows, many of whom are armed, and have been encouraged to defend themselves against any force that attempts to take them."[465] Indeed, it was a vigorous, dangerous path they were pursuing, for now the so-called Second Enforcement (or Giles) Act of 1809 went into effect, allowing for expansive governmental authority to search, seize and detain those suspected of criminal conduct, as well as permitting federal authorities to call out state militia for assistance. The draconian provisions were quickly denounced, and the Vermont countryside virtually exploded in opposition as thinly spread revenue officers, aided by a similarly sparse military presence, sought to counter their efforts.

That the authorities were not hesitant to take advantage of any opportunity to interfere with the smugglers is without question but also reveals the level to which they went in meeting force with force. One newspaper account of the time relates that in St. Albans, an individual who questioned the right of the military to stop him had his horse "stabbed with a bayonet," while another "going to the mill was threatened to have his brains blown out" if he did not allow a search.[466] Extant court records provide additional, albeit limited, insight into what took place in the first three months of 1809, and while the instances are indeed impressive, the challenges that officers faced were certainly much larger than what they describe. With the assistance of some helpful definitions (a sleigh is a "carriage without wheels," and pork is "fattened hogs killed and dressed"), they reveal a boisterous time when individuals across northern Vermont, frequently in association with many others, loaded up their sleighs and headed to various locations in Lower Quebec, constantly challenging any effort to stop them.

New Year's Day began with Ira Day, of Barre, moving 100 barrels of pearl and 100 barrels of potash, valued at several thousand dollars, to Montreal. The number of sleighs and men needed to transport such a volume is not disclosed, but on January 20, and again on the twenty-sixth, Day once again moved significant quantities of ash (another 219 barrels) utilizing the assistance of twenty unidentified men. On January 6, Thomas How and six others transported 40 barrels of pork from Williamstown to Montreal via sleigh, and on the following day, Abner Pride, aided by eight others, did the same thing with 43 barrels.

The day following the Enforcement Act's passage, on January 10, no fewer than five separate groups set off in violation of its provisions. Jonathan Bass left Braintree with a number of associates, hauling an impressive three thousand pounds of pork on their sleighs, while John Stoddard departed St. Albans carrying another forty-three barrels, assisted by five others. In Tunbridge, Joseph Yurin and friends hauled one thousand pounds of pork via sleigh, as Eleazer Walbridge took a more modest quantity of only four barrels, also assisted by others, and Shibal Converse diversified his thirty-five-barrel load of pork by adding on five hundred pounds of clover seed.

January 15 saw Charles Dana leaving Randolph for Montreal with thirty-two barrels of potash, thirty-two of pearl ash and 1,000 pounds of pork, while on the twenty-fifth, John Tyler left town with nineteen barrels of pearl ash in five sleighs. In one of the few noted successes, on January 26, Penniman's men seized nineteen barrels of potash and 1,100 pounds of pork at Swanton, while on February 1, Abner Pride repeated his prior success and directed ten sleighs northward carrying twelve barrels each of pot and pearl ash and forty barrels of pork. David Page Jr. and his friends took one hundred barrels of potash and one hundred barrels of pearl ash from Middlebury to Montreal on February 15, and on March 1, Samuel Weed and ten men transported twelve barrels of pork, one barrel of potash and one keg of butter from Sheldon into Lower Canada. Two weeks later, on March 15, Roger Hubbard of Montpelier transport nine barrels each of pot and pearl ash to St. John in six sleighs. He appears to have been particularly industrious when, upon receiving information that seized property stored at a government warehouse in Swanton was not sufficiently guarded, on June 8, he and six others raided the facility, forcibly taking twenty-seven barrels of potash, twenty-seven of pearl ash and twelve of pork out of its possession.

Hubbard's aggressive actions against the government were by no means the only instances when smugglers confronted their adversaries. The specifics of the various events are not disclosed, but on February 18, Stephen Royce, in Berkshire, "did forcibly resist, prevent & impede" customs officers in the execution of their duties, while on March 2, three other events took place in which John Waller, in Enosburgh, and George Washington Stone and Solomon Brigham Jr., in Berkshire, also obstructed their work. A week later, on March 9, Thaddeus Tuttle, John Johnson, John Berry and John Curtis raided the government's Burlington stores and removed one hundred barrels of potash, valued at $4,000.

Each of these matters received the attention of federal prosecutor Fay, who then faced the unenviable task of charging and convicting the men of violating an increasingly unpopular law. Various indictments and forfeiture actions, each consuming substantial amounts of work from court personnel, the U.S. marshal, defense attorneys, jurors, witnesses, et cetera, as well as generating fees for the participants, were instituted the following May against each of them. Simultaneously, the numerous other charges previously described (ultimately unsuccessful) were filed against the Hoxies and Taylors.

Some forfeitures actually did take place, but the underlying criminal prosecutions brought about were uniformly disastrous. First, the available law lacked any substantive penalty, leaving Fay with charging misdemeanors, most punishable by fines; certainly, treason was out of the question. Second, several cases presented to the grand jury were returned "no bill" or found lacking in evidence. Third, for those that went to trial, they were routinely acquitted; others had their cases "discharged" by the court, or Fay entered "will no longer prosecute" notes on their indictments. In the only one actually making it to the U.S. Supreme Court (John Tyler), Justice Livingston delivered an opinion in one of the government's rare victories concerning the assessment of a fine. Certainly, very few of the many men actually detained and charged had reason to complain about the outcome of their individual cases, as the government repeatedly conceded its impotence to stop them. Their jubilation at Washington's embarrassment had to have been every bit as much as that shared by one Quebec correspondent writing to a Burlington friend rejoicing at the low cost of goods and freely available money, telling him that the embargo was "certainly a very fine thing for this country."[467]

This was also the moment of reckoning for the notorious smuggling boat *Black Snake*, buried in the sand at some undisclosed location. Three days after dismissing (for an undisclosed reason) the pending case against lake merchant Gideon King's sloop *Dolphin* and its cargo of sixty-eight barrels of potash, and with no person coming forward to contest its forfeiture, on May 11, Fay obtained an order from the court directing it to be sold at public auction. Accordingly, on Tuesday, September 12, U.S. marshal Willard conducted the sale at James Sawyer's inn, in Burlington, obtaining a high bid of $13.00 from a John Pomeroy, possibly the son of local scion Dr. John Pomeroy. In deducting the $8.93 it cost to conduct the sale, the net profit to the government from the boat that had wrought so much mayhem amounted to mere pennies, and from this point on, it disappears from the historical record. The same day, Inspector Sam Buel was the successful bidder on the smuggling vessel called *Red Boat*, seized in May 1808 while hauling barrels of potash. It, and the forty pieces of abandoned leather he also purchased, became the basis for later complaints against him for engaging in questionable conduct in his official role.

The state prison in Windsor was finally ready to receive its charges, and on May 22, 1809, Judge Tyler signed an order requiring that all persons in the state serving a sentence including hard labor be sent there. The order also specifically identified the recently convicted Mott, Ledgard and Sheffield, and on June 1, Sheriff Allen delivered the three men ("having no other body or bodies in my custody under sentence as within mentioned") into the custody of Ezekiel Hanson, "Keeper of the State Prison," as, respectively, prisoners seven, eight and nine. The preceding day, six other men sentenced to terms of up to seven years for counterfeiting had arrived from the sieve-like jail in Danville; no others appeared until later in August. Notably, with the exception of Sheffield, who was born in Grand Isle, none of the first arrivals came from Vermont, listing their places of birth as outside the state. Others appeared over the next few years, serving various sentences for horse stealing, assault, highway robbery, "attempting to ravish," burglary, forgery and arson; however, none had committed such serious crimes as these three men coming from Burlington. With their departure from the town's jail, creditors submitted bills for necessities provided for their upkeep: forty-five cords of wood, 104 pounds of candles used between December and May 31 and nine dollars for a coat and pair of pantaloons for Sheffield.[468]

Life for the men was noticeably different from anything they ever experienced in the past. Gone were the days when lax oversight was provided at the porous county jails, replaced now with guards telling them to "Go here! Go there! Do this! Do that! Shut your head! Mind your business! What are you doing! Out of the vault! You shall go to solitary for that!" Armed with a sword, a guard was stationed in every shop where prisoners worked making nails, while one was located on the wall outside carrying a weapon loaded with ball and buckshot, and at night, one patrolled the prison's entrance. Treatment was humane, but solitary confinement, deemed by prisoners as equivalent to a whipping, was always available. The elements extracted their own toll as layers of frost accumulated on unheated stone walls during the winter months, allowing the men to scrape handfuls into large, icy balls. Decent clothing and food was provided, as well as access to medical care, all overseen by a board of visitors watching over the superintendent that reported its findings back to the legislature.[469] This was the existence of the murdering three from Burlington, at least for the next few years, while others proceeded on with their own interests.

THE BOTHERSOME MURDERERS OUT of the way, Cornelius Van Ness's innate sense of impending opportunity could not have been more correct, as his rise to prominence also began in 1809. He became even more conspicuous within Burlington's elite as he continued with his law practice. On March 17, he attended a massive Republican gathering in nearby Jericho, where between four and five hundred county "friends of Government" gathered to discuss their common interests. Van Ness participated as a member of a five-man committee to fashion resolutions in opposition to those objecting to Jefferson's, and now Madison's, foreign policies—something with which they were "fully satisfied." Naturally, among the dozen provisions, Federalists were condemned, but so, too, were "ecclesiastical missionaries" traveling about the countryside "under the unsuspected garb of our holy religion, exciting and encouraging opposition and insurrection against our laws." In their conclusion, the men promised they would, "so far as our political opponents are uninformed, endeavor to inform them, so far as they are deceived, undeceive them, so far as they are honest, fellowship them; but those who are ambitiously intriguing, it is our indispensable duty to frown back to their original insignificance."[470]

That effort was apparently well received, and four months later, Van Ness was the honored choice of Chittenden County's Republican Committee of Arrangements to deliver the yearly Fourth of July oration, also held at Jericho. It was another much-appreciated performance, delivered through his reading a lengthy twenty-four-page missive describing the honorable actions of the Jefferson administration. But it also ended on the mistaken note that the current times presented opportunities when "party animosities will cease to inflame the minds of neighbors and of friends against each other; and quarrels and tumults will no longer heard," not anticipating the impending war.[471]

Farther to the south, David Fay worked to prepare the yearly celebration of the Bennington Battle on August 17 and obtained a missive for the occasion from his former commanding officer, New Hampshire's General John Stark. Unable to attend the gathering because of ill health, Stark apologized and passed on some personal thoughts, dated July 31, providing a more cautious view of the times, emphasizing (emphasis in original), "FOR THERE IS A

DANGEROUS BRITISH PARTY IN THIS COUNTRY, LURKING IN THEIR HIDING PLACES, MORE DANGEROUS THAN ALL OUR FOREIGN ENEMIES." Stark told his former soldiers to strike against these domestic foes and ended with a toast to all, famously proclaiming (while providing New Hampshire with its future motto), "LIVE FREE OR DIE—DEATH IS NOT THE GREATEST OF EVILS." While the press was quick to publish his remarks and Van Ness's address, proclaiming the latter "as true as holy writ" appropriate for every Republican and Federalist to read, certainly these were not times to let down one's guard.[472]

The remainder of 1809 was relatively quiet for Van Ness, who received his first appointment as a federal employee when he was named Burlington's postmaster. He also begins to appear regularly in various lawsuits as both a plaintiff suing several others for money owed to him and as a defendant. On August 10, 1809, he was named as one of three individuals in a suit brought against them by the directors of the newly established Vermont State Bank for failure to repay a $200 loan made to them the preceding December. In October, he and several other notable individuals, including Harrington, Penniman, Fay and Buel, endorsed a petition to the legislature from Rutland's Eleazor Wheelock seeking permission to establish a stage line between that town and Burlington. Then, on October 15, Van Ness penned a quick note to brother William from Burlington (able to send it without postage in his role as postmaster), telling him he would write more later as he was leaving immediately for Montpelier because "some things are going on which are very important to me."[473]

Those "things" concerned the impending election of David Fay to the state's Supreme Court, completed two days later when he was named to replace the departing, and now governor, Jonas Galusha, joining Tyler and Harrington on the bench. Fay had received his reward for his strenuous efforts on the government's behalf during the trials the preceding year, and now what could it mean for Van Ness? The answer was not long in coming when, on October 19, Vermont senator Jonathan Robinson and U.S. representative Samuel Shaw penned a joint letter to President Madison asking that Van Ness be appointed the next district attorney, attesting that he was "a gentleman of correct habits & morals, an able attorney, and a firm and attached friend to the present Republican Administration."[474]

Between that endorsement, aided by his extensive New York connections, including family friend Supreme Court justice Livingston, and following a quiet, unpublicized moment during a legislative recess, Madison issued a commission naming him as Fay's replacement on December 18, affirmed by the Senate two days later. While he remained in that role for the next three years before resuming his remarkable climb, it marked the beginning of an unsavory period in his professional career that has received virtually no attention in the past. This was the start of Van Ness's expanded association with others in the Burlington community, which allowed him many opportunities to both exploit the vulnerabilities the times offered and to victimize others, particularly the intrepid deputy collector Sam Buel, upon whom his covetous eyes came to rest. The events he participated in were so badly tainted that they caused Buel to later explain to Madison that Van Ness and his various friends and associates constituted "the most extensive, audacious, and illegal combination, that has ever disgraced the United States."[475]

However, much had to happen before Buel's explosive allegations became known. Locally, between 1809 and 1810, Harrington instituted no fewer than thirty new lawsuits while also entering into additional agreements for the repayment of money loaned or for services rendered, which inevitably ended with more suits. Overseers of the poor brought charges against local residents Joshua Barnes and John Van Sicklen, "both men of good estate," for failing and/or refusing to provide for the necessary upkeep of relation Widow Simmons, forcing the town to expend monies on her behalf.[476]

Catlin and Jasper, while also involved in their own suits attempting to collect monies owed and Jasper's continuing presence on the lake guiding *Lady Washington* in its travels, prospered at the falls selling their many dry goods. They had clearly survived any fallout from their roles in the *Black Snake* murders and, in December 1809, advertised an eclectic assortment of goods for sale, including a shipment of "one case of Horsemen's Pistols, with brass barrels...[and] 15 pipes of Alicant and Bordeaux Brandy" and 300,000 "good brick." Meanwhile, brother Moses endowed a "donation library" with books, valued at $300, situated within the Third School District (known also as Catlinsborough or Catlinsburgh), and entered into an agreement with Peaslee and Haswell for their repaying him $97, which, of course, resulted in a lawsuit in January 1810. In October 1810, Curtis Holgate, last seen advertising in April 1808 at the embargo's onset for the delivery of potash to his Alburgh store, petitioned the legislature for an exclusive grant allowing him to build and maintain a wharf on Burlington's waterfront. The effort was heartily endorsed by the local community, which deemed him of "sufficient courage" to take on the project, and those signing on his behalf included, among others, Harrington, Staniford, Bennett and Buel.

These years also mark the period, notwithstanding his September 20, 1810 marriage to Harriot Plimpton, when former port inspector Nathan Haswell's fortunes began to spiral out of control. Personally, he, together with Moses Catlin, acted several times as an appraiser of seized goods on behalf of the district court, placing a value on them for bonding purposes, while also conducting many public auctions for his own profit. However, those efforts were not enough to sustain him, and while the timing of the demise of his association with John Peaslee is not clear, between 1810 and 1814, his name begins to appear repeatedly in court records in a more ominous tone. It was shortly after the two became embroiled in claims against others for payment of debts—those brought against the county for fees owed them for storing seized goods and in defending one seeking $300 for the delivery of three hundred pork barrels—that significant problems arose.[477]

On June 19, 1810, they, along with a Russell Jones, agreed, as so many naïvely did in these days, to act as surety on behalf of an unidentified individual to pay the United States $1,000 in the event of his non-performance. By May 1811, that unfortunate event had taken place, and U.S. attorney Van Ness instituted at least two suits against the men for payment. He had Haswell and Peaslee arrested and jailed, an event that occurred more than once. On one bizarre occasion, Haswell was actually taken out of the Burlington jail; transported to court in Rutland, where he provided testimony in an unrelated seizure case describing one of his valuations; and then returned back into confinement.[478] Their incarceration was not continuous, and as frequently happened in debt-related matters, they were allowed temporary freedom upon posting the necessary jail bonds. Haswell attempted to make a living throughout these years but became increasingly unable to do so as his financial affairs fell further into disrepair.

By 1814, Van Ness, and then his successor, Titus Hutchinson, had pursued the claims so relentlessly against the two men that Congress became involved when numerous petitions were filed on their behalf seeking assistance. It was only after an independent finding that they were virtually destitute that they were finally ordered released from their most recent confinement in the Burlington jail on June 24, 1816, by treasury secretary Alexander J. Dallas. The single condition allowing for their freedom required them to sign over to the government "all their estate, real, personal, and mixed," which meant Haswell forfeited his entire, valuable interest in the two hundred acres of local land he had purchased in the 1808 tax sale for a mere $2.19. In this era, before enlightened bankruptcy laws were passed, the two businessmen also sought assistance from the Vermont legislature for the discharge of their obligations and successfully obtained relief in 1819, when they signed over a $16,000.00 claim to their creditors. In an interesting accounting of his assets at the time, Haswell listed, among a number of other household items, "Gibbons *Roman Empire*, 5 vol., *Young's Works*, 3 vol., *Scottish Chiefs*, 4 vol."; a copy of *Ship of Fools*, a book on Indian wars; the "Works of R.T. Paine"; a horse, bridle and one "set hay scales on Court House Square"; fifteen summer hats; a fowling piece and powder horn; "3 small maps"; and one "Back Gammon Board."[479] Many years passed before debtor's laws were changed, removing their draconian outcomes in making the poor even poorer.

OUT ON WINDMILL POINT, Sam Buel remained squarely in the middle of smuggling activity and with little ready reinforcement. On one occasion, when he and a "half-witted" boy were alone, his house was surrounded by several men bent on forcibly retaking seized goods stored inside. Quickly fastening the doors and windows, Buel shouted to the boy, so those outside could hear, that he should run upstairs and bring down all the muskets, while also yelling out directions to several others—fictitious "John, James, Tom, Dick and Harry"—to also get ready. The ruse worked on that occasion, but on November 14, 1809, James Allen and Samuel Gelston, both coming from Lower Canada, successfully raided Buel's stores and made off with one hogshead of dry goods, one barrel of hardware and two casks of liquor.

In his secluded location, Buel became the brunt of efforts, ones he said were "taken to embarrass me in the execution of the laws" of both a serious and ridiculous nature. Whether he ever told anyone about this is not known, but one wag writing in the 1820s reported the exploits of smuggler Partridge Heywood during these times and of an encounter he had with Buel. On this particular occasion, Buel observed a boat entering Vermont from the north, broke off a conversation he was having and rowed out, signally it to stop. He went on board and told the master he intended to search the vessel for any contraband and went below decks. Unknown to him, those involved in the hoax had prepared a box and enclosed a small dog and cat inside, separated from each other by a board. When Buel saw it protruding out from under some lumber and removed its top, the cat suddenly sprang out, with the dog following immediately behind, as they scurried up onto the deck, where passengers took up a "snicker of laughter." When Buel returned topside, the master asked if he had found any contraband, and Buel told him, "No, but I was unaware that cats and dogs had become an article of trade amongst you. Therefore, not finding them specified in the non-intercourse act, I suppose I must let them pass, wishing you much profit of your special cargo." Buel was reportedly so embarrassed by the event that whenever the boat passed in the future, he let it go by without inspection, thereby affording the smugglers more opportunities to engage in their illegal activity. Revenue duties aside, Buel was also embroiled at that moment in a suit brought by an imprisoned Samuel Holton, a debtor owing him money, who was seeking relief from the legislature from any further confinement.[480]

By the end of 1810, Penniman decided it was time to retire from his collector responsibilities, and on February 5, 1811, despite whatever mishaps might have occurred in the past, Buel's steadfast efforts to enforce Washington's dictates were finally recognized. Madison named Buel as Penniman's replacement, taking effect two days later, when he assumed the roles of both collector for the district and inspector of revenue for the Port of Alburgh. It is indicative of the esteem many held for Buel at the time, while also ironic in light of what took place in the future, that those agreeing to stand in as guarantors in his performance of his new duties, and those witnessing the proceedings, brought together Penniman, Harrington and Stephen Pearl, who agreed to serve as sureties for the not insignificant amount of $2,000, while U.S. attorney Van Ness and his law clerk, Archibald W. Hyde, attested to the April 16 event.[481] The issue that later came to tear at each of these men concerned, not surprisingly, money. Penniman did not disappear entirely and became a justice of the peace and probate judge in the coming years, in addition to introducing, along with Heman Allen, TELESCOPE, a Long Island–bred horse brought to Colchester in 1814 to "improve the breed of horses in this country."[482]

The method of compensating the nation's revenue collectors had the attention of Congress at the time, and on March 2, 1811, those assigned to Vermont, Champlain, Sackett's Harbor and Oswego were allowed a salary increase to $500 a year, in addition to "fees and commissions allowed by law."[483] Pursuant to a 1799 law, the collector was permitted to receive a portion of fines, penalties and forfeitures, called a "moiety," determined after costs were deducted, amounting to upward of one-half of the net amount, with the balance going to the government. Unfortunately, with the possibility of having these respectable amounts of money now available to him, the honorable, hardworking and well-intentioned Buel allowed his creativity and initiative to interfere with the spirit of the law, and it contributed, in large part, to his future downfall.

As Buel explained to Madison about these particular times, the situation in Vermont was dire, with "no small perils and difficulties" presented to those enforcing the revenue laws.

> [T]*he depraved state of morals on the frontiers of this District, have not only opposed a general and weighty obstruction to the execution of the laws, but has given birth to combinations to violate them by force, as well as by fraud, which has not only required the personal exertions of* [myself], *but made it necessary for* [me] *to offer inducements* [to subordinates], *which, by interesting and influencing others to his aid, might have the effect to counteract them; and considering that to faithful and active agents it promised encouragement to give them a share of forfeitures arising from goods, &c. which they might seize (and that those that were unfaithful or negligent, merited no reward) and choosing to rely for aid on patriotic as well as pecuniary motives,* [I] *had in this manner established an extensive support to the laws, without expense to the government.*[484]

What Buel had done was set up an off-the-books method to compensate those providing assistance to the government, which included two of his deputies, Dr. James Wood (Buel's deputy at the time of the *Black Snake* murders and smuggler/informant Joshua Day's contact) and an individual named James Camp. Each of these men agreed with Buel to allow him to receive half of their salaries, for which Buel would then compensate them with his share of moieties obtained as a result of their enforcement work leading to forfeitures.

It was a creative solution to a challenging situation, as Buel sought to invigorate his subordinates' will to institute aggressive seizures by allowing them a proportionate share of the resulting profits. The arrangement lasted for only a four- to six-month period, allowing Wood to obtain upward of $1,000, but for whatever value it might have provided, it was enough to begin undermining Buel's reputation. Ironically, it was not long after Buel suffered the consequences of his imaginative payment scheme that the Treasury Department actually adopted it, citing favorably the experiences obtained in Vermont.[485]

No sooner had Van Ness witnessed Buel's arrival at his lucrative collector position than he began an effort to see to his professional demise, an outcome Buel later characterized as being "Vannessed." In a letter to treasury secretary Gallatin in 1812, the respected judge, former congressman and now Champlain collector Peter Sailly (who became Buel's father-in-law in

September 1811 upon marriage to his daughter, widow Julia Platt) responded to a request that he investigate Buel's actions. The issues Gallatin asked Sailly to look into included not only allegations contained in affidavits filed by Wood and Camp concerning their unusual compensation arrangements but also an additional one signed by lawyer Hyde. Archibald W. Hyde (1786–1847), described by Van Ness's son as his father's "confidential agent and pimp," was a newly admitted attorney in Van Ness's office and made the explosive allegations that in Buel's purchase of forfeited goods sold by the U.S. marshal pursuant to court order in 1809, "there appeared to be a combination or agreement between the said Buel and certain other bidders not to bid against each other, in order to obtain said goods as low as possible."

In declining Gallatin's request to investigate his son-in-law, Sailly was forced to acknowledge that Buel's creative method in compensating Wood and Camp was questionable but that it had not resulted in either any gain to Buel or any loss to the government. As for Hyde, his allegations were similarly rejected, as there was no proof of their having actually occurred or that the government had suffered any loss, characterizing his statements as "falsified." Sailly believed that the allegations were brought on by "intrigue and misrepresentation" by those seeking to impugn the integrity of an honorable man in order to oust him from office.

Sailly assured Gallatin that Buel was a man of integrity and "uprightness" and then went on to describe his impressions of Vermont's U.S. attorney. From his perspective, Van Ness was nothing more than a money-grabbing opportunist, a "concealed detractor" working with others who had "only their private interest in view, [taking] advantage of the early indiscretion of a very honest man."[486] However, whatever suspicions those designing others complaining to Gallatin might have raised to undermine Buel, they had to wait for the immediate future as other events unfolded.

Between August 1811 and early 1813, Van Ness instituted many dozens of forfeiture actions on the government's behalf in the district court, all the fruits of Buel's and his deputies' efforts allowing them substantial returns, none of which entitled Van Ness to a cent beyond a modest fee for filing the necessary papers. The seizures came from many towns and involved lengthy lists of goods ranging from the mundane (i.e., 924 pairs of gloves, forty-eight pieces of calico, ten shawls, et cetera), to the interesting (two hundred pounds of beaver skins, accompanying two thousand martin and two thousand muskrat skins from Canada), to the consumable (barrels of whiskey). At first, Buel thought his relationship with Van Ness was cordial and that "an esteem and confidence" existed, both professionally and personally, between the two men. But in just a short period of time, the riches coming Buel's way only raised Van Ness's envy. In the district court's May 1812 session alone, in just eight cases, Van Ness could only watch as the net proceeds from forfeitures amounted to some $6,000 to be split between the government and Buel. Many additional thousands flowed into their respective coffers later in the year, and it was something the young district attorney simply could not ignore.[487]

Becoming even more jealous of the collector, Van Ness began to delay, or fail, to pursue cases brought to him, making excuses about their legality and leading Buel to suspect that "selfish and mercenary motives" were beginning to intrude.[488] In fact, Van Ness came to display egregious signs of avarice as he pursued an outrageous, and devastating, course of action in the future, claiming a right to not only the proceeds Buel was entitled to but also to a portion of the government's own duties collected in Vermont, which in 1812 amounted to $95,330.93. It was a legal theory that officials within the Treasury Department concluded would cost the government "not far from three millions of dollars" if accepted and applied throughout the country, which it was not.[489] Aside from the monetary losses Buel might have experienced because of Van Ness's delaying or refusing to pursue cases, the lessening of income directly attributable to the work of his deputies only increased the burden on himself, as he personally sought to make up the deficiencies in order to maintain their loyalties and concerted efforts in collecting the nation's principal source of revenue. At the same time, in his personal role, Van Ness's name unsurprisingly appears alongside other Burlington businessmen in court records filing claims against others for the repayment of debts.

Only two months after his marriage, Buel was involved in the deadliest of any actions he ever personally encountered. On November 3, 1811, he was at his Windmill Point post, together with brother-in-law, John Walker, and a George Graves, when twenty-four-year-old Harrington Brooks of St. Albans (whose name also appears alongside smuggler/murderer Samuel Mott's name in an 1808 militia role), accompanied by another man, passed southward, coming from St. John, in a skiff and failed to stop and report his cargo. Buel and the other two took up pursuit of the vessel, while also being sure to unfurl the revenue cutter's distinctive ensign and pendant signifying their authority to the fleeing men. At about 9:00 a.m., Brooks navigated close to the shore of Gull Island, while Buel, unable to approach because of the deeper draft of the cutter, was forced to stand off and shout out, demanding him to surrender. Brooks called back that he had only seven bushels of salt on board, that it belonged to five families wanting only to salt their pork and that he was willing to pay whatever duties were required if he was allowed to go free.

Buel was not one to avoid enforcing the law and told Brooks that he intended to take his boat and cargo, causing the young man to start out again in flight while remaining close to shore. The chase lasted some five miles in total, during which between two and three shots were fired by the revenue men—as the law allowed a pursuing cutter bearing the ensign and pendant to do. Finally, an opportune moment arose, and Buel ordered Walker to fire once again, resulting in a fatal blast that delivered twelve buckshot directly into Brooks's chest, who called out, "See what they have done!" and fell forward, "covering the salt-bags with his blood," dying instantly. Buel and his men towed the skiff to shore, where the requisite legal inquest immediately took place over Brooks's shroud-covered body.

While passions were high and Buel and Walker were initially determined to have murdered Brooks, subsequent grand jury proceedings, ones overseen by Supreme Court judge David Fay, concluded to the contrary (eleven voting in favor and five against an indictment requiring twelve votes in order to proceed), and the two were allowed to go free. Buel never distanced himself from the affair and always assumed responsibility, but Walker was deeply affected, leaving him depressed and seeking solitude for the rest of his life.[490]

As THE NATION ENTERED into a war footing in 1812 and Burlington became a military post, attended by the arrival of some two thousand troops, nearly doubling its population, locals continued on in their efforts to defeat the non-importation and non-intercourse prohibitions with their smuggling. To address the problem, the military set up posts in Montpelier (described as "the damdest [sic] Federalist hole that I ever saw") and Swanton, even as local Federalists opposing the war sought to obstruct its recruiting efforts. In Burlington, residents quickly rallied by forming into militia companies (one captained by Guy Catlin), a company of volunteers to act as minutemen and a company of exempts, excused from military service during peaceful periods. Nathan Haswell was elected the latter's orderly sergeant and allowed federal troops the use of his business as a place to store military equipment. Attention was also paid to the ongoing problems that the illegal sale of spirits presented with the indictment of at least three local tavern keepers (and another eight the following February).[491] Later in the year, residents in St. Albans and Georgia sought to provide additional service, and on October

23, 1812, some forty local men petitioned the legislature for permission to form themselves into an independent company of light infantry, called the Franklin Blues, attaching themselves to the First Regiment of the Third Brigade of militia.[492]

In the meantime, the smugglers' actions had become so alarming to Richford's selectmen, situated immediately adjacent to the border, that on July 1 they penned an urgent request to Governor Galusha requesting that he station fifty soldiers in the town to both deal with the threat posed by the nearby British to the north and stop "the smuggling business so much carried through this place." Overt, aggressive rescues continued against revenue outposts as smugglers brazenly overwhelmed government agents working alone, which resulted in yet additional mayhem.

Just months earlier, on March 21, 1812, Lyman Painter, of Vergennes, and three other men had struck to the south, in Hubbardton, forcibly removing a quantity of shawls, muslin, scarves, gingham and other fabric out of a sleigh under the control of customs inspector Andrew McFarland. Three days later, a mêlée broke out in Milton when Jacob Davis, of that town, accompanied by unidentified others, interfered with Inspector Sardias Blodget as he sought to examine their "carriage without wheels" on suspicion that it carried a large quantity of illegal goods. The event ended as six men restrained Blodget, while Davis and his friends escaped with the goods over the snow.

On March 30, Blodget found himself a victim once again when Timothy Ashley, John Cook, Luther Darling and Archibald Ashley, assisted by Harry Shepherd of St. John, Lower Canada, forcibly removed an entire ton of nail rods he had just seized from James Allen upon his arrival in town from St. Armonds. In an interesting notation attached to these particular proceedings, on two occasions, Van Ness acknowledged the receipt of fees for preparing paperwork, thirteen dollars coming directly from the court clerk and six dollars from his successor, Titus Hutchinson. Clearly, much as William Harrington did in his business transactions, Van Ness carefully noted all monies the government might collect on cases he had anything to do with, even after he had left office, and unfailingly laid claim to sums he believed he was entitled to. The only problem with his relentless pursuit of money was that he was not always able to discern what was his and what might rightfully belong to others.[493]

Also taking place on March 30, yet another confrontation occurred when Jacob Crosset, David Sheldon and Reuben Hawks Jr. all interfered with Seeley Bennett, working on this particular day as a customs inspector, relieving him of one thousand pounds of iron wire. A few short days later, violence broke out to the south in Weathersfield when ten local men headed by Joseph Cutting "did assault, beat and wound" Inspector James Ranney and made off with fifty pounds of iron wire taken from an earlier four-hundred-pound seizure. But even when they were successful in their efforts, officers fell victim to the actions of those to whom they entrusted storing seized goods. Buel found out himself in one of several such instances when he sent two hogsheads and four barrels of whiskey, valued at $500, into the custody of Burlington's Job Bigelow, only to have him "casually" lose them, resulting in an inevitable lawsuit brought by Buel seeking restitution.[494]

One of the saddest, most blatant confrontations occurred later in the year, on September 8, 1812, once again in Hubbardton. Walter Rumsey was another of Buel's deputy collectors charged with monitoring the flow of goods on the nearby turnpike, a road barred by a gate raised and lowered as necessary by its gatekeeper, Joel Luce. At 1:00 a.m., a large contingent of eight to ten horsemen, all armed with swords, pistols and clubs and guiding seven wagons loaded with goods, emerged from the dark "in battle array." Several were later charged, including Lyman Hawley and John Hutchins of Middlebury; William Gleason, described as "a transient"; Joseph Almy of Addison; and Elisha Sears of Williston, revealing that this was a band of northerners traveling through the area with no discernible reason to be where they were at that time of night other than to violate the law.

Rumsey was alerted to their presence and quickly responded to the gate, advising the men of his authority and that he intended to search the wagons. Just as he stepped onto the first one, two of the "banditti" came out of the dark and struck him with clubs, knocking him to the ground. Several others then rode up and threatened to "blow out his brains" if he did not allow them to pass. Rumsey managed to regain his balance and ran to the gate, where he found it opened and a couple of wagons gone through even as Luce demanded that they pay the toll. Rumsey quickly closed it and told Luce he needed assistance, unaware that Luce was himself injured. More men descended, and blows rained down on them from clubs, including "an instrument commonly called a 'loaded whip,'" made particularly lethal by the pieces of lead concealed within. More threats were made against the beaten officials as the smugglers made good their escape, but not before two of them rode back to the scene concerned they had not killed Luce and threatening further to go into the house where he had been taken to "give him a little lead." They need not have worried, for the vicious wound Luce received just above his right ear, three inches long and one inch deep, had done its job, resulting in his death days later, on September 14.[495] The dispositions of cases brought against these particular defendants is not clear, but one of them, Elisha Sears, quickly went on to present additional challenges to the government on a number of levels.

Before that happened, with a state of war now declared, on October 5, orders were issued to soldiers serving in the Champlain District, alerting them to be ready to assist the civil authorities "in detecting every species of smuggling & in preventing the transportation into [Canada] the munitions of war & provisions." A new kind of smuggling was on the rise, and it involved the movement of provisions—specifically, cattle, horses and tobacco—now being boldly supplied directly into the hands of an appreciative enemy by nearby residents, even in the face of an increased military presence. A week following the order, on October 12, Asa Shaw, of Lyndon, was intercepted as he sought to herd ten beef cattle to the north, apparently escaping arrest on that occasion, but he repeated the effort two days later with another forty head.

Van Ness was immediately notified of the situation, and on the twenty-sixth, he filed papers against Shaw alleging his violations. Four days later, in a display of suspect loyalty, Derby constable James Owen not only arrested Shaw but also posted the necessary $1,000 bond to allow for his freedom. Further demonstrating exactly how the average citizen viewed the government's efforts to prosecute Shaw, the following May, a Windsor grand jury convened to consider whether formal charges should be brought; instead, it returned to Van Ness the dreaded "No bill" for his proposed indictment. Compounding his embarrassment, the grand jury wrote "Ignoramus" across it.[496]

This was not the last time government officials encountered Constable Owen, who, when he was not trying to help out a friend, boldly engaged in his own smuggling ventures. On December 5, the troops were further admonished to "be vigilant & watchful & on no account suffer any person to pass the Lines" without written permission. Accordingly, when Owen, already suspected of working to make their lives difficult, showed up in Major Jenkens Storrs's camp in Derby on February 1, 1813, lingering there between 4:00 and 6:00 p.m. and displaying no real purpose for doing so, he was immediately suspected of acting as a spy sent in to note their activities. Storrs had recently received word that cattle destined for a nighttime venture across the border were concealed in a nearby barn and was preparing to mount a raid to seize them when Owen appeared, causing him to delay for fear he would immediately alert his fellow smugglers. Frustrated, Storrs "did put [Owen] under guard & did so detain him until the rising of the sun the next morning," whereupon he was allowed to go free. Not dissuaded, Owen later filed suit in the local court against the officer, alleging trespass and that the troops "beat, bruised, & ill-treated" him during a five-day period of custody. In what should probably not be a surprise in this convoluted time, Owen eventually won a judgment of $9.00, together with costs of $13.99, against Storrs.[497]

Even high-ranking officers within this Army of the North ran afoul of the law and came under suspicion, as when a Colonel Williams and his adjutant, stationed in Swanton, found themselves court-martialed for smuggling. Witnessing these unpatriotic and obstructionist actions on the part of both citizens and his soldiers, on February 11, 1813, a thoroughly frustrated Colonel Zebulon Pike, commanding the Fifteenth Infantry, issued a dire notice to the public that nothing short of death awaited those caught aiding the enemy. However, Elisha Sears, now back in Williston after participating in the Luce murder in September, was apprehended by Pike's soldiers around this time and charged with trading with the British in Lower Canada; resisting, beating and bruising a military officer; and attempting to escape.[498] Not taking any chances with the man, soldiers closely confined him in a dark and dirty guardhouse, weighed down by some sixty pounds of iron attached to his body. Unfortunately, Pike's wishes to extract the maximum punishment for his conduct quickly met an unanticipated legal roadblock, resulting in all charges being dropped.

Pike had sought to charge Sears, a civilian, in a military court with offenses "according to the articles and usages of war" as he understood they applied. However, it was contrary to any interpretation that those in Washington recognized, and they were refusing to allow civilians to be charged even with spying. Madison pursued a hands-off approach when it came to them, and while some in Congress sought to introduce bills allowing for civilians to be tried by military courts, its efforts were unsuccessful.[499]

On March 15, 1813, Sears appeared before District Court judge Paine on a writ of habeas corpus seeking his release because he was a citizen, did not belong to the army and could not be charged with offenses in a military venue. Because nobody from the prosecution sought to introduce any evidence to support the charges, Paine had no reason to rule otherwise and allowed Sears to go free. But before doing so, he noted that the military offenses lodged against civilian Sears were simply inapplicable, wondering why they were brought in the first place. As one court observer reported, Paine believed dismissal of the case was most appropriate because to have ruled differently "would be a monstrous innovation upon principles of civil liberty, always held dear in this country." For his decision, Paine was hailed as protector of the people, for, as one writer opined, "What would have been the fate of poor Sears had our District Judge been a tool of the Administration instead of an upright and independent minister of justice."[500] One can only wonder if anyone was aware of his recent involvement in the vicious murder of Joel Luce.

Pike had other concerns at the moment when, only weeks later, he was killed during an attack in Toronto. Even then, he inadvertently became involved in the widespread ardent spirit problem plaguing the army; after his body had been put into a cask of rum for shipment back to Sackets Harbor and then removed for burial, covetous soldiers drank the contents.[501]

The embargo and arriving war also had other substantial effects in Vermont as a never before seen increase in the number of federal employees took up their various duties around the state. For a national government starved of money in order to take on the most powerful nation in the world, their money-grabbing responsibilities were widely viewed unfavorably, considered to be nothing more than a tax-collecting, penalty-imposing evil out to extract the maximum amount possible. A collector of revenue, a collector of internal taxes, an assessor of taxes, a U.S. marshal and a U.S. printer, together with their many deputies, spread out to assess and gather up various taxes imposed on saddlers, shoemakers, tavern keepers, hatters and distillers and on owners of watches, furniture, pleasure carriages, coaches, chaises and wagons. Their salaries skyrocketed; for the U.S. attorney alone, the pay went from $400 in 1801 to $4,000 in 1815, while the collectors continued to receive percentages of steadily increasing revenue in addition to their salaries. It is no wonder that many of these newly employed federal employees remained possessive of their lucrative positions. As one writer observed, there was no reason why they, estimated at no fewer than six hundred people, should ever want to see the recent travails end because "war has produced the state of things by which they have their wealth."[502]

As the state's enforcement capabilities began their increase, there were occasions when imaginative criminals actually posed as customs officers going about and relieving law-abiding individuals of their property. That is what happened to "young Emmons," from Middlebury, who was, interestingly, reported "in the service of the U. States as custom house officer, but not legally." As a result of his subterfuge, Emmons found himself occupying the local lockup, facing charges of highway robbery.[503] But even the legitimate government officers, becoming ever more ubiquitous, found themselves under continual scrutiny because of their zealous attempts to enforce the law, made all the more alarming by expansive authority granted to them.

Lamenting that such a condition could exist in Vermont so soon after 1776, one writer severely chastised the officers, calling them "a swarm of bloodsuckers" who exercised "a despotism most vexatious and deplorable, most frightful and alarming," rejecting any argument that these "high-way-men" should be allowed to do so because they were "minions of government." Taking further issue with their going so far as to extract twenty cents for each trunk they might detain and/or search, he reasonably asked, "Where is the law, which authorizes the Custom House Officers, to go on board the Steamboat, to search every chest, rummage every trunk, and even scrutinize the pockets and indispensibles of the ladies who happen to be passengers, and then to compel them to PAY for the trouble of this *friendly visit?*" And when someone was so bold as to question an officer's authority, he

> replies that "it is presumed the law contemplates it" or evades the question by saying, "you may do as you please about paying it," but by some look or intimation, giving the traveler to understand that he had better pay than risk the consequences of refusal. The consequence is, all pay and are glad to get out of the clutches of a Custom House Harpy, even so well.[504]

The writer ended by noting that the noxious officers' actions extended even beyond the lake to the highways where they were "still more vexatious, forcibly stopping STAGES, carriages, horses, &c...where no suspicion could possibly attach." Even the military was not left alone by the intrusive civilian inspectors, and when naval officers experienced nosey customs personnel inquiring into their work in 1814, Champlain collector Sailly reported he had personally been struck over the head with a musket by a soldier who, "with all the energetic swearing of a sailor," then "damned revenue boats and revenue men and wished the smugglers would destroy them all."[505]

With their increased authority, working unsupervised in this freewheeling time, came a sudden and unsettling prospect: the unspoken, though silently acknowledged, suspension of certain aspects of the rule of law—particularly those affecting civil rights as authorities attempted to deal with civilians engaged in seditious acts, accompanied by questions concerning the exercise of state versus federal authority over the militia. Overwhelmed on so many levels, customs officers, and soldiers aiding them, struck out, taking liberties they would not have considered doing in another time, portending the presence of a looming and unaccountable rising police state. These years were threatening, frightening and demanded creative solutions. However, the methods they employed were deeply felt and resented by Vermont citizens.

Despite the matter involving Elisha Sears and Judge Paine's condemnation of the use of military law to charge civilians taking place in 1813, in 1814, there is evidence that things had changed very little. Now, a leading newspaper editor began to question the commitment of the state's courts to protect its citizens, inferring the existence of party influence among members of the judiciary, elected yearly by their political peers. Decrying their inaction in countenancing the infringements by authorities, he noted its clear presence, "which has so notoriously distinguished the administration of justice in this state for several years."

Endorsing those sentiments, another editor similarly condemned the current condition, in which, in the government's "rage to enforce *restrictive measures* and to prosecute the war…many of the most vital principles on which depend the safety and the rights and liberties of our citizens have been sacrificed and lost." Specifically, he revealed the surprising new world Vermonters faced:

> *It is well known, that in violation of the plainest articles of the constitution, the property of the citizens has been wrested from them and their persons seized, confined and tried before military courts, by the minions and hirelings of the administration, without authority and without right; and all this is countenanced by "the powers that be." Such a course, if not resisted, will soon render us substantial slaves, in the habiliments of freemen.*[506]

Judge Paine's prior admonitions against the application of military law to civilians notwithstanding, Vermont's new world now consisted of secret military courts, unlawful seizures, confinements and trials instituted by those unaccountable to civil authority. And as outrageous as that was, there was more.

Seeking to address those concerns, that same year, former Federalist congressman and now Supreme Court chief judge Jonathan H. Hubbard took the unusual step of instructing an Addison County grand jury in its deliberations to always remember that civil and military officials were required to closely comport their actions within the dictates of the law. Incredibly, he noted that "nearly every homicide which has taken place in this state, for several years past" was done in what he termed "advancement of the law."

It did not matter whether it was the murders of those three men by the *Black Snake* crew as they sought to enforce the embargo's dictates or Sam Buel's pursuit of salt smuggler Harrington Brooks, virtually all deaths of a deliberative nature in these few years were the result of actions attending the enforcement of the law. But one must temper any judgment of untoward actions by officials by recalling the violent manner in which all of this mayhem was first introduced—through the vicious killings committed by the smugglers on the Onion River—which had to have had a significant psychological effect on enforcement practices thereafter. Nothing in the state's past, or future, came close to what was happening at that moment, and it was truly extraordinary.

Hubbard further instructed the grand jury to carefully consider whether a particular civilian or military enforcement effort was indeed within the letter of the law and to hold those who were not in compliance accountable for their actions. He then sheepishly ended by explaining that "it seemed necessary to make these remarks" so that officials "might conform themselves to the laws upon the subject, and thereby avail themselves of the protection which the law affords to its ministers of justice."[507] However, as unsettling as the general state of law enforcement might have been at the moment, as well as its inconsistent application to the population at large, it merely reflected the larger role that politics driven by money played, none so blatant as what was about to happen between Cornelius Van Ness and Sam Buel.

IT WAS DURING THIS time that the "illegal combination" Buel complained to Madison about began in earnest, leading to his ouster as collector months later by Van Ness. While Buel's allegations against his successor, in isolation, may appear self-serving, Van Ness had placed himself in highly suspect transactions during his tenure as U.S. attorney and then while serving as collector. Over the course of his career, Van Ness was subject to periodic inquiries concerning these years, efforts he ascribed to his political enemies. He consistently claimed that he had never done anything wrong, though he did admit, as had Buel, that much "out of the common course" had taken place. In an 1818 affidavit, he sought to distance himself from any irregularities taking place in 1813 involving a James Lloyd, whom Van Ness characterized as "a notorious and professed smuggler." Yet, with full knowledge of the nefarious nature of his character, Van Ness admitted that he entered into an agreement to purchase fabric from Lloyd with the understanding he would pay him at a later time.

Adding to the questionable transactions were accusations Lloyd himself lodged with Congress alleging that he had a secret agreement with Van Ness involving payoffs, in this case a 6.25 percent payment made to the latter if he allowed Lloyd to import goods on paying duties alone, without going through the more expensive bonding process.[508] Even if his protestations of innocence are to be believed, the fact that Van Ness agreed to enter into any kind of transaction whatsoever with a known smuggler gives some indication of the careless and reckless way he conducted himself in these years. Neither were these the only accusations; Buel made known to Washington his own suspicions during the summer of 1812, when he had experienced uncooperative behavior from Van Ness, who refused to pursue cases forwarded to him that Buel strongly believed warranted prosecution. Dismissing his claims, he was simply told "to conform to the opinion of the District Attorney."

Nonetheless, Van Ness's star remained in ascent throughout 1812, as he was chosen once again to provide the July Fourth oration to the county's assembled Republicans in Williston, taking place between a reading of the Declaration of Independence and music provided by a band, followed by no fewer than eighteen separate toasts. On August 12, he was named by the U.S. marshal as Burlington's point of contact for all British subjects residing in the area to report to and register their presence pursuant to a State Department directive, issued under the Alien Enemies Act of 1798, while he also represented the Town of Essex following its indictment for failing to maintain local roads.[509]

Buel became aware of the efforts being mounted against him at the time and later explained to Madison that his detractors consisted of a "triumvirate" of individuals. They were made up of fur merchant John Jacob Astor (he was called a "rat catcher," an admonition leveled by a Canadian judge for his exploitive trading practices), merchant and ammunition supplier to the *Black Snake* murderers Guy Catlin (referred to as "Cataline," the man associated with the first-century Catilinarian conspiracy to overthrow the Roman Republic) and Van Ness (called many things), who entered into an arrangement resulting in his removal from office. However, what Buel could not have realized at that moment as he fell victim to these men's designs was that they represented but a piece of a critical, complicated set of relationships touching on the nation's very ability to conduct war, attended by its overriding concern to right its important international credibility, so badly damaged by Jefferson's embargo.

Astor, a native of Waldorf, Germany, was not a man to be trifled with, and his influence was formidable and wide-ranging. When Madison declared war against Britain in June 1812, Astor owned a substantial amount of Canadian land, which was quickly becoming enemy territory. He immediately sold off what he could and received a substantial number of furs as payment.

However, events were moving fast, and it was critical that he get them out of Canada and into the United States before becoming embroiled in complicated customs proceedings and possibly losing his investment. The furs were taken to Montreal, and one shipment of twenty-six bales was moved immediately southward into the safekeeping of Champlain collector Peter Sailly. Realizing that he had to comport with revenue regulations, Astor set off for Washington and spoke with his good friend Gallatin about his predicament. He received a letter from Gallatin soliciting Sailly's assistance in getting Astor's furs into the country. Sailly agreed to help, and in November, and again in February and November 1813, additional shipments of Astor's goods arrived, including "20,380 marten pelts, 46 bear, 18,000 muskrat, 526 fisher, 6021 otter, 3389 mink, 2048 fox, 271 cat, and 6 wolf." For his efforts, Astor paid Sailly $500 in lieu of any fees he could have earned had the goods gone through the routine bonding procedures.[510] The emergency that Astor found himself in apparently justified his manner of compensating Sailly, and it was never thought improper; albeit, Gallatin maintained a skeptical eye toward Astor, refusing an offer to purchase a 20 percent interest in his business in 1815. Meanwhile, things took a different course on the other side of the lake.

Catlin, who had dissolved his business relationship with Joseph Jasper the preceding December while in the midst of continued litigation seeking money owed to them, was part of Astor's network and shared the same concerns over what the war would do to his trade across the border. Other problems also vexed Catlin as he and his brother Moses at the same time defended themselves in a devastating lawsuit brought in the U.S. District Court in Vermont by two New York City men seeking $3,000 for business-related activities. Moses had been arrested for the debt on November 25, 1812; jailed in Burlington; and released on a bond signed by Guy. However, on February 25, 1813, Moses fled but was captured three days later more than one hundred miles to the south, in Bennington, apparently intending to get beyond the court's jurisdiction. He was brought back to Burlington.[511] In need of cash, Guy Catlin ventured into additional shady activities.

The bonding of goods for those businessmen such as Catlin and Astor coming across the border was burdensome and required an importer to contact a customs official and post a sum equivalent to the goods' value, which allowed him to keep them in his possession and continue on his way. The merchant then had to apply to the secretary of the treasury and request a return, or "remission," of the bond amount, a result that could not always be depended on. To obtain some assurance that he would not lose his bonds in the end should the government deem his goods contraband, unsure of what might happen in Vermont, Catlin approached Buel, apparently under the assumption that he would agree to allow the importations to take place as his father-in-law had done with Astor. As Buel understood it, Catlin believed it would be "better to make you an offer, that if you would bond all the goods he might bring from Canada, and use your influence, that the bonds should not be condemned, to give you twelve and an half percent," or one-eighth the value. Catlin tried to tempt Buel with an estimate of personal profit of the huge sum of "at least, twenty five thousand dollars," but the honorable Buel deemed the plan improper and quickly refused to go along with the scheme. In describing what had taken place to Madison, Buel explained that with the untoward effort to circumvent revenue laws now exposed and his firm rejection in participating, a coup de main was launched against him personally.[512]

As the plan was later explained to Buel by Giles Chittenden, son of Governor Thomas Chittenden, Catlin confided in him that, following Buel's refusal to assist in the ruse, he had approached Burlington attorney Stephen Mix Mitchell to act as an intermediary with U.S. attorney Van Ness to inquire of his interest in participating in the scheme if he could be assured of being appointed in Buel's place. Van Ness agreed, and Catlin made known to Astor that there was a way around the obstructing Buel, resulting in Astor, accompanied by other merchants, going to Washington to make the change a reality. Most importantly, all of this took place at precisely the moment the United States government was on the verge of bankruptcy following its ill-considered decision to declare war on the strongest power in the world without a plan, a military or money. The nation was facing dire circumstances at the end of 1812, and Gallatin had only marginal success convincing Congress that it needed to provide additional funding, forcing him to look elsewhere. Fortunately, Astor and two other Europeans financiers, David Parish, from Hamburg, Germany, and Frenchman Stephen Girard, all agreed to underwrite some $9,000,000 in loans to the government, thereby warding off the embarrassment attending a default because of the "ineptitude" of American policymakers.[513] With so much dependent on Astor's willingness to stand by the country, it is not surprising that Gallatin agreed to Buel's removal—certainly a small price to pay in returning a favor to so important a friend, and one who conveniently allowed Van Ness to pocket an estimated $60,000 as a consequence.

After Buel made his explosive allegations revealing the triumvirate's schemes to the public in 1819 with the publication of *The Book*, Catlin, writing from Quebec, quickly and disingenuously denied any such participation. For Van Ness, the allegations struck deeply, and he called Buel's effort a "contemptible and ridiculous thing," "a vile production" and "an unexampled mass of scurrility against me," while also characterizing Chittenden as "a vagabond" who had commiserated with Buel over a bottle of rum and dismissing Judge Sailly's allegations out of hand.

But Van Ness saved his most damaging assessment for Buel himself and referred to his killing salt smuggler Harrington Brooks, disingenuously stating that his life was (emphasis in original) "cruelly and unnecessarily taken, whichever way the <u>letter</u> of the law affecting the case might be determined to be," calling it "beyond the pale of any restrictions imposed by the laws of God or man." In attacking Buel's defense that the death took place as he acted under the strict dictates of the law requiring that no shots be fired unless he displayed the revenue service's ensign and pendant, while he himself made it a continuous practice to split legal hairs in virtually all manner, Van Ness displays his adroit, nimble, albeit sanctimonious, ability to go on the offensive when the situation required it. When he wrote to Heman Allen in 1818 to address lingering questions about his own conduct as collector, Van Ness continued in his protests that no laws had been broken during this time, emphasizing that (emphasis in original) "every person must remember the course of this great question concerning the <u>merchants bonds</u>, and the feeling and interest which it excited throughout the country."[514] But this was just more legal hair-splitting on his part, as there was certainly more at stake than mere merchants' bonds when one considers the man's voracious appetite for accumulating wealth.

AS THE NATION STRUGGLED with its finances, the fall of 1812 saw continued petitions from murderers Samuel Mott and David Sheffield seeking release from their confinement and terms of hard labor at the state prison. Their early days in residence, dating from June 1809, required them to assist with remaining construction projects as the facility neared completion, leveling the ground in and outside the surrounding wall and making and assembling needed tools and furniture. The work was apparently not so onerous as to stop other prisoners being held in county jails from seeking to join them. In 1810, Lowel Pope, serving a sentence in the Woodstock gaol for counterfeiting, successfully obtained permission from the legislature "to be immediately made an inhabitant" of the prison.[515]

After the men began initially making nails out of the many tons of metal rod delivered to the facility, in 1811 monetary concerns necessitated a change to weaving and significant efforts ensued to procure the necessary equipment and expertise to instruct them. Thousands of pounds of yarn began arriving from Boston by cart and sleigh for processing at the more than twenty looms the men erected, all overseen by a "Mr. Fagan" of Dublin, Ireland, while the men also converted such things as 1,044 cow horns into other domestic items. They were able to weave so much cloth that there was no problem in fulfilling the prison's needs, and the balance was purchased by the Lippett Manufacturing Company of Providence, Rhode Island. Their efforts became so well known that some deemed the prison "one of the best weaving factories in the New England states," and by the 1820s, its goods were being sold as far away as South America.[516]

The new innovations presented by this state-of-the-art facility posed wholly new challenges for administrators. Only months after the first arrivals took up residency, they had questions for the legislature about "the legality of taking the life of a prisoner, in case of a determination on their part to make an escape by force." In 1811, they sought permission to install "a suitable bell…in order to give the alarm to the inhabitants in case of fire, of insurrection among the prisoners, of attempts to escape, or whenever foreign aid should become necessary." Keeper Jabish Hunter maintained six swords and six guns at his home for any eventuality, charging the state $2,296.74 in pay for himself and his several guards that particular year. Even so, by the time the facility had grown to eighty prisoners in 1815 (including a single woman and many occupants described as "old and feeble"), when stoves consumed well over two hundred cords of wood a year to ward off frost-covered walls and rations of tobacco were being provided, five managed to escape.

Prison administrators also rejected calls to turn the results of the men's production into a profit-making operation, arguing in 1811 that the "infant institution" was ill-suited to do so because it was "so far in the interior of the country…[and] made up of such a variety of characters, who have followed no regular occupations." Rather, the more appropriate benefit came from the hard labor required of the men, allowing them "time for serious reflection and to form resolutions for future reformation." And to instill those desires even deeper, they called for the services of a chaplin to speak on each Sabbath "to impress more strongly on their minds the importance of leading honest, sober and exemplary lives; and to warn them of the consequences which must inevitably attend a different line of conduct…[which] would have a great tendency to reclaim, reform, stimulate and encourage them to good conduct and peaceable behavior."[517]

Francis Ledgard was fortunate to gain his freedom in 1811 (receiving three dollars upon his discharge) shortly after providing his telling account of the hours before the murders. Mott also unsuccessfully sought his own release at the time, ingratiatingly thanking the people of Vermont for their kindnesses while asking for their mercy. A year later, he was able to obtain the endorsement of, predictably, Sam Mix and over sixty additional friends, while also, most surprisingly, that of Buel's deputy inspector and current adversary James W. Wood, for his release. Wood had joined with five others attesting that Mott was a "good natured, industrious, honest man" and deserved to be released—an effort that again met without success. Young David Sheffield's father, Charles, was apparently a well-thought-of man, advanced in years and greatly in need of his son's help for both him and his wife. While he was able to convince several local notables, including Daniel Farrand, Daniel Staniford, Samuel Hitchcock, John Pomeroy, Lyman King and Heman Allen, to endorse his petition for his son's release, it, too, met without success. Only months later, Samuel E. Godfrey, of Burlington, a man who was to leave an indelible, devastating mark on the prison, a mark that involved Mott, arrived to begin serving a three-year term following his January 15, 1813 conviction for stealing.[518]

As the prisoners worked at their looms, the challenges presented by the larger events of 1812 had posed so many problems for state officials on so many levels that the legislature decided it had to do something to aid in stopping the never-ending smuggling problem. On November 6, 1812, it took bold action, but the resulting, unintended consequences proved so devastating that it was repealed only a year later. This was "An Act, to Prevent Intercourse with the Enemies of This and the United States, on the Northern Frontier," which, among other provisions, sought to avoid the problems posed by federal law. Of particular concern was having to prove a smuggler's guilt by showing he had actually crossed over the line in order to demonstrate that a violation had occurred, clearly making a subsequent arrest impossible for a pursuing officer. Now, the new state law made it illegal for anyone acting in such a manner as "to create a reasonable suspicion" of their intention to do so. More importantly, authority to apprehend suspected violators and their goods extended to not just recognized enforcement officers but also members of the general population. As a reward for their efforts, they were permitted to obtain half of the value of any goods seized, with the remainder going to the state.[519]

Of the many cases quickly brought by industrious citizens seeking their own profit from their neighbors' illegal acts was the diligent overseer of troops along the border, Major Storrs. Only a month following the act's passage, on December 11, he intercepted Justice Smith and Orin Puswell, of Browington, as they tried to move eight kegs of tobacco, weighing eight hundred pounds and valued at $400, across the border, seizing and instituting forfeiture proceedings against the cargo, as well as the two horses, their harnesses and the sleigh they were pulling.[520]

However, these constituted only the more benign kinds of efforts to stem the illegal trade for, as well intentioned as the law may have been, a period of ill will, attended by acts of vigilantism, was just unleashed. It also contributed to the deaths of others, which no doubt constituted one of the reasons Judge Hubbard spoke up following the act's repeal when he condemned the many homicides taking place these years, those committed in the "advancement of the law."

Ramon Manzuco
of Cadiz

The winter of 1812–13 was particularly cruel to Vermonters, as many died of pneumonia, eventually killing 6,400 statewide. While Sam Buel and his bride escaped that tragedy and celebrated the arrival of their firstborn child, Julia, in November and then the arrival of the New Year, whatever good times he experienced were about to end. For U.S. attorney Van Ness, acting on his own behalf, the conflict between the United States and Canada presented a unique opportunity in December 1812 for him to obtain the dismissal of a case against his Canadian client Abraham Quackinboss. The matter extended back four years and concerned a disputed ninety-five-dollar promissory note between Quackinboss and another Canadian, Peter Richard, arguing over where the debt had been incurred—in Vermont or Lower Canada—and which jurisdiction should decide the matter. For the adroit Van Ness, who lost in the lower courts, the intervening declaration of war in June 1812 allowed him to creatively argue to the Vermont Supreme Court that because Richard, a Canadian subject owing allegiance to the British Crown, was complicit in providing "aid and comfort" to the enemy, his case should be dismissed. The court agreed.[521]

Two months later, Van Ness made his move on Buel, and on February 15, 1813, the long-suffering, steadfast, honest collector was summarily, without any explanation, dismissed from his position, replaced by the upstart he had once counseled in his work and believed his friend. The triumvirate's insinuations and baseless allegations finally succeeded when, two weeks earlier, on January 27, in the same quiet manner in which he had appointed him U.S. attorney three years earlier, Madison named Van Ness (who turned thirty-one the day before) to replace Buel, making him the youngest person to ever serve in the lucrative post during the nineteenth century. It was a coordinated effort that allowed for Woodstock attorney and moderate Republican Titus Hutchinson to then become the district's next attorney when the president named him on February 25. Now able to operate out in the open, Van Ness moved with extraordinary speed in assuming his new responsibilities while also implementing plans contemplated for some time.

Only three days after Buel's dismissal, on February 18, Van Ness appointed one of his accusers, loyal law clerk Archibald Hyde, as inspector of customs, who swore an oath that he would "diligently and faithfully" execute his duties and use his "best endeavors to prevent and detect frauds" in relation to the customs laws. Another of his first appointments included a second accuser, and opportunist, the devious Dr. James Wood, also named as an inspector. Van Ness then took the unusual step of allowing Wood, who ran a ferry between New York and Vermont, to reside not in the state where his duties existed but on his New York farm, together with two more deputies, as he pursued his personal, medical and mercantile interests. As Judge Sailly concluded in his assessment of this favorable treatment, Wood's suspicious arrangement was "considered pretty generally as a sinecure, and as a recompense for having lent his aid to overthrow Mr. Buel."[522] Clearly, a new way of conducting the government's business was not far off.

Bound in their mutual dislike of the troublesome Buel, Van Ness and Hyde then began to relentlessly pursue him. Now they sought evidence of suspected criminality beyond the unfortunate arrangements he had used to compensate his deputies, moving on to also lay claim to money he had earned during his tenure as collector. Their zealous efforts had a devastating effect on not only Buel but also, inadvertently, the entire revenue system itself as they exposed significant defects in the way customs officials were being compensated nationally. The fallout from their monumental contest eventually involved both state and federal courts, including the U.S. Supreme Court, the U.S. Congress, numerous high-level administration officials and Presidents Madison and Monroe, finally resulting in significant changes in the law in 1822. Most notably, of the 136 private suits brought in Vermont's federal circuit court for a ten-year period between 1815 and 1825, 133 were instituted by plaintiffs living outside the state, while the remaining ones originated from a single Vermonter as Sam Buel sought to correct wrongs inflicted on him by Van Ness and one of his former deputies, Roger Enos.[523]

However, just before Van Ness set off on his quest for Buel's assets, he entered into a suspiciously comfortable business relationship that had a great impact on trade taking place over the lake. Less than a month after his appointment, abandoning any hesitancy he might have had in associating with someone involved in the *Black Snake* murders, Van Ness entered into an agreement with Guy Catlin and several others to establish the Lake Champlain Steamboat Company, chartered by the State of New York on March 12, for the purpose of building and operating steamboats on the lake. Two years later, on November 10, 1815, Van Ness and his associates succeeded in obtaining an exclusive right from the Vermont legislature to navigate steamboats on the lake for an extraordinary period of twenty-three years. It was an amazing arrangement not found anywhere else, as the very man now charged with monitoring the flow of goods across an important international boundary in a time of war was a leading principal in the very mode of transportation making that possible. The potential for shenanigans was unlimited, and as Buel noted incredulously, when Congress also allowed these vessels exclusive commercial privileges, thereby affording Van Ness additional opportunity to act in a clearly conflicted role, it was no wonder that the next boat built was named *Congress*.[524]

The opening salvo in the contest between the two men began sometime in early April 1813, only days after Van Ness lost a March 31 statewide election to become one of the ten members of the Council of Censors, placing twenty-second in a field of twenty-seven with 11,774 votes. That political contest now behind him and the way cleared to pursue his personal interests, Van Ness wrote to comptroller of the treasury Richard Rush seeking his advice concerning the distribution of money he had recently received from the court clerk. While the sum was not disclosed, it came from the proceeds of a seizure and sale of property taking place while Buel was in office and constituted a moiety to be distributed according to law. For the sharp Van Ness, there was no question in his mind that he alone should assume ownership of the money, as there was no provision requiring him to distribute it to anyone not currently serving as collector.

Van Ness received a reply from Rush the following month, dated May 6, 1813, agreeing with his interpretation, but Rush wisely cautioned him, "It is easy, however, to conceive of cases, in which a strict adherence to this opinion, would work considerable individual hardship; but in all such, it is to be presumed, that the collector in office, would act with liberality suited to the occasion." Van Ness seems to have understood that suggestion to share with a predecessor, even if the law did not require it, for when he received

$500 from the court as part of an 1808 case taking place under the authority of retired collector Penniman, Van Ness gave him $100. Penniman later attested that while Van Ness had indeed provided him with some of the money, he "often said, previous to the payment…that he felt himself under no legal obligations to pay them, considering himself entitled to the same; but that he did it in consideration of the trouble and expense, which [I] had been at."[525]

However, cordial relations and sharing certainly did not extend to Sam Buel, and on May 10, Van Ness received a substantial $1,202.64 from the court clerk and immediately split it between himself and the government. The money was the result of condemnation proceedings that had begun the preceding fall when one of Buel's inspectors, Joshua Peckham, seized a quantity of furs and wine brought illegally into the country. With Buel now out of office, Van Ness had no qualms about taking possession of the money, but when confronted on August 5 by Buel, who had penned his first letter to Madison a month earlier laying out his suspicions of his successor, he appears to have promised to turn at least some portion of it over to him. When that did not happen, despite repeated requests and assurances that it was forthcoming, on August 30, Buel instituted suit against him, alleging that Van Ness was "contriving and fraudulently intending craftily & subtiley [*sic*] to defraud" him, and served him with a $1,500.00 writ of attachment. In a second case, Buel challenged the claim of one of his former inspectors, Roger Enos, to his purported right to a moiety of goods seized under Buel's authority in 1812.

The case against Van Ness continued on to the Vermont Supreme Court, where Buel took an appeal after receiving an adverse ruling in the county court. There, a trial was conducted before a jury, which returned a most unhelpful verdict, telling the court that if it determined the law meant one thing, then its verdict was for Buel, but if it meant another, then Van Ness should prevail. On that, the court ruled in Van Ness's favor, but that decision was later overturned by the U.S. Supreme Court after the case made its tortuous way through the system, finally ending in Buel's favor in 1823. Buel instituted additional suits in the intervening years, seeking the return of other moieties belonging to him—staggering sums of $10,000, $20,000 and $30,000, which were apparently reduced to but a portion when Van Ness, who had gone on to higher political office, was ordered to pay those significantly lesser sums.

Buel might have won those wars, but Van Ness was not done with him by any means. With regard to the Enos claim, while the Vermont Supreme

Court noted in its 1820 decision that it involved two federal officials arguing over federal law and was "one most peculiarly proper" for decision by the federal courts, and after questioning its own authority to do so, it ruled in Buel's favor. However, it also strangely confessed that it had done so "without taking that time for consideration, which the difficulty of the subject requires."[526] Clearly, challenges presented by smugglers aside, there were substantial questions throughout these years regarding the precise interpretations of the law as it applied to those charged with its enforcement, and it was into this void that Van Ness unabashedly plunged.

CONDITIONS REMAINED DIFFICULT WITHIN Burlington as the local population sought to accommodate the many soldiers' demands. Nathan Haswell, when not otherwise confined for debt, was readily employed by the U.S. Army to assist with the staggering amount of provisions flowing into town, stored in "every vacant store, cellar and shed" available, including his. While Van Ness later described the quartermaster's operations during the summer of 1813 as "entirely deranged and completely without credit," Haswell did what he could to alleviate any problems. One effort involved his conducting an inventory of goods, described as a "herculean task," revealing the scope of the challenge he faced in storing and distributing 10,000 barrels of beef and pork, 3,500 barrels of flour and rye and 4,230 gallons of whiskey. At one point, a shortage of barrels needed to store salted beef resulted in his building a large vat in his cellar capable of holding 300 barrels of meat that was filled by dropping freshly slaughtered flesh down through a trapdoor cut into the first floor.

Sometimes, distributions of provisions to the soldiers did not always go as planned. On one occasion, when horseflesh was reportedly provided instead of the requisite beef, it prompted Haswell to indignantly respond to an equally indignant commander's accusations that if it was indeed horse, the fault lay "at some other's door." On another occasion, when liquor stores became depleted, two thousand gallons of a bad version of potato whiskey arrived from Barre, resulting in at least one outlandish display of conduct. As Haswell explained it, he walked out of his store one day to see an inebriated Irish soldier digging a hole in the ground and pouring whiskey into it, exclaiming, "By Jasus [*sic*], cover it up, or she will be sprouting in a minute." Taking pity on the man, Haswell gave him some "superior tobacco" to stem his loss.[527]

Smuggling problems persisted in the countryside unabated, despite the work that Van Ness and his cadre of inspectors, spread around the state, were doing. In August, fifteen zealous agents descended on Charles Hatch's store in Williston to inspect his goods after they experienced "a few jokes put on them" by smugglers, suspecting Hatch as being one. He was able to produce invoices proving that his merchandise came from the south, and they abruptly departed. However, unbowed by the invasion, Hatch related that if it happened again, "I may, next time pursue a different course to satisfy their curiosity, which possibly might not please them."[528] What Hatch had in mind is not revealed, but it is clear that resorting to violence remained a viable option.

Watching their neighbors shepherd goods northward was just too tempting a target for those otherwise law-abiding Vermonters, and with the legislature's recent approval of their stopping those activities through the non-intercourse act, their ensuing interventions ranged from the benign to the deadly. On March 17, no fewer than three hundred pounds of cheese, valued at $160, were seized and charges instituted against two men, and their goods, by unnamed claimants who alleged they intended to convey it to Canada. Only days later (and a month following his detention by Major Storrs as a spy), Derby's intrepid constable, James Owen, was intercepted by troops, acting on information provided to them by civilian Ralph Parker, who removed eight kegs of tobacco (weighing eight hundred pounds) from him as he attempted to take it over the lines. Owen continued to disobey the law and was indicted in August for transporting two oxen northward. However, all of this conduct paled in comparison to the grand intentions of renowned smuggler Chauncey Brownson, from Winchester, Connecticut.

Brownson did not deal in trivial amounts of contraband. He was well experienced in getting goods across the lines via routes in northern New York and on Vermont's west side, meeting with great success. It may have been because of the increased military presence in the northwest that he was now forced to consider routes up the east side of the state. He hauled a staggering twenty thousand pounds of tobacco up the Connecticut River and stored it at Wells River. Leaving his goods in storage, Brownson traveled farther to the north, making inquiries about new routes to cross the line, and learned that, while teams hauling sleighs would meet with difficulty, it was possible to do so using horses.

Word of the impending arrival of a large amount of tobacco into the area aroused the interest of locals, and associates (including a Captain Samuel Smith acting on behalf of his smuggling brother Justus) went out into the countryside soliciting interested purchasers and receiving advance payments in the form of either money or furs. Plans began to go awry on March 29, when James Parker took it upon himself to suddenly appear and successfully removed six kegs (weighing 629 pounds, numbered 142, 100, 73, 100, 95 and 99 and bearing a telling and incriminating "B" burned into their sides) disguised as flour from Brownson's possession. Undeterred, on April 5, Brownson immediately arranged for teamsters to bring an additional 2,100 pounds forward and apparently succeeded in getting it across the lines. When Brownson later contested Parker's claims to his share of the goods he had seized, while also bringing his own suits against two government agents involved and protesting any contention that he intended to cross into Canada, he argued that he should be pitied because he was not from the area and, essentially, adrift in this "land of strangers." A jury determined otherwise, and the goods were duly condemned in Parker's favor.[529]

Horses were also in demand by the British in Canada, and Vermonters did what they could to satisfy that need. On June 1, Samuel Eaton, of Westmore, drove twenty of them north and then repeated the effort the following day.[530] For those not inclined to blatantly break the law, getting the military to assist them remained an option. Samuel Burnham, described in court documents as "a notorious smugler [sic]," and brother Charles, residing in Canada, arranged to have a Captain Thomas Matteson and Constable Owen take possession of horses on the Vermont side of the border and then convey them over the line, where they would then turn them back over to Charles. Learning of the impending violations, over the course of several days in June, citizen Ira Williams, of Derby, intruded in their efforts and succeeded in removing some seventeen of the animals out of the smugglers', and soldiers', possession and instituted court proceedings seeking his share of the profits from their subsequent condemnation and sale.[531]

For those seeking to excuse their criminal conduct, their explanations took on a most simplistic tone. After soldiers seized one hundred pounds of tobacco from the Canaan home of John Weeks on July 5, 1813 (he had already stored over six hundred pounds there the preceding month), the evidence from his prosecution revealed he did not believe himself responsible, "for it was not his property." Whether he used the same explanation in his suit against Christopher Bailey and Hail Whiting when they entered his house the preceding day and confiscated an initial four kegs concealed in "a secret place" in his chimney, while also allegedly beating him for four hours, is not disclosed. For these backwoodsmen, simply acting as a conduit for the crimes of others was not, in their minds, at least, a punishable offense; thus, it provided them with a ready way of rationalizing to themselves their own culpability. But when Inspector John Beckwith (who later met with a devastating injury as part of his duties) detected Benjamin Robinson, of Brownington, driving a yoke of oxen into Canada on August 20, Robinson's futile attempts to explain his conduct by giving conflicting testimony on a couple occasions sealed his fate. Though noted "a worthy character destitute of property excepting a small piece of land for which he yet owed," and telling authorities he simply needed the animals for his work, Robinson was convicted at trial and received a most harsh sentence, one out of all proportion to his crime: of a year of hard labor at the state prison in Windsor and to pay costs of prosecution, $53.28.[532]

Of all the commodities heading into the enemy's hands, none generated the high degree of emotion that cattle provided. Indeed, having ready access to Vermont's beef was of such importance to British military commanders that they restricted their immediate operations to the Lake Champlain vicinity in order to maintain close contact with their supply. The rough, narrow roads available to herd the animals northward provided some problems, but industrious Vermonters simply pushed them onward as the geography allowed, likened by one British soldier who watched in astonishment to "herds of buffaloes, they press through the forests, making paths for themselves."[533]

For Collector Van Ness, enforcement was a virtual impossibility, accurately assessing local civil authorities' capabilities as "wholly incompetent" to deal with the problem without the intervention of military assistance. In July 1814, he sought the assignment of a roving squadron of fifty to one hundred mounted soldiers to keep the smugglers off balance and to stop "this traitorous practice." He was understandably concerned, as only a month earlier the so-called Smugglers Riot had broken out in Georgia, also called Hells Gate, during which dozens of lawbreakers—including a local merchant, a physician and a grand juror—came together and went on a rampage searching out customs officers, calling them highway robbers, and severely injured several of them before fleeing.[534]

More recently, Van Ness explained that he had conducted a seizure of 117 head of cattle just four miles east of Burlington in their northward course, telling the local commander that

> *if they are stopped a distance of forty or fifty miles from the lines, it is extremely difficult to prove they are destined for Canada, particularly as they are almost altogether drove by persons living near the frontiers who own farms and who pretend they are driving them to stock their farms. If they are suffered to pass, those men take them home in the first place, and*

*the cattle slip off a few at a time, or else a large body of men is suddenly
collected together, all armed, and before it is possible to rally anything like
an equal force, a large drove of cattle is hurried across the lines.*[535]

The numbers of animals involved were indeed huge; only a week later, Van
Ness wrote again, explaining that he now retained "about 200 cattle and
the number will be 3 or 4 times as large within a few days." His problem
at that moment was the "serious danger of them being forcibly taken &
drove to Canada unless I have force enough to check them."[536] Though not
mentioned, certainly the potential for loss of life was also a factor.

On September 4, 1813, two customs officers, Samuel Peckham Jr. and
Augustus Wright, along with others, learned that a herd had recently been
driven into Canada and were determined to watch for anyone returning
south. At some point that evening, John Smith, of Fairfield, accompanied by
two friends, was observed and immediately confronted by the officers. The
facts surrounding the encounter are not known, and extant court papers
provide little information, but the meeting was not cordial, and Smith "was
shot and immediately expired." While Peckham and Wright were detained
and held for a court of inquiry, the disposition of their case is not noted.

Public condemnation of the smugglers' actions continued, lamenting the
seeming absence of aggressive punishment, notwithstanding the attention
that counterfeiters received. One paper noted in September 1813 that when
four smugglers were caught trying to pass a military flotilla on the lake, "none
of these wretches, or of those constantly employed in driving cattle, &c.
across the line, have yet been taken and hung."[537] Part of the problem with
enforcement concerned the added scrutiny now being applied to the officers
themselves and away from the lawbreakers. Within the military, Captain
John Hall, commanding one of the two gunboats patrolling the lake, was
removed from Burlington in July and taken to Plattsburgh, where he was
court-martialed and convicted for falsely imprisoning an American citizen.

When Hoxie trial judge U.S. Supreme Court justice Livingston was
sitting on his circuit duties in Rutland in October, he imposed heavy fines
on citizens involved in seizing contraband and bringing smugglers to justice.
It raised such concern that many now questioned whether the judiciary was
siding with those in "the smuggling interest" and "being partial to the class
of people concerned therein."[538] In light of the many inherent deficiencies
within the system and conflicting signals being sent to the public and those
charged with enforcement, it is not surprising that extra-legal methods were
employed out of the public's sight, such as those unauthorized military courts

run by the "minions and hirelings of the administration" and by citizens themselves in order to right the wrongs so clearly in evidence. And that is what appears to have happened at one particularly tragic moment.

All indications are that Samuel Beach, living on the border in Canaan, had done nothing wrong. He took the trouble to obtain a permit from the governor allowing him to go a short distance into Canada in order to repair a sawmill and had sent some workmen on ahead. On October 9, 1813, Beach and his brother, Heman, followed after them, driving what court documents vaguely refer to as cattle but which might have been nothing more than an ox team for use in their work. Unfortunately, the men ran into local residents John Dennet, Micajah Ingram and John Morrison, who, perhaps sensing an opportunity for quick profit by instituting legal claims against property, removed the animals out of their possession and took them to Ingram's home.

The Beaches followed, and when Samuel sought to retake them, Dennet threatened that if he did, "he would blow him through." Beach persisted, and Dennet, described as thirty-eight to forty years old, six feet tall, with sandy hair and light eyes, walked up to him carrying a loaded ten-dollar musket, placed it against Beach's left breast and brazenly blasted him with a single lead bullet and two buckshot. The rounds traveled entirely through his body, leaving a half-inch-wide path and exiting below his left shoulder blade, killing him instantly. Dennet was quickly arrested, appeared before the local court and was ordered held for trial before the Supreme Court the following September, while confined in the Guildhall jail, located some forty miles to the south.[539] Whether it was this incident in particular, the adverse rulings being rendered in the U.S. District Court against those engaged in self-help remedies or some other factor is not clear, but the following month, the Vermont legislature rescinded its one-year non-intercourse experiment.

On June 27, 1814, Dennet managed to escape, and deputy jailer Daniel Dana immediately posted a $100 reward notice for his return, describing him as wearing black woolen pantaloons, buttoned on the outside from top to bottom; a brown jacket without sleeves; and an "almost new" felt hat with a large brim. When Dennet's presence became known in the Canaan area after he unwisely returned to familiar grounds, local men Giaus Kibbe, Elihu Forrest, Richard Morgan and Ebenezer Sperry decided to take up the chase. Their effort may have been directed toward either the reward or simply avenging Beach's murder, as they expended great effort to track him down, finding him on July 21 some ten to twelve miles deep in the woods of Averill, alone and chopping on a fallen tree.

As the four men slowly approached, Dennet detected them and called out for them to stand off or he would shoot. Kibbe reportedly told him that it was Dennet who was to stop what he was doing or he would shoot him. The men appear to have gotten relatively close when Dennet decided continued flight was in his best interests, and as he turned, two shots rang out. Who fired the second is not disclosed, but court papers involving Kibbe reveal that he was carrying a five-dollar loaded pistol, with a single lead bullet, which he placed against Dennet's lower back "a little below and to the right of the lower hip… back bone or spine" and fired. While the bullet was able to travel almost all the way through his body, cutting a half-inch-wide path and stopping just behind his navel, Dennet's adrenalin propelled him forward, and a chase of one-half to three-quarters of a mile ensued farther into the woods.

Of the men in pursuit, Morgan was the fastest, covering ground, as Kibbe estimated, at a rate of three rods to Dennet's two. When overtaken, Dennet turned bearing his axe, and Morgan delivered at least two severe blows with a club to his head, knocking him to the ground. Dennet abandoned any thought of escaping further and submitted. But that is when his suffering began.

While Kibbe described it as nothing more than a flesh wound, Dennet was certainly in no condition to walk, but his captors uncaringly prodded him on to cover the many miles back to the road. When Dennet protested that he could not go on, he was simply told that they would "let him fall," abandoning him to his fate. The return to the men's wagon, pulled by a two-horse team, took some time, and it was not until the following day that the party finally arrived in Guildhall. It had not been a good experience for the "wounded, bruised & mangled" Dennet as his captors made it a point to maneuver the wagon in such a "manner as most to increase the pain of & render incurable & mortal" his wounds. Many residents witnessed their arrival that afternoon and saw the severely injured Dennet sitting on some straw in the wagon, looking, as Joseph Berry observed, "extremely pale" with "a wild deathlike stare in his countenance."

Someone called out to the arriving men, "Who shot Dennet?" and Kibbe replied it was he and that it was done in "God's service," telling the crowd, "By God, I meant to place the ball so as to stop him." Dennet was then manhandled, forcibly picked up by the shoulders and, "with great rapidity," dragged out of the wagon, up the steps to the jail and taken inside and then downstairs. Someone then called out that "he should never come out of the dungeon by God without he comes out dead or for trial." Dennet's sister, Olive Morrison, was allowed inside and observed the men "laughing, pointing their fingers at him and attempting to make fun of him." She said that they "appeared to be gratified and exult in the groans & distress of the said Dennett." Three days later, Dennet died while lying in the dungeon of injuries inflicted by a combination of the gunshot, clubbing and rough treatment received during the trip back to town, described by officials looking over his body as inflicted in a "cruel & barbarous" manner, leaving him in a "mangled" condition.

Unsurprisingly, despite all of the ensuing court proceedings, nobody involved in either of the two murders was ever convicted, as grand juries either refused to return indictments or trial juries rendered "not guilty" verdicts for what were clearly egregious violations of law. Notwithstanding, there was yet another obstacle to officials enforcing the law. This concerned the availability—and unabashed manner in which they were used by smugglers—of lawsuits brought directly against their enforcers. It was not a new phenomenon, as treasury secretary Gallatin noted years earlier in 1808 that these "vexatious suits…not only perplex faithful officers, but have the effect of intimidating others, and prevent an energetic performance of their duties." New York authorities were also experiencing the same thing, and the problem persisted on both sides of the lake.

Van Ness, now in the center of the fray, deemed the suits a constant threat, writing in 1814, "Whenever any number of cattle are seized, the officer seizing them is immediately sued, and in the present state of things suits of this nature are extremely dangerous." On that particular occasion, he had just taken a large number of cattle and resignedly wrote, "I expect to be sued tomorrow; what will be the result I cannot say." His concerns were certainly correct; in a recent separate event involving the seizure of goods traveling between Montreal and Boston, a staggering forty lawsuits were filed against his men alleging assault and battery. Practically, requiring so many officers to step aside from their duties and travel far distances to address frivolous suits not only significantly interfered with enforcement efforts but also presented opportunities for yet further confrontations when they met their accusers at courthouses. The problem became so bad in Vermont that in November 1814, treasury secretary Dallas sought legal reforms from Congress, citing "the terror" these officers felt at being exposed to suits sanctioned by Vermont courts bizarrely concluding that customs officers were not authorized to make seizures.[540]

In the fall of 1813, Inspector Richard Jennes, assigned to the Memphramagog district, was one of those men actively engaged in enforcement activities. He had already found himself a named defendant in an unsuccessful trespass suit brought against him by tobacco smuggler

Chauncey Brownson and was now further embroiled in a ridiculously lengthy case involving the seizure of a small quantity of fabric, which consumed an inordinate amount of court time to conduct trials and appeals. Working on behalf of the beleaguered agents were attorneys with whom Van Ness had already established relationships, including one in particular who was frequently called on and who also served with Van Ness as one of the U.S. marshal's point of contact for aliens to report living in the Montpelier area. Timothy Merrill, of Barre, was the recipient of several letters from Van Ness in these years in which he provided advice concerning cases involving customs officers in Washington County. Only two weeks after he had received his appointment earlier in 1813, Van Ness wrote to Merrill recommending a new attorney to his attention. Then, over the course of the next few years, Van Ness made a number of suggestions to him ranging from issues relating to arranging for bail for his arrested men to how to handle particular issues in the various courts.[541]

The letters further reveal a fully engaged legal mind, insightfully distinguishing various legal principles and how they might be applied in a particular case. Van Ness refused to accept any defeat in a trial court and directed Merrill to appeal adverse rulings, while also anticipating and forwarding on any evidence he might need in the proceedings. He repeatedly assured Merrill of payment for his services while also demonstrating a remarkable familiarity with how to extract the maximum amount of money from the government for each case: "If neither of them [referring to two inspectors] appears at Montpelier to give you the necessary evidence, you cannot get double costs...you must take up with single costs. You will of course tax separate time & travel fees for each defendant." As he explained in a knowing manner, "This is the practice in trespass in all the higher courts."

Problems within his own ranks are further revealed as Van Ness confessed to Merrill he could not tell whether these two particular inspectors, sued for seizing cattle, were acting in their official roles or otherwise, indicating the possibility that they were engaged in criminal activity. In fact, in June 1813, in his role as Burlington's postmaster, he was deeply involved in uncovering a significant smuggling operation utilizing the mail as a front while operating between there and Highgate to the north. Burlington constituted the northernmost mail facility in the country at the time, and in addition to acting as an important hub for communications in general, it also functioned as the Office of Interchanging Mails for those coming from and going to Canada.

Van Ness became aware that several suspicious men had been employed by Middlebury postmaster Asa Nevin to carry some of this mail, prompting him to convey his concerns to Postmaster General Gideon Granger in Washington. This led to a blazing response in which Granger ordered Nevin to immediately dismiss the men, calling them "a set of unprincipled smugglers who make use of the cover of the mail to keep up constant intercourse with the enemies of the United States." From that point on, Granger instructed, Nevin was only allowed to employ carriers approved by Governor Jonas Galusha, former representative and future governor Martin Chittenden and Van Ness, ending with a sharp warning that "of this you will not fail."[542] For his part in dealing with his inspectors engaged in questionable behavior, Van Ness told Merrill that, while he wanted him to assist them when possible, "in the assault and battery suits, I prefer to have the defendants find their own bail."

Even Van Ness's adversary, the previous collector, was discussed with Merrill on one occasion when he instructed him not to deal with a particular matter Buel was involved with because it was "not a seizure under me."[543] Tellingly, Van Ness distanced himself from any possible problems with Buel's cases, but he was not hesitant at all in pursuing monies derived from them.

SAM BUEL'S LUCK WAS particularly bad in 1813. He had been summarily dismissed from his distinguished position in February and replaced by a young arriviste seeking further acclaim, followed by his initiating a lawsuit for the return of money he had previously earned as he stood helplessly by and watched his personal property in the customhouse on Windmill Point be destroyed by invading British troops. He no doubt received some solace in seeing his once-trusted-deputy-turned-adversary Dr. Wood seized by British troops on July 30 and held as a hostage in Beaufort, Quebec, where he remained jailed for the next six months, in apparent retaliation for the arrest of a Canadian lawyer by American troops. Those events aside, Buel now witnessed the unfolding of a series of yet more questionable transactions involving his replacement, which came to cast dark shadows on the new collector's credibility for years to come.

By this time, the government had recognized that a blanket prohibition on the importation of goods was simply unenforceable and, incidentally, not particularly in its own interests. Too much was at stake for the economy and those of the merchant and business classes if it should be entirely shut down. So, in Vermont at least, some allowances were made through the bonding and remission processes to give a winking appearance of enforcement as the needed goods filtered through the border. Buel had already suffered the consequences of his refusal to be a part of any scams avoiding established procedures, but for his replacement, whose later protestations that the times presented such complex challenges that he was forced into actions that might appear suspicious but were lawful, they only clouded issues concerning his underlying ethical conduct. That Van Ness had an astute and nimble faculty in recognizing the fine details and loopholes contained within the existing revenue laws is without question. That he further recognized attending opportunities for profit at the same time is also in evidence. For Van Ness, as with many in the business community, if the law did not specifically exclude a particular course of action, then it was not his fault if he profited from its inherent inadequacies. In short, the morality of his actions represented but a distant concern in his persistent pursuit of money and station.

When Buel published *The Book* in 1819, a 158-page missive describing the circumstances of his fall from grace, all attributable to Van Ness, he related several instances of his successor's questionable conduct, a process he called the "Science of Vannessing." When a congressional committee investigated him in 1828, Van Ness protested that any insinuation remotely attacking his reputation, then or in the past, was baseless, telling one member, "I have suffered much persecution from the smugglers for my exertions [while serving as collector]. My life and my property have frequently been in jeopardy. I was placed in a situation peculiarly critical and difficult." However, accepting those protestations as true, the questions remain.

In the first instance, why one would abandon the prestigious position of U.S. attorney, so recently obtained, for that of collector appears to have been but for a single reason: to accumulate money. Not only Judge Sailly called the move into question, but so did the secretary of the treasury (Buel does not say which one, but it appears to be Gallatin), who "took occasion repeatedly to remark, that he could not imagine any honest motives" behind Van Ness's seeking the position. As Buel further explained, Van Ness's personal finances at the time were not good and revealed how he had misappropriated "a few thousands" of the public's money to cover debts (obligations Van Ness's own son said rendered him virtually destitute during these times) while he was U.S. attorney, using them in the interim as he sought the collector's position.

However, in his pursuit of gain, Buel observed that Van Ness erred by failing to first note that the law had anticipated the possibility of a collector's untoward enrichment and placed limitations on his "emoluments." In 1802, Congress passed a law making $5,000 the maximum he could accumulate, with anything in excess going directly to the government. But it was Van Ness's astute legal mind that came to his rescue, allowing him a solution, for, as Buel related, he simply "proffered the residue…to his subordinate officers, thereby offering a compromise to his conscience, inasmuch as what he took unlawfully from one party, he offered unlawfully to another."[544] Indeed, the close relationships Van Ness shared with his various associates were ripe for collusion on a number of levels.

One of the ways around the law's vagaries came in the manner of exploiting letters of marque and reprisal, permitted by the Constitution, allowing civilians to obtain governmental permission to search out and seize enemy shipping.[545] Buel explained that during the summer of 1813, captains fortunate enough to obtain them made "valuable captures" on the lake, which then "went through the formality of a legal adjudication; and as the government required no duty on prize goods, it was a profitable way of importing them, after paying liberally agents and collector." One historian refers to the presence of collusion between holders of such letters and officials reciting the protestations of Champlain collector Judge Sailly in December 1813 that prearranged "seizures" by authorities permitted importers to avoid paying expensive duties or post bonds.[546] Sailly's allegations ring true when one considers the suspicious circumstances of one incident in particular involving Van Ness and (putting aside any conflict of interest issues) his friend, fellow steamboat investor and the *Black Snake* murders' ammunition supplier Guy Catlin.

On September 23, 1813, Catlin became the second of three captains authorized that year to seize enemy shipping on Lake Champlain when Commission No. 830 was issued to him by collector of the Port of New York David Gelston. Now, he was permitted to "cruize [*sic*] on the Lakes, or interior waters of the Country," which allowed him to venture as far away as the Great Lakes via the St. Lawrence River. In his application for the commission, Catlin described himself as the sole owner of a vessel called the *Alert*, being "ten tons or under," originating in White Hall and carrying a crew of "seven men…armed with muskets." Accompanying him on the lake's waters were two other vessels, the sloop *President* (eighty tons, two guns and a twenty-man crew) and the *Lark* (three tons, with a six-man crew).[547]

On November 26, Catlin experienced an extraordinary bit of "luck" when he sailed into Canadian waters in Missisquoi Bay in search of prey. There, he came across an unnamed boat and, upon stopping it and opening its hold, discovered a most fortunate cargo of seventy-seven bundles of fur and a small amount of dry goods. The subsequent condemnation proceedings in the U.S. District Court in Rutland resulted in Catlin receiving, after deducting marshal's fees of $271.25, an eye-popping windfall of $61,417.46. U.S. attorney Hutchinson, who brought the action on Catlin's behalf, received only $12.00 for his efforts, while Van Ness, who appears to have done nothing but hold the statutory collector position, allowing him a 2 percent portion, was able to pocket a respectable $1,253.41. There is no indication that any duties were ever paid.[548]

Catlin's encounter could have been entirely fortuitous in his stumbling across an unguarded boat carrying a king's ransom in goods, but when one considers Buel's and Sailly's allegations that something more was afoot, the continuing presence of the triumvirate's fur-trading John Jacob Astor working alongside Catlin and Van Ness to evade paying duties or posting bonds becomes a very real possibility. Interestingly, Catlin's venture was particularly short-lived, as Collector Gelston became suddenly concerned with what the three captains possessing their lucrative commissions were up to on the lake. Only weeks after Catlin's seizure, on December 22, he ordered each of them, without explanation, to "surrender them immediately."[549]

Sam Buel also explained another aspect of the "Science of Vannessing" that involved Burlington land. Once an importer promised to pay bonds on goods brought into the country, he was allowed to take his merchandise and proceed on his way with the expectation of paying his obligation before a certain date. Failure to do so resulted in the collector himself becoming obligated to pay that amount, and to avoid such a result, Van Ness reportedly instituted court proceedings against anyone standing in the role of surety for those bonds, thereby placing the burden on them rather than himself. As Buel explained, the problem was that Van Ness delayed so long in bringing these suits that, in the intervening time period, merchants were able to remove their goods so far away that any surety was unable to seek any recourse against them. Since the sureties' assets frequently included real estate, they then became ripe for court-ordered sale, resulting in their subsequent loss, together with an up-close experience at being Vannessed. In fact, Van Ness's own encounter with smuggler Lloyd, from whom he personally purchased goods, involved some of Lloyd's land being levied against by the government. Buel does not say that Van Ness personally profited from these transactions but strongly infers he did and that an examination of Burlington land records "may afford some explanation." While Van Ness is indeed named in many purchases and sales of land, any description of their underlying particulars is frustratingly absent. However, it is a reasonable assumption that some degree of complicity existed between the collector and those merchants able to escape their bond obligations, leaving the sureties in the cold.

Of Van Ness's several exploits, none was as tantalizingly suspicious as those involving one "Ramon Manzuco of Cadiz in the Kingdom of Spain," further identified by Buel as "Mon Zucco, a descendant, perhaps, of a Hebrew," a close associate of the Catlins with whom he shared an "intimate connection."[550] The scheme left Buel, and others, in wonderment that it was possible to pull off. As he recounted, even those who were friends of the administration "could not believe that a commerce of this nature had the approbation of the government, particularly when they knew it was elsewhere, under similar circumstances, expressly disallowed."

A resident of Burlington at the time, operating Gideon King's fifty-ton sloop the *Saucy Fox* (built in Whitehall, New York, in 1810) and displaying the Spanish flag, Manzuco was uniquely able to walk the fine line separating legal from illegal utilizing his status as a purported "neutral" individual, allowing him to operate outside the dictates of onerous customs regulations. On his travels, steering the *Saucy Fox* along the north side of the lake, Manzuco ordered two mounted guns fired, serving as a signal to local residents to bring their furs and skins down to the shore, where they were loaded on board "in large quantities." From there, Manzuco reported to the customhouse in Burlington and presented invoices bearing the names of local individuals as the purported owners of the property that had just assumed a "neutral" status upon coming into his possession and paying only modest fees before proceeding. In a similar ruse, Buel explained that others had escaped paying duties by telling officials the goods they bore were for "personal" use rather than intended for the commercial market, thereby removing them from any assessment. As Buel further recounted, "millions" of dollars in goods were brought in by these subterfuges, estimating that Van Ness was able to extract a handsome $100,000, "more or less," over the course of three years because of them.[551]

Despite newspaper accounts reporting the presence of boats also bearing Danish and Swedish flags on lake waters, any allegation that he allowed "neutrals" to operate during his tenure were simply not true, according to Van Ness. He admitted that treasury secretary George W. Campbell suggested this was permissible but that he had chosen instead to proceed "in a more cautious way, so as to have the legality of the importations tried by the court."[552] That Campbell, who served but a brief eight months in office, countenanced skirting the law in this fashion does appear a legitimate claim and was probably one agreed to by Washington officials in their zeal to lessen the burdens merchants experienced along the border. However, his successor, Alexander J. Dallas, wanted no part in even the appearance of engaging in any deception. One month after assuming office, in October 1814, he wrote to Congress explaining that he disagreed with one of Campbell's earlier decisions concerning a Vermont case that implicated his office in abetting a suspect importer in his efforts to obtain a remission of bond money. In concluding his letter, Dallas forcibly and unequivocally stated that

> *no man is ever permitted to obtain relief in the courts of justice, upon a claim founded in his own willful violation of the law; and it would be an extraordinary, and, I presume, a novel application of the equitable powers of the Secretary of the Treasury, to legitimate a trade with the enemy, through the medium of remitting penalties and forfeitures incurred by a breach of the non-importation acts.*[553]

But Secretary Dallas, located so far away in Washington, clearly had not run into the likes of Vermont's chief customs official.

In office only a short time, Van Ness rejected the stringent "by the book" procedures utilized by Champlain collector Sailly and Sam Buel, choosing instead to pursue a noticeably lax enforcement posture. Whereas British-made goods were offered for sale at prices cheaper than in the United States just over the border in Canada, Sailly prohibited his men from taking advantage of that opportunity, something that Van Ness allowed his deputies to do. His dealing with neutrals was also clearly opposed, as evidenced by the presence of vessels flying various European flags. Whereas Sailly insisted on strict proof of their claims, Van Ness turned a blind eye so often that people claiming neutral status, such as Manzuco, simply "avoided the Champlain district… and entered such goods where greater laxity prevailed"—on the east side of the lake. Certainly unsurprising in light of his conflicted role as a steamboat investor, the same thing happened with those vessels plying the waters between St. John and communities around Lake Champlain; they chose to make whatever declarations were necessary in Vermont, "where the regulations and the administration of the law were too lax to protect the Government."[554]

However, Van Ness was particularly sensitive to any insinuation that he abused his authority, and on August 19, 1814, an article signed "CORRECTOR" appeared in the local paper addressing the presence of neutrals. The tone, and telltale specific and definitive references to customs practices and procedures, leaves no doubt that Van Ness penned the missive. Assuming the legal, hair-splitting posture of an attorney, he denied that anything untoward had taken place with regard to neutral *vessels* but acknowledged that subjects of a foreign country living in the United States could import goods and had been permitted to do so—*but over land*. Once they arrived in Vermont and notified officials of their intentions, he explained, the practice was to send a customs representative to meet the importer and bring the goods by boat to Burlington, where they were then subjected to court proceedings to determine whether they should be condemned.[555]

The fact that Van Ness chose to make a distinction between land and water importations is specious and wholly irrelevant to the issue of whether any particular mode of travel was lawful, unless one considers the timing of his article. It had been only three months since he received his substantial windfall from the court stemming from Guy Catlin's escapades into Canadian waters on the *Alert* and his seizure of those many thousands of dollars worth of suspicious furs. Accordingly, it appears Van Ness became concerned over the possible appearance of any impropriety taking place between himself and his business partner and chose instead to go on the offensive with his water/land distinction. But a closer examination of the underlying facts fails to sustain him.

Van Ness does not relate whether Manzuco appeared by land or water on one particular occasion, but months later, in November 1814, he reported to authorities that he was bringing 61 chests of tea, followed in the next few days by an additional 137 chests, into the United States. As Van Ness explained in 1828 to the congressional committee inquiring into his conduct, "It was supposed [Manzuco] meant to protect them against condemnation under his neutral character, as he did other goods, but finding that by being entitled to the informer's share it would be somewhat better to let them be condemned than to pay the high duties…he concluded to take that course."

Who came up with the idea that a merchant self-reporting his very own importation was now transformed into a third-party "informant," providing authorities with notice of an offense, is not disclosed, but it was an exceedingly creative and highly questionable claim—certainly, one not seen in the literature for other customs districts. Someone witnessing a crime and telling enforcement officers what he knew was encouraged, and the law permitted him to receive a portion of any subsequent forfeiture, but how an importer walking into a customhouse to report his goods in compliance with the law became similarly entitled is absolutely suspect. Coincidently, the collector was allowed to receive a portion of any subsequent condemnation, thereby allowing Van Ness yet another avenue for enrichment. It was all part of a continuing scam contributing, in part, to Van Ness's subsequent accumulation of "a splendid fortune."[556]

There was yet another problem with Van Ness's protestations that he passed these questionable importations off to the court for impartial decision, thereby insulating himself from the fray. When one examines the twenty-six cases in which Manzuco was involved in the U.S. District Court between 1814 and 1815, his story falls apart. It was true that Van Ness took the necessary bonds from Manzuco in these many cases and that his friend, U.S. attorney Hutchinson, instituted court cases against them. They are described variously in huge quantities—"393 Packages Dry Goods," "361 Packages Dry Goods," "176 Packages Merchd," "89 Packages of Merchandize," etc., totaling a staggering 1,082 individual bundles—with virtually all defended by yet another friend (and counsel to the triumvirate), attorney Stephen Mix Mitchell.

If the importations were indeed suspect and deserving of the substantial time and money it took to prosecute them, then one has to seriously question why, in thirteen of those cases, 50 percent of the total, the court clerk entered final dispositions stating that "the District Attorney in Court here says he will not further prosecute this [case]," with the goods then being returned to Manzuco.[557] Of the few that actually went to trial before a jury, their astonishing verdicts that these substantial amounts of goods constituted his personal, or "sole," property, and that they be returned to him, defies logic unless one further considers the possibility that Hutchinson was not as vigorous in seeking actual forfeiture verdicts as he might otherwise have been in the case of other merchants, those not as well as connected as Manzuco. And in one of the most brazen schemes imaginable, that is precisely what happened.

In 1834, after a career that included his serving as chief judge of the Supreme Court, Hutchinson sued Woodstock printer B.F. Kendall, alleging he was libeled when reports of his misconduct while serving as Vermont's U.S. attorney in 1817 were published. As Kendall explained in a later release, Hutchinson, known locally as "the everlasting candidate" for his repeated failure to win elected office, displayed a marked inclination to institute suits against Federalists, only to later dismiss them as having "flash'd in the pan." The reason, Kendall explained, was the availability of the "golden harvest" that fees paid by the court allowed him for simply filing forfeiture paperwork.

More importantly, evidence introduced during the trial through the statement of U.S. District Court judge Elijah Paine demonstrated conclusively ("I have a perfect recollection," he said) that while Van Ness was the district's collector and Hutchinson the U.S. attorney, he had personally received applications from individuals seeking the forgiveness ("remission") of forfeitures and penalties "when no suit was pending." How is it possible for a federal court to have claims filed with it as part of a pending action when there was no such thing in existence? As Kendall's defense attorney explained to the jury, Hutchinson (who had adopted Van Ness's practices), incredibly instituted claims against violators without notifying and involving the court of the cases, while surreptitiously filing fraudulent papers ("smuggling of a high handed character," he called it) that would have allowed his receipt of fees. By doing so, his actions allowed for the possibility of "smothering and suppressing [suits] behind the curtain" while he extracted illegal off-the-book payments without the court even becoming aware in the first place.[558] If Judge Paine, the man taking an early stand for civil rights in the case of Elisha Sears, intimates that Van Ness and Hutchinson colluded in some fashion to illegally obtain revenue monies, there is little more that can be said concerning the lackadaisical manner in which they administered the nation's customs laws.

Yet further suspicions arise concerning Manzuco in his role as informer for his 198 chests of tea when that case, along with many others, all came before the court during its May 1815 term. Of the twenty-one matters in which Manzuco was the claimant, fifteen were dismissed by Hutchinson outright and three returned to him upon paying duties and costs, one with an undisclosed disposition, while the tea (named in two entries) received the only peculiar disposition. When nobody stood up in response to the clerk calling the case to make a claim, the court ordered the goods condemned and the $5,147.00 bond that had been paid disbursed, with $30.12 going to Hutchinson. The recipients of the remainder of the money is not disclosed, but there is no reason to believe it went to anyone other than Manzuco, as had been previously arranged, and to Van Ness, the collector.

The ending seemed so strange that it triggered additional concerns with the 1828 investigating congressional committee, which also turned its attention to Van Ness's handling of over seven thousand pounds of pork, seized on three occasions between January and February 1814. Van Ness vigorously defended his actions and even went so far as to impugn the integrity of Vermont's current U.S. attorney, as well as the committee's chairman and those counseling him, protesting that he was being hounded by a "trio of inquisitors" out to cause him substantial harm. Just a week earlier, the district court itself had inquired of Van Ness about where his records were, indicating it, too, was looking into the matter. In responding, Van Ness wrote back "in haste," telling the clerk he could not respond at the moment because his records were unavailable, "packed in the office under the house" he occupied on Burlington's Courthouse Square. Attacks on Van Ness's integrity while collector continued, and he found himself on the defensive for many years. Buel threw off all restraint and called him, variously, a monster, a crocodile, a mammoth and possessed of a "sheep-faced" countenance and reported an incident in which another individual caught Van Ness "in a state of vagabondizing" and threatened him that "if he should find him any more trespassing upon his premises, he would treat him as he would a wolf that might be caught in his fold."

On March 13, 1818, Van Ness swore out an affidavit defending himself against accusations concerning his suspicious relationship and reported receipt of percentages of illegally imported goods with notorious smuggler James Lloyd. A month later, he dismissed another challenger's assertions of improper bookkeeping in the collector's office, characterizing him as a "tool" of New York governor Dewitt Clinton and saying that he "sold himself (and the sacrifice is not a great one) soul and body to this clan." Even his wife, Rhoda, was quick to take offense at a perceived slight when, in October of that same year, she lashed out at a woman she believed had slandered her during a visit to her home, telling her she had "committed what I consider an unwarrantable breach of hospitality" and concluding that she was "determined that all intercourse between us must cease." To that, the feisty recipient gave as good as she got and wrote back, "Nothing but a deep sense of your own guilt, or absolute insanity could have produced from any modest female" a letter such as the one Rhoda had penned. Ending out the year, in December, Van Ness found himself again explaining his prior conduct to Heman Allen and, again, justifying his every move as lawful. The questions continued, and in 1823, he wrote to an associate telling him that unnamed persons working in Boston "in conjunction with my enemies in this state" sought "some attempt to blow me up (as they will it) for something I did while Collector." He indeed became a lightning rod for many; an undated "Whig" resolution identifies him as "the administration's special agent," guilty of engaging in "misrepresentations, gross attempts at deception and unmeasured falsehoods and slanders" during his public service. His reputation had risen, or fallen, to such a level at the time that Whigs resolved to recommend Van Ness to the administration "as a suitable person for their employment in any dirty jobs which they may have on hand in this state."[559]

Buel was certainly not the only one recognizing Van Ness's crafty ways in those early years, and they included others located in Washington. Castleton's Colonel Isaac Clark, affectionately named "Old Rifle," was a well-known, respected and vigorous soldier who first led troops into Burlington and settled them in along the heights overlooking Lake Champlain. He then led them on forays into Canada, seizing smuggled goods and cattle. When he was being considered for an important command, his son, Satterlee, then in Washington, had some words of caution for him. Writing in March 1814, only a year after Van Ness had taken over as collector and days after his father successfully seized and returned twenty-three sleighs of smuggled goods from across the border and was preparing to do so again, the younger Clark wrote that he intended to refuse an impending promotion to major serving under his father in a newly raised regiment of volunteers. Satterlee explained that Vermont's entire congressional delegation was "unfriendly" to his father and that he believed the source of the problem was Van Ness, "whose hostility to you has originated in the most selfish, base and dishonorable feelings." Fearful of committing specifics to a letter that might be intercepted (Van Ness was the postmaster), Satterlee warned him that he had "many and bitter enemies, and the most dangerous are those who profess to be your friend and the friends of the administration, selfish, narrow minded, unprincipled hypocrites who have not one generous or noble sentiment."[560] Only thirty-two years old, it is clear that Van Ness's rising reputation and influence was not something to trifle with, and any efforts, no matter how well intentioned, that might overshadow them were destined to meet with vigorous opposition conducted behind closed doors and, in the end, leave the recipient bewildered.

Despite whatever reservations some might have had, on March 28, 1814, Van Ness was named, along with Harrington and one other, to a committee to meet with the local commander of U.S. forces to deal with an ongoing, perplexing problem. Beginning the previous summer, soldiers had been forced to hastily occupy buildings on the University of Vermont grounds to store "a large quantity of arms," watched over by guards who had no hesitation in vandalizing their new homes and the surrounding area. Much to the chagrin of university officials, finding themselves in "a similar state with several of our Colleges during the Revolution" unable to oppose the occupation, they helplessly stood by and watched as soldiers "laid waste and destroyed" the land around the president's home, broke open doors of vacant dormitories, pilfered absent students' books and, through their "tumultuous behavior," rendered the locale "extremely unpleasant."[561] The problem extended out into the community, forcing officials to create the committee after an allegation was made that "the soldiers stationed at this place being permitted to roam at large thro' the village, [were] entering the dwelling houses of the citizens at nighttime" to "their great inconvenience and annoyance."

During the elections the preceding fall, soldiers were also implicated in voting irregularities in Colchester, resulting in Harrington and Penniman becoming personally involved in getting to the bottom of the controversy. As several affidavits disclose, a Major McNeal, from New Hampshire, associated with the "republican or war party," marched 190 men from their encampment eight miles away into the town to cast their votes. Questions arose concerning the fact that thirty Federalist soldiers were left behind at camp and that the others had been threatened by McNeal that if they did not vote the Republican ticket, they would be severely punished, or "cobbed," as one soldier attested. Cobbing was a new form of punishment being inflicted on the men as a substitute to flogging the bare back, employing the use of a stick to strike a soldier's exposed buttocks.

Moses Catlin happened to be present at the voting place and reportedly heard McNeal tell a soldier that if he did not vote the Democratic ticket, as he planned to, he was a "damned rascal," threatening further that if anyone else in his command did otherwise, "he would mark him, & remember him for it." Citizens watching the gathering soldiers were ordered to stand off and not get close or question the men "or there would be difficulties." Judge Heman Allen was called to appear before the assemblage, formed into three large circles, to stand in the center of each and administer an oath en mass without inquiring of each man individually of their legal status. Eight to ten officers then handed out pre-marked ballots for Republican candidates to each of the men who then cast them in a nearby box, after which they were supplied with rum. Of their approximately 170 votes, all but 4 or 5 were for Republican candidates. It then fell to Harrington and Penniman to inquire into the circumstances and to obtain affidavits from "every Republican voter" in town to verify their votes had been accurately recorded in the final tally.

Yet additional significant problems arose when large numbers of Vermont militiamen deserted from federal ranks, leaving behind such a disproportionate number of officers that they found themselves unneeded and dismissed from service and losing expected pay. "We have had so much confusion, sedition, mutiny, & desertion since the troops arrived in Burlington that it beggars all description," Sandford Gadcomb (law associate of Van Ness's mentor, Asa Aldis) wrote in October 1813, assigning blame to "the unexampled efforts, and insidious measures of the internal enemies of the country," meaning Federalists. Even Harrington, in his important role as state councilor, fell under suspicion when he was implicated in controversial voting irregularities within the council itself involving fellow member Carpus Clark, of Worcester, leading him to file an affidavit of denial on November 17, 1813.[562]

Aside from politics, much more discord was taking place when Van Ness and Harrington met the local commander to express their concerns over the situation at the university, which appears to have been to no avail. As one student wrote in April 1814, upon visiting, "it presented a spectacle from which every friend of Science must turn with indignation and disgust; infant children squalling, soldiers swearing, 'camp ladies' in the last stage of intoxication, belching forth the contents of their filthy stomachs upon the floor" were more than he could stand. The problems persisted throughout the summer and fall as dismayed commanders sat on numerous court-martials taking place in university buildings of soldiers refusing to stop their many "depredations" against both public and private property. Theft was rampant, desertions continued, "riotous conduct" took place and insubordination exhibited to senior officers persisted as sentences ranging from dismissal to confinement, loss of pay, suspension of whiskey rations and wearing "a ball and chain for one month" were imposed.

Those problems aside, for the nimble Van Ness, other pursuits called, and on June 22, he and Penniman, working on the Committee of Arrangements, attended a meeting in Essex to prepare for the upcoming July 4 celebrations.[563] One name notably absent from those in attendance was fellow Republican Harrington, for he was preparing to die.

OF THE MANY PROBLEMS the military presented, none was as dangerous to the community in general as the disease accompanying its every move. A quarantine camp was established south of town in late 1813, and afflicted soldiers were sent there, lessening the possibility of their infecting the local populace. Unfortunately, it did not help Seeley and Amy Bennett's daughter, twenty-year-old Pamelia, who died that winter on February 6, 1814. Only two months later, on April 2, Seelely himself, at age forty-six, joined her, and the two were interred in Elmwood Cemetery, the scene of Dean's execution.[564]

Following the death of his wife, Roxselana, occurring only days after completing the Hoxie and *Black Snake* trials in November 1808, William Harrington married widow Mrs. Abiah Smith, of Rutland, on September 9, 1811, the last year he served as state's attorney. Over the next two years, he was elected to the state's twelve-man council and was one of eight Democrats chosen in the fractious 1813 elections. He vigorously continued in his law practice, bringing many more lawsuits for debts owed to him on his book accounts and in real estate transactions, experiencing much success, most recently taking place in the February 1814 terms of court. Business remained good, and as he had done previously, the preceding year he retained the services of an unidentified individual to go out into surrounding communities to track down absconding debtors owing him money. While the current state's attorney, George Robinson, continued to battle the illegal sale of spirits coming from unlicensed taverns and obtained indictments against a number of individuals in February 1814, the same thing was taking place farther to the south, in Rutland County. There, officials were faced with an onslaught of similar conduct during the summer and fall as several individuals were charged in federal court with selling alcohol and foreign goods without a license, all fleeing when the U.S. marshal attempted to serve them with court papers.[565]

Amid all of this, on June 29, 1814, Harrington decided to write out a will, and then, two weeks later, at age fifty-eight, on Friday, July 15, he died. His ill health, perhaps caused by the dysentery that Burlington experienced on a yearly basis or influenza spread by the roving military, was apparently already noted by others, as Republican officials did not recommend him earlier in the month for reelection as a councilor. Despite all the years of honorable service to his state as colonel of militia and now on the council; to his local community as state's attorney prosecuting murdering smugglers; and as selectman overseeing the poor, a friend to those of color and to women seeking to assert nascent legal rights, the local paper noted his passing with a brief, three-line insertion. Located immediately next to it were notices from Nathan Haswell describing an upcoming auction of beef and pork and court-appointed individuals handling Seeley Bennett's estate, "represented insolvent," advising creditors to file their claims. When administrators later tasked with handling Harrington's estate came to examine his intricate, detailed accounts of credits and debits, the best they could do the following November was to also advertise to potential claimants that it, too, was "represented insolvent."[566] However, that was not accurate.

The relationship is not clear, but Harrington made provisions in his will directing that $1,000 of his assets go to the children of local attorney Phineas Lyman upon their turning twenty-one years of age and to other relatives. A vigorous court battle ensued years later, finally ending in 1837 (a year after his wife, Abiah, passed away), concerning the manner in which Lyman administered the money on his children's behalf, and it constituted one of the more important early cases in Vermont legal history dealing with executors' obligations. During the proceedings, it was established that at the time of his death, Harrington's estate was far from insolvent, valued at a respectable $60,000.[567] His attention to detail and continual pursuit of obligations owed to him over the years, while leading a modest lifestyle in the meantime, demonstrated that it was possible to live in an upright manner, even if highly placed government officials and others within the business community chose to do so less honorably.

The man Harrington had tried so hard to kill during the course of two hard-fought trials lived on. At forty years of age, and in the fifth year of his ten-year sentence for manslaughter, on October 9, 1813, Samuel Mott petitioned the governor for a full pardon, arguing that "the great end of public justice and the peace of community" had been met in his case, warranting his release. While the attending Visitors attested that he "has been obedient to the laws of the prison, faithfull [*sic*] and industrious," the effort was denied. Fellow *Black Snake* convict, twenty-three-year-old David Sheffield, filed a similarly unsuccessful petition at the time, telling the governor his prior conduct was the result of his "not thinking the consequences…and not using forethought."[568] Other prisoners also sent in their requests for pardon, and in the fall of 1814, the wife of fellow convict thirty-eight-year-old Samuel E. Godfrey, serving a three-year sentence for stealing a watch, a small amount of change and some rum from his landlord, did so on his behalf and was awaiting a decision when a most unfortunate event took place.

Weaving cloth constituted a substantial portion of the prisoners' boring, relentless hard labor punishment as each man sought to produce the specific number of yards assigned to him each day by the master weaver. A year earlier, one of them, identified in the newspaper only by his initials, S.G. (either Godfrey or fellow inmate Sam Green Jr., also serving a three-year term for stealing), exhibited such enthusiasm for his work that officials drew the public's attention to the occasion. On June 23, 1813, they wrote, "Owing to the great improvements made in weaving machinery, and to the spirit of emulation existing among the convicts to excel each other in activity and skill in the loom," over the course of fifteen hours, the man wove "fifty eight yards and a quarter of gingham No. 16 Factory yarn; plying three shuttles… with the astonishing quickness of 112 times a minute," finishing with fifteen and a quarter pounds of the product. "If such are the fruits of an institution, while in its infancy, what benefit may not the State expect to derive from future improvements?" they proudly proclaimed.[569]

By November 5, 1814, the work had become so monotonous that when Godfrey handed in his work to the "superintendent of the weavers" one morning, he unguardedly made a comment to the effect that he had done more than he intended. Officials already suspected "there was a combination among the prisoners not to weave over a certain quantity," and when

Thomas Rogers, keeper of the Upper Shop, took offense upon overhearing the comment, Godfrey quickly corrected himself, clarifying that he meant to say he had only done more than he thought he had. The damage was done, and Godfrey's offense was forwarded on to the head keeper, Thomas Hewlet, to deal with.[570]

Facing a lonely, cold punishment sitting in solitary confinement in a stone cell "as dark as a tomb," being fed four ounces of bread a day, for a period lasting "seldom less than a week" before having to admit guilt and grovel for mercy constituted Godfrey's immediate future, and he quickly sank into a state of desperation. When Hewlet pulled him aside as he was leaving the dining hall shortly after the exchange, Godfrey panicked and ran to the nearby weaving shop; picked up a two-foot-long, inch-and-a-half-diameter leg from a loom bench; placed a ten-cent "common shoe-knife" with a blade six to eight inches long into his left hand; and confronted nearby Rogers.

"God damn you, was you the one that reported me?" Godfrey demanded, and when Rogers told him he had, indeed, Godfrey raised the leg to strike him but was thwarted by a parrying blow to his wrist from Rogers's sword. Hewlet had arrived by this time, and with the addition of his own sword, the two jailers rained down blows on the prisoner. During the mêlée, Godfrey's knife found its mark, sinking six inches into Hewlet "in and upon the left side of him...near the end of the second false rib." Hewlet called out, "You have stabbed me!" turned pale and was taken out of the room by two other men to his quarters. Godfrey, who had himself received severe head wounds, was knocked down by Rogers and restrained, ending the confrontation. Hewlet quickly received the attention of local doctors, who supplied him with opium, cordials and bleeding, but after a long, agonizing four weeks, with "great pain, and...sick at his stomach and puking a great part of this time," he died on December 2.

While the specific location of *Black Snake* triggerman/double murderer Samuel Mott during the fray is not known, he did go to the hospital where Godfrey was confined to meet with him. No words were exchanged between the two because of Godfrey's injuries, but Mott returned the following day. As Godfrey complained of his pains, the wise Mott, who had so much experience in these kinds of matters, as he later explained to a jury, simply told Godfrey not to say anything about the confrontation, "as he might commit himself unnecessarily." Advising a murder suspect not to cooperate with authorities was hardly consistent, but certainly not surprising when considering Mott's past, with his having written to the governor in his 1813 pardon petition that he was "determined in the future to lead an honest and inoffensive life."

Even without Godfrey's assistance, authorities promptly instituted a murder charge against him and then, over the course of the next three years, put him on trial as many times. Former U.S. attorney Hutchinson represented him throughout but was ultimately unsuccessful upon the last trial, taking place in Woodstock on November 14–15, 1817. After the case was received at ten o'clock on a Saturday evening and the evidence considered for three hours, Godfrey was found guilty and sentenced days later to be hanged on Friday, February 13, 1818. With months to consider his fate, Godfrey spent the ensuing time commiserating his end with his wife and, in eleven typeset pages, wrote out his sorry life's story, together with a "Final Address to the World."

Notwithstanding the military's execution of Private Baily in 1813, this was Vermont's second execution following Dean's ten years earlier and was said "to be the first instance of the kind which has ever occurred on the East side of the Green Mountains in Vermont; and consequently excited an unusual interest," also receiving ample attention in newspapers. When the day finally arrived, an estimated seven to twelve thousand people crowded in and around Woodstock's Green, in front of the local courthouse, to witness the proceedings. At 11:00 a.m., his latest request for a fourth trial rejected by the Supreme Court days earlier, Godfrey was escorted out of the local jail by the sheriff. A military guard composed of some one hundred soldiers stood by and, together with the "officiating Clergyman, the officers of justice, &c. with appropriate martial music, solemn as death," the assemblage marched to the local meetinghouse to hear a sermon delivered by Windsor's Leland Howard.

Following those proceedings, the company then moved to the Green, where the gallows, built three years earlier following Godfrey's first overturned conviction, stood. The condemned climbed the stairs and was joined at the top by Howard, who then knelt and "addressed the Throne of Grace, imploring Divine mercy on the unhappy sufferer." The executioner placed the rope around his neck and allowed him time to make some last words. His Final Address had been delayed at the printer and, not having those last words before him, he called out, "I have no remarks to make, only that I declare before God and man, that I am innocent of the crime for which I am about to suffer."[571] When the sheriff offered to delay the proceedings for a half hour, Godfrey told him that since "the weather was excessively cold [and] his clothes were thin," he wished not to delay a moment longer. A cap was then

drawn over his face, the plank on which he stood suddenly dropped, and let him down a distance of about three feet, when he instantly expired, with no apparent agony, and very trifling motion. After hanging about 20 minutes, his remains were deposited in a coffin, and delivered to his friends, agreeable to his request.[572]

For the man counseling a murderer to keep his mouth shut, his persistent requests for leniency were finally answered. David Sheffield had successfully obtained his pardon in 1815, and Mott continued in the intervening years to petition Montpelier, the latest in October 1816, when he sought release because "his health is greatly impaired in consiguence [*sic*] of so long a confignment [*sic*]." When Governor Jonas Galusha and the council, which included former prosecutor U.S. attorney David Fay, met at 9:00 a.m. on Saturday, October 11, 1817, the petitions of fourteen prisoners from the state prison were considered. All of them were dismissed except Mott's, who received a favorable response granting his request, nine voting in favor (including Fay) and two opposed.[573]

THE SUMMER OF 1814 continued to present Collector Van Ness with numerous challenges. His efforts to obtain mounted assistance from the local military commander to deal with the smuggling in the Burlington area proved so successful that his counterpart in the northeast part of the state, Roger Enos, working hard along the line in Derby, requested that he obtain similar aid that August. Enos was challenged on multiple levels in dealing with the smuggling going in both directions, including—incredibly—money. In what has to be one of the most unusual smuggling incidents taking place during these years (one has to wonder on how many other undetected occasions it succeeded), noted briefly in a single court document, on January 15, 1814, Alexander Ferguson, described as "a transient person," was intercepted driving a sleigh into Canada while in the possession of $1,500 in ready cash. What was the purpose of his attempt is not described, but it further conveys the blatant methods smugglers used in their relentless, illicit trade.[574]

Rescues of goods continued. On January 11, 1814, John McLaren, William Boss and Moody Beard all forcibly removed several items from Enos's possession, including "two pieces of superfine broadcloth...one pair of saddlebags filled with silks, two bear skins, two cub's skins, one buffaloe's skin [and] one hundred sable skins" valued at $2,000. Even when authorities went to the trouble to obtain search warrants seeking contraband, others persisted in interfering with their execution. On July 29, Inspector Benjamin Fisk suspected that Canadian goods were concealed in a Williamstown store and, when he appeared to conduct his search, was met by Benjamin Cutter and five other men, who obstructed him "by pushing back the said Fisk as he would pass behind the counter in said store." Violations were now so commonplace that the U.S. attorney had forms printed allowing him to quickly fill in the necessary blanks depending on whether a particular incident involved the seizure of dry goods, cattle, a rescue or something else.[575]

Of all the obstructive incidents, none compared to the bizarre events taking place in 1815 involving customs inspector and lawyer John Beckwith of Sutton. Originally from New Hampshire, and later a local representative to the state legislature, Beckwith began his employment with the revenue service during this period, remaining until at least 1833. Then he is identified as working alongside Enos for Van Ness's protégé Archibald Hyde, who himself eventually ascended to the collector's position. Noted as "a vigilant inspector during the war, [who] seized many cattle and great quantities of provisions destined for the enemy in Canada," Beckwith certainly accumulated his share of ill will from local residents who resented the presence of an enforcer in their midst.[576] In 1813, he was responsible for the arrest of Benjamin Robinson, "a worthy character destitute of property," as he drove a yoke of cattle toward Canada, earning him a year of hard labor at the state prison, which no doubt did not sit well with his neighbors.

Court documents convey only a bit of the criminal activity that Beckwith and his fellow deputies were faced with at that time. Samuel Smith, Clement Eaton, Cyrus Eaton, Michael Bly, Justus Smith and Oran Persival all drove 250 "fat cattle," valued at $4,000, toward Canada in October 1814, while in November, Noah Sanborn tried to take ten more, as Moses Wright and Vine Taylor moved forty head and Samuel How did the same with an additional twelve. In December, James Way tried to herd fifteen head, while Edward Burt and Josiah Parmilee chose to move a respectable four tons of pork northward. These were people not at all dissuaded by displays of authority, even when draconian punishments were imposed on counterfeiters and others such as that visited on three men recently sentenced for stealing twenty-four sheep, receiving a staggering term of two years of hard labor at the state prison.

For those steadfast smugglers, taking matters into their own hands continued as a viable option, and simply banding together, bearing their clubs and guns, taking from one another and rescuing back from others what they believed their property while embellishing their efforts with continual death threats was a daily way of life. It certainly put the fear of God into Robert Man, of Irasburgh, in October 1814, when he was stopped by a group of men headed by Ira Day as he herded four cattle from Barton.

Responding to demands about where he got the cattle, Man told Day that Ezekiel Little had hired him to move the animals, given him a gun and then ridden off only moments before their arrival. In what appears to have been a smuggling effort by Little utilizing an unsuspecting Man, Day was not at all happy, and the men threatened to go after Little to "put a stop to his driving cattle." One of the men told Man that the only thing that "saved me from the whip was that I was old and grey headed."

Only weeks later, on November 1, Little struck again, apparently in retaliation for Day's interference, when he, together with several others, using "guns, bayonets, swords & fists," assaulted Aaron Rood and inflicted serious injuries on him, all leading to the inevitable lawsuits. Mobs of men continued to gather together disturbing the public's peace, and to the west, in Huntington, in June 1815, John Ambler and eleven other individuals found themselves indicted for participating in a riot of unnamed intention. Clearly, increases in manpower notwithstanding, those charged with enforcing the law in lonely isolation had an uphill battle when they were unable to even rely on the aid of nearby citizens as the law required them to assist when called upon. Such a case unfolded when Jonathan Dells was charged in federal court with refusing to assist Inspector David Nutting in February 1816 as he tried to seize a sleigh suspected of customs violations.[577]

But all of this paled when considering poor John Beckwith on the night of July 6, 1815. As he slept in his house, John Atwood, together with John Atwood Jr., William Goodwin, David Sanger, Joseph Spalding and Elijah Bundy, equipped themselves for a long night. Taking their knives, shears and razors, they broke into Beckwith's bedroom, dragged him from his sleep and, over the course of six hours, beat and choked him before doing the unimaginable. What other injuries they inflicted are not described, but court papers concerning both the subsequent prosecution of, and suit for damages against, Atwood disclose that Beckwith sustained permanent disfigurement when the men viciously severed the right ear from his head. The injuries were so traumatic that Beckwith was unable to resume his daily activities for at least the next six months.[578]

As Beckwith writhed in pain, a grand jury immediately convened, and charges were instituted against Atwood, resulting in his eventual conviction after two trials. Incredibly, he was able to avoid any type of incarceration, receiving a sentence consistent with those involved with other egregious assault cases: a fine of only $200. In the suit Beckwith later filed against him for his injuries, he received a favorable verdict in June 1818 ordering his attacker to pay him $1,500. What the connection might be, if any, is not known, but only months later, on the night of November 11, Beckwith was victimized once again. This time, Jacob Webster and John Gore targeted a barn he owned and carried a tin can containing hot embers to the side of the building. There, they pried off a board and set the contents down inside, destroying the entire structure, including twenty-five tons of hay, five tons of clover, one yoke of oxen and a horse. Following yet more lawsuits, finally ending in 1822, Beckwith obtained a $737 judgment against Webster for the fire.

The lawlessness present in these remote locations was no doubt exacerbated by the ever-present problem posed by the ready availability of alcohol. Its pernicious effects became of greater concern and forced policymakers to begin looking for solutions. In 1817, Van Ness was named to a prestigious committee including the governor, lieutenant governor and members of the council and House of Representatives looking into the adverse effects alcohol had on the state at large. In "An Address to the Inhabitants of the State of Vermont on the Use of Ardent Spirits," the committee estimated that some $1 million worth of the liquid had been purchased in the preceding year, causing severe hardships on many towns that had to raise taxes to support those, and their families, falling victim to alcoholism and pauperism. They further called on all levels of society, particularly ministries, to enlist in remedying the problem, constituting one of the opening salvos that gave rise to the creation of temperance societies around the state in the next few decades.

Clearly, the embargo, the war, alcohol and all of their attending problems were having a marked effect on the state. In the years between 1810 and 1820, Vermont saw only an 8 percent increase in population (from 217,895 to 235,966), a figure distinctly at odds with the 80 and 40 percent increases taking place between 1791 and 1800 and 1800 and 1810, respectively. The stagnation in growth was only slowly shrugged off in later years as those in the countryside transitioned away from self-sufficiency toward a market economy and the state put into place effective laws and institutions allowing for increased order and stability to settle in.[579]

But those changes were for the future as, for now, certain vendettas remained to be satisfied.

11

ENDINGS

Even as British forces assembled the largest, strongest and best-equipped army to ever appear on the North American continent in the summer of 1814, preparing for their southward advance, Collector Van Ness found time to engage in personal business. In June and August, he entered into various arrangements with others to pay their debts in the future, which later became lawsuits. He also became embroiled in a difficult case in which he sued, and was sued in turn for trespass, for the possession of a piece of black cloth, a portmanteau containing dry goods and other items valued at $1,200, seized during an August 26 confrontation in Swanton. It did not go well for him; he lost in the local court, and then, inexplicably, later defaulted when he failed to appear in the Supreme Court after appealing those judgments. That same day, his men seized thirty-seven packages of unidentified merchandise and two kegs of rum in Highgate from Middlebury merchant Jonathan Hagar and, after instituting forfeiture proceedings, watched as the secretary of the treasury decided to return them to him. What he felt upon learning that Sam Buel's father-in-law, Peter Sailly, had lost both his home and customs storehouse (holding several thousand dollars' worth of seized goods) earlier that month when British troops burned them to the ground is not known. But there must have been some smug satisfaction in evidence at the distress inflicted on his adversary's supporter.[580]

Aside from those matters, things turned around substantially following Thomas Macdonough's victory across the water at Plattsburgh on September 11. Two weeks later, as Nathan Haswell supplied the local military hospital with sixty-two dollars' worth of urgently needed cotton and ten gallons of cognac for its patients, Van Ness became involved with putting together the city's festivities, set to begin at 10:00 a.m. on Tuesday, September 27. The day before, Macdonough and his staff had been boisterously received, accompanied by "a roar of cannon," at the waterfront after arriving via one of the lake's steamboats. Van Ness was probably present, but he also made certain that day to file suit against James Evarts for failing to settle accounts owed to him.

Described as "an immense concourse of citizens of this and neighboring towns," the assemblage gathered at the Courthouse Green, where Haswell assigned them their places in a parade. From there, the body, "escorted by a large and elegant company of Cavalry," moved to the meetinghouse for a religious service of thanksgiving and then on to a local hotel.[581] There, the attendees were met by lavish displays, "the room was beautifully decorated with festoons of evergreen and wreaths of flowers; the words 'T. Macdonough *the Hero of Champlain*,' in gold letters were conspicuously displayed at the head of the room in transparency." Following "an elegant and sumptuous dinner," Van Ness and four others "conducted the ceremony of the Table" (a Masonic-tinged reference to consuming "refreshments"), to the accompaniment of "heavy peals of Artillery, reiterated cheers, and appropriate music from the bands." Lasting until the "early hour" of the following day, round after round of toasts were made, including to "The 11th of September 1814," "The Union of the States," "Washington," "The Navy," "American Sons of Ocean, Nature's Noblemen," "The Army" and "Agriculture, Commerce & Manufactures," all receiving a series of cheers, much music and more drinking. The festivities were greatly appreciated by all, and Van Ness certainly received his share of accolades.

Sam Buel, the persistent thorn in his side, could never be far from Van Ness's mind as he defended himself from claims of absconding with money rightfully owned by his predecessor. Estimated by Sailly to be in the vicinity of $18,000 to $20,000, Buel dogged Van Ness with suits seeking vindication and their return. Only days after Macdonough's victory, on September 17, Van Ness, together with Hyde, appeared in court on behalf of Elisha Clark in a suit brought by Buel for the repayment of a $156.43 debt Clark owed. The fact that Van Ness acted in an individual capacity representing others while also serving as the district's collector provides interesting insights into the state of these types of relationships, revealing that government officials were not necessarily expected to provide full-time attention to the public's needs. Certainly, he could not have appreciated the outcome of Clark's case in particular when Buel received a $185 judgment in his favor.[582] Regardless of whatever success Buel might encounter, it was short-lived.

While Buel struggled on, advancing a claim for reimbursement to Congress in January 1815 for his Windmill Point property destroyed by the British, and celebrated the birth of daughter Sarah in September, these were particularly good times for Van Ness. Of the dozens of seizure and forfeiture cases filed in Vermont's federal courts between 1814 and 1815, a vast majority of them resulted in condemnations, and money flowed directly to him, including a portion of fines assessed in other matters. Despite Hutchinson's repeated dismissals of many cases, which retain the taint of being prearranged, there were a few instances in which juries actually rendered verdicts. Demonstrating their independence, some made discerning decisions that certain goods were not subject to forfeiture when they concluded that "horses were not employed in conveying," or "pork was not put on a sleigh" or cattle were not intended for transport into Canada, thereby rejecting the government's case.

Regardless, of the few outcomes not otherwise favorable to him, literally tens of thousands of dollars found their way into Van Ness's pocket during this time period. He may very well have been able to account for the money as he continually protested to repeated investigations, but Buel's allegation that amounts he received above the statutorily allowed $5,000 limit were being filtered to his associates cannot be discounted in this time of loose interpretation and enforcement of the customs laws under Van Ness's watch. Interestingly, records for the years immediately following the war's end reveal that very little was done in this regard, and it resulted in a significant drop in revenue flowing into government coffers, as well as consequent riches going to the collector. In 1816, only sixteen cases were filed; in 1817, seven cases; and in 1818, four cases. Things continued in that manner through, at least, 1828.[583] This lack of an ability to garner easily obtained money and the sudden opening of opportunities made possible by the war's close might very well have influenced the next steps Van Ness took in his incredible rise.

Between 1797 and 1837, the Treasury Department questioned the accounts of 114 collectors, naval officers and surveyors responsible for collecting duties, including several U.S. marshals also handling money on their behalf. In many of the cases, officials ordered the respective U.S. attorneys to institute suits against them seeking its return, alleging maladministration, or defalcation, as a legal basis. On October 12, 1815, Vermont's U.S. attorney was directed to seek the return of $9,441.87 the department believed was owed to it by one of them, Sam Buel.[584] The timing and circumstances of this particularly onerous suit, filed in December, reveal just how deeply the Van Ness interests, those of Cornelius and his two brothers, penetrated into Washington's decision-making.

Earlier that spring, Buel had become aware of the government's claim against him and made two trips to Washington to meet with various treasury officials to discuss the matter in detail. It was only then that he learned of more serious allegations being made—specifically, that his accounts constituted more than mere recordkeeping oversights but involved criminal activity. There was only one person making such a charge, and that came from Van Ness's "confidential agent and pimp" Archibald Hyde. Taken aback, Buel found himself defending the imaginative, albeit admittedly "indiscreet," way he compensated his deputies, taking a portion of their salary in exchange for their receiving a larger share of monies recovered from their seizures. Even so, after presenting evidence that a large part of the government's claim should have been offset by some $5,000 in credits, Buel negotiated what he believed an amiable resolution that required him to repay only $1,903.15. However, it was an ending that quickly evaporated with the department's October order that suit be brought against him.

Buel was not alone in his struggling efforts at the time, as former sheriff Daniel Staniford, noted earlier, advanced his own petition to the Vermont legislature on October 10, 1815, seeking relief from being personally seized and incarcerated as a debtor. Pressed by several creditors, including Van Ness, Staniford explained that many of his troubles "originated in his becoming security for others," revealing the tragic consequences attending anyone, even those in positions of authority, naïvely believing that ensuring the future performance of another was a wise decision. He further explained, as his suits against Seeley Bennett demonstrated, that his problems also came "from the neglect of his deputies." A sympathetic assembly agreed with the hardworking man and allowed him a three-year reprieve from being subjected to the embarrassing incarceration suffered by a debtor.[585]

Even with the riches his position afforded, Van Ness was not satisfied with simply discrediting his predecessor with vague and questionable allegations of serious wrongdoing. Now, he fought back against Buel's claims seeking the return of moieties he believed were his by instituting his own set of charges. On December 5, 1815, Van Ness brought seven separate suits alleging trespass and conversion of goods, seeking some $10,000 in damages against his predecessor in the U.S. District Court, reaching back to February 20, 1813, the opening days of his tenure as collector. Even though he had just experienced his own set of difficulties in July when he stored

$223 of seized goods with a Stephen Pettis in Alburgh, someone he trusted and who later refused to return them ("casually lost" was the legal term), Van Ness, now represented by Hutchinson, alleged that Buel did the same thing with the goods he held in his custody.[586] As Buel later explained to the Treasury Department, many of these items were simply forcibly rescued from his custody—exactly what happened to Pettis. Unspoken in any of Van Ness's papers, but certainly a motivating factor, concerned his ever-present contention that Buel's ineptness deprived him of an opportunity to claim some of his moieties.

Fighting both the Washington establishment and Van Ness became too much for the belabored Buel, and on February 22, 1816, Vermont's Asa Lyon presented a petition to the House of Representatives seeking relief on his behalf. In it, Buel's situation was laid out, "complaining of injuries and oppressions from public officers," resulting in "large sums of moneys to which he was legally entitled" being withheld. The House took no action at the moment and referred the matter to a five-man committee for further consideration.[587] Buel was then living "in a remote part" of New York when the contested Treasury Department claims were scheduled for a local court hearing. Relying on incorrect instructions from his attorney that the proceedings were postponed, he departed for home only to have the court clerk then call the matter in his absence. With nobody there to respond, a default judgment was entered against him, thereby making an already complex set of circumstances even more difficult when he sought assistance from Congress in 1823, having already been "imprisoned about five years," to unravel all of the conflicting claims.

In the meantime, by May 17, 1816, Buel experienced his first incarceration, occupying one of Burlington's debtor cells because of Van Ness's seven suits against him. Nathan Haswell's problems with the government also took place at this moment, and the two men no doubt crossed paths several times going into and out of jail. Two weeks later, Buel obtained a brief respite when Congress ordered his release, but by July, he was back in.

As Buel came to quickly learn, fighting against these many claims coming from faceless, evasive bureaucrats became a losing proposition, no matter how legitimate and honorable his past actions might have been. In 1817, he lamented that they "derived from an uninterrupted current of calumny and misrepresentation" coming from Van Ness, who possessed an "object of deriving and retaining to himself large sums of money, the result of the perils, the labors and the sacrifices of myself and associates," all allegations he said were "fraught with falsehood."[588] And so began a difficult, dizzying period of many years as Buel found himself jailed, freed and then re-jailed again, still fighting those battles in 1829, when he once again petitioned Congress for release. He received limited successes in the lower courts, obtaining some judgments against Van Ness and fellow collector Roger Enos (who was, in turn, represented by Van Ness), while being forced to pay in others.

Buel's difficulties hardly mattered to Van Ness at any point in time. The December 24, 1814 Treaty of Ghent settling the war contained three articles concerning lingering disputes along the northern boundary line separating the United States and Canada. Article V provided for the creation of a commission to meet at St. Andrews, New Brunswick, to establish a line from the source of the St. Croix River to the St. Lawrence River. On March 18, 1816, Madison nominated Van Ness as United States commissioner "to carry into effect" this particular article, agreed to by the Senate two weeks later. Coincidently, the following month, Madison also nominated his brother, John, a resident of Washington, D.C., as a commissioner to deal with public works issues in the city but was rejected by the Senate the following day.

Prior to his departure for Canada, in April, Van Ness corresponded with attorney Timothy Merrill, in Barre, and asked him to immediately forward a list of all smuggling cases pending in the local courts because, despite his pending absence, he wanted "to assist in the preparation of those kind [sic] of crimes."[589] Those matters aside, the boundary work requiring Van Ness's presence in St. Andrews actually did not begin until September 17, when he traveled to that city from Portland, Maine. On the twenty-fourth, the respective parties met, exchanged commissions, made arrangements for necessary surveys and, because of the lateness of the season, adjourned until the following spring.

With Van Ness conveniently out of state, yet more troubles arose for Buel when, on September 16, 1816, U.S. attorney Hutchinson instituted suit against him, Jabez Penniman and Stephen Pearl; Harrington escaped being named only because he was dead. Now, the government turned to the living to obtain the $2,000 promised by the men in 1811, when they agreed to act as sureties for Buel's faithful performance at the time of his appointment as collector, a promise Hutchinson alleged had been breached by Buel's indiscretions. He successfully obtained a judgment against the men the following month and then secured warrants for their arrests until the money was received, eventually seeing Buel and Penniman taken into custody (Pearl had died in the interim) and lodged in Burlington's jail in July 1817. The specific disposition is not noted, but papers do indicate that a substantial portion of the $2,000 was indeed paid over to the government by at least one of the defendants.[590]

Notably, in the two cases involving Van Ness that actually reached the U.S. Supreme Court in these years, Buel was fully vindicated in his various claims. On the overriding issue concerning his right to a moiety for work done before his removal as collector, the court decided in February 1819, in a one-paragraph decision read out by Justice Joseph Story, that he had "an absolute vested title to his share in the forfeiture." That finding no doubt instilled in him the strength and resolve needed to publish *The Book* later that year to advance his arguments of unjust dismissal at the hands of a vindictive Van Ness and obstinate treasury officials. Those problems never reached a full determination because of persistent bureaucratic obstructions, the departure of officials with particular knowledge and, in the end, Buel's own death in Burlington on August 11, 1831, at age sixty-five, causing the government to write off entirely any claims against him.[591]

For Van Ness and his oversight of the critical boundary dispute, the work of the commission and several British and American astronomers and surveyors in the next few years created their own set of difficulties. No treaty provision addressed exactly how much money the effort was allowed to conduct its business, and on November 21, 1820, virtually excluded from any consultation, an exasperated Senate sent a resolution to President Monroe seeking detailed information disclosing the amounts expended—and when money was in issue, Van Ness's name was not far off. When he read in the newspapers of their concern, on November 25, he quickly dashed off a letter to Secretary of State John Quincy Adams in explanation. Only a year after Buel's *The Book* appeared, and during the course of launching his defense of those allegations ("an unexampled mass of scurrility against me"), a penitent Van Ness told Adams he never understood that any accounting was necessary until the completion of his work. However, he offered that, "being at all times not only willing but anxious to satisfy any branch of the Government as to my public conduct," he would forward the necessary information.

Certainly, one of the more noteworthy lines of Van Ness's accounting concerned his exceedingly generous yearly salary of $4,444.44, one he received in addition to his collector's stipend in the early years of the commission. Notwithstanding, even in the face of Congress's concerns, Van Ness unashamedly told Adams the money was not enough, pointing out that his British counterparts received pay of some $5,333.28, and he wanted the same. However, it certainly was not the consensus of another diplomat working on other treaty issues who told Congress "neither considerations of justice nor national etiquette" required comparable pay. Then, in a statement that might have been correct with regard to the matter at hand but certainly suspect if one looked further back in time to his involvement with Samuel Buel, Van Ness told Adams, "I have never claimed on my personal account anything over my salary, whatever that may be."

Belying any contention of altruism on his part, Van Ness certainly possessed an unattractive persistence in his quest for money, efforts that later included long missives on the unconstitutionality of acts limiting his pay and going so far as to bring pressure on President Adams through the efforts of Vermont congressman William C. Bradley. Bradley probably never told Van Ness after meeting Adams that the president viewed the commission's conduct as "unfit" or that Bradley himself was "utterly ashamed of them himself." It was all to no avail, for with his expenses exceeding $99,000, no boundary resolution in sight and Congress's backhanded slap that his salary was already "far greater, in proportion to the services performed, than those which are usually given to any officers of Government," Van Ness gained nothing more. It all fell apart in 1821, when the parties agreed not to agree, leaving the dispute lingering for years awaiting a resolution.[592]

Van Ness was, if anything, a force to be reckoned with. The young man who had attained such high levels of responsibility so early, exploited each step along the way for further gain, employing the strategy of "an ardent, or rather, a violent politician."[593] In 1818, sensing the time was right, he resigned his collector position and was elected as Burlington's representative to the General Assembly (Penniman joined him in 1819). He remained there for the next three years and developed a marked reputation for distributing political patronage.

In 1821, Van Ness was elected chief justice of the Supreme Court and served in that role until 1823. Now, his past returned to haunt him, and in January 1823, his own court ordered him to pay $513.24 to Buel for three separate moieties he received improperly. More significantly, the following month, he lost his second case involving Buel before the U.S. Supreme Court, which had an immediate impact on any hopes he had for further judicial advancement.

On March 18, 1823, Justice Brockholst Livingston died, leading Van Ness to quickly write a letter, marked "confidential," to Monroe only days later seeking appointment to the Supreme Court in his place. Telling the president he would be "extremely gratified" should he receive a positive decision, Van Ness briefly laid out reasons in his favor, explaining further that "the present delegation in Congress from this state are all my warm friends, except

Mr. Mallery [Representative Rollin Carolas Mallary of Rutland County]. They will of course give me their support." In ending, Van Ness apologized for writing without previously consulting anyone and carefully suggested that (emphasis in original) "if there is any impropriety in it, I must throw myself on your kindness to overlook it, and to attribute it to other motives than those of <u>designing</u> the least impropriety or disrespect." Whether he actually did not seek the assistance of others is not known, but on April 3, District Court judge Paine, setting aside any previously held reservations he might have had over the way he and Hutchinson had handled revenue receipts, stepped in to endorse him for the role. It could have been for any number of reasons, ranging from Buel's devastating descriptions of his past behavior; any number of personal failings he simply could not distance himself from; or his more recent involvement in litigation concerning land on Pennsylvania Avenue or those associated with his well-known, politically connected brothers, but Monroe ultimately declined the invitation, choosing instead secretary of the navy Smith Thompson of New York.[594]

Undeterred, Van Ness then turned his sights to higher state political office, becoming governor and remaining in office until 1826, when he became embroiled in the race for the Senate, seeking to replace incumbent Horatio Seymour. Despite whatever good will he might have garnered in the meantime, those making the final decision in Montpelier had the benefit of more particular knowledge of him—that he was "more careless than he was wise and prudent in provoking enmities," possessed of "careless predilections"—thereby causing "a mass of latent and smouldering [sic] hostility" to rise against him, resulting in Seymour's reelection.[595]

Down, but not out, in June 1829, Van Ness received a recess appointment (confirmed the following year) from President Andrew Jackson as the country's minister plenipotentiary and envoy extraordinary (a rank between ambassador and minister resident) to Spain, widely viewed as a sop for his prior service. His departure was gratefully noted by one St. Albans newspaper, "as it will for a few years relieve us from intrigues and machinations."[596] However, that assignment also became mired in its own controversy. Following Rhoda's death in 1834 during an outbreak of cholera in Madrid, according to his son James, Van Ness refused to erect any kind of headstone in her honor at the local graveyard and immediately began to carouse the local brothels. He finally settled in with, and eventually married, a Madalena Allus, and the two had a daughter, Mary Magdaline Christina, in 1836. James relates that the affair had been kept secret from Washington officials and that when Jackson learned of it, he became "excessively enraged," resulting in Van Ness being excluded from the mission, whereupon he "took leave" from his post in December of that year.[597] He returned to Vermont, became involved once again in state politics and later moved to New York City in 1841.

In March 1842, Congress began yet another investigation into Van Ness's conduct, this time looking into whether during his time in Spain he had "received a larger amount of money than he was entitled to receive by law, and what steps (if any) are necessary to recover back the money so improperly paid." The result of that inquiry is not recorded, but in 1844, President John Tyler appointed him as collector of the Port of New York, which post lasted but a year before Tyler lost faith in him and sought, and received, his resignation—a result obtained only after Van Ness tried to retract it.

Van Ness's brother, General John P. Van Ness, former mayor of the city of Washington, died in 1846, leaving an estate worth some $500,000, a substantial portion going to him. Now very wealthy, and following a difficult course of litigation over John's estate that generated substantial headlines and crowded courtrooms, Van Ness began to consider the distribution of his own assets, an effort that caused significant dissent and ill will within the family. James explained in 1849 that his father refused virtually all meaningful support for him and his brothers, Cornelius (who acted as his father's secretary during the Spanish mission and was an important participant in settling the raucous Texas frontier in the 1830s) and George, and sisters, Marcia (married to Britain's minister to the United States, Sir William Gore Ousley) and Cornelia (married to Judge James Roosevelt of the New York Supreme Court and great-uncle of Theodore Roosevelt). Whatever led to the split is not revealed, but James related that his father's interests no longer attended the needs of his Vermont-born children and now extended only to his Spanish family. In August 1851, Van Ness wrote out a short will naming Madalena and Christina as the sole beneficiaries of his entire estate, excepting a gold watch destined for son George. He died in Philadelphia on December 15, 1852.[598]

THE STORY OF CORNELIUS Peter Van Ness is indeed extraordinary. None of his constituents experienced close to the opportunities he encountered, and even if they had, their outcomes could not possibly have tracked his many successes. Coming from a family with so many high-level political connections recommending him for early advancement certainly afforded him a convenient stage on which to put his creative talents on display that might not otherwise have been available to him. His many flaws aside, he was perhaps the most remarkable person surviving the disruptions Vermont experienced between 1808 and 1815, problems that allowed him to exercise creative interpretations of the law in his ambitious pursuit of gain and fame while also displaying an unsettling inclination toward avarice.

Van Ness represents only one aspect of what was taking place. His sharp, legalistic mind may have been admirable for its ability to maneuver around troublesome issues, leading him to desired resolutions, but it also interfered with his ability to fully understanding the impact it had on others, at least in the early years. The law may have allowed for him to do something simply because it did not prohibit the act, as when he relentlessly pursued Buel's moieties, but in doing so, he failed to observe its countering, underlying spirit, which did not preclude the application of compassion. To be fair, these times did not necessarily recognize that equitable resolutions as sharp interpretations and practice were the accepted norm; albeit, Van Ness took those opportunities to higher levels than most others. He simply represented one extreme in a unique period of time, in an environment that fostered unremitting ambition. Perhaps he was the esteemed man later in life that history has painted him, but it was a reputation he grew into and certainly one he did not possess early on following his arrival in Vermont. "Scoundrel" might be too strong a word to characterize him for this particular time, but it is not far off.

With William Harrington, who both sued and defended so many and prosecuted those who offended, while also serving the less fortunate, voiceless blacks and women in the community, the differences could not be greater. For Van Ness, it was about winning at all costs, leaving the loser often wallowing in despair, while for Harrington, there was the other side of the law that allowed room for compassion. Van Ness bulled and bullied his way to the front, creating both admirers and enemies, while Harrington stood back, taking a much less aggressive stance. While he may not have gained the heady rewards of his counterpart, he certainly had the unyielding respect of many.

In these times when practical application of the letter of the law was so unsettled, Vermont became a showcase revealing its many inadequacies. When Thomas Jefferson launched his verbose embargo in December 1807, it constituted but a paper tiger, lacking virtually any threat of enforcement, let alone meaningful effect on either Britain or France. It required the appearance of dire problems that should have been considered before its passage to make its many inadequacies and misguided intentions known.

Few of the far-off bureaucrats in Washington appreciated the difficulties these policies posed, leaving the enforcers on the Vermont frontier to their own devices to create mechanisms to fulfill their overseers' directives. Short of manpower and desperately in need of intelligence concerning smugglers' intentions, the honorable Sam Buel, alone on Windmill Point, engaged others as deputies and informers, including some who later posed so many problems. Nathan Haswell constitutes one of the bright moments in these times because he demonstrated that, while personally ambitious as an inspector and businessman, it was not necessary to drop to the cutthroat level that some, such as Van Ness, sought to go.

Jefferson declared the area around Lake Champlain in a state of insurrection, but that was certainly an overblown assessment of the actual situation. His resort to such an inflammatory language, even if necessary to fulfill the dictates of the law allowing the call-up of the militia, together with the halting of all trade, marks the moment when Vermonters suddenly realized the existence of an intrusive, distant power. In their history as a state, they had never before experienced the fact that they could be told not to do something and that, if they did it, there would be consequences. So, in their fright, state officials rejected any intermediate measures to deal with the purported unrest and immediately summoned the militia. And in doing so, they made real a latent hatred many had for Jefferson's policies that might otherwise have never become known.

Jabez Penniman was certainly surprised at the call-up and had never anticipated Jefferson's proclamation. His report to Washington in April 1808 describing the existence of "combinations" along the border came only after he consulted with those two attorneys possessing the most intimate knowledge and experience with the lawless set: Van Ness and Aldis. They clearly had great insights worthy of attention into the intentions, and abilities, of smugglers through their many court cases representing them, and it is difficult to imagine that any of them ever thought the situation so bad as to constitute an insurrection. Yes, bands of men joined together to counterfeit, riot, assault and smuggle, but it was only that, certainly not a threat to the physical overthrow of government that an insurrection envisions. Theirs was simply an attempt to maintain a bare-knuckled level of existence selling their valuable commodities to nearby Canadians while utilizing long-established trade routes that, unfortunately for them, crossed an international border, playing an integral role in interfering with Jefferson's embargo.

But none of these things particularly mattered to the soldiers called out to enforce its provisions. St. Albans and Rutland troops responded readily to Governor Smith's call, and despite the various troubles within their own ranks, each contingency performed as well as could be expected under those challenging conditions. For the few men selected to venture out on the *Fly* in pursuit of the *Black Snake*, displaying their ensign and pendant or not, their unwelcome appearance in Burlington's Federalist enclave along the Onion River on August 3, 1808, could not have been more tragic. They certainly did not understand the true level of hatred that many along the river had for what they represented. There, they faced full on everything that these trying times brought, as young, desperate, drunk men, divided even among themselves about the rightness of their actions, fought to maintain possession of their boat while equally young troops struggled to satisfy the law's requirements and take it from their grasp while inflicting the least amount of harm possible. The fright that every man, whether soldier, smuggler or watching farmer, possessed that day was palpable. It was all, as witness Stephen Pearl Lathrop observed, a matter where "one is afraid and another is scared."

Local businessmen were similarly concerned by what the embargo meant for them. Their secret, nighttime counsel to the *Black Snake* crew to protect their boat from government interference might have been the most some were willing to do, but others went further to facilitate that opposition by providing the necessary ammunition, powder and alcohol to overcome lingering inhibitions, while promising the rising of hordes of others in their defense. The devastation wrought by Mott's big gun took the contest to an even higher level and violently jolted everyone involved into the new realities of what it meant to challenge government's authority here on the frontier.

Unfortunately, despite their best intentions, the rushed results obtained by state and federal prosecutors in the many criminal trials taking place over a compressed period of time were inconsistent and, for Cyrus Dean hanging at the end of a rope, irrational. The murdering Samuel Mott, also involved in rioting, assaulting and counseling another murderer to not cooperate with authorities, served a much-deserved nine-year sentence before dropping out of the historical record—this at a time when counterfeiters and sheep thieves received lengthy jail sentences while smugglers, and those involved in vicious assaults and forcible rescues of goods from officials, paid only fines. Meanwhile, good people such as Sam Buel and Nathan Haswell suffered inordinate discomfort because of ambitious others and onerous debt-related laws changed only many years later.

Following the tragedies of 1808, the problems hardly abated. Conflict continued in Europe, and that meant the implementation of yet additional restrictive trade policies seeking to maintain the country's neutrality following repeal of the embargo in 1809. As a result, Vermonters remained on the front lines, experiencing more of the same, made all the more dire by the havoc wrought from their ill-advised non-intercourse act passed in the months following Madison's declaration of war in June 1812. Without effective enforcement measures in place, the smuggling and death continued, and many on the border saw no reason to halt the trade they so dearly needed to survive, moving now into clearly treasonous conduct as they supplied provisions directly into the hands of the British army.

Federal troops arrived in Burlington to address their possible intrusion across the border and to assist civil authorities in halting the illicit trade. The national government stepped up its revenue-collecting efforts to pay for the woefully underfinanced war effort by significantly increasing the number of its employees engaged in that work around the state, generating further discord among the population. Great uncertainty ensued with inconsistent, and oftentimes overly aggressive, enforcement measures being taken, sometimes ending in death. Illegally constituted military courts, searches, seizures and detentions took place as unsettled questions concerning federal, state and martial law presented themselves, all demanding coherent resolution from a legal system itself in need of direction. These moments represented a violent awakening to Vermonters, revealing that, despite anyone's chimerical beliefs that they possessed some unique form of "independence" apart from others, in actuality, they were but a part of a much larger whole.

It took time for the smuggling to abate and become less obvious after 1815, but it never truly disappeared, lingering on to the present time. Now, it has become a more ominous prospect as not only tons of drugs and other contraband find their way into the United States but also human beings seeking freedoms not present in other parts of the world. It is a condition that will remain for as long as there are borders separating disparate economic and social conditions, allowing covetous eyes to indulge a "grass is greener" mentality. And as long as those borders exist, there will be those trying to maintain their integrity, even to the point of sacrificing their own lives.

Untitled Period Ballad

(AUTHOR UNKNOWN, CIRCA 1809)[599]

In the year eighteen hundred and eight,
The Embargo Law in Vermont state,
Did so enrage our furious Feds
They would cross the line or lose their heads.

Our rulers meant to be obeyed,
And sent some men to stop the trade;
Some of our soldiers did combine
In arms, to guard the northern line.

A smuggling set in the Black Snake,
Resolved to sail upon the lake,
They armed themselves to fight their way,
And thus they thought to win the day.

The men who laid this smuggling plot,
Was Sheffield, Mudgett, Dean and Mott,
And many more, who were not clever,
Spread out their sails on Onion River,

All for to load their boat again,
And then to sail across the line;

But soldiers were so well agreed,
Their plan did not so well succeed.

Our officers found where she lay,
The orders were, take her away;
The Revenue *was then sent on,*
Commanded by one Farrington.

And when this smuggling rebel crew,
Heard of the boat, the Revenue,
Unto the house of Joy's they went,
And there one night in private spent.

There each agreed upon a man,
And Mudgett took the sole command;
He, like a tory or a friend,
The lives of many meant to end.

To carry on this wicked deed,
With a large gun they did proceed,
And by the Snake *they made a stand,*
To guard the same stood on the land.

Then Farrington sailed from the lake,
And thus he to the rebels spake,
"Orders I have to take the Snake,
And all the smugglers on the lake."

This raised their blood, to arms they flew,
For to keep off the Revenue,
And execute this wicked deed,
That did from rebels' hearts proceed.

Then Mudgett gave the threatening word,
To all the men that was on board,
"The first that steps into the Snake,
A lifeless corpse of him I will make."

But Farrington feared not his threats,
Into the smuggler boat he steps;
There, like a warrior bold and brave,
His blood and honor thought to save.

Now let us turn and view the scheme,
And who begun this bloody scene;
It was Sheffield, with his Indian skill,
The crimson blood of Drake did spill.

With hearts unfeeling they went then,
To spill the blood of honest men;
Ormsby and Marsh then prostrate fell,
Before these wicked imps of hell,
And bold and warlike Farrington,
His crimson blood they caused to run.

These men were tried all for the same crime,
Why not alike their sentence find;
Dean was sentenced to the halter,
The rest convicted of manslaughter.

NOTES

ABBREVIATIONS

NARA: National Archives and Records Administration at Boston, Waltham, Massachusetts
UVM: Special Collections, University of Vermont, Burlington, Vermont
VHS: Vermont Historical Society, Barre, Vermont
VSARA: Vermont State Archives and Records Administration, Middlesex, Vermont

PREFACE

1. *United States v. William Greer aka "Thomas William Dodds," Stephen Hutchins, Thomas Cook aka "George Wright," Gregory Stevens, and Glen Koski*, Docket No. 2:95-CR-72, United States District Court for the District of Vermont.
2. Officer Down Memorial Page, United States Department of the Treasury, Customs Service, http://www.odmp.org/agency/3948-united-states-department-of-the-treasury-customs-service-us-government (accessed April 27, 2014).

CHAPTER 1

3. *State of Vermont v. Cyrus B. Dean*, August 1808 term, Chittenden County Supreme Court dockets and case files, 1794–1829, VSARA, *passim*.

4. *Moses Catlin v. Spafford, Chamberlin & Hallock*, February 1805 term; *Reuben Harmon v. Content C. Hallock & Eli Baker*, February 1808 term, Chittenden County Court judgments, 1806–1836, VSARA.

5. Rann, *History of Chittenden County*, 227.

6. American State Papers, Finance, 1:735; Innkeepers Licenses, 1791–1849, series A-123, VSARA; Hemenway, *Vermont Historical Gazetteer*, 870.

7. *Vermont Sentinel*, April 14, 1803; Stillwell, "Migration from Vermont," 109.

8. *Spooner's Vermont Journal*, March 6, 1804; *Middlebury Mercury*, February 6, 1805; *Rutland Herald*, March 21, 1807; *Middlebury Mercury*, April 6, 1809.

9. *John Broome & Son v. Daniel Staniford*, Chittenden County Court, February 1806 term, court judgments, VSARA.

10. *Vermont Sentinel*, December 9, 1807; February 24, 1808.

11. *State of Vermont v. Chittenden County*, January 1808 term, Chittenden County Supreme Court, VSARA.

12. Entry, Chittenden County Court, September 1803–February 1806, Vermont State Papers [hereafter VSP] 5:556, VSARA.

13. Stillwell, "Migration from Vermont," 95.

14. Fanis, *Secular Morality*, 76; Roth, *Democratic Dilemma*, 71–73.

15. Caledonia County Petition, dated October 24, 1807, Petitions, VSP 65, VSARA.

16. Sherman et al., *Freedom and Unity*, 143.

17. *The Lake Region of Western Vermont* (Morrisville: Vermont Bureau of Publicity, 1918), 15.

18. Samuel de Champlain, *Voyages of Samuel de Champlain, 1604–1618* (New York: Charles Scribner's Sons, 1907), 161–62.

19. Maria Jeannette Brookings Tuttle, *Three Centuries in Champlain Valley: A Collection of Historical Facts and Incidents* (Plattsburgh, NY: Saranac Chapter DAR, 1909), 179.

20. Michaela Stickney, Colleen Hickey and Roland Hoerr, "Lake Champlain Basin Program: Working Together Today for Tomorrow," *Lakes & Reservoirs: Research & Management* 6, no. 3 (September 2001): 213–17.

21. Albers, *Hands on the Land*, 168.

22. Chandler Parsons Anderson, *Northern Boundary of the United States* (Washington, D.C., 1906), 12.

23. Bemis, "Relations Between the Vermont Separatists," 557.

24. *Laws of the United States of America*, vol. 1 (New York: Childs and Swaine, 1795), 296–98.

25. *Records of the Governor and Council of the State of Vermont*, vol. 4 (Montpelier, VT: J. & J.M. Poland, 1876), 463–65.

26. Paul Leicester Ford, ed., *The Writings of Thomas Jefferson, 1792–1794*, vol. 6 (New York: G.P. Putnam's Sons, 1895), 99–100.

27. U.S. Circuit Court–VT Case Files, 1792–1869, NARA.

28. *Vermont Gazette (Bennington, VT)*, November 19, 1787.

29. Herbert P. Putnam, "Vermont Population Trends, 1790 to 1930, as Revealed in the Census Reports," *Proceedings of the Vermont Historical Society* 9, no. 2 (March 1941): 14–16; Sherman et al., *Freedom and Unity*, 627; Bassett, "Rise of Cornelius Peter Van Ness," 5; Stillwell, "Migration from Vermont," 125.

30. Williams, *Natural and Civil History*, 88.

31. Ibid., 87–89.

32. Williamson, *Vermont in Quandary*, 141–44, 156, 243.

33. Memorial of Levi Allen to Lord Sydney, May 4, 1789; Bemis, "Relations Between the Vermont Separatists," 554.

34. Donald Grant Creighton, *The Empire of the St. Lawrence* (Boston: Houghton Mifflin, 1958), 104.

35. Stanley Pargellis, ed., *Military Affairs in North America, 1748–1765* (New York: D. Appleton-Century Company, 1936), 70–71.

36. Stratton, *History of Alburgh, Vermont*, 326–28; Guy Omeron Coolidge, *The French Occupation of the Champlain Valley from 1609 to 1759* (Fleischmann, NY: Purple Mountain Press, 1999), 93–95; Hemenway, *Vermont Historical Gazetteer*, 488; *Wickwire v. Butler, Vorthrop*, December 1806 term, Franklin County Supreme Court, VSARA.

37. *Francis Childs v. Moses Catlin*, February 1808 term, Chittenden County court judgments; *Francis Childs v. Moses Catlin & Maynard Chamberlin*, September 1805 term, Chittenden County court judgments, VSARA; Williamson, *Vermont in Quandary*, 148.

38. E.W. Judd to John Johnson, April 13, 1810, John Johnson Collection, UVM.

39. Horace Greeley, *The Autobiography of Horace Greeley, or Recollections of a Busy Life* (New York: E.B. Treat, 1872), 57.

40. Albers, *Hands on the Land*, 156; Taylor, *Civil War of 1812*, 21.

41. Nathan Perkins, *A Narrative of a Tour Through the State of Vermont from April 27 to June 12, 1789* (Woodstock, VT: Elm Tree Press, 1920), 27; Hemenway, *Vermont Historical Gazetteer*, 517–18; Timothy Dwight, *Travels in New England*

and New York, vol. 2 (New Haven, CT: published by author, 1821), 425; Albers, *Hands on the Land*, 156.

42. Joseph Robert Cozzi, "The Lake Champlain Sailing Canal Boat," PhD diss. (Texas A&M University, 2000), 24.

43. John Lambert, *Travels through Lower Canada and the United States of North America in the Years 1806, 1807, and 1808*, vol. 1 (London: T. Gillet, 1810), 249.

44. Stratton, *History of Alburgh*, 265.

45. *Vermont Sentinel*, December 7, 1804.

46. Hemenway, *Vermont Historical Gazetteer*, 497.

47. Stratton, *History of the South Hero Island*, 721–22; Stratton, *History of Alburgh*, 208–11.

48. Muller, "Floating a Lumber Raft," 116–24; Muller, "Jay's Treaty," 40–41.

49. *Norfolk Repository* (Dedham, MA), January 5, 1808.

50. Stratton, *History of Alburgh*, 266; *Vermont Sentinel*, May 20, 1808; *Weekly Wanderer* (Randolph, VT), January 13, 1809; *Spooner's Vermont Journal* (Windsor, VT), December 14, 1807; *Rutland Herald* (Rutland, VT), April 30, 1808.

51. Wright, *Potash and Pine*, 52; *North Star* (Danville, VT), February 29 and June 18, 1808; Judith Lucey, "Celebrating Centuries of Food and Dining," *American Ancestors* (Fall 2013): 26–31.

52. *The Acts and Resolves, Public and Private, of the Province of the Massachusetts Bay*, vol. IV (Boston: Wright & Potter Co., 1890), 996–1,000.

53. *A Digest of Patents Issued by the United States from 1790 to January 1, 1839* (Washington, D.C.: Peter Force, 1840), 86.

54. David Townsend, *Principles and Observations Applied to the Manufacture and Inspection of Pot and Pearl Ashes* (Boston: Isaiah Thomas, 1793), 3, 9.

55. Williamson, *Vermont in Quandary*, 246.

56. *Columbian Sentinel* (Boston, MA), January 14, 1809; *Merrimack Intelligencer* (Haverill, MA), January 14, 1809; *Freeman's Friend* (Portland, ME), February 18, 1809.

57. Hugh Gray, *Letters from Canada, Written During a Residence There in the Years 1806, 1807, and 1808* (London: Longman, Hurst, Rees and Orme, 1809), 277–78.

58. *National Intelligencer* (Washington, D.C.), March 22, 1809.

CHAPTER 2

59. United States Department of the Treasury, *Report of the Secretary of the Treasury*, 4.

60. Ibid., 8.

61. Robert Fulton to Albert Gallatin, December 8, 1807; United States Department of the Treasury, *Report of the Secretary of the Treasury*, 117–23.

62. United States Department of the Treasury, *Report of the Secretary of the Treasury*, 127.

63. Sofka, "Jeffersonian Idea," 519–44.

64. Taylor, *Civil War of 1812*, 82, 118.

65. Ibid., 112.

66. Thomas Jefferson to John Taylor, January 6, 1808; Dumas Malone, *Jefferson the President: Second Term, 1805–1809*, vol. 5 (Boston: Little, Brown and Company, 1974), 483.

67. Wood, *Empire of Liberty*, 647–49.

68. Steele, "Thomas Jefferson," 830–31.

69. Congressional Record, *Proceedings and Debates of the 105th Congress Second Session*, vol. 144 (Washington, D.C.: Government Printing Office, 1998), 18:448.

70. *Public Statutes at Large of the United States of America*, vol. 1 (Boston: Little and Brown, 1845), 706; Futrell, *American Customs Jurisprudence*, 83.

71. Albert Gallatin to Senator W.B. Giles, November 24, 1808, *Annals of Congress*, Senate, 10th Congress, 2nd session, 233.

72. Gallatin to Madison, September 9, 1808, in Perkins, *Prologue to War*, 161.

73. Orrin Peer Allen, *The Allen Memorial, Second Series* (Palmer, MA: Fisk and Co., 1907), 258–59.

74. Udney Hay Papers, VHS.

75. Ibid.; Duffy, *Ethan Allen and His Kin*; *Jabez Penniman v. Silas Hathaway and Heman Allen*, Udney Hay Papers, VHS.

76. *Penniman v. Hathaway and Allen*.

77. Ibid.

78. Buel, *The Book*, 150; Stratton, *History of Alburgh*, 329–30.

79. Penniman, *Penniman Family*, 132.

80. Welles, *History of the Buell Family*, 63, 116.

81. Buel, *The Book*, 5, 151.

82. Stratton, *History of Alburgh*, 331.

83. American State Papers, *Finance*, 2:255–56.

84. *U.S. House Journal*, 20th Congress, 2nd session, February 26, 1829.

85. Bellico, *Sails and Steam*, 259.

86. Guy Catlin Papers, 1789–1873, UVM.

87. Hamilton Child, *Gazetteer and Business Directory of Chittenden County, Vermont for 1882–1883* (Syracuse, NY: The Journal, 1882), 151.

88. *Vermont Sentinel*, May 2, 1806; Nathan Haswell Papers, UVM.

89. *National Intelligencer and Washington Advertiser* (Washington, D.C.), August 10, 1807.

90. Ibid., January 20, 1808.

91. E.P. Walton, ed., *Records of the Governor and Council of the State of Vermont*, vol. 5 (Montpelier, VT: J and J.M. Poland, 1877), 182; *National Intelligencer*, January 20, 1808.

92. *Vermont Sentinel*, February 3, 1808.

93. *Gazette*, June 27, 1808; *The Supporter* (Chillicoth, OH), March 9, 1809.

94. Lionel Curtis, ed., *The Commonwealth of Nations*, pt. 1 (London: Macmillan and Co., 1916), 409.

95. McClellan, *Smuggling in the American Colonies*, 27.

96. Ibid., 58, 86.

97. Anonymous, "Smuggling in 1813–1814: A Personal Reminiscence," *Vermont History* 37, no. 1 (Winter 1970): 22–26.

98. *Political Observatory* (Walpole, NH), December 26, 1808.

99. Matthew Bacon, *A New Abridgment of the Law*, vol. IV (Dublin: Luke White, 1793), 523.

100. *Pittsburgh Gazette*, May 31, 1808.

101. *The Supporter*, April 13, 1809.

102. *United States v. Sheldon*, October 1814 term, U.S. Circuit Court, VT Docket entries, USCT-VT, NARA; 15 U.S. 119 (1817).

103. Buel, *The Book*, 115.

104. John Howe, "Howe's Journal," 264–70.

105. Mueller, "Floating a Lumber Raft," 116–24.

106. Papers of Cornelius Peter Van Ness, 1809–1827, VHS.

107. *The Supporter*, March 9, 1809.

108. *Pittsburgh Gazette*, August 31, 1808.

109. Muller, "Smuggling into Canada," 17.

110. John J. Duffy, Samuel B. Hand and Ralph H. Orth, *The Vermont Encyclopedia* (Lebanon, NH: University Press of New England, 2003), 79; Feeney, *Great Falls on Onion River*, 25–26; VSP, 43:170, VSARA; *Vermont Sentinel*, April 29, 1808.

111. *Vermont Sentinel*, November 20, 1806.

112. Ibid., December 30, 1807; Catlin & Jasper to Johnson, December 10, 1807, Papers of John Johnson, 1790–1842; Guy Catlin papers, UVM; Ward to

Catlin & Jasper, April 22, 1807, and December 20, 1810; Ames to Catlin & Jasper, Burlington Land Records, vols. 3:212, 4:102.

113. *Moses Catlin v. Daniel Staniford*, January term 1808, Chittenden County Supreme Court, VSARA.

114. *Daniel Farrand v. Moses Catlin & Guy Catlin*, August 21, 1808, Chittenden County Court, VSARA.

115. *Vermont Sentinel*, December 16, 1807; September 2, 1808.

116. *State of Vermont v. Samuel Fitch*, January 1807 term, Chittenden County Supreme Court, VSARA.

117. Rush, "Enquiry into the Effects," 335.

118. Stillwell, "Migration from Vermont," 109; *Vermont Intelligencer*, November 17, 1817; Wood, *Empire of Liberty*, 340.

119. Walter Hill Crockett, *Vermont, the Green Mountain State*, vol. 3 (New York: Century History Company, 1923), 154; *The World*, December 7, 1808; *Vermont Sentinel*, July 15, 1808; *The Reporter*, May 23, 1812; Hemenway, *Vermont Historical Gazetteer*, 1:870; Stillwell, "Migration from Vermont," 109.

120. *Vermont Sentinel*, January 20, 1808; September 2, 1808.

121. Ibid., February 10, 1809.

122. Ibid., June 18, 1806.

123. *United States v. A Certain Boat called the* Black Snake; *A Sloop & sixty-eight barrels of potashes; Red Boat and twenty-five barrels of potashes; Three bateaus & long canoe; Forty pieces of leather; Bateau and three barrels and one hogshead of potashes; Perogue and fifty-one barrels of potashes; Black boat and twenty barrels of potashes; Black boat and twenty-one barrels potashes; The Sloop* Hope, *alias The* Governor Craig; *Vessel called the* Fly *and twenty barrels potashes; Sloop and sixty-eight barrels potashes; Sloop* Dolphin *and sixty-six barrels potashes; Five barrels sugar*, U.S. District Court Dockets, October 1808 term, USDC-VT, NARA.

124. *United States v. Sloop* Hope, *alias* Governor Craig, October 1812 term, USCC-VT, NARA.

125. *U.S. v. Fifty-one barrels of potashes; Twenty-five barrels of potashes*, U.S. District Court Dockets, October 1810 term, DC-VT, NARA; *Vermont Mirror* (Middlebury, VT), April 21, 1813; *Vermont Sentinel*, June 24, 1814.

126. *U.S. v. Twenty-one barrels potashes; Sixty-eight barrels potashes; Twenty barrels potashes; Twenty barrels potashes*, U.S. District Court Dockets, May 1812 term, USDC-VT, NARA; Nathan Haswell Papers, UVM.

127. *Journals of the General Assembly of the State of Vermont…October 1808* (Bennington, VT: Anthony Haswell, 1809), 145.

128. *Reports of Cases Argued and Determined in the Supreme Court of the State of Vermont,* vol. 3 (St. Albans, VT: J. Spooner, 1832), 213.

129. Jesse S. Myer, *Life and Letters of Dr. William Beaumont* (St. Louis: C.V. Mosby Company, 1912), 31; Lewis Cass Aldrich, *History of Franklin and Grand Isle Counties, Vermont* (Syracuse, NY: D. Mason & Co., 1891), 260; *Vermont Sentinel,* February 4, 1807; *North Star,* September 5, 1807; *Gazette of Maine,* July 14, 1808.

130. *Lazarus Tousey v. Truman Powell,* September 1806 term; *Stephen Noble, Stephen Butler & Truman Powell v. Peter A. Schenck & Co.,* February 1808 term, Chittenden County Court Judgments, 1806–1836, VSARA.

131. *Journals of the General Assembly of the State of Vermont,* 40; *State v. Horatio Powell, David Tracey, Elijah Littlefield, Joseph Farnsworth, Benjamin Chandler, Truman Powell, Paul Eager,* December 1807 term, Franklin County Supreme Court, VSARA; Oliver S. Hayward and Constance E. Putnam, *Improve, Perfect, & Perpetuate: Dr. Nathan Smith and Early American Medical Education* (Hanover, NH: University Press of New England, 1998), 86–101.

132. Dutcher, *History of St. Albans,* 345; *Vermont Sentinel,* November 13, 1806; *Acts and Laws Passed by the Legislature of the State of Vermont…October 1809* (Randolph, VT: Sereno Wright, 1809), 83–84.

133. *Gazette of Maine,* November 14, 1805.

134. Eliakim Persons Walton, *Records of the Governor and Council of the State of Vermont,* vol. 4 (Montpelier, VT: J & J.M. Poland, 1876), 531.

135. *Post Boy* (Windsor, VT), October 8, 1805.

136. *Samuel Mix v. Samuel Plumb,* January 1806 term, Chittenden County Supreme Court, VSARA; VSP, 49:103; 50:36; 55:19; 74:84; VSARA, passim; *Rutland Herald,* May 30, 1807.

137. *Rutland Herald,* February 21, 1807.

138. *Paul Dodge v. Alpheus Hale & Samuel Mix,* September 1805 term; *Enos Brown v. Samuel Mix,* September 1807 term, Chittenden County Court judgments, 1806–1836, VSARA.

139. *State v. Bradley Wilson, State v. Moses Wilson, State v. Richard Wheeler,* January 1808 term, Chittenden County Supreme Court, VSARA.

140. *Spooner's Vermont Journal,* February 22, 1808; *Rutland Herald,* October 10, 1807; *Journals of the General Assembly of the State of Vermont…October 1808,* 34; Certificate from Amesa Howe, January 27, 1811; Certificate from Joseph Gillotson and John Leonard, Park-McCullough Papers, Box 100C, UVM; Williamson, *Vermont in Quandary,* 254; *North Star,* February 22, 1808; Israel Grovenor Petition, October 20, 1808,

Petitions to the General Assembly, 1806–1808, VSP, vol. 46; Jabez Burnham Petition, October 10, 1808, Depositions, October 1808–September 1831, VSARA.

141. Paul S. Gillies, *Uncommon Law, Ancient Roads, and Other Ruminations on Vermont Legal History* (Barre: Vermont Historical Society, 2013), xvi.

142. Roth, *Democratic Dilemma,* 21; H.J. Conant, "Imprisonment for Debt in Vermont: A History," *Proceedings of the Vermont Historical Society* 19, no. 2 (April 1951): 68–69.

143. William Slade Jr., *The Laws of Vermont of a Publick and Permanent Nature* (Windsor, VT: Simeon Ide, 1825), 200–06.

144. *Vermont Sentinel,* September 2, 1807.

145. Ibid., December 30, 1807.

146. Rann, *History of Chittenden County,* 158–59.

147. *Daniel Staniford v. Elias Buel, et.al.,* September 1806–February 1811 term, Chittenden County Court, VSARA.

148. *Daniel Staniford v. The Inhabitants of Chittenden County,* September 1808 term, Chittenden County Court, VSARA.

149. Appointments, Chittenden County Court Records, 5:557–60, VSARA.

150. *Daniel Staniford v. Benjamin Adams,* September 1809 term, Chittenden County Court, VSARA.

151. Slade, *Laws of Vermont,* 225.

152. *Darius Jacques v. Joseph Griswold* in *Reports of Cases Argued and Determined in the Supreme Court of Judicature of the State of Vermont,* vol. 2 (New York: L. Riley, 1810), 235.

153. Depositions of Major Amos Morrill and Alfred Hathaway, Franklin County Court files, 1798–1806, Henry Sheldon Museum, Middlebury, VT.

154. Slade, *Laws of Vermont,* 234.

155. *Indictment of the Gaol in Burlington,* January 1809 term, June 1818 term, June 1819 term, June 1820 term, January 1821 term, January 1822 term, January 1823 term, January 1825 term, Supreme Court of Judicature, VSARA; Wm. C. Harrington to Heman Allen, August 15, 1809, Papers of John Johnson, 1790–1842, UVM; *Woodstock Observer,* March 13, 1821.

156. *Vermont Sentinel,* December 2, 1807.

157. *New England Palladium* (Boston, MA), December 1, 1807.

158. *Spooner's Journal,* November 30, 1807; *Rutland Herald,* February 6, 1808; *Journals of the General Assembly of the State of Vermont…1807,* 277–79; *The Laws of the State of Vermont,* vol. II (Randolph, VT: Serano Wright, 1808), 401–03.

159. Constitution of the State of Vermont, ch. II, sec. 64.

160. Woody Holton, *Unruly Americans and the Origins of the Constitution* (New York: Hill and Wang, 2007), 43–44.

161. Windsor Prison architectural drawings and documentation, circa 1806–1808, MAP A-35.5, VSARA; *Journals of the General Assembly of the State of Vermont, 1807* (Randolph, VT: Sereno Wright, 1807), 202–03; Rewards, VSP, 78:1–2, VSARA.

162. *Rutland Historical Society Quarterly* 30, no. 1 (2000): 3–4; *Washingtonian*, February 11, 1811.

163. *Bee* (Hudson, NY), December 1, 1807; *Middlebury Mercury*, October 28, 1807; *Spooner's Vermont Journal*, October 5, 1807; *Rutland Herald*, July 11, 1807; June 11, 1808; October 29, 1808; *North Star*, July 23, 1808; Petitions, VSP, vol. 65, VSARA; Joseph Armington petition, October 20, 1808, Petitions to the General Assembly, 1806–1808, VSARA.

164. *Journals of the General Assembly of the State of Vermont...October 1808*, 466–70.

165. Russell, *Authentic History*, 15.

166. *Middlebury Mercury*, August 24, 1808.

167. Ibid., September 28, 1808.

168. Russell, *Authentic History*, 138.

169. Ibid., 25.

170. *Elnathan Keyes v. Theophilus Morrill*, February 1807 term, Chittenden County Court Judgments, VSARA.

171. Vermont State Prison, Index of Prisoners, 1809–1975, June 1809, VSARA; Stratton, *History of Alburgh*, 67; VSP, 46:134, VSARA.

172. *State v. Ryan, et. al.*; *State v. Morrill, et. al.*; *Samuel Holton v. Zenos Clark, Medad Lyman, Amos Morrill, Jr.; Stevens v. Crane*, December 1807 term, Franklin County Supreme Court, VSARA; *Journals of the General Assembly of the State of Vermont...October 1808*, 40.

173. *Pittsburgh Gazette*, April 19, 1808; McMaster, *History of the People*, 286.

174. Penniman letter, January 11, 1808, Nathan Haswell Papers, 1805–1810, UVM.

175. *State v. Sael Bumpers, State v. Daniel Carey*, May 1808 term, Chittenden County Supreme Court, VSARA.

176. *State v. Beriah Cleeland, State v. Joseph Hurlburt, Jonas Nye, Samuel Lewis*, May 1808 term, Chittenden County Supreme Court, VSARA.

Chapter 3

177. *Vermont Sentinel*, April 29, 1808.

178. *Rutland Herald*, April 23, 1808; *Vermont Sentinel*, April 22, 1808.

179. *Vermont Sentinel*, April 15, 1808.

180. Dutcher, *History of St. Albans*, 323.

181. Peyton Farrell Miller, *A Group of Great Lawyers of Columbia County, New York* (N.p.: privately printed, 1904), 128–37; Hemenway, *Vermont Historical Gazetteer*, 1:609.

182. Ibid.; William Raymond, *Biographical Sketches of the Distinguished Men of Columbia County* (Albany, NY: Weed, Parsons and Co., 1851), 34–35; John Wood, *A Correct Statement of the…Administration of John Adams* (New York: G.F. Hopkins, 1802), 45–46; Van Ness, *Examination*; *Daily Advertiser* (New York, NY), September 24, 1803; *Albany Register*, March 16, 1804; *Bee*, April 23, 1805; Hemenway, *Vermont Historical Gazetteer*, 1:609.

183. Entry, December 17, 1806, December term, Franklin County Supreme Court, VSARA.

184. John Whittemore, "The Autobiography of John Whittemore, 1796–1885," *Proceedings of the Vermont Historical Society* 6, no. 4 (December 1938): 327–28.

185. Unsigned letter, September 23, 1849, from New Orleans, Papers of Cornelius Peter Van Ness, 1809–1827, VHS.

186. Hemenway, *Vermont Historical Gazetteer*, 2:475.

187. Penniman to Haswell, May 8, 1808, Nathan Haswell Papers, UVM.

188. *The Reporter* (Brattleboro, VT), May 21, 1808.

189. *St. Albans Advisor*, April 21, 1808.

190. *Vermont Centinel*, April 15, 1808.

191. Ibid., April 22, 1808.

192. Ibid., May 6, 1808.

193. Notice, M. Woolsey, April 24, 1808, Nathan Haswell Papers, UVM.

194. Marvin A. Kreidberg and Merton G. Henry, "History of Military Mobilization in the United States Army, 1775–1945," Department of the Army, pamphlet 20–212 (November 1955): 30–40.

195. Malone, *Jefferson the President*, 518.

196. U.S. Statutes at Large, 1:424.

197. Kreidberg and Henry, "History of Military Mobilization," 30.

198. John Ferling, *A Leap in the Dark: The Struggle to Create the American Republic* (Oxford, UK: Oxford University Press, 2003), 372–74.

199. Jefferson to Rodney, April 24, 1808, in Paul Leiscester Ford, ed., *The Works of Thomas Jefferson*, vol. 11 (New York: G.P. Putnam's Sons, 1905), 30.

200. Jefferson to Gallatin, April 19, 1808, in Thomas Jefferson, *The Writings of Thomas Jefferson*, vol. 5 (Washington, D.C.: Taylor and Maury, 1853), 271.

201. Ibid.

202. Insurrectionary Combinations in the Neighborhood of Lake Champlain, November 30, 1808, American State Papers: Miscellaneous, 1:940.

203. Penniman to Haswell, May 8, 1808, Nathan Haswell Papers, UVM.

204. Ibid., Notice, M. Woolsey, April 24, 1808.

205. U.S. Statutes at Large, 1:499–502.

206. *The Reporter*, August 27, 1808.

207. *New Bedford Mercury* (New Bedford, MA), May 27, 1808.

208. Haswell to Penniman, May 2, 1808; Penniman to Haswell, May 3, 1808, Nathan Haswell Papers, UVM.

209. *The Reporter*, May 21, 1808.

210. *Rutland Herald*, May 14, 1808; *St. Albans Advisor*, July 14, 1808.

211. *St. Albans Advisor*, May 5, 1808.

212. Penniman to Haswell, May 8, 1808, Nathan Haswell Papers, UVM.

213. Haswell work records, July–September 1807 and April–September 1808, Nathan Haswell Papers, UVM.

214. *Peaslee & Haswell v. Abraham Hollenbeck*, September 1808 term, Chittenden County Court judgments, VSARA.

215. *United States v. Nathan B. Haswell*, May term 1811, U.S. District Court, Vermont, USDC-VT, NARA.

216. Penniman to Haswell, May 8, 1808, Nathan Haswell Papers, UVM.

217. *The World*, June 13, 1808.

218. *New Bedford Mercury*, May 27, 1808.

219. *St. Albans Advisor*, July 14, 1808.

220. McMaster, *History of the People*, 304.

221. Heman Allen to John Johnson, May 22, 1808, Papers of John Johnson, 1790–1842, UVM.

222. *National Intelligencer*, May 23, 1808; *Maryland Gazette*, May 26, 1808.

223. *Middlebury Mercury*, June 1, 1808.

224. Gallatin to Jefferson, May 28, 1808, Henry Adams, ed., *The Writings of Albert Gallatin*, vol. 1 (Philadelphia: J.B. Lippincott & Co., 1879), 390–97.

225. James Sullivan to Thomas Jefferson, January 7, 1808, in Louis Martin Sears, *Jefferson and the Embargo* (Durham, NC: Duke University Press, 1927), 58.

226. *Spooner's Vermont Journal*, June 2, 1808.

227. *New York Herald*, June 22, 1808.

228. Ibid.

229. *Pittsburgh Gazette*, May 31, 1808; Penniman to Haswell, May 19, 1808, Nathan Haswell Papers, UVM.

230. *Middlebury Mercury*, June 1, 1808.

231. *North American* (Baltimore, MD), July 30, 1808.

232. *Maryland Gazette*, April 2, 1807; March 8, 1809.

233. Williams, *Natural and Civil History*, 2:413–14.

234. Larned Lamb, *The Militia's Guide: Exhibiting a More Comprehensive Explanation, Than Before Published, of the Posts and Duties of the Several Officers on a Review, from a General to a Sergeant, Designed for the Instruction of a Young and Undisciplined Militia* (Montpelier, VT: Samuel Gross, 1807), 3–4.

235. *The Reporter*, August 27, 1808; Aldrich, *History of Franklin and Grand Isle Counties*, 332.

236. *The Reporter*, August 27, 1808.

CHAPTER 4

237. Pratt to Adjutant General Alexander Macomb, July 19, 1812, Letters Received by the Adjutant General, 1805–1821, NARA, Roll 0014, Folder 1857.

238. Malone, *Jefferson the President*, 519; *Albany Gazette*, July 14, 1808.

239. *The Pension Roll of 1835*, vol. 1 (Baltimore, MD: Genealogical Publishing Co., Inc., 1968), 848.

240. Benjamin Pratt testimony, *United States v. Frederick Hoxie, et. al.*, October 1808 term, U.S. Circuit Court, USCC-VT, NARA.

241. Hiram Carleton, *Genealogical and Family History of the State of Vermont*, vol. 1 (New York: Lewis Publishing Co., 1903), 28–29; Walter Thorpe, *History of Wallingford, Vermont* (Rutland, VT: Tuttle Co., 1911), 55.

242. Jacob Houghton to A. Miller, September 28, 1805, Alexander Miller Letters, Orders, Bills, &c., VHS.

243. Houghton to Miller, May 23, 1802, Alexander Miller Papers, 1797–1829, Park-McCullough Collection, UVM.

244. Fred Fuller to Miller, December 21, 1805, Alexander Miller Papers, 1797–1829, Park-McCullough Collection, UVM.

245. Orders, May 23 and 24, 1808, Alexander Miller Letters, Orders, Bills, &c., VHS; Orderly Book, First Company, Second Brigade, Second Division of Vermont Militia, 1801–1830, Squadron Orders, May 24, 1808, Rutland Historical Society.

246. *Rutland Herald*, May 28, 1808.

247. Ibid., June 4, 1808.

248. Stratton, *History of Alburgh, Vermont*, 67.

249. *Elizabeth Hoxie v. Job Hoxie*, December 1817 term, Chittenden County Supreme Court, VSARA.

250. Hemenway, *Vermont Historical Gazetteer*, 2:491.

251. Ibid., 344; Thompson, *History of Vermont*, 117.

252. *St. Albans Advisor*, August 4, 1808; *The Trial of Cyrus B. Dean, for the Murder of Jonathan Ormsby and Asa Marsh, before the Supreme Court of Judicature of the State of Vermont, at their Special Sessions, begun and Holden at Burlington, Chittenden County, on the 23rd of August, A.D., 1808* (Burlington, VT: Samuel Mills, 1808), 28.

253. Penniman affidavit, August 9, 1808, *United States v. John Taylor, et. al.*, October 1808 term, USCC-VT, NARA.

254. *The World*, June 13, 1808; *Spooner's Vermont Journal*, June 20, 1808.

255. Alexander to Lucretia Miller, June 3, 1808, Alexander Miller Letters, Orders, Bills, &c., VHS.

256. *Middlebury Mercury*, June 1 and 8, 1808.

257. *Spooner's Vermont Journal*, June 20, 1808.

258. Alexander to Lucretia Miller, June 6, 1808, Alexander Miller Letters, Orders, Bills, &c., VHS.

259. Lucretia to Alexander Miller, June 4, 1808, Alexander Miller Papers, 1797–1829, Park-McCullough Collection, UVM.

260. Alexander to Lucretia Miller, June 2, 1808, Alexander Miller Letters, Orders, Bills, &c., VHS.

261. Ibid., June 7, 1808.

262. Ibid., June 6, 1808.

263. Ibid., June 7, 1808.

264. *The Reporter*, June 3 and 11, 1808.

265. *Pittsburgh Gazette*, May 31, 1808.

266. *Vermont Sentinel*, June 3, 1808.

267. *The Reporter*, June 18, 1808.

268. *Maryland Gazette*, May 19, 1808; *The Reporter*, May 21, 1808.

269. *National Intelligencer*, June 24, 1808.

270. Williams to Miller, June 9, 1808, Alexander Miller Letters, Orders, Bills &c., VHS.

271. *United States v. John Taylor, Ezekiel Taylor; United States v. Frederick Hoxie*, October 1808 term, May term 1809, U.S. Circuit Court, USCC-VT, NARA.

272. Ibid.

273. *Rutland Herald,* June 18, 1808; *Gazette,* June 27, 1808.

274. *United States v. Frederick Hoxie, et. al.,* October 1808 term, U.S. Circuit Court, USCC-VT, NARA, *passim; Commercial Advisor,* June 25, 1808; *Boston Commercial Gazette,* July 4, 1808.

275. "Payroll of Capt. Benjn. Pratts Company of infantry…," Alexander Miller Letters, Orders, Bills, &c., VHS.

276. Lucretia to Alexander Miller, July 12, 1808, Alexander Miller Papers, 1797–1829, Park-McCullough Collection, UVM.

277. *Spooner's Vermont Journal,* July 4, 1808.

278. *Columbian Phoenix* (Providence, RI), August 3, 1808.

279. *Middlebury Mercury,* June 22, 1808.

280. *United States v. Frederick Hoxie, et. al.,* October 1808 term, U.S. Circuit Court, USCC-VT, NARA.

281. *St. Albans Advisor,* July 14, 1808.

282. *The Reporter,* July 9, 1808.

283. *United States v. Joseph Tinkham,* October 1808 term, U.S. Circuit Court, USCC-VT, NARA.

284. Solomon Miller to Lucretia Miller, June 8, 1808, Thomas Towner to A. Miller, June 7, 1808, Alexander Miller Papers, 1797–1829, Park-McCullough Collection, UVM.

285. Houghton to Miller, June 13, 1808, Alexander Miller Papers, VHS.

286. Reward notice, July 23, 1808; "Payroll of Capt. Benjn. Pratts Company of infantry…," Alexander Miller Letters, Orders, Bills, &c., VHS.

287. Miller Deposition, 1814, Alexander Miller Papers, 1797–1829, Park-McCullough Collection, UVM.

288. Alexander to Lucretia Miller, June 13, 1808, Alexander Miller Letters, Orders, Bills, &c., VHS.

289. Lucretia to Alexander Miller, June 12, 1808, Alexander Miller Papers, 1797–1829, Park-McCullough Collection, UVM.

290. T. Miller to A. Miller, June 17, 1808, Alexander Miller Papers, 1797–1829, Park-McCullough Collection, UVM.

291. Williams to Miller, June 20, 1808, Alexander Miller Letters, Orders, Bills, &c., VHS.

292. Reward notice, July 23, 1808, VHS.

293. *St. Albans Advisor,* August 18, 1808.

294. Ibid., July 21, 1808.

295. Ibid.

296. Ibid., July 14, 1808.

297. Ibid., June 23, 1808.

298. *The World*, July 4, 1808.

299. *Maryland Gazette*, May 26, 1808.

300. *Rutland Herald*, July 30, 1808.

301. A. Miller to L. Miller, June 18 and 25, 1808, Alexander Miller Letters, Orders, Bills, &c., VHS.

302. *Albany Gazette*, July 14, 1808.

303. Receipt, signed N.B. Haswell, June 24, 1808, Nathan Haswell Papers, UVM.

304. Hurd, *History of Clinton and Franklin Counties*, 48.

305. Nathan Haswell Papers, UVM; *The Reporter*, July 9, 1808.

306. *St. Albans Advisor*, June 23, 1808.

307. Silas Hamilton to A. Miller, July 23, 1808, and Captain Benjamin Pratt payroll ending July 31, 1808, Alexander Miller Letters, Orders, Bills, &c., VHS.

308. Receipt, Alexander Miller Letters, Orders, Bills, &c., VHS.

309. Penniman affidavit, August 9, 1808, *United States v. John Taylor, et. al.*, October 1808 term, U.S. Circuit Court, USCC-VT, NARA.

310. *Rutland Herald*, July 30, 1808.

311. Alexander to Lucretia Miller, July 2, 1808, Alexander Miller Letters, Orders, Bills, &c., VHS.

312. *Rutland Herald*, July 23, 1808.

313. L. Miller to A. Miller, July 2, 1808, Alexander Miller Papers, 1797–1829, Park-McCullough Collection, UVM; A. Miller to L. Miller, July 8, 1808, Alexander Miller Letters, Orders, Bills, &c., VHS.

314. Reward notice, July 23, 1808; "Payroll of Capt. Benjn. Pratts Company of infantry…," Alexander Miller Letters, Orders, Bills, &c., VHS; Blunt confession, August 16, 1808, Alexander Miller Letters, Orders, Bills, &c., VHS.

315. *Rutland Herald*, June 25, 1808; A. Miller to L. Miller, July 13, 1808, Alexander Miller Letters, Orders, Bills, &c., VHS.

316. Reward notice, July 23, 1808; Wm. Fox to Miller, July 21, 1808, Alexander Miller Letters, Orders, Bills, &c., VHS; *Rutland Herald*, July 23, 1808.

317. S. Hamilton to Alexander Miller, July 23, 1808, Alexander Miller Letters, Orders, Bills, &c., VHS.

318. Penniman statement, July 22, 1808, Alexander Miller Letters, Orders, Bills, &c., VHS.

319. Thomas Miller to A. Miller, October 1, 1808, Alexander Miller Papers, 1797–1829, Park-McCullough Collection, UVM.

320. Miller to Bostwick, September 1, 1808; Randall statement, undated; Penniman statement, July 22, 1808, Major William's order, July 23, 1808, Alexander Miller Letters, Orders, Bills, &c., VHS.

321. *United States v. One Boat called the Black Snake*, U.S. District Court Docket, May 1809 term, USDC-VT, NARA.

322. Hemenway, *Vermont Historical Gazetteer*, 2:344; *North Star*, July 30, 1808; *Gazette of Maine Hancock Advisor*, July 28, 1808.

323. *The World*, July 25, 1808.

324. Jefferson, *Writings*, 9:275.

325. Malone, *Jefferson the President:*, 603; Wood, *Empire of Liberty*, 654; Gallatin, *Writings*, 397, 403.

326. *Pittsburgh Gazette*, June 28, 1808.

327. Payroll ending July 31, 1808, Benj. Pratt Company, Alexander Miller Letters, Orders, Bills, &c., VHS.

CHAPTER 5

328. Hemenway, *Vermont Historical Gazetteer*, 1:498.

329. William C. Harrington lawyer's account book, 1799–1814, Large Bound Manuscript, UVM, passim; Burlington Records of Town Meetings, 1787–1820, vol. 1, Fletcher Free Library, Burlington, VT, passim.

330. First and Second Census of the United States, 1790, 1800, Records of the Bureau of Census, NARA, Washington, D.C.

331. *Spooner's Vermont Journal*, March 8, 1791; Rann, *History of Chittenden County*, passim; *Journals of the General Assembly of the State of Vermont, 1808*, 144; *Columbian Patriot*, August 3, 1814.

332. Alden M. Rollins, *Vermont Warnings Out*, vol. II (Camden, ME: Picton Press, 1995), passim.

333. Harrington to Sawyer, February 11, 1802, no. 802161, Sheldon Museum, Middlebury, VT.

334. Chittenden County Court Judgments, 1806–1836, VSARA, passim; *Vermont Sentinel*, August 20, 1806.

335. Prince Robinson pension file, no. R8894, Revolutionary War Pension and Bounty-Land Warrant Application Files, 1800–1900, NARA, Pub. No. M804, roll no. 2067.

336. *Journals of the Adjourned Session of the Legislature of the State of Vermont…1804* (Windsor, VT: Alden Spooner, 1804), 74.

337. Nathan Haswell Papers, UVM.

338. *Vermont Sentinel*, Aprril 15, 1808.

339. *Harrington v. Samuel Johnson*, December 1807 term; *Harrington v. Burbank, et. al., Harrington v. Green, et. al., Harrington v. Cole, et. al.*, January 1808 term; *Harrington v. James Sawyer*, September 1809 term; *Harrington v. Elijah Herrick*, May 1809 term; *Staniford v. Newell*, September 1809 term, Chittenden County Judgments, 1806–1836, VSARA.

340. *Harrington v. Staniford; Harrington v. James Heaton, James Heaton, Jr.; Harrington v. Sawyer, et. al.*, September 1808 term; *Sax v. Bennett; Sax v. Staniford; Miller v. Staniford*, Chittenden County Judgments, 1806–1836, VSARA.

341. Nathan Haswell Papers, UVM; "*Black Snake* Affair" papers, 1805–1809, MSA 263, VHS, passim; *Trial of Cyrus B. Dean*, passim.

342. Nathan Haswell Papers, UVM; Stratton, *History of Alburgh*, 59; Buel, *The Book*, 18–20.

343. N.B. Haswell Memorandum, Nathan Haswell Papers, UVM.

344. *United States v. John Taylor; United States v. Ezekiel Taylor*, May 1809 term, USCC-VT, NARA; Penniman affidavit, August 9, 1808, *United States v. John Taylor, et. al.*, October 1808 term, U.S. Circuit Court, USCC-VT, NARA.

345. *Vermont Sentinel*, August 12, 1808; May 25, 1810.

346. *Public Statutes at Large*, vol. 1:700; Anne Saba, "Tradition, Service, Honor: The Customs Ensign," *U.S. Customs Today*, January 2000, http://www.cbp.gov/custoday/jan2000/tradtn.htm (accessed January 12, 2014).

347. *Public Statutes at Large*, 1:700–01.

348. Ibid., 316.

349. Guillaume LeBlond, *The Military Engineer: or, A Treatise on the Attack and Defense of All Kinds of Fortified Places* (London, 1750), 7, 108.

350. "*Black Snake* Affair" Papers, 1805–1809, MSA 263, VHS, passim.

351. *Silas Hathaway v. Samuel Mix*, December 1811 term, Franklin County Court, VSARA.

352. *Francis Ledgard Statement*, October 21, 1811, VSP, 78:5, VSARA.

353. January 30, 1809 warning out list, *Burlington Records of Town Meetings*, March 26, 1798, 1:293; Baker to Hurlbert, Pearl & Peaslee, *Burlington Land Records*, March 30, 1798; Pearl, Hurlert, Peaslee to Tuttle, December 17, 1811; April 13, 1814, 2:243–44; Jacob Ormsby to Van Ness, May 26, 1814; Penniman to Van Ness, January 19, 1815; Staniford to Van Ness, June 2, 1812; Catlin to Van Ness, 5:36, 67–68, 83, 158.

354. Indictments, Town of Chittenden, Town of Essex, Chittenden County Court Records, 8:529, VSARA.

355. Petition of Charles Sheffield, October 23, 1813, 50:49, VSARA.

CHAPTER 6

356. *United States v. An Old Sloop and Sixty-eight barrels of potashes*, Oct. term, 1808, U.S. District Court, USDC-VT, case files, 1791–1906, NARA; *Moses Catlin v. Theophilus Morrill*, September term 1808, Chittenden County Court dockets and judgments, 1788–1840, VSARA; *Vermont Sentinel*, August 5, 1808; *Catlin & Jasper v. Justus Warner*, September 1811 term, Chittenden County Court documents and judgments, VSARA.

357. *Vermont Sentinel*, August 26, 1808.

358. Taylor, *Civil War of 1812*, 343, 268.

359. *Acts Passed by the Legislature of the State of Vermont at Their October Session, 1821* (Middlebury, VT: Copeland and Allen, 1821), 110.

360. Louis Stoughton Drake, *The Drake Family in England and America, 1360–1895: and the Descendants of Thomas Drake of Weymouth, Massachusetts* (Boston, 1896), 87.

361. *State of Vermont v. David Sheffield, et. al.*, Chittenden County Supreme Court dockets and case files, 1794–1829, VSARA.

362. Jonathan Ormsby service record, Compiled Service Records of Soldiers Who Served in the American Army During the Revolutionary War, NARA, Publication No. 881, Record Group 93, Catalogue No. 570910; *Ira Allen, Administrator of Ethan Allen against Gideon and Jonathan Ormsby*, Reports of Cases…in the *Supreme Court of Judicature of the State of Vermont*, 1:345.

363. *State v. Cyrus B. Dean, et. al.*, August1808 term, Chittenden County Supreme Court dockets and case files, 1794–1829, VSARA.

364. Inquisition, December 1808 term, Vermont Supreme Court, Franklin County, 2:190, VSARA.

365. David Russell affidavit, October 22, 1808, 78:3, VSARA.

366. Russell attestation, September 10, 1808, *State v. Cyrus B. Dean, et. al.*, August 1808 term, Chittenden County Supreme Court dockets and case files, 1794–1829, VSARA.

367. Seeley Bennett expenses, September 1, 1808, James Cummings invoice, August 3, 1808, *State v. Dean, et. al.*, VSARA; *John Taylor v. Jabez Penniman*, October 1808 term, U.S. District Court, USCC-VT files, NARA.

368. Asa Bulkley invoice, October 21, 1808, *State v. Dean, et. al.*, VSARA; *Vermont Sentinel*, August 5, 1808; *State v. Dean, et. al.*, August 1808 term, Chittenden County Supreme Court dockets and case files, 1794–1829, VSARA.

369. *Journals of the General Assembly of the State of Vermont, 1808*, 144.

370. Youngman invoice, August 16, 1808, Nathan Haswell Papers, UVM; Youngman invoice, undated, Staniford invoice, undated, *State v. Dean, et. al.*, VSARA.

371. "*Black Snake* Affair" Papers, 1805–1809, MSA 263, VHS.

372. *Laws of the State of Vermont*, vols. 1–2, ch. 24, 257.

373. Nathan Haswell expenses, Nathan Haswell Papers, UVM.

374. William C. Harrington lawyer's account book, UVM; *Farmer's Cabinet*, August 16, 1808.

375. Letter, Haswell to Penniman, October 4, 1808, Nathan Haswell Papers, UVM.

376. *Rutland Herald*, August 13, 1808; *Middlebury Mercury*, August 31, 1808; *The World*, August 8 and 23, 1808; *The Reporter*, August 20, 1808; *Rutland Herald*, September 23, 1809.

377. *Rutland Herald*, September 23, 1809.

378. *St. Albans Advisor*, August 18, 1808.

CHAPTER 7

279. *Records of the Governor and Council of the State of Vermont*, 1:174

380. *Records of the Grand Lodge of Free and Accepted Masons of the State of Vermont* (Burlington, VT: Free Press Assoc., 1879), passim; By-laws of North Star Lodge, No. 2, and Records of Hiram Lodge, No. 8, courtesy of Grand Lodge of Free and Accepted Masons, Barre, VT; H.L. Haywood, *Well-Springs of American Freemasonry: A Historian Looks at Our Forty-Nine Grand Lodges* (Silver Springs, MD, Masonic Service Association, 1953), 44.

381. *The World*, July 11, 1808; August 22, 1808.

382. Buel to Haswell, August 5, 1808, Nathan Haswell Papers, UVM.

383. Haswell invoice, July 27, 1809, Nathan Haswell Papers, UVM.

384. Letter, Buel to Haswell, August 13, 1808, Nathan Haswell Papers, UVM.

385. Malone, *Jefferson the President*, 519.

386. Jefferson to Governor Daniel Tompkins, August 15, 1808, in Jefferson, *Writings*, vols. 11–12, 131.

387. *U.S. v. Taylor, et.al.*, October 1808 term, U.S. Circuit Court, USCC-VT, NARA.

388. *Harrington v. Azariah Painter; Harrington v. Winthrop Hill, John Porter & Eleazer Hubbell; Harrington v. John H. Burton & Thomas Russell; Penniman v. James Brisman & Horatio Bethsong; Stephen Pearl, Dan Farrand & Jabez Penniman v.*

Asa Converse, September 1808 term, Chittenden County Court judgments, 1806–1839, VSARA.

389. *Moses Catlin v. Daniel Staniford,* September 1808 term, February 1809 term, Chittenden County Court judgments, 1806–1839, VSARA.

390. *Staniford v. Chittenden County; Enos v. Inhabitants of Chittenden County; Peck v. Chittenden County; Peaslee & Haswell v. Chittenden County; Bennett v. John Bean & John Wood,* September 1808, February 1809, Chittenden County Court judgments, 1806–1839, VSARA.

391. *Trial of Cyrus B. Dean,* 37–44; Staniford expenses, September 10, 1808, Chittenden County Supreme Court dockets and case files, 1794–1829, VSARA.

392. Blunt confession, August 16, 1808, Alexander Miller Letters, Orders, Bills, &c., VHS.

393. Alexander Miller to Lucretia Miller, August 22, 1808, Alexander Miller Papers, VHS.

394. Jefferson to Gallatin, September 9, 1808, in Jefferson, *Writings,* vols. 11–12, 160.

395. Receipts, August 29 and 30, 1808, Alexander Miller Letters, Orders, Bills, &c., VHS.

396. Letter to Alexander Miller, March 1809, Alexander Miller Papers, 1797–1829, Park-McCullough Collection, UVM.

397. *United States v. Sloop* Dolphin *& 66 Barrels potashes,* May 1809 term, U.S. District Court, USDC-VT, NARA.

398. Buel to Haswell letter, August 20, 1808, Nathan Haswell Papers, UVM.

399. "A Guide to the Royall Tyler Collection, 1753–1935," Vermont Historical Society, Montpelier; *Salem Mercury,* March. 3, 1787.

400. *Spooner's Vermont Journal,* July 16, 1799.

401. *Jonathan Janes v. Levi House; David Thompson v. Jonathan Atwell & John Simons; Curtis & Foot v. Reuben Evartts; Silas Hathaway & Heman Allen v. Levi Hungerford,* August, September and December 1808 terms, Franklin County Court and Franklin County Supreme Court, VSARA.

402. *U.S. v. Forty Pieces of Leather,* May 1809 term, USDC-VT, NARA.

403. Harrington invoice, September 10, 1808, Chittenden County Supreme Court dockets and case files, 1794–1829, VSARA.

404. *Vermont Sentinel,* September 2, 1808.

405. Ibid.

406. "*Black Snake* Affair" Papers, 1805–1809, MSA 263, VHS.

407. *Vermont Sentinel,* September 2, 1808.

408. *The Reporter,* September 17, 1808.

409. Dutcher, *History of St. Albans,* 346–47.

410. Ada Lou Carson and Herbert L. Carson, *Royall Tyler* (Boston: Twayne Press, 1979), 67.

411. Correspondence, Royall Tyler to Vermont House of Representatives, contained in Vermont General Assembly resolution, October 25, 1808, 68:10, VSARA.

412. Russell S. Taft, "The Supreme Court of Vermont," *Green Bag: An Entertaining Magazine for Lawyers* 7 (1894): 185.

413. *St. Albans Advisor,* September 8, 1808.

414. Journals of the General Assembly of the State of Vermont…1808, 135–36.

415. Motion to Set Aside Verdict, undated, "*Black Snake* Affair" Papers, 1805–1809, MSA 263, VHS.

416. "Reasons Why Cyrus B. Dean Ought to Claim the Attention of the Legislature," *State v. Dean,* August 1808 term, Chittenden County Supreme Court dockets and case files, 1794–1829, VSARA.

CHAPTER 8

417. *U.S. v. Hoxie, et. al.,* October 1808 term, U.S. Circuit Court, USCC-VT, NARA.

418. Caledonia County petition, October 18, 1808, Orwell Petition, October 20, 1808, Groton Petition, October 1809, Petitions to the General Assembly, 1806–1808, vol. 46, VSARA.

419. *St. Albans Advisor,* September 8, 1808.

420. Haswell and Woolsey letters, September 21 and 22, 1808, Nathan Haswell Papers, UVM.

421. *Daniel Staniford v. William C. Harrington; Indictment v. Elias Buel,* January 1809 term, Vermont Supreme Court, VSARA; Harrington Account Book and Guy Catlin Papers, UVM, 47:7, VSARA.

422. Lawrence Friedman, *Crime and Punishment in American History* (New York: Harper Collins, 1993), 66.

423. James Willard Hurst, *The Law of Treason in the United States, Collected Essays* (Westport, CT: Greenwood Publishing Corp., 1945), passim.

424. *United States v. John Taylor, Ezekiel Taylor,* October 1808 term, U.S. Circuit Court, USCC-VT, NARA.

425. U.S. District Court, Vermont Dockets, 1798–1816, USDC-VT, NARA.

426. VSP, 68:11, VSARA; *Vermont Patriot & State Gazette,* November 7, 1826.

427. Prentiss Cutler Dodge, *Encyclopedia, Vermont Biography* (Burlington, VT: Ullery Publishing Company, 1912), 56.

428. Jefferson to Gallatin, August 1808, John P. Foley, ed., *The Jefferson Cyclopedia: A Comprehensive Collection of the Views of Thomas Jefferson* (New York: Funk & Wagnalls Co., 1900), 292–93; Gallatin to Madison, September 9, 1808, Perkins, *Prologue to War,* 161; Gallatin to Sen. William B. Giles, November 24, 1808, American State Papers, *Annals of Congress,* 10th Congress, 2nd session, 236.

429. *Libel v. Three Bateaus & Long Canoe; United States v. One Bateau and Three Barrels and One Hogshead of Potashes,* May 1809 term, U.S. District Court, USDC-VT, NARA.

430. *Records of the Council of Safety and Governor and Council of the State of Vermont,* V: 398–99.

431. *Vermont Sentinel,* October 21, 1808; *Middlebury Mercury,* October 26, 1808.

432. *Journals of the General Assembly of the State of Vermont…1808,* passim.

433. *State v. Dean,* August 1808 term, Chittenden County Supreme Court dockets and case files, 1794–1829, VSARA.

434. *Records of the Council of Safety and Governor and Council of the State of Vermont,* V:212–13.

435. *Journals of the General Assembly of the State of Vermont…1808,* 49.

436. *Vermont Sentinel,* November 4, 1808.

437. Kermit L. Hall, ed., *The Oxford Companion to the Supreme Court of the United States* (Oxford, UK: Oxford University Press, 1992), 507–08.

438. Elijah Paine, Jr., *United States v. Frederick Hoxie,* in *Reports of Cases Argued and Determined in the Circuit Court of the United States for the Second Circuit,* vol. I (New York: R. Donaldson, 1827), 283.

439. *Vermont Sentinel,* November 4, 1808; *U.S. v. Frederick Hoxie,* October 1808 term, U.S. Circuit Court, USCC-VT, NARA.

440. Robert F. Eldredge, *Past and Present of Macomb County, Michigan* (Chicago: Clark Publishing Co., 1905), 682; Term Papers, U.S. Circuit Court, October 1810 term, USCC-VT, NARA.

441. *Rutland Herald,* August 29, 1810.

442. Harrington to John Johnson, January 6, 1810, Papers of John Johnson, 1790–1842, UVM; *Free Press,* August 14, 1858; Taylor, *Civil War of 1812,* 349.

443. United States Bureau of the Census, 1810.

444. Dutcher, *History of St. Albans,* 347; David Blow, *Map of Burlington, circa 1812,* Fletcher Free Library, Burlington, VT.

445. Burlington Records of Town Meetings, 383, 389.

446. Andrew Beers, *Franklin's Legacy; or, the New York & Vermont Almanack, for the Year of our Lord 1808* (Troy, NY: Oliver Lyon, 1808).

447. *Weekly Wanderer,* November 21, 1808.

448. *Vermont Sentinel,* November 18, 1808; *Spooner's Vermont Journal,* November 21, 1808.

449. Staniford claims, November 11, 1808; October 16, 1810, VSP, 48:82, 73:33, VSARA; *Staniford v. Chittenden County, Staniford v. Bennett,* February 1809 term, Chittenden County Court, VSARA; Staniford letter, August 3, 1812, Henry Sheldon Museum, no. 8124.53.3; *National Standard,* November 29, 1815.

450. *State v. Thomas Green, Jr.,* September 1809 term, Chittenden County Court, VSARA.

451. *Vermont Sentinel,* February 24, 1809.

452. Ibid., May 25, 1810.

453. *State v. Nancy Blackmore; State v. Abiather Smith; State v. John Haynes; State v. Alexander Palmer,* December 1808 term, Franklin County Supreme Court, VSARA.

454. *State v. Samuel Smith,* December 1809 term, *State v. Eber Baldwin,* Dec. 1811 term, Franklin County Supreme Court, VSARA.

455. Harrington to Tyler, January 25 [*sic*], 1809, "*Black Snake* Affair" Papers, VHS.

456. *Rutland Herald,* September 23, 1809.

457. *Vermont Sentinel,* February 24, 1809.

458. *Indictment v. Samuel Fitch,* January 1807 term, Chittenden County Court, VSARA.

459. William Harrington Account Book, 1799–1814, UVM.

460. *Vermont Sentinel,* January 20, 1809.

CHAPTER 9

461. Jefferson to Judge St. George Tucker, December 25, 1808, in Malone, *Jefferson the President,* 657.

462. Haswell to Penniman, February 19, 1809; Haswell to Penniman, November 21, 1808; Haswell to Buel, November 22, 1808; Buel to Haswell, November 17, 1808, Nathan Haswell Papers, UVM.

463. Haswell to Penniman, March 9, 1809; Penniman to Haswell, April 22, 1809, Nathan Haswell Papers, UVM.

464. Burlington Records of Town Meetings, 337–38.

465. *Vermont Sentinel,* February 24, 1809.

466. *Pittsburgh Gazette,* March 1, 1809.

467. See generally, May 1809 term, U.S. Circuit Court, Windsor, VT, USSC-VT, NARA; *U.S. v. Tyler,* 11 U.S. 285 (1812); Bennett to John Johnson, February 15, 1809, John Johnson Papers, UVM.

468. Names of Convicts received into the State Prison in Windsor, Vermont, in the year 1808, 1809 & 1810, F-04551; VSP, 73:16, VSARA.

469. John Reynolds, *Recollections of Windsor Prison*, 3rd ed. (Boston: A. Wright, 1839), 15–24.

470. *Vermont Sentinel*, March 24, 1809.

471. Cornelius P. Van Ness, *An Oration Delivered at Jerico, July 4, 1809* (Rutland, VT: W. Fay, 1809), 24.

472. *Green Mountain Farmer*, August 21, 1809; *Rutland Herald*, August 5, 1809.

473. *Van Ness v. James Brown; William Lewis; Theophilus Mansfield; The President & Directors of the Vermont State Bank v. John Burton, C.P. Van Ness, Elnathan Keyes*, September 1809 term, Chittenden County Court, VSARA; Petition of Eleazor Wheelock, September 28, 1809, VSP, 47:125, VSARA; C.P. Van Ness to William Van Ness, October 15, 1809, Papers of Cornelius Van Ness, VHS.

474. Robinson and Shaw to Madison, October 19, 1809, Presidential Appointments, Letters of Application and Recommendation, James Madison, microfilm M0438, NARA.

475. Buel, *The Book*, 13.

476. *Overseer of the Poor in Burlington v. Joshua Barnes & John Van Sicklen*, February 1810 term, Burlington County Court, VSARA; *Vermont Sentinel*, May 26, 1809; December 22 and 29, 1809; Petition of Curtis Holgate, VSP, 48:56, VSARA; *Moses Catlin v. Peaslee & Haswell*, February 1810 term, Chittenden County Court, VSARA.

477. *Peaslee & Haswell v. Inhabitants of Chittenden County*, January 1813 term, Supreme Court of Judicature; *Green v. Peaslee & Haswell*, February 1811 term, Chittenden County Court, VSARA.

478. *U.S. v. Nathan Haswell, et al.*, May 1811 term, U.S. District Court, USDC-VT, NARA.

479. Ibid.; Chittenden County Records, accession no. PRA-00990, 8:550, VSARA.

480. Buel, *The Book*, 10; James John, *Partridge Haywood, the Smuggler: A Story of Non-intercourse Times*, Ms. 813, VHS; Hurd, *History of Clinton and Franklin Counties*, 48; *U.S. v. James Allen & Samuel Gelston*, May 1812 term, U.S. Circuit Court, Vermont, USSCT-VT, NARA; Petition of Samuel Holton, October 14, 1809, VSP, 47:207, VSARA..

481. *Senate Executive Journal*. 11th Cong., February 5, 1811, 166; *U.S. v. Samuel Buel, Stephen Pearl & Jabez Penniman*, October 1816 term, U.S. Circuit Court, Vermont, USSC-VT, NARA.

482. *Columbian Patriot*, May 25, 1814.

483. U.S. Statutes at Large, 2:656,1:697.

484. Buel, *The Book*, 7.

485. Ibid., 18–19, 30.

486. Ibid.

487. U.S. District Court, Vermont, May 1812 term, USDC-VT, NARA.

488. Ibid., 9.

489. Cornelius P. Van Ness, *Claim of C.P. Van Ness* (Washington, D.C., 1852), 16–17.

490. Hemenway, *Vermont Historical Gazetteer,* 2:495; Dutcher, *History of St. Albans,* 294; *Vermont Sentinel*, November 7, 1811; *Washingtonian*, February 17, 1812.

491. V.R. Goodrich to Col. Isaac Clark, June 5, 1812; Isaac Clark, Jr. to Col. Isaac Clark, June 17, 1812, Col. Isaac Clark Papers, 1781–1821, UVM; *Burlington Free Press*, August 13, 1858.

492. Petition of the Undersigned Inhabitants of St. Albans, October 23, 1812, VSP, 49:126, VSARA.

493. Petition of the Selectmen of Richford (Vt.) for Military Aid, Col. Isaac Clark Papers, 1781–1821, UVM; *U.S. v. Lyman Painter, U.S. v. Jacob Davis, U.S. v. Timothy Ashley, U.S. v. Harry Shepherd, U.S. v. James Allen*, May 1812 term, Vermont U.S. Circuit Court, USCC-VT, NARA.

494. *U.S. v. Crossett, et.al., U.S. v. Cutting, et. al.*, May 1813 term, Vermont U.S. Circuit Court, USCC-VT, NARA; *Buel v. Bigelow*, June 1816 term, Vermont Supreme Court of Judicature, Chittenden County, VSARA.

495. *State of Vermont v. Lyman Hawley, et. al.*, February 1813 term, Vermont Supreme Court of Judicature, Rutland County, folder 317 (dispositions not noted); *Green Mountain Farmer*, October 7, 1812.

496. *U.S. v. Asa Shaw*, May 1813 term, Vermont U.S. Circuit Court, USCC-VT, NARA.

497. *James Owen v. Jenkins Storrs*, August 1815 term, Orleans Country Court, VSARA; William Sweetser to Elihu Luce, November 5, 1812, David Sumner Papers, 1807–1888, VHS.

498. *Vermont Mirror*, April 7, 1813; *Spooner's Vermont Journal*, April 5, 1813.

499. Hickey, *War of 1812*, 167.

500. *Spooner's Vermont Journal*, April 5, 1813; *Vermont Mirror*, April 7, 1813.

501. *Vermont Sentinel*, February 11, 1813; Taylor, *Civil War of 1812*, 343.

502. *Bennington News-Letter*, July 31, 1815.

503. John Reid to Alexander Miller, June 28, 1812, Alexander Miller Papers, VHS.

504. *Washingtonian*, August 3, 1812.

505. George S. Bixby, "Peter Sailly (1754–1826): A Pioneer of the Champlain Valley with Extracts from His Diary and Letters," *University of the State of New York Bulletin* 680 (February 1, 1919): 48.

506. *Washingtonian*, February 14, 1814.

507. *Columbian Patriot*, February 9, 1814.

508. Van Ness affidavit, March 13, 1818, Papers of C.P. Van Ness, UVM.

509. *Green Mountain Farmer*, August 12, 1812; *State v. Town of Essex*, February 1813 term, Chittenden County Court, VSARA.

510. Bixby, "Peter Sailly," 40; J.J.Astor to W.H. Crawford, Secretary of the Treasury, May 31, 1819, 88.

511. *Benjamin and Joseph Strong v. Moses & Guy Catlin*, October 1813 term, Vermont U.S. Circuit Court, USCC-VT, NARA.

512. Buel, *The Book*, 83–90.

513. Nicholas Dungan, *Gallatin: America's Swiss Founding Father* (New York: New York University Press, 2010), 96.

514. Ibid.; Guy Catlin affidavit, October 7, 1819, C.P. Van Ness papers, VHS; Van Ness to Allen, December 15, 1818, Papers of C.P. Van Ness, UVM; "To the Public," undated, Papers of C.P. Van Ness, VHS.

515. *Washingtonian*, November 5, 1810.

516. *Journals of the General Assembly of the State of Vermont…1811*, 21–21; …*1819*, 110.

517. Windsor State Prison inventories, 1810–1811, VSP, 67:27, VSARA; *Journals of the General Assembly of the State of Vermont…1811*, 80…82; …*1815*, 85.

518. Samuel Mott petitions, September 16, 1812, and undated, VSP, 49:12, 48; Petition of Charles Sheffield, VSP, 49:35; *Schedule of the Convicts*, October 14, 1814, VSP, 67:31, VSARA.

519. *Laws of the State of Vermont*, 3: 272.

520. *Indictment of Orin Puswell* and *Storrs v. Smith*, August and September 1813 term, Vermont Supreme Court, VSARA.

CHAPTER 10

521. *Peter Richard v. Abraham Quackinboss*, December 1812 term, Franklin County Supreme Court, VSARA.

522. Archibald Hyde Appointment, February 18, 1813, Hyde Papers, 1813–1839, VSARA; Buel, *The Book*, 20.

523. *Vermont Patriot & State Gazette*, November 7, 1826.

524. Rann, *History of Chittenden County*, 319; *Burlington Gazette*, November 17, 1815; Buel, *The Book*, 114.

525. Van Ness to Richard Rusk, April 11, 1813, in Buel, *The Book*, 57–59; *Vermont Mirror*, May 12, 1813.

526. *Buel v. Van Ness*, September 1813 term, Chittenden County Court, accession no. PRA-560, VSARA; *Buel v. Enos, Buel v. Van Ness*, Reports of Cases Adjudged in the Supreme Court of Vermont, 1815–1819 (Middlebury, VT: Copeland and Allen, 1821), 56–59; *Buel v. Van Ness*, 21 U.S. 312 (1823).

527. C.P. Van Ness to Col. Wm. Cummings, September 20, 1815, Letters Received by the Office of the Adjutant General, 1805–1821, NARA, ID No. 300368; *Burlington Free Press*, August 18, 1858; Haswell to Gen. Chandler, March 8, 1813, Nathan Haswell Papers, UVM.

528. Charles Hatch to Jonathan Hagar, August 17, 1813, doc. no. 813467, Henry Sheldon Museum.

529. "Judgment of the Court," June 18, 1813, Orleans County, accession no. SUPR-CA-00005, VSARA.

530. *State v. Samuel Eaton*, September 1813 term, Caledonia County Court, VSARA.

531. Complaint, *Ira Williams v. Samuel Burnham*, Special Court holden at Derby, June 18, 1813, Orleans County Court, VSARA.

532. *John Weeks v. Bayley & Whiting*, July 1815 term, Essex County Court, VSARA; Affidavit of Anna Tode, June 14, 1814, *State v. Benjamin Robinson*, September 1813 term, Vermont Supreme Court, accession no. SUPR-CA-00005.

533. John Bach McMaster, *History of the People*, 4:66.

534. Hemenway, *Vermont Historical Gazetteer*, 2:245; *Columbian Patriot*, August 22, 1814.

535. C.P. Van Ness to Col. Wm. Cummings, July 29, 1814, Letters Received by the Office of the Adjutant General, 1805–1821, ID No. 300368, NARA.

536. C.P. Van Ness to Col. Wm. Cummings, August 6, 1814, Letters Received by the Office of the Adjutant General, 1805–1821, ID No. 300368, NARA.

537. *Vermont Mirror*, September 15, 1813; *State v. Augustus Wright*, December 1813 term, Franklin County Court, St. Albans, VT; *Columbian Patriot*, October 6, 1813; *Gazette* (Portland, ME), July 19, 1813; *Bennington News-Letter*, July 20, 1813.

538. *The Reporter*, October 30, 1813.

539. *State v. Dennet, State v. Kibbe, et. al.*, September 1814 term, Caledonia County Supreme Court, accession no. SUPR-CA-00005, passim.

540. Albert Gallatin to Senator W.B. Giles, November 24, 1808, Annals of Congress, Senate, 10th Congress, 2nd session, 233; Van Ness to Col. Wm. Cummings, July 29, 1814, Letters Received by the Office of the Adjutant General, 1805–1821, NARA, ID No. 300368; Hemenway, *Vermont Historical Gazetteer*, 2:673; Dallas to U.S. House of Representatives, November 19, 1814, American State Papers, 2:881.

541. Van Ness to Merrill, March 7. 1813; December 20, 1814; January 29, 1815, C.P. Van Ness Papers, VHS.

542. Gideon Granger to Asa Nevin, July 17, 1813, Letters Sent by the Postmaster General, 1789–1836, H0601, roll 18, NARA.

543. Van Ness to Merrill, June 8, 1815, December 10, 1815; June 4, 1816, Van Ness Papers, VHS.

544. Buel, *The Book*, 10, 111–12; *Laws of the United State*s, vol. III (Philadelphia: Bioren, Duane and Weightman, 1815), 495.

545. U.S. Constitution, Art. I, sec. 8, cl. 11.

546. Muller, "A 'Traitorous and Diabolical Traffic': The Commerce of the Champlain-Richelieu Corridor During the War of 1812," *Vermont History* 44, no. 2 (Spring 1976): 95–96.

547. War of 1812 Papers, 1789–1815, Letters Received Concerning Letters of Marque, 1812–1814, microfilm M0588, roll 1, NARA.

548. *Guy Catlin v. 77 Packs of Furs & One small bale of dry goods*, May 1814 term, U.S. District Court, USDC-VT, NARA.

549. War of 1812 Papers, Letters of Marque, microfilm M0588, roll 1, NARA.

550. Muller, "A 'Traitorous and Diabolical Traffic,'" 94; Buel, *The Book*, 112; Hemenway, *Vermont Historical Gazetter*, 1:670.

551. Buel, *The Book*, 112–13.

552. Van Ness to Heman Allen, December 15, 1818, Papers of Cornelius Van Ness, UVM.

553. A.J. Dallas to J.W. Eppes, November 4, 1814, American State Papers, part 3, 2:875.

554. Bixby, "Peter Sailly," 49–51.

555. *Vermont Sentinel*, August 19, 1814.

556. *New York Times*, January 8, 1853.

557. *United States v. 87 Packages Merchandize, 184 Packages Merchandize, 34 Packages Merchandize, 198 Chests of Tea, 34 Packages Merchandize, 127 Packages Merchandize, 99 Packages Merchandize, 37 Packages Merchandize, 46 Packages Merchandize, 25 Casks Hard Ware, 117 Packages Merchandize, 28 Packages*

Merchandize, 41 Packages Merchandize, 170 Boxes Tin, 137 Boxes Tea, 96 Packages Merchandize, 51 Packages Merchandize, 6 Packages Merchandize, May 1814 term, U.S. District Court, Vermont, USDC-VT, NARA.

558. Kendall, *Ex-Chief Justice,* vi, 42, 56.

559. Van Ness to unnamed recipient, April 28, 1828, and Van Ness to Jesse Gore, April 17, 1828; Van Ness to D.P. Parker, August 14, 1823, Papers of C.P. Van Ness, VHS; Buel, *The Book,* 111; C.P. Van Ness to George Cleveland, April 30, 1818, Henry Sheldon Museum, doc. no. 818880; Rhoda Van Ness to Mrs. Hickok and Mrs. Hickok to Van Ness, October 1, 1818, VSARA; Resolution, undated, Papers of C.P. Van Ness, 1802–1852, UVM.

560. Satterlee Clark to Col. Isaac Clark, March 20, 1814, Col. Isaac Clark Papers, 1781–1821, UVM.

561. Report of the Corporation of the University of Vermont, M. Chittenden and Heman Allen, October 22, 1814, VSP, 74:49.; Burlington Town Meeting Minutes, March 28, 1828, Fletcher Free Library.

562. Depositions, October 1808–September 1832, VSP, vol. 72, VSARA; Affidavit of George Deming, October 11, 1813, VSP, 72:19, VSARA; Heman Allen to John Johnson, October 16, 1813, John Johnson Papers, UVM; Sandford Gadcomb to Asa Aldis, October 6, 1813 and January 15, 1814, Sandford Gadcomb Papers, 1811–1819, UVM; *Vermont Mirror,* December 15, 1813; Harrington affidavit, November 17, 1813, Depositions, October 1808–September 1832, VSP, vol. 72, VSARA; Hoskins, *History of the State of Vermont,* 180; Taylor, *Civil War of 1812,* 348–49.

563. *Vermont Mirror,* April 27, 1814; Orderly Book, United States Army, Thirtieth Infantry, vol. 1, unnumbered, UVM; *Vermont Sentinel,* June 24, 1814.

564. Vermont Vital Records through 1870, New England Historic Genealogical Society.

565. Unidentified to William Harrington, April 3, 1813, doc. no. 813252.2, Henry Sheldon Museum, Middlebury, VT; Chittenden County Court Records, February 1814 term, vol. 9, accession no. PRA-00991, VSARA; U.S. District Court, Vermont, 1791–1906, October 1815–May 1816, USDC-VT, NARA.

566. *Vermont Sentinel,* July 22, 1814; *Spooner's Vermont Journal,* July 25, 1814.

567. *Sparhawk v. Administrator of Ozias Buell,* 9 Vt. 41 (1837); *Vermont Sentinel,* November 18, 1814.

568. Mott Petition for Pardon, October 9, 1813, VSP, 49:215, Petition of David Sheffield, October 23, 1813, VSP, 49:213, VSARA.

569. *Bennington News-Letter,* July 6, 1813.

570. Godfrey, *Sketch of the Life*, passim, document no. G543gp, VHS; Reynolds, *Recollections of Windsor Prison*, 38; *Journals of the General Assembly of the State of Vermont...1815*, 128–34.

571. *Vermont Intelligencer*, February 23, 1818.

572. Godfrey, *Sketch of the Life*, 35, VHS.

573. Samuel I. Mott Petition for Pardon, October 3, 1816, VSP, 51: 248, VSARA; E.P. Walton, *Records of the Governor and Council of the State of Vermont*, vol. VI (Montpelier, VT: J Poland, 1878), 177.

574. C.P. Van Ness to Col. Wm. Cummings, August 15, 1814, Letters Received by the Office of the Adjutant General, 1805–1821, NARA, ID No. 300368; *United States v. Alexander Ferguson*, May 1817 term, U.S. Circuit Court, Vermont, USCC-VT, NARA.

575. Ibid., *United States v. McLaren, et. al.; United States v. Cutler, et. al.*

576. *Weekly Museum* (New York City), September 19, 1815.

577. *United States v. James Way; Samuel Smith, et. al.; Noah Sanborn; Moses Wright, Vine Taylor; Samuel How; Edward Burt, Josiah Parmilee*, May 1817 term, U.S. Circuit Court, Vermont, USCC-VT, NARA; *State of Vermont v. Francis Pilker, Louis Pilker & Antoine Dubois*, February 1815 term, Chittenden County Court, VSARA; *Treasurer of the State of Vermont v. Benjamin Derby, et. al.*, June 1818 term, Supreme Court of Judicature, accession no. PRA-00982, VSARA; Deposition of Robert Man, June 21, 1816, misc. Vermont Supreme Court papers, SUPR-CA-00005; *Aaron Rood v. E. Little, et. al.*, June 1816 term, Vermont Supreme Court, VSARA.

578. *State of Vermont v. Atwood, et al.*, June 1816 term, Vermont Supreme Court, SUPR-CA-00005, VSARA.

579. Sherman, *Freedom and Unity*, 167–70; *Vermont Intelligencer*, November 17, 1817.

CHAPTER 11

580. *Van Ness v. Daniel Smith & Josiah Tuttle*, February 1816 term, Chittenden County Court; *Van Ness v. C. Danforth & J. Bostwick*, September 1815 term, Chittenden County Court; *Van Ness v. Nathan Row & E. Mitchell*, February 1815 term, Chittenden County Court, VSARA; *United States v. 37 Packages of Merchand. & 2 kegs of rum*, September 1814 term, U.S. District Court, USDC-VT, NARA.

581. *Bennington News-Letter*, October 10, 1814.

582. *C.P. Van Ness v. James Evarts*, February 1815 term and *Samuel Buel v. Elisha Clark*, September 1814 term, Chittenden County Court, VSARA.

583. United States Congress. *United States Congressional Serial Set* (Washington, D.C.: Government Printing Office, n.d.)

584. "A Report in Relation to Public Defaulters," Levi Woodbury to James Polk, January 15, 1838, 25th Congress, 2d Session, Doc. No. 111, in House Documents, Otherwise Published as Executive Documents: 13th Congress, 2d Session—49th Congress, 1st Session, 12.

585. Daniel Staniford's petition, October 10, 1815, VSP, vol. 51, 18.

586. *Van Ness v. Pettis*, June 1818 term Vermont Supreme Court, VSARA; *Van Ness v. Buel*, May 1815 term, U.S. District Court, USDC-VT, NARA.

587. Petition of Samuel Buel, February 22, 1816, Journal of the House of Representatives, 14th Congress, 1st session, 386.

588. Buel, *The Book*, 67.

589. Van Ness to Merrill, April 18, 1816, Papers of C.P. Van Ness, VHS.

590. *U.S. v. Buel, Pearl & Penniman*, October 1816 term, U.S. Circuit Court, USCC-VT, NARA.

591. *Van Ness v. Buel*, 17 U.S. 74 (February 8, 1819), *Buel v. Van Ness*, 21 U.S. 312 (February 18, 1823); *Daily National Intelligencer*, December 25, 1829; *Vermont Sentinel*, November 18, 1825.

592. *Providence Patriot*, November 29, 1820; Van Ness to Adams, November 25, 1820, Documents, Legislative and Executive of the Congress of the United States, American State Papers, Second Series, 5:66; *The Miscellaneous Documents of the House of Representatives for the Second Session of the Fifty-third Congress, 1893–1894* (Washington, D.C.: Government Printing Office, 1895), 72–82; Great Britain: Execution of the Treaty of Ghent, February 3, 1821, American State Papers: Foreign Affairs 4:647; Bassett, "Rise of Cornelius Peter Van Ness," 8; John Quincy Adams, *Memoirs… Comprising Portions of His Diary from 1795–1848*, edited by Charles F. Adams (Philadelphia: J.P. Lippencott & Co., 1874), 334.

593. *New York Times*, January 8, 1853.

594. *Buel v. Van Ness*, January 1823 term, Vermont Supreme Court, VSA; *Buel v. Van Ness*, 21 U.S. 312 (February 18, 1823); Van Ness to Monroe, March 27, 1823, Papers of C.P. Van Ness, UVM; Paine to Monroe, April 3, 1823, Presidential Appointments, Letters of Application and Recommendation, James Monroe, microfilm M0439, NARA.

595. *New York Times*, January 8, 1853.

596. *American Repertory*, May 28, 1829.

597. List of U.S. Diplomatic Officers, 1789–1939, microfilm M0586, NARA.
598. Will of Cornelius Van Ness, Vermont Probate Files, 1800–1921, Chittenden County, 1854.

APPENDIX

599. Hemenway, *Vermont Historical Gazetteer*, 1:503–04.

SELECTED BIBLIOGRAPHY

Albers, Jan. *Hands on the Land: A History of the Vermont Landscape.* Cambridge, MA: MIT Press, 2000.

Bassett, T.D. Seymour. "The Rise of Cornelius Peter Van Ness, 1782–1826." *Proceedings of the Vermont Historical Society* 10, no. 1 (March 1942): 3–20.

Bellico, Russell P. *Sails and Steam in the Mountains: A Maritime and Military History of Lake George and Lake Champlain.* Fleischmanns, NY: Purple Mountain Press, 1992.

Bemis, Samuel F. "Relations Between the Vermont Separatists and Great Britain, 1789–1791." *American Historical Review* 21, no. 3 (April 1916): 557.

Bixby, George S. "Peter Sailly (1754–1826): A Pioneer of the Champlain Valley with Extracts from His Diary and Letters." *University of the State of New York Bulletin* 680 (February 1, 1919): 48.

Buel, Samuel. *The Book, or Fragments of Modern Chronicles: Being a Delineation of New and Successful Ways and Means to Merit Contempt, Detestation, Damnation, or Any Other Term of Reprobation in the Above Scale of Degradation which the Charity of the Reader May Substitute; Derived from Authentic Documents and Recent Examples, Both in Public and Private Life and Illustrated by Distinct Notes and References of the Translator, by Whom It Is Respectfully Inscribed to the Public.* Burlington, VT: published by the author, 1819.

Duffy, John J. "Broadside Illustrations of the Jeffersonian-Federalist Conflict in Vermont, 1809–1816." *Vermont History* 49, no. 4 (Fall 1981): 193–222.

———, ed. *Ethan Allen and His Kin, Correspondence, 1772–1819.* Hanover, NH: University Press of New England, 1998.

Dutcher, L.L. *The History of St. Albans, Vermont.* St. Albans, VT: Stephen Royce, 1872.

Fanis, Maria. *Secular Morality and International Security: American and British Decisions about War.* Ann Arbor: University of Michigan Press, 2011.

Feeney, Vincent Edward. *The Great Falls on Onion River: A History of Winooski, Vermont.* Winooski, VT: Brown and Sons Printing, 2002.

Futrell, William H. *The History of American Customs Jurisprudence.* Union, NJ: Lawbook Exchange, 1998.

Hemenway, Abby Maria, ed. *The Vermont Historical Gazetter: A Magazine Embracing a History of Each Town, Civil, Ecclesiastical, Biographical and Military.* Burlington, VT: published by the author, 1871.

Howe, John. "John Howe's Journal, November 1812–April 1813." *Vermont History* 40, no. 4 (Autumn 1972): 264–70.

Hurst, James Willard. *The Law of Treason in the United States, Collected Essays.* Westport, CT: Greenwood Publishing Corp., 1945.

Kendall, B.F. *The Ex-Chief Justice, and the Printer; Being a Report of a Trial for Libel, Titus Hutchison vs. B.F. Kendall.* Woodstock, VT: J.B. & S.L. Chase & Co., 1836.

McClellan, William S. *Smuggling in the American Colonies at the Outbreak of the Revolution.* New York: Moffat, Yard and Co., 1912.

McMaster, John Bach. *A History of the People of the United States from the Revolution to the Civil War.* New York: D. Appleton and Co., 1892.

Muller, H. Nicholas, III. "Floating a Lumber Raft to Quebec City 1805: The Journal of Guy Catlin of Burlington." *Vermont History* 39 (1971): 116–24.

———. "Jay's Treaty: The Transformation of Lake Champlain Commerce." *Vermont History* 80, no. 1 (Winter/Spring 2012): 33–56.

———. "Smuggling into Canada: How the Champlain Valley Defied Jefferson's Embargo." *Vermont History* 38, no. 1 (Winter 1970): 5–21.

———. "A 'Traitorous and Diabolical Traffic': The Commerce of the Champlain-Richelieu Corridor During the War of 1812." *Vermont History* 44, no. 2 (Spring 1976): 78–96.

Penniman, George Wallace. *The Penniman Family, 1631–1900.* Baltimore, MD: Gateway Press, 1981.

Perkins, Bradford. *Prologue to War: England and the United States, 1805–1812.* Berkley: University of California Press, 1961.

Rann, William S. *History of Chittenden County, Vermont, with Illustrations and Biographical Sketches of Some of Its Prominent Men and Pioneers.* Syracuse, NY: D. Mason and Co., 1886.

Records of the Grand Lodge of Free and Accepted Masons of the State of Vermont. Burlington, VT: Free Press Association, 1879.

Reynolds, John. *Recollections of Windsor Prison.* Boston: A. Wright, 1839.

Rollins, Alden M. *Vermont Warnings Out.* Camden, ME: Picton Press, 1995.

Roth, Randolph A. *The Democratic Dilemma: Religion, Reform, and the Social Order in the Connecticut River Valley of Vermont, 1791–1850.* Cambridge, UK: Cambridge University Press, 1987.

Rush, Benjamin, MD. "An Enquiry into the Effects of Ardent Spirits Upon the Human Body and Mind." In *Medical Inquiries and Observations.* Philadelphia: J. Conrad & Co., 1805.

Russell, John. *An Authentic History of the Vermont State Prison.* Windsor, VT: Wright and Sibley, 1812.

Sherman, Michael, Gene Sessions and P. Jeffrey Potash. *Freedom and Unity: A History of Vermont.* Barre: Vermont Historical Society, 2004.

Sofka, James. "The Jeffersonian Idea of National Security: Commerce, the Atlantic Balance of Power, and the Barbary War, 1786–1805." *Diplomatic History* 21, no. 4 (Fall 1997): 519–44.

Steele, Brian. "Thomas Jefferson, Coercion and the Limits of Harmonious Union." *Journal of Southern History* 74, no. 4 (November 2008): 823–54.

Stillwell, Lewis D. "Migration from Vermont." *Proceedings of the Vermont Historical Society* 5, no. 2 (1937): 109.

Stratton, Allen L. *History of Alburgh, Vermont: An Account of the Discovery, Settlement, and Interesting and Remarkable Events.* Barre, VT: Northlight Studio Press, 1986.

———. *History of the South Hero Island Being the Towns of South Hero and Grand Isle, Vermont.* Burlington, VT: Queen City Printers, 1980.

Taft, Russell S. "The Supreme Court of Vermont." *The Green Bag: An Entertaining Magazine for Lawyers* (1894).

Taylor, Alan. *The Civil War of 1812: American Citizens, British Subjects, Irish Rebels & Indian Allies.* New York: Alfred A. Knopf, 2010.

Thompson, Zadock. *History of Vermont, Natural, Civil and Statistical.* Burlington, VT: Chauncey Goodrich, 1842.

Thorpe, Walter. *History of Wallingford, Vermont.* Rutland, VT: Tuttle Co., 1911.

The Trial of Cyrus B. Dean, for the Murder of Jonathan Ormsby and Asa Marsh, before the Supreme Court of Judicature of the State of Vermont, at Their Special Sessions, Begun and Holden at Burlington, Chittenden County, on the 23rd of August, A.D., 1808. Burlington, VT: Samuel Mills, 1808.

United States Department of the Treasury. *Report of the Secretary of the Treasury on the Subject of Public Roads and Canals Made in Pursuance of a Resolution of Senate, March 2, 1807.* Washington, D.C.: William A. Davis, 1816.

Van Ness, William Peter. *An Examination of the Various Charges Exhibited against Aaron Burr, Esq.* New York: privately printed, 1804.

Welles, Albert. *History of the Buell Family in England.* New York: Society Library, 1881.

Williamson, Chilton. *Vermont in Quandary: 1763–1825.* Vol. 4, *Growth of Vermont.* Edited by Earle Williams Newton. Montpelier: Vermont Historical Society, 1949.

Williams, Samuel. *The Natural and Civil History of Vermont.* Burlington, VT: Samuel Mills, 1809.

Wood, Gordon S. *Empire of Liberty: A History of the Early Republic, 1789–1815.* Oxford, UK: Oxford University Press, 2009.

Wright, Leigh. *Potash and Pine: The Formative Years in Randolph History.* Randolph, VT: Randolph Historical Society, 1977.

INDEX

INDEX

ABOUT THE AUTHOR

G ary Shattuck is a retired prosecutor (U.S. Department of Justice), having served thirty-five years in the law enforcement field, including work as a state police officer and legal advisor to Kosovo and Iraq governments. A magna cum laude graduate of the Vermont Law School, he is currently pursuing a master's degree in military history, concentrating on the American Revolution.

Visit us at
www.historypress.net
....
This title is also available as an e-book